FOR FAITH AND FREEDOM

FOR FAITH AND FREEDOM

THE GIFFORD LECTURES, 1955—1957
IN THE UNIVERSITY OF GLASGOW

LEONARD HODGSON

VOL. I

SCM PRESS LTD
BLOOMSBURY STREET LONDON

Originally published by Basil Blackwell Ltd
Part I : 1956; Part II : 1957

First cheap edition 1968
Published by SCM Press Ltd

SBN 334 00449 7

Printed in Great Britain by offset by
Fletcher & Son Ltd, Norwich

FROM THE PREFACE TO THE FIRST EDITION

THESE lectures are printed precisely as they were written for delivery. I trust that they will explain themselves as they go along and need no further advance elucidation in a preface. My title is plagiarism naked and unashamed. It comes from a book I read in my Victorian boyhood, a story by Sir Walter Besant about the Monmouth rebellion, in which the chief characters either perished at Sedgmoor or were haled before Judge Jeffreys and transported to the West Indies. The details of the story I have long ago forgotten, but the title has always lingered in my memory as a felicitous phrase, and it so aptly describes the theme of these lectures that I have no hesitation in appropriating and reviving it.

L.H.

PREFACE TO THE PAPERBACK EDITION

TEN years have gone by since these lectures were composed, delivered and originally published. During this time there has been a good deal of movement in the world of theological thought. So much so, indeed, that in some circles it has become the fashion to speak of the 'new theology' and the 'new morality'. Why then reprint this ten-year-old theology which by now must surely be out of date?

Actually there are a number of 'new theologies' representing different schools of thought, with one deep cleavage of which the importance is too easily overlooked. For many of us here and in America the phrase is apt to suggest theology associated with such names as Bultmann, Bonhoeffer, Tillich, the Bishop of Woolwich, van Buren and Altizer. But according to a review in the *Times Literary Supplement* of Jacques Maritain's *Le Paysan de la Garonne*; 'in France, as with other themes in history, Teilhard de Chardin has become an either-or. Either you are a Teilhardist or you are an anti-Teilhardist. And according to whichever you are, you are progressive or conservative.'[1] The contrast is well summed up by C. F. Mooney when he writes:

> The whole Modernist movement in fact tended to create the impression that between modern thought and traditional church teaching there could be no compatibility at all. If Teilhard de Chardin has a special mission in the Church, it would seem to be to remove this impression once and for all. Nor is it without significance that, whereas such modern thinkers as Rudolf Bultmann can see only rupture between today's world outlook and the 'mythical' data of the New Testament, Teilhard keeps insisting that this same world outlook can ultimately be understood by the light of this data, and that in the last resort only Christian faith can grasp the full meaning of the obscure human searchings present in every scientific achievement.[2]

[1] *T.L.S.* March 23rd, 1967, p.248.

[2] C. F. Mooney: *Teilhard de Chardin and the Mystery of Christ* (London, 1966), p.198.

The deep cleavage is this. For the one group the 'newness' springs from the radical rejection of much that traditionally has been thought to be basic to the truth of the Christian faith. Much in the New Testament that has been taken as historical must be 'de-mythologized'. The later metaphysical constructions of patristics, scholastics, reformers and others no longer have meaning in the twentieth century. The new theology is heralded by such headlines as 'Our Image of God must Go', or 'But that I can't Believe!', or 'The Death of God'. But to the members of the Teilhardist *avant-garde* all this is as irrelevant as the proverbial water to a duck's back. The Christian faith which they seek to present as interpreting a scientific understanding of the universe and providing a hopeful future for man is the original faith as it has been received and developed through successive generations of theological research.

To my mind the most important movement of theological thought in these ten years is not associated with any one of the big names that have hit the headlines. Beneath the surface a new current has been mingling with the stream. It is beginning to exert its influence and we are beginning to see something of the course which in future it will have to take.

For more than a century our biblical studies have mainly been concerned with exegesis, that is, with the attempt to determine the date and provenance of the various documents and what they meant in the minds of their original authors and readers. The background of this in the general history of human thought was the development of 'modern' scientific theory based on observation of the *data* provided by the natural world in the present instead of reliance on the *dicta* of acknowledged authorities in the past. Thus in the seventeenth century zoology made a fresh start when study of the nature and habits of actual animals displaced descriptions by Aristotle and pictures preserved in bestiaries and the traditions of heraldry.

In one respect the mingling of the streams came to a head with the nineteenth-century Darwinian controversies. In respect of

God's creative activity we learned to accept the observed evidence of the actual behaviour of the natural world as one of the channels of His self-revelation. We take, for example, this way of understanding the Genesis account of creation. For specifically Christian faith in God's redemptive activity the channel of revelation is the history of the biblical Chosen People leading to the gospel story and issuing the life of the Christian Church.

So far, so good. But as yet we have hardly begun to grasp what it will mean to graft the study of this history into the stock of our theological thinking. We are at a turning point in the history of Christian theology comparable to that which in the wider field gave birth to modern science in the seventeenth century. Let me quote from what I wrote last year:

> We shall find it hard to accustom ourselves to the uprooting of traditional habits, as hard as it must have been for the compilers of bestiaries in the early seventeenth century. For so long we have taken it for granted that in the New Testament, in the teaching of Jesus, and in the understanding of their faith by St. Peter, St. Paul, St. John and the rest, we have the genuine statement of what Christianity really is; that the subsequent history of the Church is the history of a falling away from the original high level of faith and practice; and that what we need is to get back to the understanding of our faith which those New Testament Christians had. It is hard to get used to the fact that in the sense in which we are seeking it they never had it. They were Jews, most of them Palestinian Jews. They had the outlook of their time, place, and culture. Their creed was the Jewish creed of that age. The original Christianity was the faith of a few of them who had followed Jesus of Nazareth in the hope that he might be the promised Messiah. That hope had been shattered by his arrest and execution, revived by his resurrection and transformed into faith that somehow or other, in spite of appearances, he had been the Messiah after all, and was now their heavenly Lord through whom God was carrying out his purpose of reconciling the world to himself. The New Testament shows them trying to make head or tail of what had happened on the basis of their Jewish understanding of God and the universe. So far from having given us a full and final explanation of the meaning of our faith they were taking the first steps towards its discovery, initiating a process which under the guidance of the Holy Spirit has been continuing ever since and is still going on. To answer the question 'What is the Christian view of anything?' we have to take into account how the understanding of it by the New Testament Christians has been deepened and enriched

in the experience of their successors, and is still being deepened and enriched by our experience of life in the world of today.[1]

For the theologian actual history is what takes the place of the zoologist's actual animals as the object of study. To realize this opens the door to a reconciliation of the truths for which both iconoclasts and Teilhardists stand. Both were moved by a healthy reaction against an unhistorical view of God's method in revelation.

We have no ground for supposing that the first Christians themselves ever asked, considered, or attempted to answer all the questions which were dealt with at Nicaea and Chalcedon, which have perplexed Christians down the ages, and which exercise our minds to-day. First must come a genuinely historical attempt to understand the kind of men they were, leading up to the question: 'What must the truth have been and be if that is how it looked to men who thought and wrote like that? This has to be done over and over again, as we take up the study of successive generations of Christian scholars. We ourselves are in the succession: all we can do is make our contribution from our own point of view, leaving it to be similarly revised by those who come after us. But theology is bedevilled by the illusion that somewhere, sometime, someone really knew the full truth and that what we have to do is to study what he said or wrote, find out what he meant by it, and get back to it. Both schools are in reaction against this assumption, but in different ways: the iconoclasts as men who, having come of age, must put away childish things and start afresh; the Teilhardists as men whose maturer vision gives them a fuller understanding of what they had thought and said in their youth.

Paradoxically both are controlled by the assumption against which they are reacting, the assumption that somewhere at some time it is possible to have a finally satisfactory statement of the truth. The iconoclastic demand to substitute the new theology for the old presents them as rival claimants for this untenable position. The Teilhardist reinterpretation of the faith in terms of

[1] *Sex and Christian Freedom* (London, 1967), p.41.

evolutionary science reads back into the minds of our ancestors ideas they never had. But God alone knows all the truth, and in this space-time universe is communicating it to us human beings as our growing minds grow in ability to receive it.

We must make a fresh start from the historical picture of the first Christians as Palestinian Jews trying to fit their faith in the risen Lord into their inherited Jewish theology. From them we go on to their successors. In each case our first aim is to learn what kind of minds they had, being the men of their age and culture. Then we ask how far their outlook helped or hindered them in seeing more deeply into the meaning of their faith. Their Jewish background gave the first Christians penetrating insights which have stood the test of time. It also closed their minds to aspects of the truth which had to wait for others to discover. The patristic age brought contributors from minds both enlightened and beclouded by Greek and Roman culture and the influence of oriental religious piety. So it has been ever since; until to-day it is mainly progress in scientific research which opens our eyes to fresh insights while doubtless blinding us to much that waits to be seen by theologians yet to be born. At every stage the study of the history of Christian doctrine involves the effort to discriminate between enduring insights into truth and passing reflections of the spirit of the age.

I have been asked by what criterion or standard we can tell the one from the other. In the sense in which the question is asked, there is none. We have to make up our own minds, reviewing in the light of to-day's knowledge what we have inherited from our fathers. The Christian faith is a unique thing in the world, working out its development for the first and only time in history. We are, as it were, inside the first acorn that ever became an oak. How can we tell the right way to be going so as not to be an elm or a beech? When Christopher Columbus set off to sail beyond the sunset he could not tell till he got there what kind of a land he would find across the ocean. He sailed by faith and not by sight. To-day Sir Francis Chichester has a multitude of navigational aids which he would be a fool to ignore because they were not known to Columbus.

Among theories and formulae 'time will show' well describes the method by which the Church has actually lived and grown. It was prescribed many years ago by an unknown writer in Deuteronomy xviii. 21, 22. In orthodox Catholic tradition an ecumenical decision is one which is promulgated by a constitutionally convened council of the Church and ratified by being accepted by the faithful. 'The ratification of conciliar decisions by catholic consent' is a translation into ecclesiastical language of the maxim 'time will show'.

This is not to deify time, for time is not God but God's, the order of successiveness through which God makes Himself known to man. 'Time will show' means 'God will show in His own time'. It is a useful phrase because it bids us wait on Him for the solution of our problems, recalling us from the impatience which would demand, like Marcion of old, that God shall do everything on a sudden.

It needs patience, the patience required first to get to know the minds of our predecessors in the context of their own age and then to consider what the thought of our age will allow us to endorse and what it will bid us revise. It is the discipline which will save us both from iconoclastic extravagance on the one side and from too facile an echoing of tradition on the other. This is what I had come to see when I wrote these lectures. What I have learnt since then from my share in the life and thought of the theological world makes me want to re-affirm it to-day.

Moreover, what I have read and heard during these ten years has confirmed me in three convictions.

1. When we think of God as personal this is not a mythological personification of some more ultimate reality. It is penetrating more deeply into thinking of Him as He really is. A corollary of this is that ultimate explanations will be found in terms of God's will and purpose which underlie the regularities investigated in scientific research.

2. This thinking of God as personal is not the same thing as thinking of Him as a Person, a distinction clearly brought out by C. C. J. Webb in his 1918 Gifford Lectures on *God and Personality*. Hesitation to think of God as personal is largely due to confusion on this point, and to failure to grasp the philosophical significance of the Christian doctrine of the Trinity. It is reinforced by a prevalent tendency to imagine it to be more 'scientific' to subordinate the personal to the impersonal, as when a man's personal action is explained to be the inevitable expression of an impersonal system of complexes.

At its worst this tendency lures theologians into a woolly-mindedness which substitutes arguments about depersonalized abstractions for wrestling with the mystery of God's revelation of Himself in the Person of Jesus Christ. Discussion of 'the Christ event', 'the resurrection experience', 'the new being', and 'the love which is the ground of our being' takes the place of any attempt to enter into and share in the personal relation of the disciples to our Lord. Too often it seems to be forgotten that what is called the resurrection experience was a matter of personal intercourse with a personal living Lord.

3. I have never been the same since I learnt from R. G. Collingwood to recognize the existence of scientifically knowable change. The combined influence of the scientific naturalism and the Hegelian idealism of my youth had tended to make it axiomatic that whatever could not be explained as either caused or reasonable could not really be what it appeared to be. A sudden shaft of light revealed the fact that so far as this space-time universe is concerned, this is not so. There may be actual events of which as they stand no reasonable account can be given; it is a waste of time to try to give one, as futile as an attempt to give a geometrical definition of a square circle. The element of truth for which the pragmatists stand is that such things must be accepted as what they are, wrestled with and changed in fact, in order to be made transparent to thought.

I would like to end by quoting a slightly altered version of a prayer ascribed to Bishop Ridding, published in 1915 in G. C. Binyon, *Prayers for the City of God*:

In times of doubts and questionings, when our belief is perplexed by new learning, new teaching, new thought, when our faith is strained by creeds, by doctrines, by mysteries beyond our understanding, give us the faithfulness of learners and the courage of believers in Thee; patience and insight to master difficulties; stability to hold fast our tradition with enlightened interpretation, to admit all fresh knowledge of truth unknown to us, and in times of trouble really to grasp the new knowledge and to combine it loyally and honestly with the old. Alike from stubborn rejection of new revelations and from hasty assurance that we are wiser than our fathers,

Save us and help us we humbly beseech Thee, O Lord

August 1967 L.H.

CONTENTS

Part I
INTRODUCTORY: FOR FAITH

Volume II contains

Part III: *CHRISTIAN THEOLOGY: FOR FAITH AND FREEDOM*

Part I

INTRODUCTORY: FOR FAITH

LECTURE I

Retrospect: Theological

I

SEVENTY years have passed since the munificent founder of these lectures defined in his will the task to which his lecturers should set themselves and the terms by which they should hold themselves bound. To enter upon their delivery is to be conscious of mingled feelings of gratitude and awe. There is gratitude to Lord Gifford for his benefaction, to the University of Glasgow for the honour of the appointment, and to previous lecturers for all that they have contributed to one's own mental growth. Of those who have lectured here in Glasgow I am in private duty bound to mention three to whom I am much indebted for their formative influence on my own thinking: Samuel Alexander, William Temple and John Laird. It is not surprising that the memory of such men should beget a sense of awe at being called upon to follow in their footsteps, to seek to deal with the high themes propounded by Lord Gifford, and to do so in the presence of so august an assembly. The only thing to do is to remember St. Paul's picture of the Christian warrior girding himself for the fray, to seek for truth with no ulterior motive, and having acknowledged one's own unworthiness to put one's trust in God and go forward.[1]

To go forward we must first go back. We must see how the present has grown out of the past in order to know where we stand as we look to the future. I propose to begin by trying to recall the study of philosophy and theology in Oxford when I was first introduced to Gifford Lectures by reading Bernard Bosanquet's *Principle of Individuality and Value* in 1912.

[1] Eph. vi. 14–16.

The fact that these lectures were being delivered, and that this book was recommended to a man reading for Greats as the most up-to-date source in which his examiners might be quarrying material for questions, shows to what extent in philosophy Hegelian idealism was still among the dominant forces in this island. But its star was already on the wane. While the influence of the Cairds lingered on in such teachers as J. A. Smith, and Hastings Rashdall maintained a Berkleian type of subjective idealism, violent revolt was manifest in the pragmatism of F. C. S. Schiller. Schiller, however, in his drastic leap to the opposite pole, was playing a lone hand. The more solid advance was made by such men as H. W. B. Joseph, H. A. Prichard, W. D. Ross, C. C. J. Webb and, above all, John Cook Wilson. Of these I shall have more to say hereafter.

But first, and before going on to speak of the contemporary study of theology, I must say something of the background of thought in the life of the university as a whole. The outstanding feature in the history of English education between the two wars has been the growth of the municipal and county secondary schools, opening the door to grant-earning university education for numbers of boys and girls who in earlier years could have had no such prospect. This has had a double effect on university life: it has increased out of all proportion the number of undergraduates who come up for the purpose of serious study, and it has ensured that the members of the university should no longer predominantly be drawn from the somewhat sheltered circles of the older public schools. Between 1918 and 1939 the undergraduate population, from whom in the main the dons of succeeding generations would be chosen, came to represent a much wider section of their fellow countrymen.

It is difficult to now realize the extent to which in general, in 1912, the members of the university were familiar with the language and practices of Christian worship according to the rites of the Church of England. Individuals and groups, both senior and junior, might make mental reservations or be bold enough to utter open criticisms of the faith officially professed, but for the most part they came from schools where chapel services and divinity lessons had made them familiar with the Bible and the Book of Common Prayer.[1] Undergraduates were required to attend services in their college chapels as a matter of obligation, and a good proportion of their teachers would be found there too.

A fading Hegelianism, in the setting of this general acceptance of Christianity, was the background of the academic study of theology, a study which was more a matter of antiquarian research than of theology proper. That it had this character was due in the main to two factors.

1. Biblical criticism was still a comparatively new discipline. There was much discussion and great uncertainty about the sense in which the Bible could be regarded as a divinely revealed source of Christian doctrine. The general tendency was to lay stress on its nature as a record of human religious experience, showing the progress made by our spiritual ancestors in the discovery of truths about God. Meanwhile the undergraduate students were coming into residence in more or less complete ignorance of the critical approach to biblical study. Among those who came to read theology, the Christian faith of many was wedded to a wholly uncritical use of the Bible. Rumours of the destructive activities of so-called critics had produced in others a state of unease which they hoped that their theological teachers would be able to dispel by showing them what in the Bible could still be relied on as authoritative in the old way. It was necessary that they should be made to see for themselves the grounds on which the critical reading of the Scriptures was based. For this purpose an incredible amount of time had to be spent in disentangling, with the aid of coloured paints or crayons, the different penta-

[1] I remember my predecessor Dr. Headlam mentioning a remark by the Principal of one of the women's colleges to the effect that whereas in her youth most of the students came from churches where Mattins was the regular Sunday morning service, now they were more familiar with choral Eucharist.

teuchal and synoptic sources. There was little time left to use them, when disentangled, for any other purpose than that of attempted historical reconstruction.

2. If biblical criticism was a comparative novelty, so also was the problem of the constitution of a theological faculty on a fully interdenominational basis. Barely half a century had passed since the university had been opened to others than professing members of the Church of England. In 1912 degrees in divinity, and examinerships for an arts degree in theology, were still subject to that restriction. There was uncertainty about the extent to which, and the manner in which theology proper, the doctrinal interpretation of revealed truth, could be treated with academic objectivity. It was generally agreed that in the university the study of the Bible and of Christian Doctrine should concentrate on the historical question of who said what, and what at the time had been meant by it. The interpretation of it with a view to determining the truth for our present believing had better be left to unofficial discussions and denominational agencies.

It was remarked in my hearing by a teacher of philosophy: 'There is more real theology talked in Greats than in the Theology school nowadays'.

While in the interests of academic objectivity university examination papers were confined to questions about the historical evidence which should not directly raise the theological issues, there was much discussion in theological circles of subjects such as the divinity of Christ and the gospel miracles. Here, too, the emphasis was on historical investigation. Just as in the Bible as a whole the question was whether man's discovery of truth about God was such that it could rightly be described by the use of such words as 'inspiration' and 'revelation', so we had to ask whether the evidence for the human life of Jesus was such that this man could in a unique sense be thought of as divine. The credibility of the miracle stories seemed to depend on the extent to which they could be shown to be outstanding instances of phenomena that could be paralleled elsewhere.[1]

Looking back on those times one can see in both theology and philosophy a single movement of the spirit which can be described as a resurgence of empiricism. I shall have more to say later about the meaning of this term and the significance of this trend of thought. I want now simply to call attention to the kinship between the philosophical questioning of idealism and the theological questioning of traditional orthodoxy. The philosopher no longer starts from some such principle as that the rational is the real, using it as a criterion whereby to judge the validity of our actual experience: his first care must be to ensure that no detail of our actual experience shall be ignored, explained away, or distorted in order to make it fit into a coherent scheme of thought. The theologian no longer sets out to expound a system of doctrine based on the conflation of various biblical texts: he scrutinizes the evidence for what men have actually believed with a view to discovering what remains as credible for himself. For both philosopher and theologian, the admission of loose ends and even contradictions in his system of thought is a more venial offence than carelessness about or indifference towards the evidence for what actually occurs in the history of this world.

As we now look back on those days we can see how in this both philosophy and theology contained the seed of what has come forth in the following years. But even in England, even in Oxford, thought does not develop in isolation, uninfluenced by pressure from events in the world around. For Great Britain, the British Empire, Western Europe and North America, August 1914 marked the end of an era. It would be foolish to ignore the effect of this century's political convulsions on the history of its thought. What I shall hope to show is that, while

[1] I can remember a paper read by a theologian to the effect that intercessory prayer could reasonably be thought to produce results in the body of a sick friend by acting on that body through the telepathic influence of mind on mind. Thus healing miracles were in general held to be more credible than nature-miracles.

in their effect on philosophy and theology the results were widely different, in each case they were produced by working upon that element which in 1912 was common to both.

II

In the first of his Lowell Lectures, delivered at Harvard in 1925,[1] A. N. Whitehead said: 'Faith in the possibility of science, generated antecedently to the development of modern scientific theory, is an unconscious derivative from mediaeval theology'. His point was this. So long as the world was thought to be governed by gods and goddesses, by incalculable angelic and demonic powers, it offered no field for scientific inquiry. Scientific research rests upon the 'belief that every detailed occurrence can be correlated with its antecedents in a perfectly definite manner exemplifying general principles', and this belief came from 'the medieval insistence on the rationality of God, conceived of as with the personal energy of Jehovah and with the rationality of a Greek philosopher'.

This phrase: 'the rationality of a Greek philosopher', reminds one of how for Plato this world of things and events in space and time was only partially patient of scientific knowledge, only partially embodied the intelligible forms which were truly knowable. For science to mean what it meant in 1912 a long development was needed not only from Plato but from medieval theology, a development in which the meaning of the words 'reason' and 'rational' suffered a sea-change. For the medieval theologian this world was a fallen world, and the divine rationality referred to by Whitehead was to be explored by deductive arguments based on principles roughly comparable to Platonic forms rather than on the observation of what actually exists and occurs. Science in the modern sense of the term means generalizing on the basis of this latter kind of observation, and to-day a rationalist is one who arrives at his conclusions by a method which at first

[1] A. N. Whitehead: *Science and the Modern World* (New York, 1925), pp. 17, 18.

was regarded as the forsaking reason for attention to irrational matters of fact.[1]

It was the success of the new method which led to the change in the use of the word reason, and in 1912 we were still under the spell of the nineteenth-century reverence for the certainty to be attained in this way. This world was neither the fallen, and therefore disorderly, world of the medieval theologian, nor the self-contradictory, and therefore unknowable world of Plato. Observation, experiment, and induction had shown it to be so dependable in its habits, so controllable by human intelligence, that God's creation was taken for granted as embodying the rationality of its Creator.

Moreover, so far at any rate as Great Britain was concerned, we had the feeling that we could study and think in a world of assured peace. Almost a century had passed since the Napoleonic wars: such fighting as we had had to do in India, the Crimea, and South Africa, the Italian *risorgimento*, and the Franco-Prussian war, had been sporadic interruptions in the spread of enlightened civilization. There might be other such incidents—a minor one was threatening in Ireland—but major upheavals and catastrophes belonged to the bad old pre-scientific times now gone for ever.

The war which broke out in 1914 put an end to this illusion of assured peace. In 1933 a German lecturer, lecturing in Manchester, described the effect on his countrymen as follows:

> Before the war we believed that the world in which we lived was the result of a creative intelligent force. So the world appeared rational, and man seemed to be able to change and transform it according to his rational purposes. This interpretation was a result of an increasing intellectualism which had lost touch with the concrete world. The war gave us quite a new feeling of what reality is.
>
> Pre-war men usually believed they knew a thing if they knew its laws. The soldiers discovered that we have no real knowledge of a thing as long as we have not experienced its concreteness. . . . The things of this world are not subject to the spirit in such a way that those who have knowledge can be lords of creation, one cannot use a thing or even benefit the world unless one has experienced all its properties and learned how to adapt oneself to them. When,

[1] Cp. C. E. Raven: *Natural Religion and Christian Theology* (Cambridge, 1953), iv, v.

for instance, the enemies' big guns shot into our trenches, all previous instructions had but small value; we had to adapt ourselves to what little protection the ground could give us. Moreover, by the experience of modern technical battle we were taught how superficial was the causal explanation of the world given by Positivistic science. Our first need is living, not knowledge, and living involves orientation to ends. But the soldiers discovered that there is no natural harmony of ends in this world. Teleology and dysteleology are linked with one another....

Another discovery was that history develops to a large extent independently of personal will, and according to its own laws and inherent forces....

The war had been for millions the school where they learnt to deal with reality as it is. This experience once made in the relatively small scope of war-life, they became able to apply it to all the other departments of the world and of life. Whereas pre-war man thought that the universe was entirely within the limits of his comprehension, there is now no such confidence. Man may work in this world and upon this world, but there is no possibility of giving a rational account of its nature....

The main problems which arise for this new attitude are the mysterious character of the world and the existence of evil.... The world in which we live not only resists our attempt at rational transformation, there is even evidence that it has in itself a tendency to hinder and counteract the moral good. A happier time believed that this world, though imperfect in some parts, was good. But... evil is not merely a deviation of the human will from the right way. In this world there are tendencies which work against its order and harmony, and for its destruction.[1]

I have given this somewhat lengthy quotation because it helps to explain the origin of certain features in which post-war theology came to differ profoundly from that of 1912. Underlying the changes was this breakdown of confidence in the power of human reason to discover the secrets of an intelligible universe, that confidence which had led the theologians of my youth to feel that they were on most sure ground when they based their faith on the records of human discovery rather than on the acceptance of divine revelation. One expression of this breakdown was the hypothesis of the non-rationality of God, advocated in Germany by Rudolf Otto and in the United States by Paul

[1] O. Piper: *Recent Developments in German Protestantism* (London, 1934), pp. 40–47.

Elmer More.[1] Another was the exposition of the Bible as bringing from God to man an authoritative revelation demanding the response of faith. The outstanding example of this was the *Römerbrief* of Karl Barth, which appeared in 1918. Existentialism sprang from the same disbelief in the existence of the unity of truth as common to all and discoverable by the exercise of reason. I have a vivid recollection of a conversation in the 'thirties with a fervent admirer of Hitler who based her arguments on the assumption that belief in a good common to different nations was a relic of outmoded nineteenth-century liberalism. Fourthly, there was a growing readiness to admit the existence and activity of evil demonic powers which in 1912 would have been dismissed as harking back to pre-scientific medieval mythology.

We in this island did not feel the impact of these factors so immediately as our fellow-Christians on the continent of Europe. This was partly due to our being spared such deeper ravages of war as invasion, oppression, and defeat. In both wars, while through extremity of suffering the eyes of others were being opened to a keener appreciation of the mysteries of the Christian faith, our vocation has been to keep alive in Christian thought the element of balanced judgment. But this is not the whole story. Why was it that Karl Barth's *Römerbrief* which was first published in 1918 and went through six German editions by 1928 did not appear in an English translation till 1933? Why was it that when I moved from Oxford to New York in 1925 I came into a world in which Barthian theology was creating a stir as yet unfelt by the banks of the Isis? America had shared with Great Britain in remoteness from the battlefields of Europe. There must have been some further reason why both in Europe and America the voice of Barth evoked a more immediate response than here.

I am inclined to think that the answer is to be found in the conservatism and illogicality which characterize the British mind.

[1] R. Otto: *Das Heilige* (Breslau, 1917; E. Tr. Oxford, 1923); P. E. More: *Christ the Word* (Princeton, 1927). See my *Place of Reason in Christian Apologetics* (Oxford, 1925).

I suspect that on the continent of Europe the logical conclusions to be drawn from the substitution of discovery for revelation had had more widespread influence on the preaching of the Christian faith than among us. Not only did our parochial clergy and ministers continue to proclaim the gospel of God's saving grace as though this were unaffected by what was being argued by professional theologians; we theologians ourselves could not believe that our liberalism implied any weakening of our faith in the historic creed of Christendom. I remember the late Bishop of Oxford, Dr. K. E. Kirk, once telling me that when he was a member of the University theological faculty he had read Barth's *Römerbrief* in the original German: it had impressed him as a very good expository commentary for pastoral use; he had been surprised a little later to hear that in some quarters it had been regarded as marking an epoch-making innovation in theological thought. Again, the so-called 'social gospel' came to us through such teachers as Frederick Denison Maurice, Brooke Foss Westcott, Henry Scott Holland, and Charles Gore, men for whom it was a corollary of a thoroughgoing faith in Jesus Christ as God incarnate. In America, for reasons over which we need not now delay, it had tended to become a substitute for that faith rather than an expression of it.

In what I have been saying I have had in mind throughout the theology of the non-Roman churches in western Christendom. After the condemnation of modernism by the papal encyclical *Pascendi Gregis* in 1907, Roman Catholic theology was little affected by the liberalism of which I have been speaking, and for some years after 1912 little or no attention was paid by Anglican and Protestant theologians to what was being thought and taught in the Church of Rome. But undoubtedly one reason for what I have called the conservatism of British theology was the fact that the Church of England, while freely opening its doors to the winds of inquiry, welcomed them as currents of fresh air in a household which in its faith and practice maintained its essential catholicism. However much individual theologians may have been influenced by biblical criticism and liberal thought, the Church as a whole continued to worship in accordance with the Book of Common Prayer, to baptize its new members in the faith of the Apostles' Creed, to instruct them in the doctrine of the Catechism, and to affirm the Nicene Creed at every celebration of the Holy Communion.

For one reason or another different but parallel types of humanism, based on the liberal questioning of the authority of the Bible and the divinity of Christ, had penetrated more deeply into the religious life of continental Europe and America than among us here. The Barthian revival made a more immediate impact upon them than upon us because it 'spoke to their condition' more directly than to ours.

Nevertheless, though our reaction may have been slower, we have come to share in the changed outlook which distinguishes the theological world of to-day from that of my youth. I can illustrate this change from my own experience of two events which in the year 1938 brought home to my mind the contrast with 1912.

In the summer of 1937 the World Conference on Faith and Order and the Universal Christian Council for Life and Work had agreed to unite in forming the World Council of Churches. In May 1938 there was a meeting at Utrecht in Holland for the purpose of drawing up a constitution for the proposed Council. The Faith and Order Movement had always been a Conference of churches 'which accept our Lord Jesus Christ as God and Saviour', and as its secretary I was present, charged with the responsibility of explaining that it could only come into the World Council if the Nicene faith in our Lord Jesus Christ as God and Saviour were made the basis of its Faith and Order work. The Life and Work Movement had never had this restriction, and I was expecting the Council to be constituted on its wider scale, with the narrower basis written into its constitution as a requirement for its Faith and Order activities. But speaker after speaker, representing a wide variety of churches from

America, Great Britain, Germany, Scandinavia and elsewhere, demanded the acceptance of the Nicene faith as the basis of the Council itself. I took care to point out that this was not demanded by the Movement I represented as the price of our adherence. It became abundantly clear that this basis would be adopted, not because of any desire to conciliate the stalwarts of the Faith and Order Movement, but because it was the almost unanimous demand of all those present. One speaker voiced the mind of the meeting when he said that if it was intended to have a Council of Christian Churches they must be Christian churches, and Christian churches are churches which accept that Nicene faith.

The prevailing impression made on my mind was that that debate registered the change that had come over the theological world since I had begun my theological studies in 1913. There was no one present to voice the modernist liberalism which would almost certainly have been a prominent, if not the dominant, force in any similar gathering held a quarter of a century earlier.

A month before the Utrecht meeting I had come back to Oxford after an absence of thirteen years. I came back as a professor in the faculty under which I had first learned theology, in which I had begun teaching as a young tutor. I came back to find myself in a changed theological world. I can best indicate the nature of the change by noting three features of it.

1. Pupils could now be expected to grasp the critical approach to the study of the Bible more readily and more quickly than in the past: time which had been devoted to colouring or underlining passages by way of exposing their sources could now be given to better study of their contents. In this study attention was passing on from the analytical dissection of different points of view to attempts to grasp the significance of the Bible as a whole. 'The Bible is not only a collection of records describing the development of religious ideas among Israelites, Jews and Christians, but also and chiefly the story of God's saving purpose for his people begun with the deliverance from Egypt, continued in his later dealings with them recorded in Old Testament history

and prophecy, and consummated in the sending of his Son, the Messiah.'[1]

2. This quotation reflects what by 1938 was in the minds of most of the younger theological tutors. One may sum up the situation by speaking of a growing conviction that a school of Christian theology should not be so much concerned with what I have called antiquarian research as with expounding the revelation of God which has come to men through Christ. From that time to this there has been growing impatience with an examination syllabus which lays undue emphasis on the analysis of sources, the accumulation of historical data, and the cataloguing of ideas while giving little scope for the consideration of their meaning or their truth.

3. With the critical approach to the Bible taken for granted as the normal and natural Christian way of reading it, with the Bible as a whole regarded as bearing witness to God's revelation of Himself to men, and with the demand that theology should be the expounding of this revelation, the door was opened to a revival of interest in systems of dogmatics to be found in different traditions of Christendom. Interest in Protestant neo-orthodoxy was balanced by interest in Catholic neo-Thomism: it was no longer the case that the theology of the Church of Rome was left out of account.

III

It must not be thought, however, that the changed outlook was simply due to the impact on theological thinking of world events, that it represented a surrender of rational inquiry to the demand for an assurance of revealed doctrine in an age of chaos. These circumstances may have hastened the development, but the development itself was the logical working out of principles already inherent in the earlier theology. The new emphasis on Christianity as a religion in which God's revelation of Himself

[1] A. M. Hunter: *The Unity of the New Testament* (London, 1943), p. 10.

makes demands on man's response expressed the conclusion towards which the progress of liberal and critical studies was tending along at least three lines.

1. In 1912 the historical study of the Gospels was based on the method illustrated by a volume which grew out of a seminar conducted by Dr. Sanday,[1] and was given full expression in B. H. Streeter's *The Four Gospels*, published in 1924. The essence of the method was the comparison of the texts of the different gospels with a view to discovering relations of literary dependence. There was general agreement that St. Matthew and St. Luke were expansions of St. Mark, that they had both used a second document, now lost, called Q, and had added material drawn from other unidentifiable sources. Put briefly, the underlying aim in general was to isolate the earliest evidence for our knowledge of the life of Christ, on the assumption that this would bring us nearer to the rock bottom of historical fact.

When, in 1919, Martin Dibelius published *Die Formgeschichte des Evangeliums* he was moving ahead along the customary lines of critical gospel study. But his advance undermined the assumption on which had been based attempted reconstructions of the gospel story. It is no good our thinking that by comparing documents to determine the respective dates of sources we can pare away accretions and thus determine what Jesus had actually done and said. The gospels are evidence of what was thought and taught about Christ by the earliest Christians. Our faith comes to us from them as with them we enter into the worship of Him who is their Lord and ours. In their recording of His acts and words there may be elements that we have to discount as reflecting presuppositions which have not stood the test of time. But we must not think that our methods of historical criticism enable us to understand better than did His disciples what was in the mind of Christ.

One instance will serve to illustrate this point. Various

[1] *Oxford Studies in the Synoptic Problem* (Oxford, 1911).

attempts have been made by comparison of texts to determine the precise words used by our Lord at the Last Supper, and the question has been raised whether, when we have narrowed them down to the bare minimum of indubitable authenticity, they imply any intention on His part to institute any new service for future observance. In answer to this question it should now be enough to say that there is evidence in the New Testament which shows that His disciples who were there understood Him to have meant this, and that we cannot go behind that.

2. I have said that in 1912 the divinity of Christ was among the live issues in theological discussion. There was then still current the notion that the Jesus of history, the Jesus discoverable by concentration on the earliest strata among the gospel sources, was one who taught the fatherhood of God and brotherhood of man but made no claims of any supernatural kind for His own person. This position was already being undermined as a result of the attention drawn by Johannes Weiss and Albert Schweitzer to the eschatological and apocalyptic elements in the gospels. When the dust of controversy had settled it became clear that there could be no clear historical reconstruction of the life of Christ without recognition that at the heart of His thought of Himself was the conviction that He had come as God's representative for the establishment of His kingdom on earth in fulfilment of His promises to His people through the prophets.[1] Whether or no during His earthly ministry our Lord ever thought or spoke of Himself as God in the full sense of the later Nicene doctrine, the evidence is inconclusive. But messiahship implied the claim to a unique status in relation both to God and man. Here let me quote from the book in which my one-time colleague Burton Easton was among the first to introduce form-criticism to English-reading students of theology:

> Fundamental to Jesus' work was his vocation to proclaim the coming kingdom; with a message of infinite blessedness, no doubt, but equally with a message of infinite destruction . . .; man is about to confront God.

[1] On this see W. Manson: *Jesus the Messiah* (London, 1943).

B

He who is entrusted with such a message can never feel that he belongs to this world; a sense of separateness must be an integral part of his nature. Now add to this the Messianic consciousness. Too many moderns treat it as if it were something almost any religious man might possess, as if it were a normal outgrowth of a sunny piety. It was nothing of the sort. It meant that in the coming judgment Jesus felt that he would not be on man's side but on God's.[1]

In an early work of my own, published in the same year (1928) as Dr. Easton's book from which I have quoted, I wrote: 'The claim of the Christian Church is that His one thought of Himself involves, if it be true, such a supernatural office as justifies the beliefs about him stated in the Christian creeds, and that if these elements in His thought are set on one side, whatever remains is not the historic Jesus'.[2] My point at the moment is that these two questions were not dictated by the requirements of a Barthian or any other dogmatic, nor did they voice a war-weary willingness to exchange trust in the use of human reason for acceptance of the authority of tradition. They stated conclusions arrived at by continuing further along the lines of rational inquiry on which theologians were moving before August 1914.

3. The recognition of Jesus' messiahship as the key to the historical understanding of the gospels involved a new appreciation of the place of the Church in New Testament Christianity.

According to Dr. Olaf Linton of Uppsala, there had been a general *consensus* of protestant theologians in 1880 to the effect that the pious individual Christian was the *Urdatum* of the Christian religion, that the original churches were sovereign self-organizing congregations (*gemeinde*), *collegia quae libera hominum coitione constant*, and that as the individual Christians found themselves forced to organize themselves in congregations, so the congregations were driven by circumstances into confederation. The premises on which the organization of the one church is to be understood are not religious ideas but worldly

[1] B. S. Easton: *The Gospel before the Gospels* (New York, 1928), p. 160.
[2] L. Hodgson: *And Was Made Man* (London, 1928), p. 67.

necessities.[1] This reading of the New Testament evidence was by no means extinct in 1912, and as late as 1938 Dr. Newton Flew could write: '"Jesus founded no Church"—this statement has become almost a dogma of critical orthodoxy'.[2]

The messianic understanding of Christ's ministry and person came by reading the New Testament documents in the light of contemporary Jewish thought. The extended use of this same method of historical inquiry led to the realization that the messianic vocation to establish God's kingdom on earth implies the existence of the people of God, the messianic community, the *ecclesia*.[3] As under the old covenant there had been one God and one chosen people, so under the new covenant there was one Christ and one Christian Church, the 'remnant' of the old Israel reconstituted to be the new Israel by the gift of the Spirit from the crucified, risen and ascended Lord. From Pentecost onwards individuals became Christians by being baptized into this fellowship of the Spirit, and the local congregations, the churches of Jerusalem, Antioch, Ephesus and Corinth, were localized settlements of the one church.

Christianity has come down to us as the faith of the original disciples of Jesus Christ who accepted Him at His own valuation of Himself as Messiah. The books of the New Testament are those in which some of them, and others who came to share their faith, set down in writing their understanding of how that faith had come to them, and of what it meant for creed and conduct, that is, for their belief about the nature of the universe and the purpose of human life. In the words of the latest of the gospel writers: 'These are written that ye may believe that Jesus is the Christ, the Son of God; and that believing ye may have life in his name'.[4]

As they saw it, during the earthly ministry of Jesus in Palestine His original disciples had had little understanding of what His

[1] Olaf Linton: *Das Problem der Urkirche in der neueren Forschung* (Uppsala, 1932), pp. 1–8.
[2] R. N. Flew: *Jesus and His Church* (London, 1938), p. 24.
[3] On this see A. M. Hunter: *The Unity of the New Testament* (London, 1943), pp. 46–74.
[4] St. John xx. 31.

messiahship meant to Him. It was after His resurrection, when they had been begotten again into a living hope[1] and commissioned, as the new and true Israel, the Christian *ecclesia*, to go forth into the world with the charge: 'As the Father hath sent me, even so I send you',[2] that by the guidance of the Spirit, looking back over the days when they had companied with Him in the flesh, they began to understand many things that at the time had been dark to them.

The starting point for the historical study of Christian theology is the faith of the Church as set forth in the books of the New Testament. More than nineteen hundred years have passed since those books were written, and successive generations of Christian theologians have sought to expound that faith in terms of the thought of their own times. However necessary may have been that critical study of the Bible which thirty years ago bulked so large in the curricula of schools of theology, we can now see that it was propaedeutic to the study of theology proper, study of the faith these books enshrine. In later lectures we shall have to consider in what sense this faith should be called revealed, and to what extent its exposition falls within the terms of Lord Gifford's trust. My present task is to set the stage for that further work by describing what is going on in the world of theology to-day. What I have already said will explain the emergence of two features to which I must call your attention before I close.

1. In 1953 Dr. J. R. Nelson, the Secretary of the Commission on Faith and Order of the World Council of Churches, prepared for its use a 'Factual Survey' in which he wrote:

> We live in a time of the renaissance of theological studies, which has brought forth renewed interest and serious inquiry in the meaning of the biblical revelation. As part of this widespread revival, there is evident a growing consensus on the centrality of the doctrine of the Church in the New Testament. Despite the fact that the biblical basis for this doctrine is so very clear to many scholars and non-critical readers to-day, it is well-known that the whole concept of the Church was virtually ignored even by some leading scholars,

[1] 1 St. Peter i. 3. [2] St. Matt. xxviii. 19; St. John xx. 21.

one or two generations ago. This rediscovery (as it has been for some Christians) involves a serious understanding of God's plan of salvation, of the calling of His people to a special task in this plan, of the intention of Jesus Christ to form a community of faith which should continue His ministry, of the institution of the Sacraments and the beginning of Church order—and, indisputably, of the essential unity of the Church.

The conception of Christianity as the faith of the Church finds expression in a revival of patristic and liturgical studies. When an international patristic congress was held in Oxford in 1951 the number of scholars who came together from various countries and denominations exceeded all expectations, and an even larger number attended the second such congress in 1955. Nor, indeed, is this interest in the systematic formulation of doctrine confined to the period of the early councils and creeds. Lutherans and Calvinists vie with neo-scholastics in producing volumes of dogmatics which are debated among university theological students. And the study of the Church's worship, as both expressing and influencing its doctrinal thinking, is making good its claim to an increasing share of attention.

2. The typological school of New Testament interpretation is an outcome of the realization that the starting point of the historical study of Christian theology is the faith of the New Testament writers combined with the reading of their works in the light of contemporary Jewish thought. Its advocates have done good work in reminding us that these writers were for the most part Jews whose background was the Old Testament and the cast of whose thought was Hebraic. It is true, I think, that because their books are written in Greek what I may call our 'classical' commentaries tended too much to interpret them in the light of the forms of thought and linguistic usage of the Greek classics. To have been recalled from this to look in the Old Testament for the ideas which govern the thinking of the writers of the New is a positive gain, and though in the first flush of their enthusiasm for this method of interpretation some of its exponents credit them with allusions that are more ingenious

than convincing,[1] a door has undoubtedly been opened to a fuller understanding of the text.

The political convulsions of this century have produced in many quarters scepticism of the capacity of human reason to discover truth, a desire for a religion proclaiming an authoritative revelation of God which does not submit itself to man's judgment but simply demands his acceptance and obedience, for a theology which confines itself to the exposition of the revealed truth. There have been theologians who have acquiesced in this scepticism, repudiated the pretensions of critics who have sought to sit in judgment on the oracles of God, and set themselves to write dogmatics on the basis of these assumptions. I have tried to show that a theology which meets the needs of the situation by taking for its subject matter the living faith of the Church is the outcome of developing the critical methods of the theology of my youth. I propose in these lectures to maintain that this is the right path for the theologian to follow, and that the fullest recognition of the revealed character of the Christian faith is consistent with the belief that it is God's will to submit it to the judgment of human reason.

[1] See below, Lecture IV, pp. 76 ff.

LECTURE II

Retrospect: Philosophical

I

IN my first lecture I was attempting to call to mind the worlds of philosophy and theology as I knew them in Oxford in the years before 1914. I described how each in its own sphere was characterized by what I called empiricism: the exposition of doctrines or systems of thought was being submitted to the test of accurate observation of the facts in human experience which they professed to interpret. I then went on to show how in the world of theology the outbreak of war produced a demand for the revival of doctrinal teaching and briefly considered ways in which theologians have sought to meet this demand.

I must now say something about what has been going on contemporaneously in the world of philosophy. I cannot here speak with the same inside knowledge that I have of the world of theology. For some years now, for reasons which will become apparent, I have felt in philosophical circles that I am an outsider. Any value in what I have to say can only come from my occupying the stance of the proverbial onlooker who is said to see most of the game. This particular onlooker must be allowed to preface his account of the play with some general remarks about the nature of the game, and to begin at the beginning by asking what is philosophy. In university curricula the term includes metaphysics and morals, epistemology and logic, political theory and the philosophy of religion. Is it simply by convention that the same word has come to be used for a group of heterogeneous studies, or have they some intrinsic connection which is the reason for its use?

Let us look through the word to the activities that we use it to describe. Our thinking is born of the desire to know the nature of the world we live in, and often starts from the consideration of some particular things or events which provoke our curiosity. Whether or no there be any truth in the story of Isaac Newton and the falling apple, an excellent illustration of what I mean is provided by Sigismund Freud in the second of his *Introductory Lectures on Psycho-Analysis.*[1] His starting-point for the voyage of discovery which leads to the formulation of his thesis is observation of the mistakes that people make in speaking, writing and reading: slips of the tongue, slips of the pen and misreadings. What needs to be explained is not merely the fact in general that we make such mistakes, it is the fact that particular people make the mistakes they do. Why on this occasion did this man unintentionally say the particular thing that he said?

Freud will not allow that any event can be dismissed as inexplicable because sheer accident. 'Does he mean to maintain that there are occurrences so small that they fail to come within the causal sequence of things, that they might as well be other than they are? Anyone thus breaking away from the determination of natural phenomena, at any single point, has thrown over the whole scientific outlook on the world'. Later on we shall have to consider whether Freud is right in thus denying the occurrence of genuinely contingent events: the point to notice at the moment is that scientific inquiry is born of the desire to see how the immediate objects of attention are related to all the other things that exist and go on in the world.

There is a story of a boy who was out for a walk with his father in the country and asked: 'Father, what is a phenomenon?' 'You see that cow', said his father, 'that's not a phenomenon. You see that tree; that's not a phenomenon. But if you saw that cow climbing that tree, that would be a phenomenon'. This quasi-ostensive definition explains the popular, and not the philosophical, use of the word, but the anecdote serves to illustrate my point. Our thinking starts when we are intrigued by

[1] London, 1949; pp. 19 ff.

something which catches our attention: the falling of an apple, a slip of the tongue, an unfamiliar word. We want to know more precisely just what it is in itself, and we find that we cannot accept a thing as being what it looks like until we see how it fits in with the rest of our experience. If we seemed to remember having seen a cow climbing a tree, we should say: 'That must have been a dream cow up a dream tree'. In the passage just quoted Freud speaks of this as a requirement that everything that happens must fall within 'the causal sequence of things'. At the present stage of our inquiry we cannot be so specific, or attempt to prejudge the question whether the required explanation is to be in terms of causality, sufficient reason, or any other principle. What we need is a colloquialism whose value to us is its philosophic vagueness. For this purpose I propose to use the phrase 'make sense'. We want to see how the various objects of our experience fit in with one another so as to make sense.

Once upon a time I was trying to do a cross-word puzzle in Boston, Massachusetts. Finding myself baffled in a measure exceeding the limits of my normal stupidity, I discovered on further inspection that by some printer's error the diagram of one puzzle had been combined with the clues of another. I wasted no more time on it: there was no point in trying to solve a puzzle when the parts did not belong to each other. If the world were like that it would not make sense, and it would be a foolish waste of our time to 'scorn delights and live laborious days' in scientific or philosophical inquiry.

> Were it not better done, as others use,
> To sport with Amaryllis in the shade,
> Or with the tangles of Neaera's hair?

Our thinking starts with the desire to know more about things in the world which excite our interest. For the most part we assume that they do fit in with one another in a pattern that makes sense: we assume that anything which will not so fit in cannot really be what at first sight it looks like. So long as we are simply concerned to find out what things are, and how they behave and fit in with one another in the history of this world in space and time, we are engaged on a scientific inquiry. If our desire is simply to know, we shall be pure scientists and the satisfaction we seek will be aesthetic. The successful result of an experiment which confirms a hypothesis, or the discovery of a formula which expresses the relation between various observed occurrences, will give us a satisfaction analogous to that which a man of aesthetic sensibility finds in the contemplation of a work of art. It is alleged in Oxford that at an annual dinner of mathematicians in Cambridge the toast is 'To the higher mathematics, and may they never be of any use to anyone'. We may, however, in our search for knowledge, be moved by the desire to extend human control over the course of events: our interest in pure science may be the contribution it can make to applied science. The contrast between the two is dramatically portrayed in Sinclair Lewis' novel *Martin Arrowsmith*, where the doctor employed by a research laboratory finds himself unable to carry out his instructions to inoculate only fifty per cent. of the inhabitants of a plague-stricken island in order that the others may be used as controls in testing the efficacy of the newly-discovered vaccine.

So long as the world produces sights and sounds which satisfy his need of aesthetic creation and enjoyment the artist can pass through life without ever bothering his head about whether there be any pattern which makes sense of the whole. In so far as the pure scientist finds his satisfaction in similar contemplation, both he and the practical man of affairs can take for granted the assumption of the existence of such a pattern. Freud's appeal to 'the causal sequence of things' takes for granted the universal sway of a convention which has been found to work well within a certain sphere of scientific inquiry.

It is not only in scientific inquiry and aesthetic activity and contemplation that we take for granted conventions that have been found to work. The same thing is true of our moral life. Moral conventions differ widely in different ages, climes and civilizations, but within any one of them parents and teachers bring up their children and pupils to take for granted the accepted scale of values, to have the appropriate feelings of admiration or shame. Where different conventions meet and clash a *modus vivendi* has to be found—a problem familiar, for example, to missionaries and civil administrators in connnection with the marriage customs of African tribes. In practice such problems are usually dealt with without raising the question whether the different customs can be fitted into some unifying pattern of moral values.

But sometimes it does occur to some minds to raise questions concerning these conventions and assumptions, and when a man is so intrigued by these questions that he cannot but pursue where they lead, a philosopher is born. It makes no difference whether he starts from questioning conventions and assumptions in the field of ethics, politics, religion, science or art, he will soon find himself face to face with the fundamental dilemma: do the things that exist and happen in the field of the natural sciences, do the things that we say and do in the worlds of ethics, politics, religion, and art, belong to a universe that makes sense, or are they clues in a puzzle which has no diagram with a pattern into which they fit?

I have called this fundamental question a dilemma because I do not see any way of proving demonstratively the truth of either possible answer, and whichever we adopt we embark upon a sea of troubles. If we abandon further inquiry on the ground that it is a fruitless waste of time in a patternless universe, we shall not escape the nagging of our intellectual conscience: we may either lose the respect of our fellows by trying to stifle it with Amaryllis and Neaera, or invite psychological distress by denying ourselves such solace without sufficient reason. If we decide to go forward, our questioning of departmental conventions and assumptions has led us to make one fundamental assumption, the assumption that the universe makes sense; the convention within which we work will be an act of faith that this is so.

Faced by this dilemma, the only way to avoid both horns of it is to maintain an attitude of suspended judgment. The philosopher would be the man who is inquiring whether the so-called universe has any unifying pattern, and if so, what. But so long as he knows what he is doing, knows that he is making an act of faith, a man does not cease to be genuinely philosophical if he takes for granted an affirmative answer to the former of these questions, and in that faith directs his attention to the second. He can plead at least this much in justification: that all human thinking, even those first strivings of curiosity which lead on to the development of the sciences, imply this faith, and that the progress which has resulted gives ground for holding that the confidence was not misplaced. I, at any rate, now affirm this faith, and shall take it for granted in what follows in this course of lectures. Philosophy, assuming that everything that exists and happens exists and happens in a universe that makes sense, is the attempt to understand how this can be so.

I do not as yet wish to affirm anything fuller or more specific. I want simply to introduce the philosopher as a man who is intrigued by the thought that all human thinking implies that the objects of thought fit into some sort of a pattern that makes sense. I would remind you that I deliberately use the phrase 'make sense' as a philosophically vague colloquialism which implies nothing as to what the nature of the supposed pattern may be.

Nevertheless, this introductory description of philosophy has at least four important implications for our present purposes.

1. We can see how the various branches of study which in a university are grouped together and labelled 'philosophy' spring from a common root. Their internal differentiæ are of two kinds. One is related to different fields of human thought and action. Thus we can speak of the philosophy of morals, of politics, of religion. We ask what are the grounds of the conventions and assumptions which are taken for granted in each field, how they are related to one another, and whether the investigation of them

can throw any light on the nature of the pattern in which everything must be seen to fit together so as to make sense. According to this differentia philosophy is asking the same kind of questions about different fields of study. Then, within all the fields, it sub-divides itself into different kinds of inquiry. In its aim to discover the universal pattern it is metaphysical; in its scrutiny of ethical or aesthetic value-judgments it is axiological; in its critical reflection on our ways of perceiving, thinking, and speaking it takes the form of epistemology and logic. The underlying purpose of the philosopher is to seek for the answer to the question of metaphysics, and in every field of human thought and action he must ask whatever questions are relevant to that purpose, questions concerning their assumptions and conventions which other men ignore.

2. I want to stress the point that essentially philosophy is an asking of questions, the quest for an explanation of what exists and happens. It can find no ultimate satisfaction until it finds such an understanding of the pattern of the whole as will provide a criterion whereby to judge of the reality and the value of everything that appears to exist or occur. Moved by this underlying aim, the history of philosophy is marked by the rise of different philosophical systems, and proceeds by the method of trial and error. A philosophical system is born when in his quest for the desired understanding a thinker conceives the idea that some element within our experience may give us the key to the nature of the whole. In Platonism, for example, it is 'the idea of the good'; in positivism what Freud calls 'the causal sequence of things'; in Marxism, the development of history in accordance with the interplay of economic forces. Then comes the attempt to see whether by the use of the proposed key we can account for all the objects of our experience without having to ignore, distort or explain away any of them. That is what I mean by the method of trial and error: the advocates of a system try to make it cover all the ground, and in so doing expose it to criticism which brings to light their errors.

Sooner or later I shall have to declare where I stand with regard to the truth or falsehood of different systems. But the time for that is not yet come. My sole aim at the moment is to make clear the distinction between philosophy itself in its fundamental nature, and the philosophical systems to which it gives birth. This distinction is obscured by the fact that we commonly use the word 'philosophy' to mean some particular system. We speak, for example, of the Platonic, the positivist and the Marxist philosophy as though they were particular instances of a universal, each exhibiting its essential characteristic in its own way. This conceals the distinction that later on we shall see to be of cardinal importance: the distinction between philosophy itself as the quest for understanding, the asking of questions, and particular philosophies as experimenting with hypothetical answers. It would be better to call them children of a common parent than instances of a universal.

3. Springing, as it does, from the desire to know the true nature of things, and why they behave as they do, the philosophic quest is a quest for objectivity. The philosopher wants to be assured that things really are what he thinks them to be, that neither in his perceiving them nor in his thinking about them has he misconceived their nature or their behaviour. He may start by being interested in falling apples or slips of the tongue, and not in himself as perceiving or thinking about them. But sooner or later his thought will turn in upon himself: he will begin to wonder whether he is deceived by his senses or has his ideas coloured by his passions and prejudices. When such questions arise in his mind, he realizes that, although they are secondary questions and a distraction from the pursuit of his primary quest, they are germane to it, and are genuinely philosophical questions which cannot impatiently be brushed aside. This is why philosophy includes epistemology and logic, and has a special interest in psychological research in so far as it has a bearing on those studies.

4. So far I have been trying to describe what I may call the archetypal philosopher. It is a long time since the questions he asks first began to be asked. The history of philosophy is not only the history of successive attempts to discover the pattern in which all things fit together in a whole that makes sense; it includes the history of attempts to deal with such relevant questions as those in epistemology and logic. Sometimes these secondary questions are of such importance and complexity and engage so much attention that their study feels like an end in itself: one tends to forget that they are subsidiary to the philosopher's primary quest. In the years before 1914, for example, when I was being introduced to the study of philosophy, this was the case with the study of the theory of knowledge as we traced its course from Descartes through Locke, Berkeley and Hume to Kant.

In various directions some positions have been secured, their grounds examined so that they are no longer uncriticized assumptions; some blind alleys have been explored and signposted 'No Road'. To be a competent philosopher it is not enough to have been bitten by the *bacillus philosophicus* and be plagued by the itch to know the answer to the philosophic questions; one must know enough about what has already been done to be able to profit by the discoveries and mistakes of our predecessors in the field.

As a result of all this the study of philosophy is exposed to two dangers, the production of view-tasters and of parlour-gamesters. Philosophy only comes into being and has a history because of the existence of men for whom its pursuit is a matter of life and death, for whom its questions are of such importance that they can have no peace of mind until they feel that they are at least on the way to an answer. One thinks of the Platonic Socrates searching in an age of general scepticism for a rock on which to stand and finding it in his conviction of the security of certain moral principles. One thinks of Descartes doubting the existence of everything except his own thinking self, of Kant awoken by

Hume out of his dogmatic slumber. To be a competent philosopher to-day one must know what these and many others thought and taught, and much that has been said and written about them; one must know the relevant literature and be at home in the vocabulary and technical terms that have become conventional in it; and one must have that mental acumen which enables a man intelligently to grasp the significance of points in philosophical arguments. With these qualifications a man may obtain high examination honours in philosophy, and may even become a teacher of the subject. But if this is all there is to him, he will never become more than either a dilettante view-taster, or at the best an extremely skilful parlour-gamester. To pass beyond this, the necessary knowledge and skill must be at the service of one for whom the subsidiary questions are of importance through their relation to the central quest, one who is possessed by so passionate a concern for truth that he can never find satisfaction in knowing who said what, or in the exercise of dialectical skill, unless these are contributing to his growth in understanding the why and wherefore of the world he lives in and of his own existence.

II

I must now try to define rather more closely the goal of the central quest. Can we, at the present stage of our thinking, have any idea of what kind of a pattern would satisfy us as making sense of everything that exists and occurs?

Who are we, that we should expect our demand for satisfaction to be honoured by the universe? Should we not rather take Carlyle's advice and be content simply to accept it? The answer is paradoxical. We are the mouthpiece of the archetypal philosopher, and the archetypal philosopher is possessed by two apparently contradictory passions. On the one hand it is his sole aim simply to accept the universe: it is to this end that he engages in such studies as epistemology and logic, turning aside to make sure that none of his thoughts are the children of his wishes or the dupes of his senses. On the other hand, he finds that he cannot begin thinking at all, he cannot even begin to examine his own perceptions and thoughts, without making his act of faith in the fundamental assumption that the things he is trying to think about fit in together so as to make sense. In so far as this is a demand upon the universe, it is a demand that he must make if he is to think at all, a demand which he must make if he is to be able intelligently to accept the universe. The paradox is that only what will satisfy the demand can be accepted as objectively real, as being what it is in itself, uncoloured and undistorted by any demand that he may have made upon it.

I touch here the rock bottom which is the foundation of all that I shall attempt to build in the lectures that follow. It is the fundamental act of faith to which I have already confessed: the assumption that everything that exists and happens exists and happens in a universe that makes sense. It is not only the foundation on which I shall build my own construction, it is also the basis for what I shall have to say in criticism of others, both in philosophy and theology. I shall not, therefore, be wasting our time if, before going further, I pause to say three things about it.

1. First let me repeat my conviction that this paradox is implicit in all serious human thinking. There is always a quest for objectivity which can only be satisfied by the object fulfilling the demands of the thinker's canons of thought. Two children of a friend of mine were overheard discussing what kept their arms and legs fastened to their bodies. Was it glue or screws? 'If it was glue', said one thoughtfully, 'they would come off in the bath. It must be screws'.

The quest for objectivity is illustrated alike by the questions of children, by scientists who repeat experiments with a view to eliminating the possibility of error, and by theologians who seek to find in the Bible or the Church an authority whose acceptance will silence all further questioning. Even the lover cannot help asking

Nay, but you, who do not love her,
Is she not pure gold, my mistress?

Each and all will only accept answers which are consistent with their categories of thought. This is seen most clearly in the children and the scientists, for whom their categories may be derived from experience of the tragic fate of cherished toys in hot bath water, or of the 'causal sequence of things'. In the case of the theologians and the lovers it does not lie so openly on the surface, but it is there nevertheless. They may glory in holding to their beliefs in spite of the available evidence, but the lover's question and the theologian's faith augur a secret hope that in that world where the secrets of all hearts shall be revealed and we shall know even as we are known, we shall find that the evidence now available has been not only inadequate but misleading, and that when all is known those who disagree with them may have to revise their categories to meet the situation.

The suggestion that in the course of interaction between categories and evidence the one may be subject to revision as much as the other will be found, before long, to be of great importance, but must not detain us now. Nor am I raising the Kantian question whether the demand that objects of thought shall conform to canons of thought must invalidate any claim to be able to discover the nature of things as they are in themselves. All I am saying at the moment is that all thinking is fundamentally the paradoxical quest for an objectivity which we can allow to be such.

2. Secondly, I want to affirm my conviction that in so far as a man exemplifies the archetypal pure scientist or philosopher, his demand for an objectivity which shall satisfy his canons of thought is not to be dismissed as either selfishness or pride. The error here is one to which in these days theologians are more prone than philosophers. Bishop Butler, it is true, had to wrestle with the corresponding contention in moral philosophy,[1] and from time to time it recurs in the works of sophists who make

[1] E.g., in the Preface to the *Sermons at the Rolls Chapel*.

play with the apparent contradiction involved in such a phrase as a disinterested interest in truth. But its main advocates are certain theologians whose idea of revelation is such as to leave man no right to decide between what he can and what he cannot honestly accept as true. The antithesis they draw between the humility which accepts the revelation, and the pride which dares to criticize it, or the selfishness which demands the satisfaction of its desires, rests upon a profound misunderstanding of the psychology not only of scientists and philosophers, but also of artists and of would-be decent citizens. Here I must anticipate what I shall have to argue more fully in a later lecture, and say that on both sides of his paradoxical activity, in the demand for the satisfaction of his canons as well as in his passion for objectivity, the honest thinker is not seeking to impose upon the universe his own personal will, to satisfy his pride, or to indulge his desires. Often, indeed, if his convictions are out of harmony with the spirit of the age, pride would be better served by dishonesty and desire by abandoning his studies for Amaryllis and Neaera. In his own consciousness he knows that fidelity to his convictions is not self-assertion but submission to a demand made upon him by a something other than himself. Philosophy is the examination of assumptions habitually taken for granted by men in their various activities. One of my chief tasks in this course of lectures will be to inquire into the implications of this consciousness of submission: my concern at the moment is that we should recognize it as being what it is, and not confuse it with something else.

3. This quest for objectivity implies faith in the existence of an objective reality which is patient of discovery by different inquirers. From the point of view of the inquirer its objectivity means that neither its existence nor its nature depends upon his having this or that idea of it. His aim is to discover what it is in itself so that he may revise his ideas and make them conform to the discovery. To this end, if the subject admits of it, he may test his ideas by laboratory experiments, and if he discusses his

problems with other inquirers it is on the ground that by comparing his ideas with those of others each may be enabled to discount what is purely subjective to himself.[1]

When Freud set himself to find out why particular men make particular slips of the tongue, he took it for granted that the explanation to be discovered was one which would be recognized, understood and accepted as satisfactory by all intelligent fellow-seekers. Whether or no he was right in thinking that he had found it within the limits of the 'causal sequence of things' in which there is no place for chance is beside the present point: what matters is that when he gave his *Introductory Lectures on Psycho-analysis* he certainly believed himself to be doing something more than merely narrating a diary of his own personal reactions to the behaviour of his patients. Whatever may be the truth in existentialism, if in any field of inquiry it is carried to the length of denying the possibility of different inquirers usefully discussing a common object with a view to agreeing about its nature, it renders any further discussion within that field a waste of time.

Taken together, the three points amount to this. If we hold it to be worth while to try to think at all (and our presence here suggests that we do), even if our thinking only goes so far as to ask such questions as how our arms are attached to our bodies, or why people make mistakes, in so doing we assume that we and the objects of our thought belong to a world in which we and they fit together in a pattern such that we can accept it as satisfying the demands of an understanding which we share with other inquirers.

This assumption, or act of faith, is, as I have said, my starting point. Now I want to use it not merely as a starting point but as a jumping-off ground for a leap which will carry me over territory much of which will need to be secured in detail later on. I want to assert the conviction that there can be no end to the philosopher's quest until he has discovered the pattern to be one

[1] On this see my *Towards a Christian Philosophy* (London, 1942), pp. 28-37.

which approves itself to him as good, and that only this discovery can finally justify as worth while that asking of elementary questions which constitutes the first step in our thinking.

Questions at once well up in our minds. What definable sense can be attached to so vague and general a term as 'good'? Good for whom or for what? These questions must wait for the attention they deserve. For the time being I must content myself with saying that by 'good' I mean that which we can accept as justifying its own existence without needing to be referred to something else to answer the question why it should be so. We all of us, in our everyday lives, make use of this criterion. In the spheres of aesthetics and ethics, for example, when we are presented with a sublime work of art or with nobility in act or character, we do not ask why they should be: we cease to question, and find our satisfaction in the contemplation of them as being what they are. To a certain extent we find a similar satisfaction, the satisfaction of the pure scientist, whenever we feel that we have freed ourselves from mistakes and illusions and really grasped some objective truth about the nature of things. But so long as what we have discovered is such that it can adequately be described as brute fact, we shall still find ourselves asking why it should be. Our questioning will not be stilled until we can find some further explanation of it which shows how it fits into the pattern of a self-justifying whole.

If we ask who is to be the judge of its goodness, I can at this stage only refer to the figure whom I have called the archetypal philosopher. Who is this archetypal philosopher? He is the ideal philosopher whom in all our philosophizing we are seeking to emulate, and, indeed, ourselves to become. We know by experience something of the interaction of thought and things, of categories and evidence, of which I have spoken; we know how further consideration of evidence can lead to the revision of categories: we have learned, for example, that there are other means of attachment besides screws and glue, we have learned (in Whitehead's language) to correlate occurrences as exemplifying general principles instead of regarding natural phenomena as 'governed by gods and goddesses, by incalculable angelic and demonic powers'.[1] From our experience of the possibility of progress in our imperfect achievements we form an idea of the perfection at which we aim, the complete understanding of all things by a mind which needs to ask no further questions because it finds complete satisfaction in the contemplation of what it knows.

Whether or no there be any such mind, whether or no it is conceivable that any man should receive such knowledge, are questions which for the present I must leave in the air. What I am trying now to establish is that all our thinking—indeed, all our actions—that means all our living—imply and require for their justification faith in the possibility of an affirmative answer to them. Occupied in their immediate concerns, men of affairs, artists and scientists may never be called upon to examine the implications of what they think and say and do. It is the philosopher's task to analyse and seek for the justification of their unexamined assumptions, and when once he is started on the quest there can be no end to it short of the discovery of the self-justifying pattern of the whole.

Now we can see more clearly what is involved in the fact that the history of philosophy has been the history of systems begotten to struggle for survival by the method of trial and error. Each system has to be tried out with a view to determining to what extent, by taking some element in our experience as the key to the interpretation of the universe, we can see the whole as transparently self-justifying in all its details. Since our thinking proceeds by the interaction of thought and things, of categories and evidence, its task at any stage of the process is the reconciliation of the two sides; the exposition of the categories to show how they can assimilate the evidence, the examination of the evidence to insure that it shall not be misdescribed in order to

[1] Cp. above, Lecture I, p. 8.

make it fit the categories. All this springs from the double-sided character of the longing for objectivity which lies at the heart of the philosophical quest.

III

If, then, a fading Hegelianism was characteristic of the world of philosophy as I knew it in 1912, this means that we were coming to the end of a period in which that system had been on trial, had been given the opportunity of showing how far it could go towards opening our eyes to the understanding of all things. It is probably too soon for us to be able to assess the value of its contribution, though some attempt will have to be made later on in this course of lectures. Here and now our concern is with what has been going on since 1914.

We have seen the beginning of one of the recurrent swings of the pendulum which mark the history of philosophy, reversing the direction in which it had begun to swing a century before.[1] Stated in terms of what I have just called the double-sided character of the philosopher's quest for objectivity, what has been happening may be described as the shifting of emphasis from the demand that reality shall conform to the categories of our minds to the demand that our minds shall conform to the evidence as it comes to them, whether or no it can be assimilated by the categories as they stand. The underlying principle of the idealism which had been on trial was that the rational is the real: the law of contradiction was the key with which to lay bare the secrets of the universe and throw light upon the mysteries of our existence. The task before exponents of the system had been to show how it could explain the fact that these secrets and mysteries appear as they do in our experience.

Of earlier Gifford lecturers whom I have mentioned, Bernard Bosanquet was one of these exponents, and a very gallant attempt he made. The influence of the school was still strong in the

[1] See John Jones: *The Egotistical Sublime* (London, 1954), pp. 35–46.

thought of William Temple.[1] Samuel Alexander and John Laird, more clearly heralds of days to come, were at that time unknown to me. As I look back on the study of philosophy in Oxford in the years before 1914, the three names which stand out most clearly in my memory as having had a formative influence on my mind are those of my own tutor, H. H. Williams (afterwards Principal of St. Edmund Hall, and Bishop of Carlisle), H. A. Prichard, and John Cook Wilson.

I can never adequately express what I owe to H. H. Williams, nor can I say anything of what he taught me beyond that he taught me to think. He was a tutor for whom teaching did not mean the imparting of information or indoctrination in the views of any school of thought. His aim was to teach his pupils to think for themselves, as week by week in the reading of their essays any loose thinking or shoddy construction was relentlessly laid bare. It was not to tutor but to books and lectures that one turned for the material to think about.

I must have been among the last of those who sat at Cook Wilson's feet, caught the inspiration that came from the flashing eyes and snapping fingers which accompanied his most incisive thrusts, or shrivelled inwardly as some callow suggestion of one's own was exposed in all its naked foolishness. In his *Idealistic Logic*[2] Sir C. R. Morris treats Cook Wilson's criticism of idealism as a reaction to the views of a bygone age. In my recollection of him he stands out as a precursor of what was to follow.

Take, for example, his criticism of the traditional formal logic, his analysis of its notion of the proposition as the unit of thought which led him to prefer the use of the term statement to either proposition or judgment. The essence of it was that no form of words can be taken as expressing thought without reference to the question in the mind of the thinker. In the sentence 'That building is the Bodleian', which term is subject and which predicate depends on whether the question asked was 'Which is

[1] See my *Doctrine of the Trinity*, pp. 131–4. [2] London, 1933.

the Bodleian?' or 'What is that building?' The subject is that which is in the mind to begin with, that about which one is seeking further information; the predicate is the new information which is acquired. 'Statement' was adopted as a non-question-begging term, one which would neither, like proposition, imply that the form of words was by itself an adequate indication of the thought nor, like judgment, imply that the thought was of a particular kind.

In thus calling attention to the importance of considering the relation between words and thoughts Cook Wilson opened the door to the detailed analysis of linguistic usage which has largely occupied the time of philosophers in these last thirty years. Cook Wilson's ground for the choice of the word statement as the logical term for the kind of grammatical sentence which can be made the basis of inference implies the existence of sentences expressing other forms of mental activity which were for his purpose irrelevant. He rejected the term judgment because it involved an unnecessary element of doubt or wonder followed by decision. But if the meaning of words and sentences is to be determined by the purpose for which they are used, we cannot stop short at apprehension, doubt, wonder and decision; we must further distinguish and recognize such uses as valuation and prescription.

Cook Wilson used the term apprehension for the mental act which should include nothing beyond what was necessary for its statement to be the basis of valid inference. Moreover, he used the same word for the inferring itself. Having apprehended the premisses severally, the thinker looks at them together and apprehends the conclusion involved in them. This apprehension was for him the starting-point and goal of all thinking, an immediate grasping of fact or truth which is *sui generis*, known to all men by experience but indescribable in terms of anything other than itself.

What is meant by calling this the goal of all thinking is clear from what I have been saying about the passion which animates the archetypal philosopher. His quest for objectivity is a quest for the kind of knowledge, of grasping of reality, for which Cook Wilson used the word apprehension. What of its use for the starting point, and for intermediate steps taken in the course of the quest?

Cook Wilson used it indifferently of apprehensions belonging to two distinct fields, those of sense-perception and of mathematics and logic. Now, as I understand it, philosophy in the last thirty or forty years has largely been occupied with the investigation of the problems here involved. On the one hand there has been analysis of the language and thought characteristic of the natural sciences, undertaken with a view to discovering to what extent through our sense experience we may be said to gain genuine knowledge of objective reality. On the other hand there has been analysis of the language and thought used in abstract reasoning, with much interchange of ideas between logicians and mathematicians.

In my first lecture, when speaking of the impact of the political convulsions of this century on the progress of theological thought, I said that while in their effects on philosophy and theology the results were widely different, in each case they were produced by working on that element which in 1912 was common to both.[1] That common element was what I then called empiricism, meaning by the word a turning of interest from the exposition of revealed truths or metaphysical systems to the investigation of the actual facts of human experience. When, a few minutes ago, I spoke of Alexander and Laird as heralds of the future, it was because in their attempts at metaphysical construction they started from this empirical end. But in so far as they made such attempts at all they showed that they were not wholly carried away by the rising currents of opinion. For while among theologians a growing scepticism with regard to the capacity of human reason was engendering a demand for its supersession by a divinely guaranteed revelation, the parallel movement in

[1] Above, p. 7.

philosophy was a tendency to deny the possibility of metaphysics and confine the scope of reason to the investigation of events in space and time. Thus in his *Essay on Metaphysics*[1] the late R. G. Collingwood (so often my companion at Cook Wilson's Informal Instructions) reduced that study to the empirical study of the presuppositions of different thinkers characteristic of different ages, climes and cultures.

One exception to this denial of the possibility of any metaphysic was the emergence of logical positivism. Logical positivists regarded themselves as among those who denied the possibility, but the name positivism, with its reminiscence of Comte, describes a materialistic metaphysic, the position that in argument about the objective nature of reality the only valid premisses are those guaranteed by the kind of apprehensions made in the natural sciences. It was the aim of exponents of this theory to show by linguistic analysis that statements which had been held to bear witness to the existence of another order of reality had been misunderstood, that 'philosophical propositions are not factual but verbal'.[2] For the most part, however, philosophers engaged in linguistic analysis have not so much been concerned to establish this or any other metaphysic, as to track down and expose errors in thought due to verbal confusion. Naturalism has been taken for granted rather than explicitly affirmed. There was work enough to be done without turning aside to inquire whether all that we experience can be seen to fit together into a pattern which will satisfy our understanding.

Existentialism has been another product of this empirical age; a further illustration of the complexities involved in the relation of words to thoughts. So long as the form of words, the proposition S. is P, could be taken by itself as the starting point, the traditional logic could go happily on its way. But when we realize that a sentence can only be understood by reference to the

[1] London, 1940.
[2] M. Macdonald, in Flew: *Essays on Logic and Language* (Oxford, 1951), p. 80.

question it is intended to answer, we are in another world. The same form of words may express different thoughts. We have to be concerned with the thoughts, and the thoughts are the thoughts of different human beings, each of whom looks out on the world from his own standpoint, conditioned by the circumstances of his birth and growth and experience. What ground have we for thinking that some truth which is common to all is more important than the realization and affirmation of that which he is empowered to contribute through his individuality?

I have said enough to show how the run of the play appears to me as I view it from the theologians' seats in the pavilion. It is an illustration of what I was saying a few minutes ago, that the history of philosophy is not only the history of successive attempts to discover the pattern in which all things fit together in a whole that makes sense; it includes the history of attempts to deal with such relevant questions as those in epistemology and logic. Sometimes these secondary questions are of such importance and complexity and engage so much attention that their study feels like an end in itself: one tends to forget that they are ancillary to the philosopher's primary quest.

This is what I believe to have been happening in the period through which we have been living. Logical positivism and existentialism are incidental accompaniments of what is in essence a necessary attention to epistemology and logic, without which certain sources of error and confusions of thought might never be exposed and avoided. In such a period philosophy is in danger of so developing the specialized study of details, with an esoteric growth of technical terms, that it ceases to be of interest to any but its own professional practitioners, encouraging the production of view-tasters among its pupils and parlour-gamesters among its teachers. Nevertheless, it is a necessary stage in the history of philosophy, as necessary as was the antiquarian research stage in that of theology. Without the latter we should not have our present freedom to preach with full conviction the biblical revelation of God's redeeming grace. That passion for an understanding of all existence which is the well-spring of philosophy will not for ever be restrained from asking its fundamental questions, and in the future those who shall seek for answers with a genuine desire to avoid pitfalls on their way will often have cause to be grateful to Ludwig Wittgenstein and his disciples.

LECTURE III

Puzzles and Clues

I

OUR fundamental act of faith is that the universe of our experience somehow or other makes sense. It is worth while trying to study it and think about it on the assumption that the clues to its puzzles coherently indicate the pattern of the whole. In this empirical age we do not proceed by assuming a theoretical pattern and trying to show how it can assimilate the facts. We begin by trying to observe and describe as accurately as possible the things which have to be accounted for. In other words, we start with the puzzles. We are not in the position of a man who is tackling a crossword puzzle, for he is confronted by a single puzzle for which he is provided with both diagram and clues. We are confronted by a multitude of puzzles in which we have to search for our own clues, and the trouble is that clues which seem to hold out hope of solving different particular puzzles often lead in different directions, making more and more difficult the puzzle of puzzles, the reconciliation of them all.

Our first task, then, is to survey the field and take note of the puzzles. Here must be made a preliminary disclaimer. In my second lecture I have spoken of how the advance of knowledge is by way of interaction between the objects of observation and the observer's categories of thought: sometimes categories have to be revised in the light of fresh observations, sometimes observations have to be discounted as untenable in the light of rational reflection.[1] In all our observing, as well as in our thinking, our minds are conditioned by the presuppositions of our age and

[1] Above, Lecture II, pp. 34, 37.

clime and personal upbringing. Of this I shall have more to say in the next lecture. I mention it now in order to disclaim any pretention to be free from these limitations. I can do no more than attempt to call attention to the puzzles as I see them, knowing that I see them with the eyes of a Christian theologian of twentieth-century western Europe, and that inevitably this must give some colouring to what I see. I make my contribution to what must be our joint quest for objectivity, the quest which will only reach its goal if all, by contributing their insights, correct what is distorted in the vision of each.[1] This being understood, I will now try to put before you, as I see them, some of the puzzles which provoke the mind of one who is trying to make sense of his experience.

The first of these is that we live in a world which makes demands upon us that do not conform to the requirements of logical consistency. It is hard to think of any good principle of action which, if carried to its logical conclusion, will not land us in absurdity. My good parents brought me up on two excellent maxims: 'Always finish the thing you are doing before you turn to another', and 'When your father or mother call you, stop whatever you are doing and come at once'. As a tiresome child I argued as though they were to be condemned for their inconsistency; in my riper years I have come to see that such inconsistency was the mark of their practical wisdom. It bore witness to the truth that the point at issue was one of the standing puzzles of our existence, not one to be easily resolved by reference to some aphorism about exceptions proving rules.

Take, for example, the principle 'equal pay for equal work'. This is so obviously just that we rightly seek to end the anomaly by which a woman is paid less than a man for doing the same work. At the same time we are supplementing wages and salaries by the payment of children's allowances, a practice which involves the principle: 'from each according to his ability, to each according to his need'. To follow either of these principles

[1] On this see my *Towards a Christian Philosophy*, pp. 33 ff.

to its logical conclusion would prevent us from acting on the other, and that would be absurd.

Again, it is sometimes said, as though it were the whole truth, that we should consider persons before things, including among things not only worldly wealth and objects of sense-perception but such intangibles as laws and standards. In his Gifford Lectures Dr. Charles Raven has criticized Plato on these lines, denouncing as unchristian the idea that a man's performance of his ἔργον, his contribution to the good life of the community, should be taken into account for the measure of his world.[1] This is one-sided. It is surely salutary for a man to reflect that he is only of importance in so far as he fulfils his vocation. Nor can one solve the puzzle by saying that while it may be good for a man thus to think about himself, he should adopt a different principle when thinking about others. An examiner, for example, may have the misfortune to know how much prospective happiness or misery, both for the candidate himself and for others, hangs upon his success or failure, and yet he must resolutely subordinate all such personal considerations to the impersonal standards which the examination exists to maintain.

Consideration of various instances of this kind of puzzle leads to the realization that we live in a world in which not only do 'new occasions teach new duties', but different occasions demand action on different, and sometimes logically inconsistent, principles. Circumstances alter cases to such an extent that logical inconsistency becomes the guide of life. This is one of our puzzles.

I have shown elsewhere how it affects our understanding of the relations of church and state.[2] Other instances are provided by problems concerning censorship. On the one hand there is the good principle of respect for freedom of thought and speech; on the other that of the duty of the state to safeguard standards of life including, among others, that respect for freedom itself.

[1] *Experience and Interpretation* (Cambridge, 1953), p. 199.
[2] *The Doctrine of the Atonement* (London, 1951), pp. 107 ff.

Is there never a danger that exclusive devotion to freedom of speech may be used to establish a *régime* which will proscribe it? There is also, for us Christians, our puzzlement over the question of war.

No thoughtful Christian, who is not a pacifist, can avoid being made uncomfortable by his sense of failure to accept the logical conclusions of certain principles involved in the life and teaching of Christ; of Him who said 'Love your enemies', and, so far from seeking to bring in the kingdom of God by force, followed the way of non-resistance to His death on the cross. How much simpler life would be if one could agree with those for whom this is the whole of the matter, for whom it provides the only principle of action of which account need be taken! But it is not so. To treat this one element in the example of Christ as though it were the whole is an undue simplification. In the years before 1939 many an English Christian was made acutely uncomfortable by the knowledge that the price of our avoidance of war was not being paid by ourselves but by Ethiopians and Czechoslovaks. As my one-time colleague Dr. Burton Easton used to put it: 'Christ said, "him that taketh away thy cloak, forbid not to take thy coat also";[1] He did not say, "let him have also the widow's cloak and the orphan's coat".' It is not surprising that while most Christians are agreed that war is an evil and should be abolished, there is difference of opinion about the duty of the individual until this be done. This difference bears witness to the underlying conflict of principles inherent in the situation.

To speak of the conflict of principles as something inherent in the situation introduces a new point in the relation between evidence and categories, and in what we mean by logic and logical. Truth is a quality of statements, and if we say that in our quest for objectivity we are seeking to know the truth about things, we mean that we are seeking so to apprehend the things themselves so as to be able to discriminate between what is true and what false in statements about them. We only accept things

[1] St. Luke vi. 29.

as being what they appear to be in so far as they are such as to conform to the requirements of our categories of thought: if anyone tells us that he has seen a cow climbing a tree, we simply do not believe him. But whence do we get these categories of thought? For those which prevent us from believing in such things as tree-climbing cows the answer is fairly simple: they come as the result of observation of how things like cows behave. In so far as they govern our thinking they are the result of prior apprehensions of objects of thought. But what of those which are prior to all observation and apprehension whatever, of that law of contradiction, for instance, which makes us insist that we can only accept as true and real statements and things which are consistent with one another?

We need not enter into the classic dispute over whether they are derived from experience or are innate ideas. More important for our purpose is the Kantian question whether, if they originate within the mind, we have any grounds for holding that they must hold good of objective reality. It is tempting for any pupil of Cook Wilson to answer this question by saying that the so-called laws of thought are only laws of thought because they are laws of being: they are not creations of the mind but apprehensions of the nature of reality. This answer, I believe, indicates the lines along which we should look for the truth of the matter, but it is not in itself sufficient.

It is not sufficient because we have to distinguish between our capacity for apprehension and thought at our present stage in the process of interaction between categories and evidence and that to which we aspire as the goal of our philosophic quest. Our goal is such knowledge and understanding of things as they are that it will be otiose to raise the question whether the fact that we necessarily think them so has its roots in them or in us. If we are to justify time spent on scientific and philosophical inquiry, we must believe that we are on the way to this goal. Experience shows the way to be interaction between evidence and categories, and progress made to date encourages us to believe that some at least of our categories will need no further revision in order to be valid of the objects of our thought. Among them pride of place may be given to the so-called law of contradiction, the demand that the objects of our thought shall fit together into a pattern that makes sense.

If, therefore, our ways of thinking are subject to revision in the light of growing apprehension of evidence, we cannot use the words logic and logical as though they qualified ways of thinking without reference to what our thought is about. If true thought is that which accurately grasps the nature of its objects, then whenever the thought is concerned with the relations between things, the truly logical thought will be that which accurately apprehends those relations. There is a sense in which the logic must be in the things if it is to be in the thoughts, a truth witnessed to in common speech by such a phrase as 'the logic of the situation'. The statement that a good principle of action, if carried to its logical conclusion, will land one in absurdity is not, taken by itself, entirely satisfactory: this use of the phrase 'carried to its logical conclusion' suggests that logic is a matter of thought carried on in abstraction from things. But absurdity is a logical concept, and the absurdity is not produced by anything in our abstract thinking; it is due to the discrepancy between the logic of our thoughts and the logic of the differing demands made upon us by different situations.

We may describe our first puzzle as the discovery of illogicality in the world we are trying to understand.

We have made the discovery by reflecting upon the illogicality in the form in which it appears in common experience, in the fact that all men have to live by making decisions in situations demanding apparently inconsistent actions. We can only avoid it by becoming the kind of doctrinaire fanatic who in all circumstances, whatever they may be, insists on action in conformity with the conclusions of his one-sided logic. In all probability the great majority of men and women, like my good parents in the instance quoted, remain unaware of it: they go from situation to situation meeting each with the action it calls for without any sense of inconsistency. But this is just the kind of unexamined assumption which provokes the notice of the philosopher. What can philosophy make of it?

I have affirmed my fundamental act of philosophical faith, the belief that everything that exists or occurs somehow fits into a unifying pattern which makes sense, that when we know even as we are known we shall see that perfect knowledge of the whole is knowledge wherein the logic in the things known is one with the logic in the thought.[1] I believe that this faith has always been the mainspring of philosophical endeavour, and that to see it as such explains both the course that philosophy has taken in the past, and its present condition.

Speaking generally, philosophical systems may be said to be of two kinds, idealist and materialist. While it is true to say that the idealist is more strongly moved by the demand that things shall fit in so as to make sense and the materialist by the demand that they shall be accurately observed and accounted for as they actually exist, this is not the whole of the truth. Both take for granted that whatever is real does so fit in: they differ in their conception of what is meant by 'make sense'.

The idealist lays his stress on what conforms to the canons of the logic of the mind: his criticism of reality is logical consistency and self-authenticating goodness. From Socrates onwards idealists have tended to regard the factual illogicality presented by the things of this world as evidence that they cannot really be what they seem to be: they must be the mode in which what is really real appears to us in our finite experience. For the materialist the criterion of reality is the observed behaviour of the things of this world: his presupposition is the existence in the spatio-temporal order of things of a logic, a consistency which makes them patient of rewarding study by the natural sciences. We have seen one instance of this in the passage quoted from Freud, where

[1]Above, Lecture II, pp. 28, 33.

he bases his thought on faith in the universal sway of 'the causal sequence of things'.[1]

So far as I can understand from outside what is going on in the world of the natural sciences, there is combined a continuing sense of the worthwhileness of their study with a growing scepticism about the theoretical nature of the consistency which makes this possible, or the extent to which this possibility depends on the kind of consistency implied by such a phrase as 'the causal sequence of things'. The kind of uniformity which those words would have described for our fathers half a century ago no longer obtains in a world where relativity makes it impossible to determine at the same time both the position and the mass of a moving object, where exponents of the quantum theory can speak of indeterminacy, where wave-theories and corpuscle-theories, inconsistent with one another, are both required to account for different phenomena in the realm of light. The illogicality in the nature of things which presents us with situations demanding actions based on inconsistent principles is paralleled in the phenomena which demand of scientists study based on inconsistent theories. To the doctrinaire fanatic corresponds the scientific crank. Yet neither in the conduct of life nor in scientific study is salvation to be found in indifference to logic, neglect of principle, or random guesswork. Our puzzle is to find the pattern in which the wise man of action and the intelligent scientist can both find a place and prove themselves consistent in their inconsistencies.

II

I turn now to another set of puzzles, puzzles which beset the Christian believer as he tries to grasp the meaning of his faith. We will start with that presented by contemplation of the vast multitude of men and women on the face of the earth. Here, again, the difficulty arises in the attempt to reconcile convictions that belong to different circles of thought.

[1] Above, Lecture II, p. 24.

I picture to myself Cornmarket in Oxford on a Saturday afternoon, as I push my way through the crowds that overflow from the pavement into the roadway; or Oxford Street in London, as I look down from the top of a bus on the teeming mass of people. You can picture to yourselves similar scenes in this city of Glasgow. If we ask ourselves what proportion of these thronging multitudes consists of baptized members of the Church who live up to the obligations of their membership, who are regular in the practice of penitence and thanksgiving, of reading God's word and assembling together for His worship, the answer surely must be that it is very small. Even if we reduce our list of requirements, ignore church membership and church attendance and simply ask how many read their Bibles, say their prayers and live by faith in Christ, we have to admit that a very large number, if not the majority, do none of these things. Then if we look out from the cities of this island into all the world around, asking the same question about the inhabitants of Europe, Asia, Africa, America and Australasia, will not the answer be much the same? What on earth, or in heaven, does God intend to do with so many such people? What is He now doing with all those of them who in recent years have perished in Indo-China and Korea?

I do not use the phrase 'such people' in any derogatory sense, but simply to refer collectively, without any attempt at appraisal or valuation, to all those in whose minds the faith and practice of the Christian Church are irrelevant to their lives. I have introduced the subject by picturing crowds with whom you and I are often in close personal contact because by putting it in this way I hope I may make it as clear to you as it is to me that it would drive any Christian clean out of his mind if he really believed that of those with whom he is rubbing shoulders all but the small minority of pious churchgoers were objects of God's displeasure and doomed to destruction. If God be the God revealed to us in Jesus Christ, it cannot be so. But if not, what in the will and purpose of God is the object and purpose of their existence now, and what their destiny hereafter?

This is a question which does not seem to have troubled our spiritual ancestors, a fact which in itself provides another puzzle of which we shall have to take account in these lectures later on. They apparently found no difficulty in holding that God's aim in His redemptive work has been and is the rescue for salvation of a select number of human beings while the rest—to use the only word that I can think of—can be scrapped. There is a collect in our Church of England service for the Burial of the Dead in which we pray that God may accomplish the number of His elect and hasten His kingdom, language which takes our minds back to St. Augustine's exposition of the theory that the number of the saved is to be that which will restore the optimum population of heaven by filling the vacancies left by the fallen angels.[1] Dante's Vergil had to be left in the Limbo prepared for the unbaptized heathen. There is plenty of evidence that these and others were concerned to show that such dispositions were in keeping with the justice and love of God, but they do not seem to have faced the question of their consistency with His love in the form in which it presents itself to our minds to-day. If Jesus Christ be indeed the revelation of God, if God's care for the men and women of His creation be of the same kind as that of the Lord who looked with compassion upon the multitude because He saw them as sheep who had no shepherd, how can He be content to let all these others be scrapped while He achieves His purpose of rescuing the chosen few?

But if now the Christian, turning his mind from this question and the circle of thought to which it belongs, reflects upon his own religious life in the fellowship of the Christian church, and confines his attention to the ideas germane to that circle of thought, he soon finds himself thinking in ways inconsistent with this generous attitude towards the heathen multitudes. He acknowledges that for himself his hope of rising from death to

[1] *Encheiridion*, ix. 29.

a blessed immortality is bound up with his faith in Jesus Christ as his Lord and Saviour. It is not something which he has in virtue of being a man: it has come to him as a gift of God's grace, and he only looks forward to rising again through being incorporate into the continuing life of the body of his risen Lord. This faith is the ground of his own hope for himself, and the substance of the gospel which he preaches to others. But how can it be consistent with the belief that is necessary to his sanity on a Saturday afternoon in a crowded city street?

Later on we shall have to consider how many of the assumptions commonly taken for granted in traditional theology will have to be revised for the solution of this puzzle. My aim in this lecture is simply to set before you the puzzles which provide the programme for our thought in those which are to follow. My first puzzle was the discovery of the illogicality in the world we are trying to understand; my second is the discovery of illogicality in my own religious convictions.

But although my immediate aim is to expose the puzzles, it will not be out of place to mention clues which seem to me to indicate the direction in which we may look for light upon them. I would suggest that in the present instance it may be of help to realize that the religious life of a man is like the thought of a scientist or philosopher in that it is a process which develops by interaction between subject and object. We have seen how in his thinking the scientist or philosopher—or, indeed, any kind of scholar—is seeking to grasp with his finite mind the object he wants to know and understand. In his religion a Christian is not simply seeking to know God as a matter of intellectual achievement; he is drawn to respond to the love of God by the devotion of his whole self. There are thus the two sides to the process: in him subjectively his whole faith and love are deepened as from the objective side there comes to him the quickening love of God. Now the more a man grows in understanding what the Christian religion is from within, the more he comes to realize that while what he is and does is of importance as constituting him the man he is becoming, of infinitely greater importance is what God is doing, because it is from God that he is receiving all that he has or is or becomes. At the heart of the Christian life is the puzzling paradox of St. Paul's: 'I live, yet not I, but Christ liveth in me'.[1]

The curious thing is that in the minds of those for whom justification by faith is contrasted with justification by works, so that *sola gratia* is the essence of the Christian gospel, this truth often seems to be combined with the notion that the presence or absence of the faith is what marks the distinction between those who are and those who are not on the road to ultimate salvation. One can see how this comes about. The Christian knows within himself both that the faith through which he responds to the love of God is itself a gift of God, and also that his own hope of a future life comes to him out of this relationship to God. It is easy to confuse the subjective fact that those who are without the faith are without the hope with the objective statement that those without the faith are not on the way to receive that which the others hope for. But to do this is to transfer from the objective to the subjective, from God to man, the *locus* of the action which is effective for or against a man's salvation. The antipelagianism which produced the doctrine of justification by faith has issued in the pelagian assumption that those without consciousness of the faith are devoid of justification.

More than once in later lectures we shall find ourselves driven to investigate what is essentially the same confusion. It is involved, for example, in the question whether the validity of a sacrament depends upon what God is doing, whether the worshipper is aware of it or not, or is in any way dependent upon the state of mind of minister or congregation. For the moment we must be content to list among the puzzles which confront us the fact that so many Christians, from their experience of the 'I, yet not I' have been led into the illogicality of drawing pelagian conclusions from anti-pelagian premisses.

Further ramifications of this same puzzle are illustrated by

[1] Gal. ii. 20.

Professor Paul Tillich's limitation of revelation to knowledge received 'through ecstasy and miracle'[1] and Dr. H. H. Farmer's limitation of religion to the experience of those who are conscious of being in personal relations with God.[2] This latter limitation may only be a matter of the definition of terms; but Dr. Farmer's treatment of the subject needs to be supplemented by reference to the late Dr. Francis Underhill's penetrating account of the possibility of the practice of religion by those who are devoid of what he calls the 'religious temperament'.[3]

More than once I have had occasion to refer to existentialism among current movements of thought. Existentialism calls attention to the importance of the subjective side of our development as persons, to the fact that both intellectually in our striving after growth in knowledge, and comprehensively in our seeking to find the fulfilment of our personality in communion with God, each of us has his apprehensions coloured and the character of his fulfilment conditioned by the circumstances of his birth, upbringing and status. Taken by itself, as though it covered the whole ground, it would involve denial of the possibility of apprehending any common truth or pursuing any common good: its value is its reminder to both philosophers and theologians that in attempting to make sense of the universe of our experience and to understand the way of God with His creation, we must take full account of the fact that we exist as individualized centres of consciousness, individualized in our approach both in thinking and living.

A further puzzle, suggested by the existentialist reminder, is that of the variety of moral codes acknowledged by different groups of men. We can no longer say with the confidence of John Ruskin in 1870: 'There are many religions, but there is only one morality. There are moral and immoral religions, which differ as much in precept as emotion; but there is only one

[1] P. Tillich: *Systematic Theology*, Vol. I (London, 1953), p. 143.
[2] H. H. Farmer: *Revelation and Religion* (London, 1954), *passim*.
[3] F. E. Underhill: *The Young Englishman* (London, 1927), pp. 187 ff.

morality, which has been, is, and must be, for ever, an instinct in the hearts of all civilized men, as certain and unalterable as their outward bodily form, and which receives from religion neither law, nor place; but only hope and felicity'.[1]

In an interesting discussion of the underlying problems Mr. J. O. Urmson has written: 'When we debate which of two moral codes is more enlightened there is no ultimate court of appeal, no umpire, unless some agreed religious code is treated as a *deus ex machina*. . . . We cannot, when debating what criterion to use for moral grading, grade the criteria morally. But we can grade them by enlightenment provided, of course, that the disputants have an agreed set of criteria of enlightenment. . . . If people have not agreed criteria for enlightenment, I do not know what one can do about it'.[2]

We western Europeans, born into the traditions of Hebrew-Christian teaching, may feel that we share a common outlook as contrasted, for example, with those for whom the political interests of the state are the criteria of both truth and goodness. But if we are tempted to think that the puzzle is solved for us by the *deus ex machina* of an agreed revealed religious code we are rudely reminded that among Christians there remain unsolved differences: while his disapproval of gambling leads the Protestant minister to forbid the holding of raffles at his church bazaar, the neighbouring Roman Catholic priest is raising funds by means of pools and lotteries.[3]

I come back to the point where we approached our second group of puzzles. These arose from the fact that the world contains a vast number of human beings whose existence must somehow be accounted for. We have seen reason to doubt that it is consistent with acceptance of the revelation of God in Christ to think of them as, so to speak, the chorus or supers on the stage of a divine drama which is solely concerned with the fortunes

[1] Quoted from Joan Evans' *John Ruskin* (London, 1954), p. 313.
[2] In Flew: *Logic and Language*, Second Series (Oxford, 1953), p. 185.
[3] See further below, Lecture VI, pp. 145 ff.

of the chosen few. In considering the fortunes of the chosen few we have found within Christian theology a puzzle provided by the question of the relation of the achievements in faith or morals to the objective activity of God the Disposer supreme. Whether we are thinking of Christians or Pagans, of the characters in the centre of the stage or the chorus and bystanders in the wings, we cannot be satisfied until we see how they all fit into the plot of a drama that will make sense.

III

As we look back over the puzzles we have been considering we can see their likeness to one another as variations on one theme. In different circumstances we have to act on principles that are logically inconsistent. Our conviction of God's love for all mankind is inconsistent with our belief about the grounds of our own hope of salvation, and for that hope we inconsistently combine the doctrine of *sola gratia* with an acknowledgment that our eternal destiny depends upon the manner of our life in this world of space and time. When we ask what that manner of life should be, we find, even among Christians, advocates of inconsistent moral codes. In every case the difficulty arises from the fact that while so long as we follow different lines of thought we can make sense of each taken by itself, when we try to put our various conclusions together, they will not agree.

To use a technical term, we live in a world of antinomies: that is to say, in circumstances in which over and over again we find ourselves unable to deny the truth of positions which, so far as we can see, are inconsistent with one another. I have begun by confessing the inconsistencies which I have to acknowledge in my own faith and practice, my inability, for example, to deny either the doctrine of *sola gratia* or the truth that I shall be held to account for how I have lived my life and be judged thereby. I must, of course, always carefully consider the question whether what I take to be an antinomy is indeed a genuine antinomy and not a case in which I really ought to choose between two alternatives. The antinomy is only to be accepted, the inconsistency tolerated, the mystery acknowledged when I have done my best to solve the puzzle and am convinced that to do otherwise would involve disloyalty to this or that aspect of truth.

While each of us has to face this issue for himself and achieve what consistency he may in his own life and thought, a Gifford lecturer, who by the terms of his trust is set to look out upon the whole universe and try to make sense of it, must take note of the fact that inconsistencies are not only uneasy companions in his own mind, but reappear, so to speak, in the large, possessing the allegiance of different groups of men, dividing them into groups. Just as in my own mind there are inconsistencies of which I am conscious and may be others of which I am unaware, so some of these groups are in conscious disagreement (as on the ethics of raffles and lotteries), while others may simply be unaware of their inconsistency by being out of touch with one another. Here, too, the parallel holds. I can remain unaware of my own inconsistencies so long as at different times I follow out different lines of thought and do not try to bring them together. So different groups of men, each bound together in pursuit of some particular line of truth and concentrating attention upon it, can be out of touch with one another and unaware of the puzzle presented to the Gifford lecturer who has to try to make sense of their various conclusions, inquiring whether a solution should be found in the acceptance of this and rejection of that, or whether he has to acknowledge the recognition of a genuine antinomy.

An instance of this kind of puzzle has been brought to my mind by reading Mr. E. I. Watkin's book *Poets and Mystics*. For the nourishment of his soul, for his training in devotion, for the deepening of his experience of the possibilities of prayer, a Christian turns to the works of the masters of the spiritual life: he reads Thomas à Kempis, Brother Lawrence, Lorenzo Scupoli, Madame Guyon, and their later successors down to Francis

Paget's *Spirit of Discipline* and the *Retreat Addresses* of Edward Talbot. Behind all these, and looked up to by them as having penetrated even more deeply into the mysteries of communion with God, are the great Christian mystics, such as St. Catherine of Genoa, St. Theresa, and St. John of the Cross. Now, according to Mr. Watkin this whole tradition of the Christian life of prayer takes for granted an understanding of the human soul which he describes as follows:

> The mystic's experience is an experience of union with God as He transcends all forms, whether images or concepts. This union is effected by, or rather is produced in, the central self, the root of intellect and will alike, though in this case more precisely as it is the root of the will, the fundamental orientation of the will. For the spirit is a spiritual energy, a radical volition. This centre is variously named *synderesis*, the fine point of the soul, its apex, its ground. . . .
>
> The anima which is the subject of aesthetic-artistic intuition is deeper and more obscure than the animus which is the subject of discursive and scientific thinking and of the conceptual factor in poetry. The centre or apex on the other hand which is the subject of mystical union, the union of which mystical experience is the intuition, is at a still greater psychological depth. It is indeed the ultimate depth where the very being of the human spirit is grounded in God.[1]

To the Christian believer these masters of the spiritual life clearly speak from their experience, speak as those who know what they are talking about. While one is trying to follow in their footsteps, or to expound their teaching with a view to encouraging others to do the same, one proceeds on the assumption that within oneself there is a 'depth of the soul' where God is to be found: one presents this as the doctrine which shall inspire attempts to enter on the practice of the inner life.

There are times, however, when one is neither praying nor preaching, but trying to learn something of present-day psychological research, reading the works of Freud or Jung or Köhler. Here one is in an entirely different world. In so far as spatial metaphors are used of the human soul, and it is said to have

[1] E. I. Watkin: *Poets and Mystics* (London, 1953), p. 12. Cp. pp. 14, 15, 81, 86, 203, 265 ff.

higher or lower levels, there is no suggestion of its deepest depths being an apex or fine point where God is to be found. On the contrary. In the subliminal depths of a man's self his inherited urges are seeking to erupt and express themselves in his conscious life, and many of them are such that it would be blasphemous to describe their contemplation as an entering into the presence of God.

Whatever one may think of this or that element in the theory of this or that psychologist, one cannot sweep all this research away, dismissing it as having nothing of value to contribute to our understanding of the human soul. Psychologists, like mystics, speak out of their experience, speak as men who have made discoveries and have some knowledge of what they are talking about.

Academic and practising psychologists on the one hand, conductors of retreats and students of ascetic theology on the other, so long as each group confines itself to its own concerns, can go merrily along making sense of their material. But when a man is interested in the works of both he finds that he is behaving like the physicist who alternates between wave and corpuscular theories of light.

Wrestling with this puzzle in his Tarner lectures, Professor Ryle clears up a number of misunderstandings and gives a useful warning against seeking to evade it by the use of 'Smother words', like picture and description. It may be that in many cases the apparently inconsistent statements made by workers in different fields are to be understood on his analogy of the difference between the way in which books appear on the shelves of a library and in the librarian's account book. 'It is not a question of two rival libraries, or of two rival descriptions of one library, but of two different but complementary ways of giving information of very different sorts about the one library'.[1] But to assume that this is always so is only another way of expressing the conviction that all things that exist somehow fit in together so as to

[1] G. Ryle: *Dilemmas* (Cambridge, 1954), p. 78.

make sense, and the fact remains that often the information collected from different sources remains obstinately inconsistent.

In his lecture on Perception Mr. Ryle usefully pillories the notion that seeing and hearing are parts of an observable process which occupy a stretch of time.[1] Let us grant that as activities they are *sui generis*, known to each one of us in the exercise of them and indescribable in terms of observable, time-occupying processes or, indeed, of anything other than themselves. In themselves they may be instantaneous activities. Yet in so far as I wish to use them to gain knowledge and understanding of the objective world I have to take account of the lapse of time in the processes which lead up to my acts of perceiving, of the fact, for example, that when I contemplate the starry heaven on a cloudless night I am seeing the stars at bygone dates differing proportionately to their distance from the earth. For most practical purposes of everyday life we can, and do, disregard this kind of consideration. Later we shall have to consider whether the fact that we can do this successfully gives a clue to the puzzle of the discrepancy between the worlds of physical theory and of everyday practice.

This living in different worlds, how puzzling it is! The world of everyday practice and the world of physical theory, the world of the mystic and the world of the psychologist, the world of Christian faith and the world of secular business. In this last contrast I am not thinking of the two as mutually hostile: I do not use the phrase 'secular business' to mean affairs which from the point of view of the Christian lie outside the range of his Christian interest, still less which all 'lie in the evil one'. What I have in mind is this. While I am worshipping with fellow-Christians, or talking with fellow-theologians, I am in a world in which we all take for granted the truth that this universe is God's creation, that He is the God revealed to us in Jesus Christ, that both for individuals and for society the most important thing in life is to be conformed to His will, and that to this end the

[1] *Op. cit.* pp. 102 ff.

practice of prayer and the pursuit of holiness should have chief place in the attention of our thought and the use of our time. To this world belong such books as Dr. Farmer's Gifford Lectures, to which I have already referred. But when I go out and about, shopping in shops, discussing the needs of my car with the foreman at the garage or the needs of my house with builder and plumber, reading the newspaper and talking over the affairs of the day with friends and colleagues, taking part in College business, sitting on committees, examining theses for degrees or helping to govern a school, I am in a world to which it is often hard to believe that the considerations which are so vital to the worshipper and the theologian have any relevance at all. The various pies in which I have my fingers each has its own canons and standards which must receive understanding and respect. Plumbing and examining, research in any branch of learning, the election of a professor and the conduct of the business of a school require attention to multifarious details, in the discussion of which there is seldom any reference to the practice of prayer or the pursuit of holiness.

I find myself at home in both worlds, and so, I have no doubt, do many of my fellow Christians. But, unless I misunderstand and misjudge them, I cannot help thinking that many men and women belong to one or the other, devout Christians and biblical theologians who do not know what it feels like to realize the mind-engrossing scope of secular culture, business men and politicians, scholars and men of science, for whom that engrossment leaves no time or energy to devote to the things of religious faith and practice. I find myself oscillating between this world and that, now at home in the one and now in the other, constantly tempted to seek peace of mind by enlisting in the one to the exclusion of the other, rescued from the temptation by the realization that to do so would be to deny undeniable truths, would be disloyalty to Him who if He is to be our Way and our Life must also be reverenced by the service of truth.

To find himself living in different worlds of thought is not a peculiarity of a Christian thinker. It is the form in which he experiences a prevailing characteristic of the present age, sharing the experience of all who are trying to understand the universe in the light of all that is being discovered about it in different fields of study. This has been well put by Dr. Emmet, for what she wrote in 1943 is no less true in 1955:

> We are concerned . . . with the possibility of finding relations between diverse kinds of experience such that it may be possible to co-ordinate them into some pattern which makes sense. If experience is reflected through the medium of different minds, themselves part of a shifting process of change, is it possible to find such co-ordinating ideas as will be more than metaphors expressing private associations? . . . And there is the further doubt whether the different kinds of experience are capable of being co-ordinated with one another in any coherent pattern. Our elders were (and some of them still are) full of hopes and ambitions of achieving a 'synthesis' of knowledge; science, religion, art, the practice of personal and political life were to become an orderly pattern, dominated by an agreed philosophical outlook. But it looks as if we were becoming increasingly conscious of diversities and discontinuities in our worlds of thought and experience. . . . The real problem is that our diverse worlds of thought do not make sense as a coherent unity, and probably cannot and will not do so for some time to come. For the basic suppositions underlying them are in process of a drastic reconstruction of which it is not yet possible to see the outcome. We cannot yet determine clearly what are in fact the main ideas behind the new physics, let alone their relevance or irrelevance for a wider outlook. Nor has the real scope and contribution of psycho-analysis yet been determined; nor that of the new border-line sciences of life such as biochemistry and biophysics; nor is it clear what are the dominant ideas which are to express man's life in society. When we have reached a stage when Einstein, Freud, Marx, Barth, Wittgenstein are not names for partisans to conjure with, but the contributions which these may have made to our understanding of the nature of the human mind and its relation to its world, have been clarified, sifted and assimilated, then we may begin to look towards a new synthesis of knowledge. And it may well be that by then we shall have learnt that the old-style synthesis in the grand manner is impossible. Meanwhile, as long as different departments of thought are primarily concerned with rethinking their distinctive methods and presuppositions, they are likely to grow apart rather than grow together.[1]

[1] D. M. Emmet: *The Nature of Metaphysical Thinking* (London, 1945), pp. 218–20.

It is indeed true that the time for synthesis is not yet, if by synthesis is meant a comprehensive statement which, with full understanding of them, shall relate and interpret the elements contributed by all our various worlds of thought. But the search for clues must go on, and in the circumstances of to-day I take it that it is to this search for clues that a Gifford lecturer is called by the terms of Lord Gifford's will.

IV

Lastly, let me indicate two puzzles which press most insistently upon the Christian thinker.

1. Our aim is to know and understand the nature and history of this universe in such a way as to see that all that is and happens makes sense. For the Christian this may be put in the form of the question: 'What is the will and purpose of God for His creation?' Traditional Christianity has concentrated attention on the thought of God's 'accomplishing the number of His elect', treating the rest of creation as stage-setting for the divine drama of their redemption. If to-day, as I believe, we cannot be content with this, but must try to discover what positive ends God is working for in creation as a whole, we are faced by our ignorance of His will and purpose for the future of this world in space and time. It will not do to base our theory on the assumption that it will inevitably be brought to a state of perfection before the end of its history: our exploitation of the destructive possibilities of the energies latent in physical matter remind us that it may have no such future before it. Yet it may be that we shall be preserved from such cosmic catastrophe, and that God wills to crown His creative and redemptive activity with such perfection as is appropriate to spatio-temporal existence.[1] This inability to forecast the future is an inescapable puzzle, a question to which no man knows the answer. The acceptance of this ignorance is a standing condition of all our attempts to 'justify the ways of God to man'.

[1] On this see below, Lecture X, and my *The Doctrine of the Atonement* (London, 1951 pp. 125 ff.

2. Underlying all other problems, the fundamental problem for all thinkers, whether Christians or not, is that of the relation of time to eternity. If the sequence of events in space and time be the whole of reality, we have no standard by which to determine what is better and what worse, what is progress and what retrogression. There is just one thing after another. If we postulate the existence of an eternally perfect being by reference to which (or to whom) we can judge the events of space and time, we are hard put to it to give any reasonable account of the existence of this universe at all.[1] This insoluble problem is the background of the Christian doctrine of creation; from it comes the ultimate antinomy in the Christian doctrine of God.

These two puzzles will be much before us in later lectures, and I will say no more about them now. But before we go further in our search for clues we must consider to what extent, and in what way, we may look for help from the revelation which Christians believe God to have given of Himself.

[1] On this see my *Towards a Christian Philosophy*, p. 155.

LECTURE IV

Revelation

I

'I WISH the lecturers to treat this subject as a strictly natural science . . . without reference to or reliance upon any supposed special exceptional or so-called miraculous revelation'. When Lord Gifford made his will he took for granted what was in 1885 the generally accepted way of conceiving the relation between scientific inquiry and reliance on revelation. In my first two lectures I have shown how, in both philosophy and theology, the political convulsions of the present century have been accompanied by a curious combination of reliance upon particular scientific investigations with scepticism concerning the possibility of what Lord Gifford called 'the greatest of all possible sciences, . . . that of Infinite Being'. When philosophers, denying the possibility of metaphysics, confine themselves to describing one another's presuppositions or analysing the linguistic usage of scientists, it is not surprising that theologians feel justified in looking to divine revelation for knowledge of truth beyond the reach of reason.[1]

Throughout the period covered by those lectures, that same way of conceiving the relation between reason and revelation continued for the most part to be taken for granted. It underlay the thought of those liberal theologians who sought to secure the basis of theology by substituting discovery by human reason for the acceptance of supernatural revelation; in the reaction against

[1] In this contrast, and elsewhere, I use the words 'reason' and 'rational' as general terms for man's power to apprehend truth, including both immediate acts of apprehension and reasoning processes. This usage differs from that of those who confine them to the latter activity, employing 'intellect' and 'intellectual' for the former. See, e.g., H. A. Hodges in Mascall: *The Angels of Light and the Powers of Darkness* (London, 1954), pp. 2–8.

liberalism it underlies the thought of those for whom the acceptance of revelation involves the rejection of natural theology.

The aim of this lecture is to expose this idea of revelation, to show that its prevalence is due to a combination of psychological and historical factors, to argue that it is inconsistent with the actual revelation that God has seen fit to give us, and to draw conclusions of importance both for our understanding of Lord Gifford's will and for our attempt to make sense of the world of our experience. Here on earth 'we walk by faith', said St. Paul, 'not by sight',[1] a text on which words by John Locke make an apt commentary: 'He that demands a greater certainty than this demands he knows not what, and shows only that he has a mind to be a sceptic, without being able to be so.[2]

It is at first sight a curious fact that the most virulent theological disputes are concerned with questions to which it is impossible for men to know the answers. Reflection shows that this is not really curious: on the contrary, it is what might be expected. Men do not quarrel over ascertained facts or clearly provable theories; and where the subject of an inquiry is such that patient examination of available evidence is likely to reveal incontrovertibly the truth of the matter, we are content to wait and see. Controversies concerning such subjects as predestination, transubstantiation and the apostolic ministry are disputes about questions to which God alone knows the answer, on which it has not pleased Him to supply us with evidence that places the solution of the problems beyond all manner of doubt. Quite rightly we exercise our minds in trying to understand such mysteries. Quite rightly we form theories to try to account for what evidence there is. But only too easily we slip over into treating our theoretical constructions as sacrosanct dogmas which it would be impious to impugn. For some Christians this status is given to a certain interpretation of the 'Tu es Petrus' passage in St. Matthew xvi; for others to a certain interpretation of St. Paul's teaching about justification by faith. We find it hard to

[1] 2 Cor. v. 7. [2] *An Essay Concerning Human Understanding*, Book IV, ch. ii.

live and worship together in common acknowledgment of the ignorance which God has seen fit to impose on us, to make our own, for example, the admirable self-restraint expressed in the four lines which have been ascribed to Queen Elizabeth I:

> Christ was the Word that spake it;
> He took the bread and brake it;
> And what that Word did make it,
> That I believe and take it.[1]

The field within which we have knowledge and clear understanding is surrounded by a penumbra of mystery. We peer into it and seek to extend the range of our knowledge, interpreting the unknown by the light of the known. We want knowledge so badly that we let the wish be father to the thought. We not only treat as knowledge what are in fact our own hypotheses and theories; we assume that it must have been the will of God to give us what we want so badly.

In *The Doctrine of the Trinity* (p. 20) I have traced the origin of this element in Christian theology to 'the Greek tradition in which rational philosophical thought and mythology were regarded as parallel sources (either rival or complementary) of human knowledge'. To what I wrote there I would now add this further point. It looks as though the psychological factors I have just been describing combined with the Christian belief in the goodness and love of God to give this notion a ready welcome into Christian minds. Yet I am convinced that it is one of those elements in pre-Christian Greek thought which is inconsistent with the special revelation of God that is the basis of our Christian faith. The revelation of God in Christ came in mid-history, at a time when men's minds were already well stocked with notions and ideas. Some of these it came to illuminate and confirm, others to uproot and cast out.[2] This notion of revelation I hold to be one of the latter. Its attractiveness to human psychology and

[1] Stevenson: *Book of Quotations* (1934), p. 262, also quotes a slightly different version from John Donne.

[2] Cp. *The Doctrine of the Atonement*, p. 14.

Christian belief about God were such as to give it not only an unquestioned welcome but a long persistence in Christian thought.

Just where the notion originated that the Bible is a divinely guaranteed manual of information about matters not open to human observation and reflection, I have not been able to find out. My suspicion is that it cannot be traced to any definite starting-point. Under the influence of the two-source theory of knowledge traditional in the Hellenistic world it was simply taken for granted that for Christians their Scriptures played the part assigned in the tradition to mythology. By the time of St. Thomas Aquinas this has become common stock of Christian thought: his *Summa Theologica* opens with a rationalization of the wish-fulfilment embodied in the idea that God must have given to man a revelation of this kind and that He has done so in the Bible. Four centuries later comes the following conversation between Christian and Pliable in *The Pilgrim's Progress*:

> *Chr.*: . . . If you believe me not, read here in this book; and for the truth of what is expressed therein, behold, all is confirmed by the Blood of Him that made it. . . .
>
> *Pli.*: . . . And do you think that the words of your book are certainly true?
>
> *Chr.*: . . . Yes, verily; for it was made by Him that cannot lie.

On May 10th, 1890, little more than half a century ago, Dr. Ernest Walker wrote in his diary:

> I have not read all these twelve essays yet, but as to the one of Gore's on Inspiration . . . I must say that I think his opponents have the stronger position. . . . Little by little fragments have been dropping off—and now in *Lux Mundi*, and all books of education, the old theory of 'plenary inspiration' is dead. It is seen that the Bible is no ultimate resort on all points, but when we once get there, I don't see what there is of dogmatic Christianity left.[1]

The theory of plenary inspiration has never been literally applied in a thoroughgoing fashion by responsible theologians. That has been left to the world of comic fiction, as in the story of the man who said he would believe that Jonah swallowed the whale, if the Bible said so. Instead, it has produced satellite

[1] M. Deneke: *Ernest Walker* (Oxford, 1951), p. 23.

theories of allegorical, metaphorical, mystical and spiritual interpretation. Those who, like Bunyan, might repudiate such expedients as popish subterfuges to avoid the plain meaning of the text, employ what may be called the method of eclectic quotation, the choice of texts and their interpretation being dictated by the ecclesiastical tradition in which they stand. Nevertheless, they all, catholic and protestant alike, thought that what they had to do was to discover and expound the hidden meaning which God had caused to be contained in the words of the sacred text in much the same way as the composer of a cross-word puzzle gives the key to its solution in the wording of the clues. Where they differ is in the determination of what they take to be the clues. Exponents of so-called 'biblical theology', whose motto is that the Bible should be allowed to explain itself,[1] employ the method of eclectic quotation in their choice of what passages shall control the interpretation of the rest.

It was this view of the Bible that was beginning to crumble when Ernest Walker was writing his diary in 1890, and his comment gives us some idea of the agony of soul through which our Christian forefathers had to pass in the next generation or two. To what I said of that period in my first lecture I would now add this: what was being undermined was not the theory of plenary inspiration (which no one had ever really held), but something more fundamental: the belief that in the sacred text of the Bible God has given us a manual of information about truths which lie beyond the range of human discovery.

One immediate effect was to minimize, if not to deny altogether, the element of revelation in the Christian faith. The traditional two-source theory of knowledge had postulated a disjunction between two fields of reality, assigning one to human discovery and the other to divine revelation: it seemed as though to treat a truth as a matter of human discovery were to remove it

[1] Cp. e.g., 'Wherever a non-Biblical principle derived from contemporary secular thought is applied to the interpretation of the Bible, the Bible's *Facultas se ipsum interpretandi* is violated, with fatal results'. H. Thielicke, in Bartsch: *Kerygma and Myth* (E. Tr. London, 1954), p. 149.

from the sphere of divine revelation. When the Bible could no longer be accepted as a handbook of divinely guaranteed doctrinal statements, there was substituted the thought of it as a record of man's progress in discovering truths about God. In an attempt to preserve the sense of its importance as a revelatory medium the word 'revelation' was kept in the description of it as a record of 'progressive revelation'; the Hebrews' growing discoveries about God could only have been possible through God giving insight to their prophetic leaders. But by clinging to the notion that revelation is fundamentally a communication of ideas, a matter of words rather than deeds, those who put forward this theory undermined the uniqueness of the Bible as a revelatory medium. If man's discovery of truth be the human apprehension of God's self-revelation, why should we claim that the Bible is 'inspired' or 'revelatory' in some other way than the writings of Greek philosophers or oriental sages? As I look back to meetings of Anglican and Free Church Fellowships, Church Congresses and similar gatherings, held thirty to forty years ago, I have memories on the one hand of singularly unconvincing papers arguing for the unique importance of the Bible, and on the other of proposals in our church services to place extracts from other sources on a par with the reading of Holy Scripture.

This way of reading the Bible coincided with an anti-supernatural bias current in contemporary thought. The denial that God had miraculously communicated information about Himself to man walked hand-in-hand with the denial that in the history of this world of space and time God performs any particular actions at all. If man's only way of learning the truth about God is by observation of what happens in the universe and reflection upon it, God must be thought of as the immanent spirit of the processes of evolution and history, not as one who stands over and above them, expressing His will in particular acts as well as in the general tendencies of the whole.[1]

[1] Cp. e.g., K. Lake: *The Religion of Yesterday and To-morrow* (Boston and New York, 1925).

We have lived to see this compromise rejected as unsatisfactory. In the theological world of to-day we are recovering our grasp of the truth that Christianity is a faith based on a unique divine revelation. What I now wish to maintain is that this recovery does not require the rehabilitation of the old Greek two-source theory of knowledge, that it is a mistake to try to find some up-to-date way of seeing in the Bible the kind of revelatory book that that theory requires.

The pursuit of this will-o'-the-wisp has of late taken the form of treating the Hebrew way of thinking as the key to deciphering the divine communications believed to lie hidden in the words of Scripture. As I have already said, this emphasis on the difference between Greek and Hebrew ways of thinking and on its importance for our understanding of the Bible, has undoubtedly been one of the most valuable contributions of our day to theological study.[1] It is not only that because the New Testament is written in Greek our standard commentaries in the past have tended to expound its language in the light of classical Greek thought. We in Western Europe have become so Hellenized in our thinking that we find it hard to realize that the writers of the Old Testament did not think as we do.[2] It is clearly of assistance to our grasping of the revelation contained in the Bible that we should know as accurately as possible what its books meant to those who wrote them, that we should read the New Testament as the work of men who, though they wrote in Greek, thought as Hebrews, whose traditions were not those of Herodotus, Thucydides, Plato and Aristotle, but of the Old Testament and the Apocrypha. But recognition of the importance of this aid to right exegesis should not be confused with the notion that in it we have a satisfactory substitute for discarded views of inspiration based on the two-source theory.

Hebrew thought did not proceed by taking successive steps in logical argument but by accumulating images which bring before

[1] Above, Lecture I, p. 21.

[2] On this see E. Bevan: *Hellenism and Christianity* (London, 1921), Essay I.

the mind different aspects of some complex truth. To recognize this, and not to criticize its authors as though they were trying to argue logically after the Greek pattern, is the first thing we have to learn when we try to understand the Bible. But there are passages in Dr. Austin Farrer's Bampton Lectures,[1] notably in Lecture III, which seem to suggest that the presentation of truth in images is what constitutes the Bible a revelation of divine truth. Taken by itself, this book suggests that when he was writing it, Dr. Farrer was searching for some way of re-establishing the Bible in its place in the two-source theory, and thought he had found it in the discovery of the Hebrew habit of image-thinking. The impression it gives is that it is the presentation in images that makes the Bible revelatory, and that if we would receive God's revelation we must think in images, too.

From his other works it is clear that, if at the time when he was writing his Bampton Lectures Dr. Farrer was tempted to fall into this trap, he has resisted the temptation, and does not ignore the need of a criterion by which to distinguish between images which mirror what is true about God and His universe and images which picture what is false. But other theologians have not been so successful in avoiding the snare.

I can best illustrate this by quoting what I wrote when reviewing Dr. Lionel Thornton's *Revelation and the Modern World* for the *Journal of Theological Studies*:[2]

> Starting from the principle that the content and form of revelation are bound up with one another, Dr. Thornton concludes that there is some special virtue in the thought-forms of the ancient Hebrews and early Christian Fathers. God's revelation is not only given in His actions which they and we seek to understand and to expound in the thought-forms of our own cultures; it is given in forms of words from which it is to be extracted by studying the writers' habits of thinking and writing. The next step is the hypothesis that whenever a writer whose ways of thinking were Hebraic used a word in one sense, he had in mind, and expected his readers to have in mind, all its other senses. Then the hunt is up, and Dr. Thornton is in full cry, tracking down the assumed intentions of biblical and patristic authors by the aid of lists of

[1] *The Glass of Vision* (London, 1948).

[2] October, 1951, pp. 223 ff.

synonyms in Hebrew lexicons. Examples of the fantastic results that may be reached by these methods can be seen in the references to St. Luke's 'topology' on p. 221 and St. John's nuptial symbolism on p. 251.

Dr. Thornton may or may not be right in this account of the working of the Hebrew mind. If he is, it is an important and valuable aid to exegesis. But of his use of it in developing his idea of revelation I can only repeat what I wrote in the following paragraph of that review:

> This search for hidden meanings in the words of Scripture has the same kind of fascination that one finds when reading expositions of the Baconian authorship of Shakespeare's plays, or the late Dr. T. S. Lea's interpretation of the New Testament through the numerical value of Greek letters—not to mention calculations based on the geometry of the Pyramids. The fundamental objection to (this) strain in Dr. Thornton's account of revelation is the contradiction it involves in the idea of God. If God be for us the God revealed in Jesus Christ how can we also think of Him as adopting a mode of revelation after the manner of a composer of cross-word puzzles? It would fit in with the speculations of Sir Edmund Gosse's father better than with the theology of the author of *The Incarnate Lord.*

My second example of this pursuit of the false trail is given by the Swiss theologian, Oscar Cullmann, in his book *Christ and Time.*[1] He begins to go astray in his Foreword, when on p. 12 he writes:

> In what does the *specifically Christian* element of the New Testament revelation consist? That is to say, precisely what is there which it does not have in common with philosophical or religious systems?

We shall see later that there is a right and proper way of asking and answering this question. But Dr. Cullmann takes it to mean that he must look for some metaphysical conception which may be accepted as divinely revealed and must therefore be preserved free from adulteration by other views. He finds this in the fact that the Hebrew mind had what may be called a linear conception of the relation between time and eternity. Christian theology has been corrupted by infection from Greek sources

[1] E. Tr. London, 1951.

with the idea of timelessness. It should have kept to the straight, narrow path of biblical thought in which eternity is the infinite projection before and after of temporal succession.

There is much that is valuable in Cullmann's exposition of the contrast between the Christian and the Jewish views on the centre of history, a contrast already familiar to English-reading theologians through the emphasis laid on it by Paul Tillich and Donald Baillie.[1] Indeed, his treatment of God's revelation of Himself in and through the time-series from the creation to the *parousia* is in many ways admirable. But when he tries to deal with what in his way of thinking must be called the pre-creation and post-*parousia* periods, he falls into inevitable contradictions through not having allowed himself to ask the questions which the Greeks saw to be involved.

It is, of course, true that the revelation given to us through the Bible comes through Hebrew minds, and that questions which troubled the Greek thinkers apparently never occurred to them. But to draw from this the conclusion that God wills us neither to raise these questions nor to seek to learn from those who have thought profoundly about them is ludicrously absurd. Why, in order to be a good Christian, should it be more important to have a Hebrew type of mind than to have a Hebrew cast of countenance? If we must be limited to the Jewish idea of eternity, why not also to the Jewish shape of nose?

Thinking in images, thinking by verbal associations, thinking of eternity as time prolonged: here are three expedients by which men have sought to replace the Bible on a pedestal as a manual of divinely guaranteed information about truths too high for human discovery, three keys to unlock a door which will enable us to walk by sight instead of faith. They have in common the aim they set out to achieve and their failure to achieve it.

Such attempts do at least imply awareness of a need to find new grounds for the old way of using the Bible. More dis-

[1] See the reference to Tillich in D. Baillie: *God was in Christ* (1948), p. 74.

concerting is the fact that many exponents of so-called biblical theology take for granted the assumption on which it is based, in blissful ignorance of its unsoundness—a deficiency which seems to be endemic in much contemporary continental theology, both Lutheran and Reformed.

In 1953, for example, there was published in England, under the title *Kerygma* and *Myth*,[1] a collection of essays by German theologians discussing a paper on 'New Testament and Mythology', by Rudolph Bultmann. More than one of the contributors describe this paper, and the debate to which it gave rise, as being for the best part of a decade the outstanding feature of interest in the German theological world. To my mind the whole discussion has an air of unreality. It is based on the assumption that the task of theologians is to take the Bible as a source-book of revealed truth and dispute about the interpretation of texts. The truth revealed concerns a divine economy to which the researches of scientists, historians, and philosophers are irrelevant. 'Eschatology tells us the meaning and goal of the time-process, but that answer does not consist in a philosophy of history. . . . Indeed, eschatology is not at all concerned with the meaning and goal of secular history, for secular history belongs to the old aeon, and therefore can have neither meaning nor goal. It is concerned rather with the meaning and goal of the history of the individual and of the eschatological community'.[2] This passage follows shortly after the statement that 'the chief aim of every genuine religion is to escape from the world'.[3] If theology means searching the Bible for a message from God telling us how to escape from the world, a message which is immune from criticism at the bar of science, history or philosophy, then we theologians are indeed doomed to spend our lives *bombinantes in vacuo*.

We can only be saved from this fate by a radical revision of the idea of revelation which underlies this way of using the Bible.

[1] Edited by H. W. Bartsch, translated by R. H. Fuller (London, S.P.C.K., 1953).
[2] *Op. cit.*, p. 116. [3] p. 113.

II

In one of his early works, *Problems in the Relation of God and Man*, published in 1911, Dr. C. C. J. Webb gave the quietus to the two-source theory of knowledge. He showed that the traditional division of truth into that which may be discovered by human reason, and that which must be accepted from divine revelation, cannot be maintained on either side. If God be the God of the first article of the Nicene Creed: 'Maker . . . of all things visible and invisible', all discoveries in the field assigned to human reason are discoveries about God as He makes Himself manifest in His handiwork. We cannot think that man is able to discover truths about God as it were behind God's back, nor can we approve the intellectual pelagianism involved in the idea that there is a field within which man can discover truth without divine assistance. On the other hand, it would be no use for God to give revelations to creatures incapable of receiving them, and the only way in which truth can be received is by a mind that can distinguish between truth and falsehood, in other words, by the exercise of reason. Revelation and reason are not alternatives appropriate to different fields of inquiry. They are correlative, the divine and the human sides involved in all man's growth in knowledge.

At first sight this might seem to lead straight into the evacuation of the word 'revelation', as ascribed to the Bible and the Christian faith, of any distinctive meaning—an evacuation which we have seen to have been widely characteristic of the theology of the period in which Dr. Webb's book was published. What was needed was a re-thinking of the whole question, and it was Dr. Webb who in his next book, *Studies in the History of Natural Theology*, published in 1915, pointed out the true line of advance. It is interesting to remember that professionally Dr. Webb was not a theologian but a philosopher. In those days, when theology was largely concerned with the literary and historical criticisms of the Bible, men in Oxford like Dr. Webb and Sir Walter

Moberly, the one philosophy tutor at Magdalen College, the other at Lincoln, were wrestling with the question of the status in reality of this world of space and time. Their background was the post-Kantian idealism of Lessing, Fichte and Hegel, for whom events in space and time were the mode in which the eternal reality appears to our finite minds: these events are of importance simply as illustrations of the timeless truth which is our goal in all our quest for knowledge.

It is easy to see how this idealistic philosophy fits in with views which minimize or deny the uniqueness of the biblical revelation. Turning from his philosophical studies to contemplate the world of theology, Dr. Webb found both Roman Catholic modernists and many liberal Protestants adopting an attitude to the Bible which implied the philosophy he had examined and found wanting. It was thus that he wrote words which deserve to become famous as a landmark in the history of English theological thought:

> . . . observing that, so far as by 'historical element in religion' we mean the element of sacred history, a belief in which forms an important element in some religions, it is a mark of higher development in a religion to emphasize this element. For in the recognition of such a sacred history religion comes to recognize itself as the most concrete and individual form of human experience, concerned not with mere abstract universals but with concrete individuals, those and no others, in which, and not elsewhere, the universals with which we have to do are, as a matter of fact, particularized, and apart from which they possess no actual reality. A religion which involves as part of its essence a sacred history is, in this way, at a higher level than one which, while setting forth certain universal principles, moral or metaphysical, is ready to symbolize them by anything that comes to hand, as it were, and is comparatively indifferent to the particular symbol chosen. Thus a religion which, having developed a theology, regards the narratives which are associated with it as mere illustrative stories, ranks below one which regards them as the actual form which the universal principles have taken. . . .[1]

This passage deserves to become famous because, at that critical stage in our theological studies, in pointing to the impor-

[1] *Op. cit.*, p. 29.

tance of the historical element in the Christian creed it pointed out the way to a recognition of the uniqueness of the Christian revelation which should not involve the two-source theory of knowledge. It suggests that the right answer to Cullmann's question:

> In what does the *specifically Christian element* of the New Testament revelation consist? That is to say, precisely what is there which it does not have in common with philosophical or religious systems?

may be given in the well-known words of St. Augustine:

> Thou didst procure for me ... certain books of the Platonists. ... And therein I found ... the same truth fortified with many and divers arguments. ... But that 'the Word was made flesh and dwelt among us', this I found not there.[1]

The specifically Christian element in our creed is the belief that in Jesus Christ we see God at work in the history of this world, personally incarnate for the purpose of rescuing His creation from the evil with which it had become infected. God gave the specifically Christian revelation by doing some particular things in space and time. But particular events in space and time cannot be insulated from their historical context. Jesus Christ was 'born of the Jews', and Christian faith began with the acceptance of His claim to be the fulfilment of God's messianic promises given through the Old Testament prophets. Had there been no previous history of Israel, there would have been no one to make this act of faith, and no New Testament. Hence our recognition of God in Christ involves a recognition of His redemptive activity extended backwards over the history of the chosen people. The specifically Christian revelation is not to be found in divinely given forms of words conveying doctrinal revelation, but in the divine redemptive activity shown forth in the Incarnation and in events preparatory for and consequent upon it.

But now there is a further point. Among the divine acts which appear as events in human history we must reckon the inspiring

[1] *Confessions* (Tr. Bigg), VII, ix.

of certain men to see their significance. Had there been no one to recognize in Christ the fulfilment of the messianic prophecies, and later to come to worship Him as God, there would be no New Testament. There would have been no such disciples if earlier there had been no prophets who saw the story of Abraham as his response to God's calling, who saw the story of the Exodus as God's rescuing of His chosen people, who saw the whole story of God's calling and rescuing within the context of faith in God as universal Creator and God of Righteousness—a faith which required the re-writing of inherited mythological cosmologies, and the education of man to know his moral responsibility to God and his sinfulness.

How did these men, first the prophets and after them the disciples, come to see all these things? They did not undertake the kind of investigation, argument and demonstration that we are accustomed to use in scientific research and philosophizing. What they had to say came to them by the exercise of a gift of insight, an illumination of the mind to see into the meaning of things.

The occurrence of this historical phenomenon is well described on pp. 194–6 of the late Dr. Wheeler Robinson's book, *Inspiration and Revelation in the Old Testament.*[1] Here again we have to beware of the temptation to fall back into the two-source theory of revelation, to try to establish the uniqueness of the Bible by postulating in the case of the Hebrew prophets a mental endowment of a unique kind which invests with sacrosanctity their thought-forms, their imagery, or the words in which they express them.

We are saved from this by taking note of the parallel between Dr. Wheeler Robinson's account of what he calls the 'intuitional character of prophecy', and the opening chapter of Sir Maurice Bowra's *The Romantic Imagination,*[2] in which he is explaining the sense in which the word 'imagination' was used by Blake, Wordsworth and the other Romantics.

[1] Oxford, 1946. [2] Oxford, 1950.

The Romantic emphasis on the imagination was strengthened by considerations which are both religious and metaphysical. For a century English philosophy had been dominated by the theories of Locke. He assumed that in perception the mind is wholly passive, a mere recorder of impressions from without. . . . His system was well suited to an age of scientific speculation which found its representative voice in Newton. The mechanistic explanation which both philosophers and scientists gave of the world meant that scanty respect was paid to the human self and especially to its more instinctive, though not less powerful, convictions.

For Blake, the imagination is nothing less than God as He operates in the human soul.

. . . the English Romantics . . . believed that the imagination stands in some essential relation to truth and reality, and they were at pains to make their poetry pay attention to them.

. . . poets who believe that the imagination is a divine faculty concerned with the central issues of being. . . . Their approach is indeed not that of the analytical mind, but it is none the less penetrating. They assume that poetry deals in some sense with truth, though this truth may be different from that of science or philosophy.

So far from thinking that the imagination deals with the non-existent, they insist that it reveals an important kind of truth. They believe that when it is at work it sees things to which the ordinary intelligence is blind and that it is intimately connected with a special insight or perception or intuition. Indeed, imagination and insight are in fact inseparable and form for all practical purposes a single faculty. Insight both awakes the imagination to work and is in turn sharpened by it when it is at work.

The perception which works so closely with the imagination is not the kind in which Locke believed, and the Romantics took pains to dispel any misunderstanding on the point. Since what mattered to them was an insight into the nature of things, they rejected Locke's limitation of perception to physical objects, because it robbed the mind of its most essential function.

To these quotations I may add a brief passage from *The Growth of the English Novel*, by Richard Church:[1]

. . . the novel is fundamentally an aspect of poetry, a process of the imagination of man working through imagery and not through logic, to a presentation of himself and the world of which he is a part. Writers who do this . . . are likely to hold a higher authority than all the proselytisers and doctrinaires, who seize the novel-form with zealous hands and wrench it to purposes other than that of poetry, the ever-flowering tree of truth, and of understanding.

[1] London, 1951, p. 213.

Let us assume for the moment that there are two ways of thinking by which men seek for and lay hold on truth, ways which for convenience we may call the scientific and the intuitional.[1] It is by the interaction of the two that human knowledge and understanding are advanced. We must not think that because the prophets mainly made use of the intuitional they were for that reason doing something unique. The uniqueness of the biblical revelation is not to be found in the thought-forms, the imagery, or the language used by its writers. It lies in the uniqueness of its content, the uniqueness of the events to which it bears witness, and of their significance as seen by the eye of faith.

These words, 'their significance as seen by the eye of faith' bring us to the crux of the matter. It is all very well to say that God reveals Himself in what He does, in the events which make up the history of redemption. But history consists of facts together with their interpretation, and the events which form the substance of the Christian revelation include the interpretations put on the facts by the writers of the Old and New Testaments and by successive generations of Christian believers. How can we treat as objective divine relevation what must inevitably include so much of subjective human interpretation? What in all this interpretation is to be the criterion of the objective, the divine, the revealed?

This latter question rests on the premise that if there be a revelation at all it must contain such a criterion, that if God has given us a revelation it must have been of this kind. It is this assumption which leads men to seek to find the criterion in the types of imagery, the verbal associations, or the metaphysical thought-forms which are characteristic of the Hebrew mind. But what is the ground of the assumption itself? Is it anything more than a human notion of what a revelation ought to be, a notion that needs to be corrected by attention to the kind of revelation that God has actually thought fit to give us?

[1] It would here need too long a digression to raise the question whether they are not both in fact intuitional. On this see my chapter on 'The Nature of Human Thought' in *Towards a Christian Philosophy* (London, 1942), and below, Lecture V, pp. 97 ff.

This idea of revelation was taken for granted in much of the so-called liberal theology which flourished in the days of my youth. It underlies the notion that somewhere in the Bible there are to be found irreformable statements of doctrine which by scientific criticism we can disentangle from accretions and distortions. A recent instance of this is provided by Dr. R. S. Franks. In a book published in 1953, he finds in the preaching of St. Peter in the early chapters of Acts the primitive Christian *kerygma*, as it existed before St. Paul and St. John got to work on it, and says: 'since all subsequent theologies stand as an interpretation of the original *kerygma*, it is by their faithfulness to the *kerygma* that they must be judged'.[1] But the revelation itself, the *depositum fidei*, is not to be identified with any verbal expression of it. All subsequent theologies are not to be judged by their faithfulness to the original *kerygma*, but by their faithfulness to the revelation of God in Christ to which the primitive *kerygma* bore witness. If at the time of his preaching St. Peter was not able to see in the revelation all that St. Paul and St. John came to see, that does not mean that he was entrusted with a purer form of doctrine, and that we get closer to the *depositum fidei* by ignoring their insights. What the Holy Spirit opened the eyes of St. Paul and St. John to see was part of the revelation itself, just as much as what was preached by St. Peter.

To tie up the content of the revelation with Hebrew thought-forms or linguistic usage is to perpetuate the kind of liberalism against which Thornton and Cullmann most deeply feel themselves to be in revolt. It locates the criterion of revealed truth in the human characteristics of a certain race, which was essentially what was done by those for whom all truth comes by human discovery and the claim of our Christian faith rests upon the claim that the Hebrew prophets were men specially endowed with religious genius and insight. Now I believe it to be true that we should have no revelation if there had been no men with the insight which enabled them to see the significance of what

[1] R. S. Franks: *The Doctrine of the Trinity* (London, 1953), pp. 5 ff., 195.

God was doing and to make the right response to it. It is also true that these men were Hebrews, and that what they saw they both saw and wrote about in ways characteristic of Hebrew thinking and speaking. But the substance of the revelation lies in the enduring significance of the divine action rather than in the transitory characteristic of their human thought and speech.

The first of our two questions was: How can we treat as objective divine revelation what must of necessity include so much of subjective human interpretation? I will not say much about this now, as it will form the main subject of my next lecture.

To accept the Christian revelation means to see certain events in the history of this world as the story of God in action rescuing His creation from evil. It means, that is to say, seeing in the events to which the Old and New Testament bear witness what the prophets and the apostles saw in them. The Bible becomes to us the bearer of God's revelation as our eyes are opened to share their insight and see what they saw. God reveals Himself not only in the earthly events but also in the illumination of minds to see their significance. We must hold fast to the principle that what makes the revelation revelation is the work of God and not of man. The Bible gives us the events as seen by prophets and apostles. When our eyes are opened to see what they saw it is because one and the same God the Holy Ghost 'Who spake by the prophets' has opened our ears to hear what He wills to say to us through them.

Down the ages the Bible becomes the medium of revelation as in successive generations God the Holy Spirit opens the eyes of readers to see through the words the truth to which it bears witness. Theologians of necessity think in the forms of thought and express themselves in the linguistic usage of their own age and culture. Careful exegesis of the text, seeking to understand what it meant in the minds of its original writers and readers, must be the basis of all attempts at exposition or the formulation of doctrine. But then the further question has to be asked: 'What must the truth have been if it appeared like this to men who thought like that?' St. Peter saw it with the eyes of a Palestinian Jew who up to the Day of Pentecost had not, so far as we know, travelled further from Galilee than Jerusalem; St. Paul, a Pharisee who had been born a Roman citizen, after his schooling by Gamaliel had had a university education at Tarsus; St. John (if Dr. Dodd is right) had a mind at home in the Hellenistic culture of Ephesus. If the truth about God's revelation in Christ be such that those men saw it and wrote of it like that, what must it be for us?

In traditional theology the Roman Catholic distinction between *ecclesia docens* and *ecclesia discens*, and Calvin's emphasis on the need of *Testimonium Spiritus Sancti internum*, both point to this side of the truth about revelation. Both imply that the Bible only becomes revelation to readers guided by the Holy Spirit, readers who (in Pauline language) have the eyes of their hearts enlightened, to whom the God of our Lord Jesus Christ, the Father of glory, gives a spirit of wisdom and revelation in the knowledge of Him.[1]

We who to-day in Great Britain seek to find God's revelation by reading the Bible under the guidance of the Holy Spirit with the eye of faith are not prophets of ancient Israel or Palestinian apostles or Hellenistic Fathers of the Church. We are men and women of the twentieth century, reared in the traditions of Western European civilization, our ways of thinking and speaking conditioned by the culture of our age and clime. In order to see with their eyes we need all the help that scholarship can give us towards understanding how the minds of biblical and patristic writers were conditioned in their turn. But we need this understanding of their habits of thought and speech in order to discount them, not to adopt them; in order to answer the question: 'What must the truth have been if it appeared like this to men who thought and spoke like that?' The God Who reveals Himself in

[1] Eph. i. 17, 18.

events and their interpretation is one and the same, yesterday, to-day, and for ever. We men, through whom He wills to act in thought and word as well as deed, are finite creatures of space and time. We must be content to see what we can see from the standpoint of our own circumstances. Our task is to expound the revelation as we see it to our contemporaries, leaving it to future generations to discount whatever in our vision and exposition has been of only passing worth.

What God has done cannot be altered or undone. Therein lies the unchanging deposit of the faith. But through the insights of different men in different ages and different cultures He, who never contradicts Himself, gives increasing understanding of its significance. One remembers, for example, how from their missionary experience men like Father H. H. Kelly and Canon W. E. S. Holland were impressed by the way in which Japanese and Indian Christians would seize on aspects of the character of our Lord which we Westerners might never have noticed until they pointed them out to us. Again, a paper by Mr. T. S. Garrett in the issue of the periodical *Theology* for April, 1951, opens up a whole range of questions by asking what will be the effect of taking into account as post-biblical revelation the continued action of God in the history of the Church.

'We walk by faith, not by sight'. False theories of revelation spring from a refusal to be content with our creaturely status, an insistence that the only revelation worth having is one which gives us the kind of knowledge open only to a spectator of all time and all existence. But it is not for us to dictate to our Creator. We must be content to see and think and speak as men of our own age and culture. The measure of our faith in Him is our willingness to walk by the light of the kind of revelation that He has thought fit to give us.

Faith is not simply believing that God has done certain definite things in the past. It is that, but it is also trust in the living Lord of to-day and to-morrow, trust in Him that He will fulfil His promise to send His Spirit to take of the things that He has done and show them unto us, guiding us onward into all truth. The revelation of the past is to be interpretated by the light of the revelation of the present and the future.

III

Lord Gifford made his will five years before Dr. Ernest Walker put down in his diary his thoughts about *Lux Mundi*. As a matter of exegesis it is clear that in contrasting it with science he uses the word revelation in the sense that derives from the two-source theory of knowledge. That way of drawing the contrast implied a difference of logical method between the use of human reason to scrutinize evidence and the holding of beliefs accepted on authority. On the view which I have been developing in this lecture that contrast no longer holds good. When we say that what we believe as Christians has come to us by revelation, we do not mean that it consists of doctrines taken over from some allegedly divine source, in the acceptance of which our minds have been passive. It means that to us a certain series of events in the history of the world are significant as expressing the redemptive activity of its Creator. So far as logical method is concerned, argument from the occurrence of those events to the specifically Christian doctrine of God is of the same kind as argument from the nature of the world in general to God's existence. The formulation and exposition of the Christian revelation is as much a matter of natural theology as what Lord Gifford described as 'the science of Infinite Being'.

The distinction we can draw is not between so-called natural and revealed theology, but between the revelation which God gives of Himself as Creator and that which He gives of Himself as Redeemer. The former is apprehended by observation of and reflection upon the nature of the universe in general; the latter by observation of and reflection upon certain events to which the Bible bears witness.

In studying both we have to bear in mind the fundamental truth that revelation and reason are not alternatives appropriate to different fields of inquiry, that they are the divine and human sides involved in all man's growth in knowledge. This carries with it the corollary that in the last resort the content of an alleged revelation must be the criterion of the source, and not *vice versa.* All that I have said in my second lecture about the method of our thinking in our attempts to make sense of our experience remains true when we regard the knowledge that comes to us as coming by revelation. When an idea is presented to us as claiming to come from a source that is revelatory, we must ask how it will fit in with what else we know of the nature of things. It may be that the result will be to show that our existing categories are in need of revision. It may be that the alleged revelation will have to be rejected as a false pretender. Until this question can be settled we must suspend our judgment on the credentials of its source.

I was once asked by a publisher for an opinion on a manuscript which had been submitted to him. It had been received by so-called automatic writing, and claimed to be a revelation of truth concerning profound mysteries given by supernatural beings entitled the Watchers. Unfortunately these Watchers, in their celestial sphere, were apparently ignorant of much that had been thought, said and written by human philosophers on earth during the last twenty or thirty years: their revelations were the kind of thing that might have passed for a quasi-philosophical article in a popular magazine, one of those articles in which the thoughts of the previous generation of scholars linger on and filter through to a wider public. I could not regard as revelation from heaven material which was inferior to what was being produced on earth.

To make the content the criterion of the source is the only safeguard against being at the mercy of any and every superstition. But if we are to apply it to those who bring us messages gained by automatic writing and similar supernormal phenomena, we must, if we are honest, be prepared equally to use it when considering the contents of the Bible or the decrees of councils of the Church. Why, indeed, should we not so treat the Bible and the Church when God Himself has revealed His will to submit His revelation to us in this way, when He has bidden us to be wise as serpents, to use for grasping revelation the same kind of intelligence that is used for meteorology, to find in His actions the credential of His claims?[1] The disciple who bade his fellow-Christians 'prove the spirits' was true to his Master in making the content the criterion of the source.[2]

In the historic creeds of Christendom the first two articles deal successively with the two modes of divine revelation which I have distinguished. We begin by saying 'I believe in one God, the Father almighty, maker of heaven and earth, and of all things visible and invisible'. This, by asserting the whole universe to be the creation of the one and only God there is, asserts our faith in Him as He is revealed to us in and through His handiwork in general. Then, in the second article, beginning with the words 'And in one Lord Jesus Christ', we affirm that what is specifically Christian in our belief is our understanding of certain empirical facts in the history of this world.

In the third article we say that we 'believe in the Holy Ghost, the Lord, the Giver of Life . . . who spake by the prophets'. This turns our thoughts to that element in God's revelatory action which I have spoken of as His inspiring men to see the significance of events as revelatory. One more lecture will have to be given to this side of the subject before I am done with the introductory part of my course. After that, in the remainder of this first series, I shall confine myself to the study of what I may call the universe in general, of the way in which, to us Christians, God reveals Himself in His handiwork as Creator. In the second series I shall be trying to show how the Christian understanding of the events which we believe to express His redemptive activity

[1] St. Matt. x. 16; xvi. 1–4; xii. 27; xi. 4–6.
[2] 1 St. John iv. 1–3.

throws light on our attempt to make sense of the whole. I cannot describe these as dealing successively with natural and revealed theology. If all theology is both natural and revealed, that distinction is no longer tenable. I may perhaps, however, use the phrase natural theology for the whole field within which Christian theology has its distinctive place, and follow this usage in giving titles to the subdivisions of my work.

LECTURE V

The Eye of Faith

I

I HAVE been maintaining that all apprehension of truth is by the co-operation of revelation and reason: man by his reason apprehends what God reveals. I have also maintained that the ground of the claim that Christianity is in some special sense a revealed religion is the conviction that a certain series of events in the history of the world embodies a certain activity on the part of God which is of supreme significance for our understanding of all that He does everywhere, and is therefore in a special sense revelatory. This conviction, in turn, rests upon a certain understanding of that series of events, on what I may call seeing them with the eye of faith. We must now squarely face the fact that the claim of Christian faith to be based on revealed truth includes the claim that a certain understanding of historical events, this seeing with the eye of faith, is itself part of the God-given revelation.

All thinking men share in the philosopher's desire for objectivity.[1] When it was first suggested that God gives His revelation in events rather than in propositions, the attractiveness of the suggestion lay in the fact that it seemed to substitute the objectivity of observable happenings for unverifiable statements. The preacher of the word would no longer have to call upon his hearers to accept certain doctrines on the ground that they were written in a certain book; he should direct their attention to certain historical events and bid them consider their implications. It was soon seen, however, that the matter is not so simple. What, precisely, is meant by a historical event? Is it merely the occurrence of a certain happening in time and space? If so, has it any

[1] See above, Lecture II, pp. 30 ff.

revelatory significance apart from some interpretation of it? Here are two difficulties: (i) History is an inexact science in the sense that evidence is seldom such as to provide demonstrative proof of precisely what happened, and (ii) if the revelatory character of the event depends upon its interpretation, how can it be said to possess the desired objectivity?

(i) If we hold fast to the principle that in this world we are to walk by faith and not by sight, the first of these two questions should not trouble us overmuch. Disquiet is due to the difficulty of accepting the kind of revelation that God has seen fit to give us; it comes from clinging to the notion that the only revelation worth having would be one which has the guaranteed certainty that we would provide if we were God. In later lectures I hope to show that the provision of this element of uncertainty is of a piece with God's whole method of creation and redemption as He does in fact reveal them to us.

(ii) More important, here and now, is the second question: If interpretation must be included in the idea of a historical event to make it revelatory, to what extent does this deprive the revelation of objectivity?

For an answer to this question we must look back to our earlier discussion of objectivity. Let me recall what I said in my second lecture about a paradox implicit in all human thinking, the paradox that there is always a quest for objectivity which can only be satisfied by the object fulfilling the demands of the thinker's canons of thought. All that I said in that lecture about each man's apprehensions being conditioned by his outlook is relevant now to the present issue. The existentialist may err in denying the possibility of apprehending any objective truth which is common to different thinkers; at the opposite pole it is equally erroneous to suppose that somewhere there is to be found a kind of truth which is distinguished from other objects of thought by being such that we can contemplate it uncoloured by our presuppositions.

Thinking, I then said, implies a fundamental act of faith, the faith that everything that exists or happens fits in so as to make sense. Our thinking is an attempt to justify this faith by comparing our supposed apprehensions of reality, hoping thereby to correct whatever inaccuracies there may be in our observations or in our thought about them. Sometimes a man may do this by comparing the observations and reflections upon them that he himself has made at different times. Or there may be a joint effort, two or more men pooling their ideas in the quest for clearer and fuller understanding. In this way knowledge grows by the interaction of categories and evidence. The process has gone on long enough for it to be generally agreed that quite a number of truths may safely be regarded as objective. Why do we smile at Kipling's village that voted the earth was flat and at Leacock's vestrymen who agreed that the world should be held to have been created as described in Genesis until decided otherwise by a majority vote in a meeting properly convened?[1] Kipling and Leacock can count upon it seeming ridiculous that men should argue and vote about what everyone knows to be matters of objective fact.

That this earth is a spherical planet which has arrived at its present condition through a number of changes are beliefs which belong to the world that is studied by the natural sciences. Here it is a commonplace that the objective truth of one age is subject to revision by fresh study of fresh evidence in another: Newtonian physics gives way to the relativity theories of Einstein. Yet no scientist believes, and no one of us in his senses can believe, that the history of scientific research is nothing but the history of changing fashions in subjective preferences. We have faith that by comparing our observations, and the theories that we base upon them, we are making progress towards a clearer apprehension of the objective truth about things which is the goal of our search.

[1] R. Kipling: *A Diversity of Creatures*, and S. Leacock: *Arcadian Adventures among the Idle Rich*.

When comparing the Hebrew prophets with the English romantics I drew a distinction between two ways of laying hold on truth which I then called the scientific and the intuitional.[1] These are not unrelated methods used by different people moving along parallel paths that never meet. Prophets and poets may sometimes be unscientific, but scientific research involves an element of the intuitional. It is, indeed, involved in all human thinking.

Nothing could at first sight seem more purely objective than the way in which conclusion follows from premisses in a valid syllogism. Yet to draw the conclusion a man must perform the intuitional act of looking at the two premisses and seeing in them, taken together, the conclusion implied. Now consider a line of thought more akin to a scientific inquiry. Imagine yourself waking up one morning with a cold in your head and wondering what can have been the cause of it. You remember that the day before yesterday you were in a train for a long time either with cold feet in sopping wet shoes and socks which you have not been able to change, or opposite a man with a streaming cold. If you decide that your cold has come from one or other of these sources, how have you drawn the conclusion? By inspecting the circumstances and seeing in them the explanation you accept. But how does it come about that you see and accept it? Let us suppose that you say you caught the cold from your fellow traveller. This means that you have brought to the consideration of the case a mind which takes for granted the theory of infection by the transmission of germs.

In my youth, many years ago, I was at an Anglican Fellowship conference at Lady Margaret Hall in Oxford. After breakfast one morning I was strolling in the grounds with an eminent woman doctor. The wetness of the grass was penetrating our light indoor slippers, and I remarked to my companion that perhaps we had better move on to the gravel path. She replied (somewhat in the spirit of Socrates refusing to escape from

[1] Above, Lecture IV, p. 85.

prison) that having for many years denied that there was any danger in what we were doing, her professional conscience would not allow her to take such evasive action. Doubtless she too thought that colds are caught by the transmission of germs rather than from cold wet feet. Whether she was right or wrong it is not for me, a layman in medicine, to attempt to decide. My point is that her judgment, 'There is no danger in what we are doing', was intuitional in the sense that she held together in her mind the state of our feet and the state of my mind, and looking at the combination of the two in the light of her views on the character of colds, saw in it an instance of error demanding refutation.

'The distinguishing mark of philosophy and of science', said John Laird, 'is to look for the reasons of things, and to set them down faithfully in order to show their explanatory value'.[1] We look for the reasons of things, but what we see is conditioned by what is already in our minds when we do the looking. This, however, does not destroy our belief that there is something there to be seen, and that by perseverence in making and comparing observations we can learn to discount misleading prejudices and acquire helpful presuppositions which will increase our capacity to see straight and grasp the true nature of the object. In medical matters the trained physician is more likely than the layman to give an accurate diagnosis because his training has built up the kind of presuppositions required. A layman's confidence that he has caught his cold from a fellow-traveller comes from his sharing in the general diffusion of a theory of which the trained physician knows the grounds.

The trained physician is more likely to make an accurate diagnosis. But there is no absolute guarantee that in every case he will do so; and there is a further factor which has to be taken into account. Physicians differ among themselves in that some seem more than others to have what may be called a *flair* for diagnosis. Of this I cannot say more at the present stage of our

[1] *Theism and Cosmology* (London, 1940), p. 30.

inquiry than that it is just something that happens. In all spheres of human activity, in the arts, in the sciences, and in practical affairs some men are more gifted than others. Advances are made when these gifted individuals open doors through which others may follow to share what is gained by their insight. Here again there is no absolute guarantee that a new departure is a fresh insight into objective truth. The pioneer has to lay bare his alleged discovery for criticism by comparison with other observations and insights. Little by little true paths of advance are distinguished from false trails, and we add to the store of what we can take to be objective.

What, then, is objectivity? Fundamentally it is an object of faith, the faith that by the use of our reason, if we honestly seek to discount our personal prejudices and discuss with one another what we think we see, we shall be able to pass beyond an existentialist limitation to our private worlds and to share in the knowledge of a common reality.[1] The extent to which we have such knowledge varies in different fields. Sciences are more or less 'exact': in each, as Aristotle says, we have to be content with what is attainable.[2] In all it is a matter of more or less. In the most exact of sciences, in the fields in which we are most confident that we have objectivity, it has come to us through the insights of men conditioned by the existing state of their minds, purged and clarified by comparison and discussion, and accepted because it fits in so as to make sense with what else we think we know. We who accept it accept what we can see with the eyes of twentieth-century Western Europeans, leaving whatever further purging and clarifying may be necessary to men of other climes and later ages. We may feel pretty sure that certain of our apprehensions are irreversible or irreformable, but such assurance is, strictly speaking, a matter of faith rather than of sight.

Now let us return to the thought of the Bible as the medium of revelation because it contains the witness of men who saw in

[1] On this, see further my *Towards a Christian Philosophy* (London, 1942), chap. ii.
[2] *Eth. Nic.* 1098 a 27.

certain historical events the redemptive acts of God. At the centre stands the witness of those who saw in Jesus of Nazareth God's Messiah, and saw Him exercise His messiahship in such a way as to lead men to see in Him none other than God Himself. They would have had no such beliefs if they had not been men who looked upon Him with minds conditioned by the traditions of their spiritual ancestry, men conscious of being members of God's chosen people who were looking for the fulfilment of God's promises given to His people through the prophets. Not everyone who met our Lord in Palestine saw in Him what the disciples saw; not everyone who in earlier years had to do with the Hebrews and the Jews saw their history as the history of God's chosen people. What ground have we for holding that the prophetic interpretation of the events of Israel's history, and the New Testament writers' recognition of God in Christ, were insights into objective truth and not illusory figments of imagination?

So far as I can see, God has not willed to give us any means whereby we can demonstratively prove that this is so. We have to be content with the same kind of assurance that is given to us in other fields of study. In medicine and in mathematics, and in the arts as well as in the sciences, advances in knowledge come through men gifted with a *flair* for seeing what others do not see. These open the door through which the others may pass and have their eyes opened to see it too. Their vision is accepted as genuine insight into objective truth by those who say: 'Yes, now that you have opened my eyes to it, I can see that it is so'. So too the Old Testament prophets and our Lord's disciples were men gifted with the *flair* for seeing in the events of Israel's history and in the Son of Mary what other men did not. Their vision approves itself as genuine insight, what they have seen is accepted as objective truth, by those who in reading what they have written have their eyes opened to see what they saw.

At first hearing this may sound like a revival of the religious genius view of the prophets which flourished in the liberal theology of fifty years ago.[1] If so, it is a revival with a difference so great that it would be truer to say that it has passed through death and resurrection and become a new creature. The parents of that view were the two-source theory of knowledge and the idea that revelation must take the form of statements to be accepted on authority; it was an attempt to commend the corresponding view of the Bible by investing the writings of the prophets with the required characteristics. In this it made the same mistake as is made by those who, in dealing with the New Testament, identify the *depositum fidei* with the *kerygma*.[2] It makes all the difference in the world when we locate the *depositum fidei* not in the apostolic *kerygma* or the prophetic utterance, but in that to which they point, that which they open our eyes to see.

I have already expressed my suspicion that it was the influence of the traditional idea of revelation which led Dr. Farrer, in his third Bampton Lecture, to put his trust in 'inspired images'.[3] The same lingering influence from the past is apparent in Dr. Paul Tillich's treatment of the subject.[4] 'Revelation', he says, 'radiates knowledge—a knowledge, however, which can be received only in a revelatory situation, through ecstasy and miracle'. He is then at pains to contrast the kind of knowledge which comes by revelation with that which we gain otherwise. Not only is it knowledge which can only be communicated to those who participate in the revelatory situation of ecstasy and miracle; it 'does not increase our knowledge about the structures of nature, history, and man'. It cannot interfere with, or be interfered with by, ordinary knowledge.

> There is no scientific theory which is more favourable to the truth of revelation than any other theory.... The same situation prevails with regard to

[1] See above, Lecture IV, pp. 73 ff. [2] Above, Lecture IV, p. 86.

[3] Above, Lecture IV, p. 76.

[4] *Systematic Theology*, Vol. I (London, 1953), pp. 143 ff. I may remark that for an accurate understanding of Dr. Tillich's writing it is sometimes necessary to ask oneself how it would have been expressed if it had been written in German. This is especially the case with his use of the preposition 'of'. This enables one to see that 'The knowledge of Revelation' and 'The History of Revelation' mean the knowledge that comes by revelation and history as seen from the point of view of revelation.

historical research. Theologians need not be afraid of any historical conjecture, for revealed truth lies in a dimension where it can neither be confirmed nor negated by historiography. Therefore, theologians should not prefer some results of historical research to others on theological grounds, and they should not resist results which finally have to be accepted if scientific honesty is not to be destroyed, even if they seem to undermine the knowledge of revelation. Historical investigations should neither comfort nor worry theologians. Knowledge of revelation, although it is mediated primarily through historical events, does not imply factual assertions, and it is therefore not exposed to critical analysis by historical research. Its truth is to be judged by criteria which lie within the dimension of revelatory knowledge.

Here we see the persistence of the theory of the two fields, the two sources, the two kinds of knowledge such that 'never the twain shall meet'. Yet there is the curious sentence about the knowledge which, though 'mediated primarily through historical events, does not imply factual assertions'. Taken literally, the words 'does not imply factual assertions' would mean that it would make no difference to our Christian faith if Jesus Christ never actually lived on earth or was crucified, that the gospels would be just as good a foundation for our faith if they were a myth of the kind suggested by J. M. Robertson, W. B. Smith and A. Drews.[1] But how in that case can the events through which the knowledge is mediated be described as historical at all?

We cannot have it both ways. We cannot claim both that our faith is rooted in history and that it implies no factual assertions. In so far as they are assertions of historical facts they must be subject to criticism by the canons of historical inquiry. But what of that further element in the assertions of faith, that in which they pass beyond what are usually regarded as questions of pure history and speak of the events as significant acts of God?

Here Tillich goes too far in saying that what he calls the revelatory situation is only to be found in conditions of ecstasy and miracle. Undoubtedly there have been and are occasions in which such language would be appropriate to describe the

[1] See references in M. Goguel: *Jesus the Nazarene: Myth or History?* (E. Tr. New York, 1926), pp. 15–19.

experience of prophet or disciple, or of reader or hearer who enters into their vision. But such occasions are not the only revelatory situations, and the absolute distinction between the two kinds of knowledge cannot be maintained.

Why was it given to some and not to others to see in Israel the chosen people of God? Why was it given to some and not to others to see God Incarnate in Jesus of Nazareth? To seek an answer in terms of ecstasy and miracle implies that the case is a different one from those in which similar questions arise in other departments of knowledge. But why should this be so? I have myself tried to teach the elements of Greek to classes of young men of whom some were soon at home in the language while others could never see the point of the simplest rules. We must all of us have known unfortunate students in school or college who could not pass examinations requiring a minimum of mathematical knowledge because mathematics meant nothing to them. In all the arts and the sciences men are variously gifted: in this direction or that some are blind and others see. Why should we seek a different explanation for the fact that in this or that historical event some men see the act of God and others do not? Why should a prophet or a disciple have a *flair* for diagnosis of a kind quite different from that of a Newton or an Einstein, a Lister or a Pasteur, a Michael Angelo or a Beethoven?

I see no justification for expecting that there should be such a difference. Nor would it be of any use to us if there were. We cannot render more secure the objectivity of the biblical revelation by withdrawing it from the kind of scrutiny by which we test and establish objectivity in general. We do not doubt mathematical truths because some pupils are unable to see them, and it certainly would not increase our confidence in them if we thought that they could only be grasped by miracle in ecstasy. The uniqueness of the revelation lies neither in the language nor in the forms of thought in which it has its biblical presentation nor in the mode of its apprehension, but in the substance of what is apprehended. To one man the opening of the eyes of his mind to see with the eye of faith may come in an experience that can only be described in terms of ecstasy and miracle; to another it may come by a flash of insight comparable to the grasping of a grammatical rule or a mathematical equation. All such opening of our eyes is the work of God the Holy Spirit, the Lord who spake by the prophets and who, in using what they have written to enable us to share their vision of the truth, still to-day does so in divers manners.

If we want to assure ourselves of the objectivity of what we see, we have to follow the usual method of considering it in relation to whatever else we think we know and asking how it all fits in together so as to make sense. If we want to commend it to others, all we can do is try to explain what we see and how we see it in the hope that they may be led to see it too, not forgetting to pray that the Holy Spirit who has quickened our mind to see the point of some rule of Greek grammar or apprehend some mystery of faith will give a like blessing to pupil or unbeliever.

This opening of the eyes of the mind to see with the eye of faith is not the substitution of faith for reason, or the supersession of reason by faith, as though one organ of apprehension took the place of, or overrode, another. It is the enlightenment of reason by faith enabling it to do its own work better.

In terms of this metaphor of vision, three things are necessary for knowledge: something to be seen, a mind that sees straight, and the right perspective along which to look. In a cinema, no matter how good his eyesight, a man who is sitting at the end of a row near the front will see the pictures on the screen distorted. To get the right perspective he must be moved to a seat further back and in the centre. Of these three factors the content of the Christian revelation belongs to the first: it is among the possible objects of knowledge waiting to be seen and known. The good eyesight, the mind that sees straight, is a gift of the Spirit widely shared in greater or less degree by unbelievers and believers alike. The one claim which we Christians cannot help making is that our faith gives us the right perspective. Conversion is being lifted out of the side seat in front and put down in the centre further back.

How are we to make good this claim? There is only one thing that we can do. Like John Laird's philosophers and scientists, we must try faithfully to set down what we see in order to show its explanatory value, submitting it to the criticism and judgment of all who bring to that task whatever ability in the use of their reason God may have given them.

II

Already in these lectures I have used the word faith in a number of different senses. The context in each case should have made the meaning clear enough. But it will be well to pause for a moment and consider the various uses of the word.[1]

The first distinction is between what may be called its intellectual and its fiduciary use. In the former of these it denotes a state of mind somewhere between opinion and knowledge: 'I think', 'I believe', 'I know' express successive steps on an ascending scale of certainty. One can define opinion and knowledge in purely intellectual terms, but to fix the point between the two for which the words faith and belief are appropriate, one has to bring in pragmatic considerations. By 'I believe' we should mean, 'I am sure enough of this to be prepared to act upon it'. Faith is holding that x is y with sufficient certainty to make it the basis of action. In this sense the word is sometimes used of the state of mind of the believer, and sometimes of the content of his belief. When we say that we walk by faith and not by sight we refer to this state of the Christian's mind; when we say that his godparents did promise on his behalf that he should 'believe all the Articles of the Christian Faith' we use the word to mean what is to be believed. I will call this latter usage its objective sense.

[1] On this, see also my *Christian Faith and Practice* (Oxford, 1950), pp. 2 ff.

Owing to its pragmatic quality, in sayings like 'we walk by faith' the word easily passes over from its purely intellectual into its fiduciary sense, the sense in which the state of mind would be described as 'believing in' instead of 'believing that'. In this usage the object of the faith is not a statement, such as that *x* is *y*, but a person or a cause; the believer enriches his intellectual degree of certainty with an attitude of trust, and it may be of devotion and self-surrender. When a politician says that he has faith in the good sense of the electorate, he professes to trust their judgment; when he says that he has faith in democracy or in his party leader, he professes devotion to a cause or a person. The strength of such faith will not be measured by the degree of its intellectual certainty, but by the extent to which the man's trust will impel him to surrender himself to the object of his devotion. For a man to have faith in God he must indeed share with St. James' devils the belief that God is, but the word will not have reached its full meaning until he has passed beyond that to the complete surrender of himself in trust and devotion.

Subjectively, then, from intellectual certainty enough to justify action faith may develop into personal trust and devotion. We must now look at the development on the objective side, where the word faith is used for the content of what is believed. The history of the Christian religion helps us to understand how the same word has come to be used both subjectively and objectively, to understand the relation between its intellectual and its fiduciary meaning.

The decisive step in this history was the proclamation of the righteousness of God by the Hebrew prophets, and their interpretation of God's righteousness in terms of moral judgment. Intellectually this means that in order to discover the will of God one is not to cast lots or inspect the entrails of birds or go to a sanctuary in the hope of having a revelatory dream; one is to ask oneself what one honestly believes to be the right decision to take. By taking this step our spiritual ancestors not only crossed the line which marks the boundary between superstition and the beginning of reasonable religion, implicitly they provided for the future growth and development of their faith. Every advance in moral insight, in sensitiveness to moral issues and understanding of them, will be an advance in knowledge of God, a fuller apprehension of the revelation of Himself which He wills to give us. Judaism and Christianity, if they keep true to this beginning, will be able to avoid the divorce between religion and philosophy which worked such havoc among the Greeks. On the subjective side, in morals as well as in metaphysics, faith in the intellectual sense means being sure enough of the truth of a judgment to make it the basis of action. Faith in God, in the fiduciary sense, means trusting in One who reveals Himself to us in and through our judgments of fact and value. On the objective side a man's faith in the intellectual sense of the word is the view of the nature of things which his reason and conscience lead him to make the basis of his actions; in the fiduciary sense it could mean the causes or persons in which or whom he puts his trust. This, at any rate, seems to be the use of the word by the German theologian, Dr. H. Thielicke, in his exposition of the phrase *sola fide*:

> When the Reformers made *sola fide* the *articulus stantis et cadentis ecclesiae* they meant faith in Jesus Christ, *fides Jesu* (objective genitive). The Reformers were not concerned with faith as a subjective disposition as contrasted with works but with its object, Jesus Christ. Luther was always emphasizing that what mattered about faith was not its subject, but its object, which was located *extra me*. In his exposition of Psalm 90 he even used the daring metaphor that the subject of faith was a mathematical point, so far was he from regarding faith as a subjective experience through which man's understanding of himself is illuminated, and so exclusively should faith be defined in reference to its object, the *extra se* of the historic Christ. As it became secularized, Protestantism lost sight of this, and *sola fide* became a subjective disposition of man, an emotional experience, the famous 'defiant faith' of Lutheranism.[1]

Enough has been said to show how varied are the uses of the word, how it can be used subjectively and objectively, in the intellectual and in the fiduciary sense. It would clearly be absurd to maintain that one or other of these is its proper sense, or has

[1] E. Tr. by R. H. Fuller in Bartsch: *Kerygma and Myth* (London, 1953), p. 138.

a prior claim to correctness of usage. Sometimes the word will mean one thing, sometimes another. Quite often, indeed, it will be intended to express a fusion of more than one sense, as when to say that a man has faith in God means both that he believes in the existence of God and that he puts his trust in Him. In speaking and writing the best we can do is to try to make clear by the context the meaning we intend, leaving it to hearers and readers, from their knowledge of the various uses of the word, to understand what is meant.

In this connection I cannot help remarking that to my mind the phrase 'justification by faith' has outlived its usefulness, and, except for the historical study of Christian thought in the sixteenth and seventeenth centuries, had better be dropped from our theological vocabulary. In some circles it has become the custom to take it for granted that the words express a fundamental article in Christian belief. But the above quotation from H. Thielicke shows that among Lutherans, at any rate, there is no agreement about the meaning in this context of the word faith, a fact made even more clear by Bishop Anders Nygren, who on p. 68 of his *Commentary on Romans*, quotes interpretations of the word from no less than seven of his fellow-theologians and adds the comment: 'it must be declared with utmost emphasis that nothing was further from Paul's mind than this'.[1] And on p. 129 of the same work Bishop Nygren indicates that there is similar confusion about the word justification.

Some twelve years ago, when I was writing my Croall Lectures, I tried to find an intelligible and acceptable way of understanding the doctrine. I had to begin by distinguishing justification from salvation, keeping this latter word for the final state of the blessed in the life of the world to come, and using justification for the condition of those who in this world are on the right side of the line which divides those who are on the way to that salvation from those who are not. Then, taking my stand on the

[1] E. Tr. (London, 1952).

prophetic principle to which I have referred above, I concluded that the faith which justifies is that fundamental faith which finds expression in a man's attempting to live up to the best light he has got, whether or no he has ever heard of the Christian gospel. Thus I wrote:

> Surrender to the truth of the Christian faith is an integral element in human blessedness; it is an experience in which for their own good all men ought to share. Some of us, by God's grace, may be privileged to enter upon it during this life, and all who are to be saved will be given it either here or hereafter. Meanwhile, the condition of avoiding damnation, the justifying faith which is necessary, so to speak, in order to be in the running for the higher privilege of saving faith, is of another kind. It consists in the surrender of a man's whole self in devotion to whatever claims he honestly believes to be made upon him by truth.[1]

This which, for me, is the sense in which I can say that I believe in the doctrine of justification by faith is, I fear, indistinguishable from what some people would call justification by works. Others use the phrase to mean something different. Not long ago, in conversation with an English theologian, I found that he took it as simply expressing the truth which in some lectures at Oxford I once expressed as follows:

> In all true religion, God acts first, and what we call our religion is our response to the divine activity. He creates, and we live; He calls and we respond; He comes on earth and dies for us and we are won to penitence and discipleship.[2]

Neither of these two interpretations gives what is meant by Thielicke, Nygren, or the seven Lutherans whom the latter rejects. And a further variation is suggested by the following passage from Fr. E. K. Talbot:

> The only thing which is going to disinfect us of our egoism is the gazing upon the object of our worship. 'The Catholic Faith is this—that we *worship*.' All Christian morality—the whole theory of it—rests upon that: all Christian conduct; all Christian goodness has its spring and source in the worship of the

[1] *The Doctrine of the Trinity* (London, 1943), p. 32.
[2] *Christian Faith and Practice* (Oxford, 1950), p. 70.

holy God. For only so are we going to be lured away from ourselves. And we know how St. Paul is never tired of insisting on it: that is the great difference, the life which rests on faith and the life which rests upon law.[1]

Here, then, we have five or six different interpretations of the same phrase. For this reason, while I still believe what I wrote in both Croall and Oxford lectures, I should not now describe either belief as acceptance of the doctrine of justification by faith, or make use of those words at all. Whatever may have been the case in the past, the phrase has now become so indeterminate, patient of so many different interpretations, that it no longer has any value as current coin in the theological exchange.

To cling to the use of the phrase is to yield to the theologians' besetting temptation, the temptation to think that somewhere at some time God's revelation has been given in a form of sound words, which form must be preserved while we argue about what we are to mean by it. It is to invest a certain formula of Reformation theology with the kind of sacrosanctity which in my last lecture, when discussing certain German theologians, Dr. Lionel Thornton and Dr. R. S. Franks, I maintained should not be ascribed either to biblical or patristic statements.[2] It is to forget that, as Mr. Weldon has put it, 'words do not have meanings . . .; they simply have uses'.[3] In whatever document they may occur, we have first to ask what they were intended to mean by those who used them. Then we have to try to express what they stood for in accordance with the forms of thought and linguistic usage of our own day. So far we have what I have just called historical study, and it is in this study that such a phrase as justification by faith has its proper place. If as a result of such study we find ourselves in disagreement about what the words originally meant—and still more if we are disagreed about what we to-day should believe to be the truth of the matter—what we need to do is to discuss in terms of the thought of to-day what we should believe to-day rather than to be concerned with

[1] L. Menzies: *The Retreat Addresses of E. K. Talbot* (London, 1953), p. 111.
[2] Above, Lecture IV, pp. 79, 86.
[3] T. D. Weldon: *The Vocabulary of Politics* (London, 1953), p. 19.

whether our beliefs are justifiable interpretations of a traditional formula.

Here there comes into prominence a corollary of the view of revelation which I have been maintaining in these last two lectures. I spoke at the outset of the two-source theory of knowledge being taken for granted by the original Christians as a traditional element in their world of thought. It was not alone in this. The revelation of God in Christ came in mid-history, at a time when men's minds were already governed by inherited categories of thought and well stocked with ideas. The revelation was given in the form of new evidence which had to make its way into these minds. There it would be found that some of the categories could assimilate it while others would have to be revised, some of the ideas would be established as apprehensions of truth while others would be shown to be false and have to be discarded. 'The Buddha', said Whitehead, 'gave his doctrine to enlighten the world: Christ gave His life. It is for Christians to discern the doctrine'.[1] This discovery is a process which takes time. It is still going on and its history, the history of Christian doctrine, has both a negative and a positive side. The negative is the discovery that existing ideas are inconsistent with the evidence and must be revised or discarded; the positive is the deeper and fuller understanding of what is involved in the evidence itself.

We can never take it for granted that everything we read in some patristic, scholastic or Reformation doctor, though the writer be a theologian of unquestioned authority and unimpeachable orthodoxy, is an expression of, or is even consistent with, the Christian revelation. We cannot, indeed, take this for granted in the case of Councils of the Church or of the biblical writers themselves. We have always to ask how far their attempts to express the revealed truth are coloured by their presuppositions and embody ideas whose inconsistency with it had not yet come to light.

[1] A. N. Whitehead: *Religion in the Making* (New York, 1926), p. 56.

The late Dr. Willard R. Sperry was once explaining to me the grounds on which Congregationalists refrain from prescribing the recitation of the historic creeds of Christendom in their public worship. 'You Anglicans', he said, 'all study the history of Christian doctrine in the first five centuries, whereas we jump from the New Testament to the Reformation. We know as little about the first five centuries as you know about the Reformation. It is natural to you to read the Nicene Creed as a historical document, as a statement of the biblical truth in the forms of thought current at the time; we think that if you insist on our using these words you are requiring us to accept the Aristotelian philosophy of substance'. Whether or no Dr. Sperry was right in his exposition of congregationalism it is not for me to say. The anecdote illustrates my point. In studying the history of Christian doctrine we have first to ask of any document how much of what is written was contributed by ideas already in the writer's mind quite apart from his acceptance of the revelation which he is seeking to expound. Only after this shall we be in a position to consider whether the result of their coming together has been mutual illumination, or whether the truth of the revelation has to be disentangled from a network of undiscovered inconsistencies.

The necessity of such disentangling is recognized by those who think, like Cullmann, that the primitive Christian faith was adulterated by Hellenization. But they over-simplify the problem by suggesting that it can be solved by a historical study of the filiation of ideas, by asking whether they come from Hebrew, Jewish, Greek or other sources. This question is important as a matter of scholarship, but its relevance to that of the truth of the ideas or of the rightfulness of their place in the development of Christian thought is that it helps us to know the presuppositions of those who were seeking to understand and express the significance of the revelatory acts of God. It prepares the way for the real question, and cannot be substituted for it. We cannot evade the responsibility of deciding for ourselves whether the presuppositions are to be welcomed as illuminating or discarded as inconsistent.

This task cannot be completed by the simple method of inquiring whether or no an idea can be traced to some biblical source. It is a task of almost infinite complexity. Every attempt at the expression of Christian doctrine has to be examined with a view to discovering whether its presuppositions have been a help or a hindrance towards fuller understanding of the revelation of God in Christ.

In the second series of these lectures we shall be turning our minds to the study of Christian doctrine on these lines. I shall be speaking as one who confessedly reads the Scriptures of the Old and New Testaments with the eye of faith, that is, as one who believes that he is rightly guided by the Holy Spirit to see in the events to which they bear witness the revelatory acts of God. What I shall be trying to discover and express will be the significance of that revelation for us in this twentieth century, for our understanding of the meaning and purpose of this universe and of our life in it. We shall treat the history of Christian doctrine as the history of successive thinkers seeking to grasp for themselves that significance by interpreting the revelation in terms of the thought of their age and culture. Aware that this study has both its negative and its positive side, our aim will be to disentangle insights from distortions; to answer the question: what must the truth be if men who thought as they did saw it like that? If we are asked by what criterion we are to distinguish the insight from the distortion, the true from the false, we cannot refer to a statement in some formula unconditioned by presuppositions due to the historical circumstances of its origin. To repeat what I said before: if we want to assure ourselves of the objectivity of what we believe ourselves to have seen with the eye of faith, we have to follow the usual method of considering it in relation to whatever else we think we know and asking how it all fits in together so as to make sense; if we want to commend it to others, all we can do is to try to explain what we see and how we see it in the hope that they may be led to see it too.

Near the beginning of my third lecture I spoke of how there is a logic in things before there is a logic in thought. Truly logical thinking is that which accurately grasps the nature of its objects and the relations between them.[1] If this be so, and if the substance of revelation be divine acts which come into our ken as events which are evidence for our understanding of the nature of things, then the history of Christian doctrine—indeed, of all human thought—is the history of the logic in reality working itself out in the minds of men. The real object of our study is not what the men whose works we are reading were consciously aware of thinking and saying; it is the truth which was struggling to make itself known through minds conditioned by their presuppositions. To take one example of what I mean: the doctrines of the Incarnation and the Trinity represent a revision of the notions of godhead, of manhood and of unity which were taken for granted by the first Christians. As we look back, we can see how the new evidence provided by the revelation in Christ required this revision. As we read the writings of the Fathers, and the records of the Councils, we can see how it was working itself out. But to say that at the time they realized that this was what was going on would be to read back into their minds ideas they never had.

As it was with them then, so it is with us now. We have to try to see as best we may, and to set down what we see as clearly as we can, leaving it to our successors to discover and discard our distortions, hoping that we may have contributed something of use to set them further on the way.

I have spoken of how all thinking implies the fundamental faith that somehow all things fit in together to make sense. What I have just been saying implies more than this. To speak of the object of our study as the truth struggling to make itself known in the minds of men, as the logic in things working itself out in human thought, is to pass beyond thinking of reality as passively

[1] Above, Lecture III, p. 51.

waiting for us to discover how it makes sense. We find that in our attempt to understand the nature of things we have our place in a succession of spectators of an objective process of self-revelation. Our interest is not so much in what we ourselves think, or in what other human beings are thinking or have thought; it is in that which is seeking to become known to us. But, properly speaking, for verbs like 'seeking', 'struggling' and 'working out' the subject of the sentence should be personal, not 'that which' but 'he'. We come back to where we started. All human apprehension of truth is man receiving the self-revelation of God.

Looking at it in this way, the Christian sees all who are seeking after truth as seeking after God. Like as the hart panteth after the water-brooks, so long their souls for God, yea, even for the living God. This throws light on the distinction between pure and applied science,[1] suggesting that in its sphere it is analogous to the distinction in prayer between adoration and petition. Perhaps to compare the two distinctions may bring mutual illumination. We are familiar with spiritual guides who warn us that we must never attempt to use God, to treat Him as a means to an end. But what if He has revealed Himself as wanting to be used, putting Himself into the hands of men so that they may be free to do with Him what they will? Is it possible that for errors both in petitionary prayer and in the application of scientific discoveries the corrective will come from following that line of revelation which derives from the Hebrew prophets, from looking to growth in moral insight for the direction both of our desires and of our technological skill? We here take note of these questions, but they, and others like them, belong properly to the second series of my lectures.

III

Gradually there emerges from this discussion the idea of revelation which is to take the place of that which was based on the

[1] Above, Lecture II, pp. 25 ff.

two-source theory of knowledge, which located the *depositum fidei* in a *kerygma* or a form of sound words. To the eye of faith the agent of revelation is God: God making Himself known to man through His creative and redemptive activity in nature and history. To the eye of Christian faith the revelation in Jesus Christ is the clue to the understanding of everything else. In order to be used for this end it must first be understood itself. 'Christ gave His life; it is for Christians to discern the doctrine'. From age to age men grow in this understanding as they learn to discount the colouring given by misleading presuppositions in the thought of those who went before. 'Orthodoxy', as Dr. Turner has put it, 'must always steer a difficult course between the Scylla of archaism and the Charybdis of innovation. Its upholders need to be delivered both from a facile assurance that they are wiser than their fathers, and from a blind refusal to accept new truth and to grapple with new tasks'.[1]

One instance of what I have in mind may be given here. At the time of Christ it was generally taken for granted that the purpose of religion was the benefit of the religious. To belong to God's chosen people meant for the Jew to be given a superior status in relation to God. The various mystery religions existed for the purpose of giving their initiates the assurance of a blessed immortality. It was inevitable that the Christian Church should be thought to exist for the same kind of purpose. It is now commonplace to say that Jesus wrought a revolution in the idea of messiahship and kingship. 'Ye know that they which are accounted to rule over the Gentiles lord it over them; and their great ones exercise authority over them. But it is not so among you. . . . For verily the Son of Man came not to be ministered unto but to minister, and to give His life a ransom for many'.[2] It is, I repeat, a commonplace to say that God in Christ, by revealing Himself in a kingship of service, wrought among men a revolution in the idea of kingship. Equally familiar is the idea

[1] H. E. W. Turner: *The Pattern of Christian Truth* (London, 1952), p. 132.
[2] St. Mark x. 42–5.

that among Christians each should seek to serve, and not to lord it over others; this is the obvious lesson to be learned from the words: 'It is not so among you: but whosoever would become great among you, shall be your minister'. What we have as yet hardly begun to learn is the revolution required in our thinking about the relation of the Church to the world. In my first lecture I referred to the fact that historical research shows the Christian Church to have come into existence as the messianic community, the continuing body in and through which the risen ascended Lord willed to carry on His messianic work on earth.[1] Surely the revolution in the idea of the Messiah involves a parallel revolution in that of the messianic community.

Here again I am trespassing on ground to be covered in my second series of lectures. I hope there to show how this revolution in our way of thinking about the Church throws light on the puzzle provided by our confused thinking about the ultimate destiny of those who die outside the Church militant here on earth.[2] I have mentioned it now because of its relevance to much that we have been considering in this lecture and the one before. How far do most expositions of the so-called doctrine of justification by faith rest upon the assumption that God's aim in founding His Church was to bring into existence a community within which men should have an assurance of blessed immortality? How far does the same assumption underlie any disturbance we may feel at discovering that God has not willed to give us revelation in the form of divinely guaranteed statements of truth? I will leave these questions in your minds as I end this introductory part of my course. We shall return to the subject next year.

[1] Above, Lecture I, p. 19.

[2] See above, Lecture III, pp. 54 ff.

Part II

NATURAL THEOLOGY: FOR FREEDOM

LECTURE VI

Creation

I

IN the first series of his Gifford Lectures Dr. Webb asked what relation the myths of Plato bore to his philosophy and answered the question as follows:

> The myth is not concerned, strictly speaking, with the same subject-matter as Philosophy, but rather takes the place of History, where a historical question is asked, but the materials for a historical answer are lacking.
>
> How did the world come into being? How did society begin? What will happen to our souls after death? It is to such questions as these that Plato offers replies in the form of myths. Philosophy cannot answer such questions, any more than it can tell me where I dined this day last year or where I shall dine this day next year. For an answer to the former of these two inquiries I should consult my personal memory or my journal; and if I wished for information about something that happened before I was born, I should seek for it in the history books. But if what I want to know must have happened at a time whereof there is no record extant, what can I do? The best I can do, says Plato, is to frame a myth, a story which, if not the truth, will at any rate be like the truth. But this cannot merely mean that it is to be like what actually occurred, for *ex hypothesi* I do not know what did occur, and hence cannot tell what would be like it and what not.
>
> What it means for Plato, however, is not doubtful. It means that the myth is to be in accord with those conclusions as to the general nature of things which I derive not from History but from Philosophy. Just as you could not tell me where and on what I dined this day last year, but could confidently assert that it was not in fairyland and not on nectar and ambrosia, so too we are sure that whatever took place in the unrecorded past must have been consistent with what we know to be the eternal nature of Reality; whatever we have reason to think is incompatible with the eternal nature of Reality we have reason to think did not occur in the past and will not occur in the future.[1]

This passage is the most illuminating commentary I know on the stories of creation in the opening chapters of Genesis. I

[1] C. C. J. Webb: *God and Personality* (London, 1918), p. 168.

understand from those who have studied the matter that the story in Chapter I comes down to us in the form which it took after the exile of the Israelites in Babylon in the sixth century B.C., while Chapter II contains an earlier, pre-exilic version. Both, in so far as they are narrative in character, in so far, that is, as they describe apparent happenings in this world of time and space, 'take the place of history, where a historical question is asked, but the materials for a historical answer are lacking'. The question to be asked about them is to what extent they are 'like the truth' in the sense of being 'consistent with what we know to be the eternal nature of Reality'. In view of what I have been saying in earlier lectures, this will mean to what extent they were in accordance with as much of the nature of eternal reality as had been revealed to our spiritual ancestors before and after the Babylonian Captivity.

Any attempt at a direct answer to that question belongs to a later stage in these lectures. What concerns us now is the source of the stories which have come down to us in their present form. The researches of Old Testament scholars have made it clear that they are drawn from the mythology current among the people for whom they were written, but have been revised so as to bring them in line with contemporary prophetic teaching about God. In other words, they gave for their day and generation the religious interpretation of the commonly accepted ideas about the origin of the universe and how this planet had arrived at its present condition.

The lesson to be drawn is that in order to be truly biblical theologians we should attempt to do for our day and generation what they did for theirs. We should not confuse the minds of our children by putting before them on Sunday a picture of the past completely different from that which they have been learning in school from Monday to Friday. Two things have happened since the compilation of the book Genesis. By the researches of historians and scientists some pages of the lost diary have been recovered: we may believe that the ideas about the past which we have to interpret are more like what actually occurred than were those which the biblical writers shared with their contemporaries. And we who are Christians believe that in Jesus Christ there has been given to us a fuller revelation of God than was known to the Old Testament prophets. For us the results of scientific and historical research take the place of the mythology presented to the writers of Genesis. What we have to try to do, if we would be biblical theologians, is to interpret them in the light of the revelation of God in Jesus Christ.

My task is now to set forth, as best I can, the material to be interpreted, leaving the development of its Christian interpretation for my second series of lectures next year. It is inevitable, however, that what I now say will give a description of what I see with the eye of a Christian believer, a description which involves an element of interpretation. That cannot be helped. As we have seen in previous lectures, every human utterance is coloured by the outlook of the speaker. All one can do is to avow one's standpoint, and thus give the hearers opportunity to discount one's discolouring.

I have just said that what corresponds to the commonly accepted mythology of the days in which Genesis was written are the commonly accepted results of scientific and historical research. If I now begin my description by calling our idea of creation evolutionary, I must take care to avoid misunderstanding, of the sense in which I use that term.

The word evolution first became widely current in these islands as a result of the publication of Darwin's *Origin of Species* in 1859. Owing to the then prevalent ideas of revelation and of the authority of the Bible, and to the lack of the distinction between empirical fact and its interpretation brought out by Dr. Webb in his discussion of myths in Plato, it was commonly assumed, both by followers of Darwin and by their opponents, that acceptance of his evolutionary hypothesis involved disbelief in creation by God. This notion still lingers on, especially on the other side of the Atlantic Ocean, with the result that to an

American audience what I mean by the word 'evolution' might be better understood if I used the more cumbrous term 'process character'. Again, I am no scientist: I have neither the wish nor the ability to express any opinion on questions concerning the mode of evolutionary development which may be at issue between Darwinians, Lamarckians, or other schools of scientific thought. Nor, thirdly, is my use of the word 'evolution' to be held to imply, with etymological strictness, that in the process of development the later stages have been contained within and unpacked from the former—a subject of which I have heard no better discussion than was given by Mr. Joseph in his Herbert Spencer Lecture of 1924.[1] All that I mean to assert by saying that we have an evolutionary idea of creation is that we commonly take it for granted that the world of our experience has come into its present condition through a series of changes in which inorganic matter, organic matter, vegetable life, marine life, animal life and human life followed one another in chronological sequence. This is the view which I believe the researches of scientists require us to hold, which our children imbibe from their teachers at school through the week, which we must take as material for interpretation on Sunday.

'In the history of European thought', says Professor Collingwood in the book which I have found the most valuable of his published works, 'there have been three periods of constructive cosmological thinking'. He then goes on to compare and contrast what he calls 'The Modern View of Nature' with those of ancient Greece and the Renaissance, summing up as follows:

> Modern cosmology, like its predecessors, is based on an analogy. What is new about it is that the analogy is a new one. As Greek natural science was based on the analogy between the macrocosm nature and the microcosm man, as man is revealed to himself in his own self-consciousness; as Renaissance natural science was based on the analogy between nature as God's handiwork and the machines that are the handiwork of man . . .; so the modern view of nature, which first begins to find expression towards the end of the eighteenth

[1] Published in H. W. B. Joseph: *Essays in Ancient and Modern Philosophy* (Oxford, 1935).

century and ever since then has been gathering weight and establishing itself more securely down to the present day, is based on the analogy between the processes of the natural world as studied by natural scientists and the vicissitudes of human affairs as studied by historians.

He then goes on to say that in the two earlier periods

The question was: How are we to find a changeless and therefore knowable something in, or behind, or somehow belonging to, the flux of nature-as-we-perceive-it. In modern or evolutionary natural science, this question does not arise. . . . Its presuppositions had undergone a revolutionary change by the beginning of the nineteenth century. By then historians had trained themselves to think, and had found themselves able to think scientifically, about a world of constantly changing human affairs in which there was no unchanging substrate behind the changes, and no unchanging laws according to which the changes took place. History had by now established itself as a science, that is, a progressive inquiry in which conclusions are solidly and demonstratively established. It had thus been proved by experiment that scientific knowledge was possible concerning objects that were constantly changing. Once more, the self-consciousness of man, in this case the corporate self-consciousness of man, his historical consciousness of his own corporate doings, provided a clue to his thoughts about nature. The historical conception of scientifically knowable change was applied, under the name of evolution, to the natural world.[1]

When I use the word evolution I use it in the same sense in which it was used by Collingwood in the last sentence I have quoted. When I say that it is natural to us to-day to have an evolutionary outlook, I mean that the world of our experience, of which in our thinking we have to try to make sense, presents itself to us as an observable series of changes in space and time. If I have rightly understood what has been going on in my own lifetime, there has been a change in the picture that is commonly taken for granted. When as a boy I first began to take an interest in the views of scientists, they seemed to describe the universe as a vast container within which material objects were moving about exchanging shares in a constant total supply of energy. Now the container has disappeared, and so has the ultimate distinction between the material objects and the energy. Funda-

[1] R. G. Collingwood: *The Idea of Nature* (Oxford, 1945), pp. 1, 9, 12.

mentally the universe appears to be a stream of energy flowing through space-time and getting itself differentiated into organisms of varying complexity. When the evolutionist, looking back over the process up to date, catalogues successive kinds of object as organic matter, vegetable, marine, animal and human life, he is distinguishing different forms, different modes of existence, into which the fundamental energy has become organized.

The question is not whether evolution in general is compatible with divine creation. It is whether the particular course which evolution has in fact taken is such that to interpret it by a doctrine of divine creation will enable us to make sense of it. Here one source of possible misunderstanding must be cleared out of the way at once.

In the last century the accepted notion of biblical revelation was not the only idea held in common by the disciples of Darwin and their opponents. All took for granted what Collingwood calls the renaissance idea of nature. 'Natural science was based on the analogy between nature as God's handiwork and the machines that are the handiwork of man'. This had been most clearly exemplified in the teaching of the deists, for whom the universe had been manufactured, wound up, and set going by God acting in the manner of Paley's celestial watchmaker. In the minds of Christians who revised their picture in accordance with the requirements of scientific research, substituting an evolutionary process of differentiation for the assembling of separately manufactured species, there lingered the belief that if they were to think of evolution as God's creative activity, they must think of it as having originated in some single creative act which set the whole process in motion. This belief is not yet dead. If I understand them rightly, the question whether the evolutionary process derives from some definite and datable moment of beginning is a matter of debate among physicists, some of whom seem to think that on the answer depends the possibility of thinking of it as divine creation. In this they are mistaken. It should become clear in what follows that the question whether the space-time universe is God's creation is quite distinct from the question whether or no it had such a definite datable beginning. In raising the one I must not be thought to be concerned with the other.

II

What, then, is the question before us? To understand this we must take up the second of the two problems I mentioned briefly at the end of my third lecture, what I then called 'the fundamental problem for all thinkers . . . that of the relation of time to eternity'.

Collingwood finds the clue to the contrast between our way of thinking and that of the Renaissance and of ancient Greece in our 'conception of scientifically knowable change'. The Gifford Lectures of Samuel Alexander and John Laird both illustrate his meaning. These philosophers do not assume that in order to construct a metaphysic, in order, that is, to find an intelligible meaning in the universe of our experience, they must postulate an 'unchanging substrate behind the changes'. For both of them, if the word creation were to be kept, it would not denote a relation between the universe and a transcendent Creator; it would mean that the observable history of the universe evinces developments that imply the inner working of something which it would be reasonable to call the principle of creativity, that the changing universe is 'deiform'.

I am not myself convinced that this conception of scientifically knowable change involves as a corollary the resolution of substance into function. Collingwood holds that this is so,[1] and in many quarters to-day it is taken for granted.[2] To my mind Dr. Austin Farrer's *Finite and Infinite*[3] shows that the matter is not so simple as this. It may be true of the world of sub-personal creatures as studied by the natural sciences. But the universe also

[1] *Op. cit.*, p. 16.
[2] See, e.g., W. P. Witcutt, *Return to Reality* (London, 1954), p. 51, footnote.
[3] London, 1943. See especially Part II.

contains men and women, and human personality is such that we have to recognize in it an element which persists as the subject of changes, for which the word substance is thus an appropriate term. We do not have to choose between the conceptions of substance and of scientifically knowable change. If we are to be genuine empiricists we must acknowledge within the world of our experience the existence of both: our aim must be to arrive at such an understanding of both that we can see how they fit in together so as to make sense.

I was saying in my last lecture that the history of human thought is the history of the truth seeking to find expression through minds conditioned by the outlook of their times and places.[1] We study the work of our predecessors in the hope that we may be able to discount some of their discolourings, leaving it to those who shall come after us to discount our own. As we look back, we must be as eager to conserve what is of permanent worth as we are to revise what was of transient value. To call the problem before us the fundamental problem for all human thinkers implies that what is essentially the same problem appears in different forms in different ages. In its most general form it may be said to arise from asking the question whether this space-time universe, taken by itself, will make sense by satisfying the demand of our minds for a self-justifying whole.[2] To those for whom there could be no scientifically knowable change the question took such forms as asking whether the fact of motion requires the postulate of a prime mover, or whether a world of finites wherein essence and existence are separable requires the postulate of an infinite reality in which or whom the two are one. Our starting-point is neither the fact of motion (as it might have been pictured to exist within the unmoving nineteenth-century container of energy), nor the unintelligibility of finitude. It is the conception of the universe of our experience as a stream of energy undergoing successive changes in space and time.

[1] See above, Lecture V, p. 114.

[2] See above, Lecture II, p. 37.

Our primary obligation is to grasp the nature of the process as accurately as we can, neither ignoring nor distorting any element in our account of it. But we cannot rest content with accepting the result as brute fact. If we are to justify the first steps we have ever taken towards trying to discover what happens and why, we cannot stop short in the effort to see how it fits into a pattern which is such that we are content to have it so. We cannot make an absolute divorce between judgments of value and judgments of fact, for in the long run the validation of every judgment of fact depends upon a judgment of values.

All that I have said in previous lectures of the nature of human thinking is equally true in both fields. In morals and aesthetics, as well as in science and philosophy, the history of human thought is the history of the truth seeking to make itself known to, and to find expression through, minds conditioned by the outlook of their time and place. For Christians, as for the prophets, advances in moral sensitiveness and moral insight bring a fuller grasp of God's revelation of Himself.[1] The objectivity we can claim for our judgments of value is parallel to that which we can claim for our judgments of fact. To repeat what I have said before: we 'accept what we can see with the eyes of twentieth-century Europeans, leaving whatever further purging and clarifying may be necessary to men of other climes and later ages. We may feel pretty sure that certain of our apprehensions are irreversible or irreformable, but such assurance is, strictly speaking, a matter of faith rather than of sight'.[2]

On the positive side, our moral judgments do undoubtedly claim an objectivity parallel to those of fact.[3] I may quote Mr. Weldon:

> I do not, therefore, mind saying that some political behaviour is obviously right, or wicked, or silly. 'Obviously' is used here in the way in which it is correctly used of observations made by people with normal eyesight in a good light. In these conditions it is pointless to ask 'How do you know that this

[1] See above, Lecture V, p. 106. [2] Above, Lecture V, p. 99.
[3] See appended note, p. 145.

pillar-box is red?' It seems to me equally pointless to ask: 'How do you know that it is wicked to torture human beings or animals?' But I think it is a mistake to use words like 'intuition' or 'self-evident' in describing such statements since these suggest that there is something odd about them which needs explanation. There is nothing odd about them at all. They are perfectly clear.[1]

Obvious and clear they may be to Mr. Weldon and most of his readers here. But what if there be men elsewhere for whom the political interests of the state provide the criterion for moral judgments?[2] How are we to decide between them? There is no short cut—unless we are to adopt the totalitarian maxim that might is right, and end differences of opinion by enforcing silence on opposition. In morals, as in other fields of study, we must have patience enough to lay along side of one another our various judgments, explaining what we see and how it is that we see it so, and asking which view will best fit in with the rest of our experience to make sense of the whole.

We come back to the subject of our present inquiry, this universe which through the empirical study of the sciences is revealed to us as a stream of energy becoming organized into different kinds of existents as it flows through space and time. How are we to think of it in a way which will make sense? Can we get a point of view from which we can see that every detail of everything that happens or has happened fits in and makes a coherent intelligible pattern?

If this space-time universe, this developing process, be the whole of reality, I do not see how we can ever get beyond the acknowledging of it as brute fact. Change follows change, and it so happens that among the products of the process are we human beings, with our capacity to observe and think about what is going on, to make moral and aesthetic judgments. I can see that in such circumstances our observations of matters of fact, and generalizations based on them concerning the way in which things are likely to go on happening, might achieve a certain

[1] T. D. Weldon: *The Vocabulary of Politics* (London, 1953), p. 16. cp. pp. 43, 99.
[2] See above, Lecture III, p. 59.

degree of objectivity. But I do not see how our judgments of value could ever be more than the expression of our own subjective tastes; and those the tastes of finite creatures conditioned, during the brief span of their existence, by the outlook of our time and place. In theory, the last word would rest with the existentialist; in practice, with the dictator.

How are we to find any ground for believing that when Mr. Weldon says that it is wicked to torture human beings or animals, or that it was wicked to send people to Belsen or Buchenwald, he is (to use his own words) 'at least trying to make a reliable report about the world and not one about his own emotional condition'? How are we to have any grounds for holding that the accepted standards of morals or art in any one age or culture are either better or worse than those in another? If reality be nothing more than a process of change, how can it mean anything to say that there is either progress or retrogression, either improvement or deterioration?

Now suppose that, in order to answer such questions as these, we postulate the existence of an eternal perfect reality as the standard by which to judge things and events in space and time. At once two further questions arise: (i) How could we have the knowledge of such reality which would enable us to use it for the required standard? and (ii) Would belief in it solve our fundamental problem?

(i) We need not delay long over the first of these questions. The usefulness of the postulate does not depend on our having an impossible kind of knowledge. We clearly cannot use it as a standard in the same way as one might take a piece of cloth to a shop in order to match its material, texture, colour and design. What is meant by asserting the existence of an eternal perfect reality is that value judgments are attempts to apprehend an objective reality as it is partially and imperfectly revealed to us through particular things and events. It is simply another way of saying what I have already said: that to claim objectivity for judgments of value is to make an act of faith precisely parallel to that which we make in the case of judgments of fact. In my last lecture I was arguing that on such an act of faith depends our belief that we can have assured results in scientific, historical or any other kind of inquiry.[1] When saying that advance in knowledge comes through men gifted with a *flair* for diagnosis I anticipated our present discussion by including as instances (along with Newton, Einstein, Lister and Pasteur) Michael Angelo and Beethoven. Let me once again make my fundamental act of faith that the history of human thought is the history of reality making itself known to us through human minds conditioned by the circumstances of their time and place. What I have now been saying is that in this process judgments of value are involved on a par with judgments of fact. Without this addition our judgments of fact might achieve that degree of objectivity which obliges us to acknowledge brute fact; we could not hope ever to arrive at the knowledge which will fully satisfy our desire for understanding, the knowledge that leads us to ask no further why what is should be so.

(ii) But will the acceptance of this postulate solve our fundamental problem? Will it enable us to make sense of the universe of our experience when that universe is thought of as a stream of energy flowing through space and time, manifesting itself in the things and events of the history of this world in which we play our part? Alas! no. We can no longer avoid facing the ultimate mystery of our existence, the mystery which no man can dispel, the question to which no human being has an adequate, an intellectually satisfying answer.

To justify our first step in attempting to understand the world we live in we have to assume that whatever is and happens fits together into a pattern that makes sense. If it is to make sense, the pattern must be logically self-consistent and of such intrinsic value that we welcome its existence and cease to ask further for reasons why it should be so. In order to have some ground for faith in the objectivity of our judgments we postulate the existence

[1] Above, Lecture V, pp. 99 ff.

of an eternal, perfect reality. So far, so good. But now, if indeed there be this eternal, perfect reality, what on earth is the point of the existence of this space-time process at all? If it is in any way contributing to the fullness of being, or richness of content, of the postulated transcendent reality, then we are back where we were: the ultimate reality is in process of change, there is no knowing whether for better or for worse or what those words really ought to mean. If it is not, if in the long run nothing of eternal import shall have been accomplished through the history of this universe in space and time, then all the long ages of evolution, all the strugglings and strivings of human effort, our 'life with all it yields of joy and woe and hope and fear', are nothing but a sheer waste of time. In either case, nothing makes sense. Victory goes to the existentialists and the dictators, to Amaryllis and Neaera.

We can only avoid this dilemma by not thinking deeply enough to get down to it. If, for instance, we stop short where Freud bases the whole scientific outlook on the denial that there are any occurrences which fail to come within the causal sequence of things,[1] we do not get beyond the contemplation of brute fact observed from outside. If, on the other hand, we assert the existence of a transcendent reality which is intelligible in virtue of its self-authenticating goodness, we are at a loss to see how this world and our life in it can be more than such stuff as dreams are made of. Useful work may be done in scientific research without raising ultimate questions about the intelligibility of the universe; the religious Platonist may not find in practice that his belief in the other world evacuates his earthly life of meaning. But the man who has been bitten by the *bacillus philosophicus* cannot help asking awkward questions that they have left unasked, and one question leads to another until he comes up against this one and finds it unanswerable.

The history of philosophy is the history of human thought wrestling with this problem. Idealists like Bradley, Bosanquet

[1] See above, Lecture II, p. 24.

and Pringle-Pattison, for whom the intelligibly rational is the real, strive to find ways of upholding the importance of events in space and time. Others, like Alexander and Laird, for whom pre-eminently the space-time universe is the reality which they must seek to understand, strive equally hard to find ways of discovering and expounding its intelligibility.

It is against the background of this unsolved and so far insoluble problem that we have to see the Christian doctrine of creation. It has its place among other attempts to find a way of intelligibly relating this universe to an eternal perfect reality. Its irreducible difficulties are not peculiar to itself, the wanton products of incorrigible religious obscurantism. They are shared with its fellows, and are not to be resolved by abandoning the doctrine in favour of some alternative which is free from them. There is no such alternative. The only way of escape is to stop short of thinking deeply enough to discover that the reason why these doctrines or theories have these difficulties is because they are attempting to hold within their embrace the ultimate mystery of our existence, the fundamental problem confronting all human thought, Christian and pagan, religious and secular. They do not have their origin in our thought, but in what we are trying to think about.

Given this universe of our experience, and the postulated eternal perfect reality, how are we to think of the relation between them? Attempts to answer this question inevitably proceed by experimenting with some relationship known to us within this universe which may possibly turn out to be analogous to that for which we are looking. Neoplatonism experimented with the idea of emanation, the relation of the sun to its rays, of its source to a stream. Idealism generally experiments with the relation of reality to appearance, or with that of an enduring unity of a self-conscious self to the successive phases of its experiences in time. The doctrine of creation takes for its analogy the human experience of making things, the experience of the potter with the clay, of the poet with words, of the musician with sounds. In its developed form the doctrine admits that the analogy is not complete: there is no relationship in our experience precisely similar to that required by the postulate. All our experience of making is of re-ordering co-existent material. For us to-day the straight analogy would be a modern version of ancient Greek dualism, one in which the imposition of form on matter reappears as the organization by the Creator of co-existent energy in patterns of varying complexity. We shall see later that there is a place for this idea within the doctrine of creation. But it cannot be the meaning of the doctrine itself. For it is not enough to think of the Creator as eternally co-existent with a stream of energy undergoing changes in time. It is the very existence of that stream of energy, of space-time reality, which has to be explained, which has to be shown to be more than brute fact, to be worth while. Creation must include the bringing into existence of the matter which is to take on different forms, of the energy which is to be organized into organisms.

What, then, are the essential points in the idea of creation? First and foremost comes thinking of the postulated perfect eternal reality as personal, that is to say, as One whose actions express His self-conscious intelligent will. Secondly, if creation is to mean absolutely the bringing into existence of this universe, ultimate explanations are to be sought in terms of the will of the Creator. We shall be on the wrong lines if we make it our immediate aim to discover or devise a metaphysical system in which the eternal and the temporal can be seen to be related to one another in a logically consistent pattern. It may be that there is such a pattern; indeed, the belief that there is is the presupposition of all our thinking. But for those who think of the universe as created, their primary task is to try to learn what they can from its actual nature of the aim of its Creator in creating it. Only when this has been done shall we be in a position to ask whether as a result we are on the way to the satisfaction of our metaphysical demands—demands which, perhaps, will only fully be satisfied when we pass from the limited vision open to us in this world to be spectators of all time and all existence.

So much for what the idea of creation is and what it implies. For us at the moment, as natural theologians, it is a hypothesis, a hypothetical postulate postulated in the hope that it may help us to move towards an understanding of the world we live in and our life within it. Put briefly, it is the belief that God, for some purpose of His own, calls into existence the universe, giving it the being and the mode of reality which that purpose requires. What we have to do is to examine the nature of the world, asking whether it is such that this postulate will give us its most reasonable explanation.

III

Prominent among elements in our experience which demand explanation are what we call contingency and freedom. By contingency I mean the apparent fact that often there is an open possibility of things happening this way or that; by freedom the apparent fact that it often rests with us human beings to decide which way it shall be. I call these apparent facts because we cannot without further examination take it for granted that they are what *prima facie* they seem to be. There is no place for them either in a materialist metaphysic according to which everything that happens falls within a determinate causal sequence of things, or an idealist metaphysic in which everything must be the expression of a rational good will.

Let us begin our examination with our experience of freedom at its best, i.e. when fully conscious of what we are doing, we make up our minds to do something and do it; when the explanation of why we have done it will be given in terms of the end we were aiming at. Suppose, for example, that we have been unable to shake off the cold we have caught, that it has developed into a fever, and that on reading the thermometer we have decided to call in a doctor. If anyone should ask why we have sent for him, the answer would be that it was in order to obtain the advice and treatment that would enable us to get well again as quickly as possible.

Our making of such decisions, and acting upon them, implies that we live in a world in which there are events of at least two kinds. There are those which belong to the causal sequence of things, for which the explanation is sought by looking back to happenings in the past which have produced the circumstances of the present. Of such were the catching of the cold and its development into fever. There are also those which result from our making up our minds to certain actions and carrying out our intention, for which the explanation is sought by asking what we were aiming at in the future. I shall speak of events as belonging respectively to two different orders, the causal and the purposive.

One form of determinism is the denial of this distinction, the assertion that all events 'come within the causal sequence of things', that whenever we think that we are freely making up our minds to a decision we are in fact moved to it by psychological factors of which we are not consciously aware, that the reasons we give for our actions are illusory 'rationalizations' of non-rational wish-fulfilments. No one who has studied the evidence can deny that there are cases when this is the true account of the matter. But it does not necessarily follow that it is true of all: we have to beware of the temptation to jump to the conclusion that, because some things we thought were A's turn out on examination to be B's, there are no A's at all. For practical purposes the value of the psychological analysis is the help it can give towards distinguishing rationalizations from genuine decisions.

Professor Cook Wilson used to point out the widespread confusion due to taking for granted the assumption that all things fall within this causal sequence. He would instance the naïve question of an inquirer who asked, after some particular explanation of a man's action had been disproved: 'If it wasn't that that moved him, what was it?'—a question which, in assuming that there must be some answer of the causal kind, failed to grasp the complexity of the universe of which we are trying to make sense.

To recognize the occurrence of events in the purposive order is to take a step towards a fuller grasp. It should be noted that at the present stage of our inquiry the two orders, the causal and the purposive, have equal status as postulates postulated in order to try to account for our experience being what it is. When we ask for the explanation of an event, the kind of answer we shall get to our question will depend on the order to which it is to be assigned. To the question: 'If it wasn't that that moved him, what was it?' the answer may be: 'You shouldn't ask what he was moved by, but what he was aiming at'.

The events of the purposive order are, as a matter of fact, more intelligible to us than those of the causal. We experience them, so to speak, from the inside, while the others are only observed from without. Let me quote from what I have written elsewhere about the tossing of a coin.

> When the initial impulse has been given which sends the penny spinning in the air, its movements proceed according to determinate mechanistic sequence, and whether it ultimately comes down heads or tails is only unpredictable by us because we have no instruments of adequate complexity and refinement to make the necessary observations and calculations. But suppose we discover that the coin has been loaded so as to ensure its falling with a certain side up. We should naturally think that factors of another order had entered into the situation, factors which are not patient of the same kind of measurement and calculation as those which govern the behaviour of the coin after it has left the spinner's hand. . . .
>
> In refusing to accede to the request that we should regard the loading of the coin as parallel to its subsequent movements in the air, we are not making an obscurantist refusal to abandon the unknown for the known. *We know very well what it means to cheat*—better, indeed, than what it means to be sent spinning through the air. Even when we do experience the latter sensation, it remains inexplicable brute fact to us until interpreted in terms of will; a football game is easier to understand than a railway accident, and the universe does not become more explicable if collisions on the football field are regarded as obscure examples of what happens when a crowd of people is hit by a tornado.[1]

[1] *Towards a Christian Philosophy* (London, 1942), pp. 76–8.

Certain idealists, realizing the inadequacy of mechanistic determinism to account for the whole of our experience, take as the key to its understanding the occurrence of events in the purposive order of which we can give an explanation which leaves the inquirer completely satisfied. If only we could show that everything that happens is explicable in this way, we should be in sight of our metaphysical goal. To do this, they argue, we must show that neither contingency nor evil are really what they appear to be. When the intelligibility of an event is derived from its being the fulfilment of a rational purpose which we approve as worth while, there is in it nothing either of chance or evil. If everything that happens is of this kind, then those events which appear to us to be evil or to come about by chance cannot really be what they seem. It must be that, as finite creatures whose outlook is coloured by the conditions of our time and place, we do not see them as they are. The aim of philosophy is to achieve a point of view from which it can be seen that everything happens for the best in the best of all possible worlds. It is a world which is as determinate as the world of causal sequence, but the determinism is of a different order. It may be called axiological determinism as distinguished from mechanistic.

The question before us is whether such an idealist metaphysic will give a satisfactory account of the actual world of our experience, an account in which nothing is ignored, distorted, or explained away as being something other than itself. There is some truth in it: how much, I hope to show in due course. But contingency and evil are elements in our experience too stubborn to be disposed of by finding a point of view from which they will appear not to be what they seem.

We have been thinking about our experience of freedom at its best. Unfortunately our actual exercise of our freedom is by no means always at its best. What am I to make of the occasions, the all too frequent occasions, when I stupidly made a fool of myself, or when I sin?

Some of these, as we have just seen, may rightly be explained by a psychological analysis which reveals that they fall within the causal sequence. But if the value of this analysis is that it enables us to distinguish between such compulsive behaviour and genuine decisions of our own, what am I to say of the genuine decisions which are either stupid or sinful, those which I cannot account for by explaining the worth-while end for which they were taken, of which I can only say either 'I've made a fool of myself', or 'My fault, my own fault, my own great fault'?

Take first the decisions and actions which are sinful rather than stupid. If a man comes to me with a confession of some evil deed that he has done, my first impulse may be to try to find some excuse for him which will ease his burden of self-reproach. At first sight this may seem to be the charitable line to take. 'My poor fellow', I may be inclined to say, 'you mustn't blame yourself. That's all a mistake. What you think was your own action was the inevitable reaction to those circumstances of one psychologically conditioned as you have been'. Undoubtedly I should be right to try to see how far I could go towards helping him along these lines, but if I go too far I shall reach a point at which he will rightly interrupt. 'Look here', he will say, 'I know you are meaning to be kind, but actually you are insulting me by treating me as something less than a man. Good or bad, I insist on being treated as a man responsible for what I have done, not as a thing moved hither and thither by forces acting upon it'.

'Very well', I may reply, 'we will agree that you were not moved by anything of that sort. It was your own decision, your own act. What reasonable explanation can you give of why you did it?' What am I to say if he answers: 'I can give no reasonable explanation at all. I can describe the circumstances which led me to do it—the difficulty I had got into which I lied myself out of, or the desirable object which I committed theft or adultery to possess—but I knew it was wrong. I knew it ought not to be done, and I did it. I can give no reasonable account of it because what I did was itself unreasonable. It is no good my trying to explain it away as having been something other than it was. I can only say that I am responsible for having done something of which no reasonable account can be given. I have sinned'.

So much, to begin with, for sins. What of mistakes, of actions for which I can only account by saying 'I've made a fool of myself'? Sometimes, indeed, the explanation of the particular form of the mistake may lie within Freud's 'causal sequence of things'. Such mistakes need not necessarily be the expression of hidden wishes, they may be due to the fact that our minds and physical organs form habits of moving along particular grooves. I do not think, for example, that during my life in America I was moved by patriotic or anti-republican sentiments when, in taking a service, I inadvertently said 'O, Lord, save the king', instead of 'O, Lord, save the State'. Again, in the early days of my ministry, on one second morning of the month, I remember hearing myself say in St. Mark's Church, Portsmouth, 'upon the ungodly He shall rain snares, fire and brimstone, storm and treacle'. Whether the cause be hidden wish, or habit of thought and speech, the particular form taken by the mistake may be due to factors of that kind. But in so far as words which I have been heard to utter are to be accounted for on these lines, are what we may describe as words spoken at random, they cease to be treated as *my* words. 'My' words are those which I consciously use with the intention of expressing what I have in mind to say. What 'I' contributed on these occasions was lack of attention to what I was doing and that, as an event in the purposive order, is, like sin, something of which no reasonable account can be given. The nearest we can get to it is to say that the event did not belong to the purposive order at all: my inattention was due to some physical cause such as overtiredness or dyspepsia. I can make no such excuse when my actions show that what I have contributed has not been mere inattention but positive stupidity; when it is really I who have made a fool of myself, and what I have made a fool of is really myself. All I can say is that I have acted unreasonably. How can I give a reasonable account of that?

The fundamental act of faith of the philosopher is that everything that is or happens somehow fits together so as to make sense. For this to be so it is commonly assumed by both materialist and idealist that everything that happens must be either an event in the causal sequence or the expression of a good purpose. They may differ in that for the materialist the causal order alone is ultimately real while the idealist has greater respect for the purposive, but both agree that only what is rational can really be real. The aim of philosophy is to find the point of view from which it can be seen that apparent irrationalities such as sins, random words and deeds, and stupidities are not really what they seem.

This comes out in their dealing with the idea of chance. It is taken for granted by both that there cannot really be any such thing. Genuine contingency has no place either in the determinate sequence of the causal order or in a world in which everything that happens is the expression of intelligent good will. There is, however, one sphere in which we do undoubtedly have experience of chance that really is chance, and that is when we deliberately create conditions in which it shall be so. I have already referred to the way in which we toss a coin to decide how to start a game. I have pointed out that once the coin is spun, what follows is a determinate sequence of events in the causal order. I have also reminded you that any attempt to reduce the unpredictability of the outcome would be regarded as cheating. Whether we toss coins or tennis racquets, hold out concealed pawns or cut packs of cards, we deliberately create conditions in which the decision of what is to be done is left to chance.

It has long seemed to me that this familiar experience has not been given by philosophers the attention it deserves. Philosophy, as the attempt to understand the world of our experience, must at all costs avoid the temptation to explain away awkward facts which will not fit in with theories. The *a priori* argument: nothing irrational can be real, chance is irrational, therefore chance cannot be real must come to terms with what we actually do on football fields and tennis courts, at chess boards and card tables.

The word 'real' here is equivocal. For the materialist it would mean what exists and happens in the space-time universe, what is observable through the senses and is patient of study by scientific method. To be rational and real means 'to come within the causal sequence of things'. To idealists, for whom there are events which belong to the purposive order, to be rational means to be the expression of an intelligible purpose. In so far as this space-time universe presents us with apparent irrationalities which cannot be explained on grounds either of physical cause or intelligible purpose, it cannot as it stands be accepted as real. What we call the world of our experience must be the mode in which the reality that is really real appears to us finite beings as we look out from our station within it. For neither materialist nor idealist is our *prima facie* experience of contingency and freedom an apprehension of the real. For the one it is illusion due to our not having yet discovered the causal explanation of acts we think to proceed from our free choice. For the other it is an illusion due to our inability to see with the eye of a timeless spectator of all time and all existence.

In idealist metaphysics the place of the idea of creation is taken by the thought of a process in which the eternal God is expressing Himself to Himself: we human beings are self-conscious organs of His self-expression who from our limited point of view cannot realize the rationality of the irrational things we feel ourselves to be doing or to have done. What we think to be acts of our free choice, chosen from among other possibilities in a world of genuine contingencies, are really events predetermined by God who can see, as we cannot, how luminously intelligible they are in their place in the pattern of the whole. While for the materialist what appears as the purposive order is the causal order in disguise; for the idealist both orders alike are such stuff as dreams are made of.

This idealist metaphysic is not, to my mind, really a doctrine of creation at all. To say that this universe is the mode in which the eternal God is expressing Himself to Himself in what appears to us as space and time is not the same thing as to say that it owes its existence to the will of God, that God has called it into existence for some reason of His own, and has given to it the mode of reality which that purpose requires. The idealistic metaphysic springs from an attempt to conceive a system which shall include both God and the universe, showing how each is related to the other, and how everything in each must be what it is in order that the whole may be an intelligible system. Now, if the doctrine of creation be true, this is the pursuit of a will-o'-the-wisp. The aim of philosophy is to make sense of the universe of our experience. For this the philosopher must try to take into account everything that is or happens, neither contenting himself with certain elements within it nor explaining away what will not fit in with his theories. But to include God within the universe of our experience, the universe which in every detail is to be understood, explained, and made sense of, is the parallel in philosophy to a theologian's demand for the kind of revelation he thinks God should provide.

To take the idea of creation as our clue to the understanding of the universe, is to look for its ultimate explanation in terms of divine purpose. We have to learn what we can of that purpose from the revelation of Himself which God has given us. Our immediate task is to learn what we can as natural theologians from the world in general. I have called your attention to the fact that for the rationally intelligible purpose of promoting fair play we often deliberately create conditions in which chance decides what shall be done. For a rational purpose we introduce an element of irrationality into the course of events. In the purposive order we have indubitable experience of chance that really is chance. If, then, in attempting to think of the relation of God to the universe we draw our analogy from our experience of purposive activity, perhaps we may be able to find within it a place for such irrationalities as contingency and freedom. Perhaps in God's plan of creation they are needed to perform a function similar to that for which we invoke chance, and for that reason He has given to the universe a mode of reality which admits of their being really themselves.

Our task now is to ask how far this supposition will help us towards understanding why the universe as we experience it is what it is.

Appended Note

Some fuller explanation is needed of what I think about moral judgments and what we should mean by the word conscience.

The fundamental question is whether such judgments are apprehensions (or misapprehensions) of objective fact or merely the expression of subjective feelings of disapproval or approval. This used to be put in the form of asking whether conscience is an exercise of reason or an emotion.[1]

Essentially I believe a man's conscience to be a rational activity, to be, in Kant's phrase, his practical reason. By that I mean that it is his power of distinguishing right from wrong in situations involving moral issues, and that the issues to be decided are as objective as are those between truth and falsehood dealt with by Kant's speculative reason. There is a parallel between the two modes of rational activity in that both alike need and can receive education. A child can learn the multiplication table or that things which are equal to the same thing are equal to one another, but it needs education in that field to be able to calculate strains and stresses in, for example, naval engineering. Similarly a child can be taught that if he sees someone accidentally drop a purse he should pick it up and return it to his owner rather than try to slip it unobserved into his own pocket, but there are situations in which it takes a trained mind to unravel the complexity of their moral issues.

There is, however, a difference between the use of the reason in the two fields. We are so made that the apprehension of a moral truth brings with it a specific feeling which may be called

[1] Cp., e.g., H. Rashdall: *Is Conscience an Emotion?* (London, 1914).

the sense of obligation. To learn that twice two is four may, as the saying goes, leave me quite cold; but I cannot see the dropped purse without feeling that I ought to give it back to its owner. That we have this feeling is shown by the fact that so many people regard it as the essence, if not the whole, of what we should mean by conscience. As against that I would maintain that it is a feeling consequent upon the apprehension of the moral issues of the situation. Just as to grasp the truth that an angry bull is rapidly advancing upon me would produce in me a feeling of fear, so the apprehension that something ought or ought not to be done produces in me the feeling of obligation. This truth is obscured by the fact that often we are so conditioned by the habits of our moral upbringing that in our actual reaction to a situation we may only be aware of it as a matter of feeling without realizing that our feelings are based on a tradition of moral judgment.

Ideally our reason and our feelings should always coincide, the reason rightly apprehending what ought to be done and generating the appropriate feeling. In theory, when they disagree, the decision should lie with the reason, as when St. Paul had to withstand St. Peter to the face and point out that if he had really grasped with his reason the implications of the saving work of Christ he must overcome his inherited feeling of obligation to avoid eating with Gentiles. Unfortunately the matter is not so simple. Imagine a man brought up in the traditions of Christian morality, who by his reading and thinking has reached a stage at which his reason tells him that much of that morality is based on outworn tabus no longer deserving of respect. Imagine that man, at that stage in the education of his reason, in a situation in which he has to decide whether or no to act on that conviction. I can imagine a case in which he might be withheld from so acting by the strength of inherited feeling. 'I know it is all nonsense', he might say, 'but I can't do it without feeling a loss of self-respect'. I submit that in such a case the truth may be that the tradition against which he is revolting may be based on a deeper and fuller grasp of the issues involved than he himself has as yet been able to attain. When we say that in the last resort the decision must lie with the reason we do not necessarily mean the reason of this or that particular man.

I can see no way of giving an answer to the question whether in all cases (as with St. Peter) the inherited feelings should give way to the requirements of the reason or *vice versa*. In morals, as in other fields of possible knowledge, we are in the midst of a process in which the truth is seeking to find expression through minds conditioned by the outlook of their time and place. There is always the possibility that new evidence may require the revision of existing ideas, and it is impossible to say in advance whether the truth will be found on the side of the upholder of what is old or of the advocates of what is new.

It may be worth while to add that as a matter of terminology I find it useful to make the following distinction between the use of the words good or evil and right or wrong. I try to keep good and evil for what in itself is intrinsically good or evil, using right and wrong for what ought or ought not to be done in the particular circumstances of a case. When a man is faced with a choice of evils, the choice of the lesser evil may be called right but not good. What is wrong is always evil, but what is right is not always good. The non-pacifist may agree with the pacifist that war is always evil; what withholds him from pacifism is his inability to predict that circumstances will never arise in which a country may be faced with a choice between war and an alternative which is morally worse, in which case to go to war might be evil and yet right.

LECTURE VII

Time, Space, Matter and Spirit

I

'GOD, for some purpose of His own, calls into existence the universe, giving it the being and the mode of reality which that purpose requires.' This, I have said, is what we should mean when we speak of creation.[1] It is the postulate which we are now to examine with a view to seeing how far it will enable us to make sense of the actual universe of our experience.

If we take seriously the idea of creation we shall not be attempting to devise some metaphysical system within which we shall be able to see how God and the universe are related to one another. To seek for any such system is to abandon the idea of creation, to include God as one element in a system of forces working through Him and His so-called creation. If God be indeed the Creator 'of heaven and earth and of all things visible and invisible', then it is no good looking for some further, more ultimate, reality beyond Him the knowledge of which will explain to us how He is what He is. If the fundamental truth about this universe be that it owes its existence to His will, then in our efforts to understand it, the last word will be in terms of His intention and purpose.

To take the idea of creation seriously is to treat the world of personal relations as ultimately more real than that of impersonal forces. Later on we shall have to consider the importance of this for the study of psychology, for its bearing on belief in angels and devils, and for its relevance to R. Bultmann's so-called demythologization of the Gospels.[2] Here and now we are con-

[1] Above, Lecture VI, p. 136.

[2] On Bultmann cp. E. Brunner: *Eternal Hope* (London, 1954), pp. 114 ff., 186 ff.

cerned with the one point that to examine the idea of creation means to ask how far it will help towards understanding the universe if we seek for its explanation in terms of God's will.

We do not set out to try to comprehend and explain God. We set out to try to understand this space-time universe of our experience. By itself it is not self-explanatory. In our efforts to make sense of it we postulate the existence of an eternal reality which is self-explanatory, self-authenticating in its perfect goodness, and thus intelligible. What we are now to examine is the hypothesis that it will help to make sense of the universe if we think of it as related to the eternal reality after the manner of creation, using that word in the sense which I have been trying to make clear.

We do not set out to try to comprehend and explain God. But if it turns out that we are verifying a sound hypothesis, we shall find that we learn a good deal about Him. We postulate the existence of God the Creator in order to make sense of the universe, and then we accept the universe as the medium through which He wills to reveal Himself to us. We do our best to grasp the nature of the universe without ignoring, distorting or explaining away anything that actually exists or occurs; then we ask: 'If the universe be so, what must be the character of the Creator from whose will it springs?' What can we gather from it of the purpose for which it is created?' This is the kind of inquiry on which we shall be engaged in the remainder of this course.

Towards the end of my last lecture I indicated certain facts which seem to me to favour the hypothesis of creation. We may class together such events as sins and stupidities with standing conditions such as contingency, freedom and evil—class them together under the common name of irrationalities. They are irrational in that, as they stand, they cannot be rationally explained in terms of either the causal or the purposive order. I suggested that our practice of deliberately creating conditions in which chance shall be a real factor in the determination of events may give us the clue we need. When we deliberately leave a decision to chance the rationality of the whole process is not to be discovered by discovering that the chance was not really chance but only appeared to be so. The lesson to be learnt is that in this world of space and time there can be real irrationalities whose justification is to be found in the contribution they make to the carrying out of rational purposes by being themselves and nothing else.

Once again we are beset by the difficulty involved by the use of the word 'real'. What I mean by my use of it here is that as belonging to the history of this world of space and time these irrationalities can have an equal claim to reality with other things which as they stand are explicable on either mechanistic or axiological grounds. They share in whatever degree of reality appertains in general to the things and events of this world. For the rational purpose of ensuring fair play we create conditions in which decisions shall be left to chance; for the furtherance of His purpose in creation God gives to His universe a mode of reality which admits of the existence and occurrence of such irrationalities as contingency, freedom and evil.

These particular irrationalities will be the subject of my next two lectures. We must now prepare the ground by thinking further about God's creativity in general.

As I have already said, I am not concerned with the question whether the universe had some definite datable moment of origin. I am not asking you to think about what God may or may not have done at some prehistoric moment in the past. In calling Him Creator we think of Him as the 'strength and stay upholding all creation'. Our inquiry is concerned with what He is doing now, and for evidence we have to look to the universe of His creation as it lies open to our observation.

What we see is a series of changes in space and time, a series of changes in which a stream of energy becomes organized into creatures of varying complexity, differing characteristics, and inequality of powers. In this, as Pringle-Pattison pointed out in his Gifford Lectures of 1912,[1] we have to recognize both the continuity of the process and the emergence of genuine differences of kind. I am not scientist enough to know how far the later development of the quantum theory should lead us now to think of the continuity as less absolute than it appeared to be when Pringle-Pattison was writing. The point is of no importance for my present argument. In a lecture to which I have already referred, H. W. B. Joseph showed that the problem presented to the philosopher by the evolutionary process as a whole is parallel to that presented by any instance of growth. An acorn grows into an oak tree, a baby grows into a child, a boy, a youth, a man. Whether the physical development proceeds with a smoothness which would satisfy a philosopher's canon of absolute continuity, or by a series of minute leaps and bounds, the fact remains that the creature, be it plant, animal or human being, passes on from one stage of its existence to another by steps so imperceptible that we cannot draw lines to say precisely where the one stage ends and the next begins. Yet there is a real difference of kind between a boy and a man. For practical purposes we have to draw lines. We decree, for example, that at the age of seventeen he can obtain a licence to drive a motor-car, ignoring the fact that he could do it as well a fortnight earlier or as badly a fortnight later. So, too, in the whole course of evolution. Vegetables, animals and human beings are genuinely different kinds of creatures, but there may be borderline cases in which it is difficult to decide to which kind a particular creature belongs.

Particular creatures grow by receiving and assimilating elements from their environment, weaving them into the pattern of their own structure. The chemical constituents of the soil, moisture, air and sunshine provide the material for the growing oak tree. The boy needs wholesome food and fresh air if he is to grow into a man. Moreover, in the case of living creatures, be they vegetable, animal or human, there is apparently some

[1] A. S. Pringle-Pattison: *The Idea of God in Recent Philosophy* (Oxford, 1917), pp. 103 ff.

kind of an inner urge which leads them to grasp what the environment has to offer and make use of it for their own growth.

If we try to picture the development of the whole evolutionary process by analogy from the growth of particular creatures within it, two problems arise. Writing from the point of view of a biologist, S. A. McDowall asked what for the universe as a whole can correspond to the environment which within it provides individual creatures with the material for their growth.[1] And what, in the earlier stages in which we can discern no trace of anything recognizable as life, corresponds to the inner urge which drives living creatures to grasp their opportunities of growing? What makes the whole process go forward?

To believe in God as Creator is to believe that whatever exists has been brought into existence, and is maintained in its existence, by His will and His gift. Whatever in His creation has any being, has it of such kind and in such measure as He thinks fit to give it. His creative activity is a continuing communication of their being to His creatures. In so far as He wills to give them any independence over against Himself, the fulfilment of His will involves a limitation of His impassibility, for He can now be the subject of a verb in the passive voice, being said to be loved or hated, obeyed or disobeyed, worshipped or blasphemed. He voluntarily accepts such passibility as is entailed by being in relation to a universe to which of His own free will He gives its existence in the mode of reality that His purpose requires.

The fundamental characteristic of the universe, as it presents itself to our observation, is its extension in space and time. Concentrating for the moment on the latter of these, and thinking of God (as we must) from the point of view of finite creatures who experience time in its successiveness, we find ourselves engaged in a process of giving and receiving which may be looked at from either end. *Mutatis mutandis*, the process of teaching provides the most illuminative analogy for the relation of God to His universe in His creative activity. In teaching the

[1] S. A. McDowall: *Evolution and the Need of Atonement* (Cambridge, 1912).

teacher is giving out from the store of knowledge and (let us hope) wisdom which is already there in his own mind—giving out in such measure as the pupil is able to receive. That is the process as seen from the end of the teacher. The same process, as seen from the pupil's end, is the history of the growth of the pupil's mind, as step by step he becomes capable of assimilating more of what he is given. So we may picture to ourselves the course of evolution. Our scientific exploration of it sees it from the end which corresponds to the growth of the pupil's mind. We trace its history from inorganic to organic, from vegetable through animal to human life. With the eye of faith we look at the same process as from the other end, the end which corresponds to the teacher teaching. We see it as God giving forth to His creation increasing measure of the fullness and richness of being which is eternally His own.

Our experience of this process is at the receiving end. Here we are aware of ourselves as receiving a mode of existence in which as self-conscious persons we are responsible for running our own lives. We know what it is to have desires and purposes, to seek to satisfy the one and to fulfil the other. We live in a world which also contains sub-human forms of living creatures and inanimate objects, things whose mode of existence is such that we do not commonly think of them as acting on purpose. They are moved hither and thither by impersonal forces acting upon or through them. The appearance on the scene of creatures who act on purpose comes at a comparatively late stage of the evolutionary process. At its coming creation receives from God a mode of existence embodying a measure of being fuller and richer than any that has gone before.

Through countless ages before the coming of any such beings creation has been an ongoing process. As we look back over it, we see it as leading up to their appearance. What has made it move? This is a typical instance of the kind of question that requires for its answer a Platonic myth. For some thinkers the myth takes the form of endowing all creatures with characteristics analogous to those known to us in human personality. If we cannot think of them as conceiving and fulfilling purposes, perhaps they may at least be thought to feel desires and seek their satisfaction. A. N. Whitehead's use of words like 'prehension' to characterize his units of creaturely existence seems to imply this kind of panpsychism. I find myself unable to credit this particular mythology. I cannot see that there is any evidence to justify it, and, given the hypothesis of creation, as I am trying to expound it, it is unnecessary. Descartes may have gone too far in his treatment of the physical universe as a machine, but there is some truth in the suggestion. The idea of creation is based on an analogy from our experience of making things. We are becoming increasingly familiar with the marvels of man-made machinery, with intricate machines in which every part functions unwittingly in accordance with the purpose of its maker. We live among persons whom we have to treat with respect as persons, things which we manipulate as we will, and forces of nature which we harness and control. All draw our being from God who gives to us our different modes of existence. He who gives to us our self-conscious personality with its accompanying freedom and responsibility gives to the forces of nature their habits and to the things their manipulable passivity. When we think of these latter as functioning in His creative process in accordance with His will, we have no need to think of them as individual centres of desire or purpose.

II

We are examining the hypothesis that to postulate its creation by God will help us to make sense of the universe of our experience. To postulate creation means thinking of God as communicating existence to the universe in a manner analogous to a teacher communicating knowledge to a pupil. We must now ask in what way it will help us to make sense of certain features of the universe, and we will begin with the fact that it exists in space and time.

The puzzles involved in the notions of space and time are notorious. There is the Kantian difficulty of the impossibility of thinking of them without self-contradiction: we cannot think of time or space as either finite or infinite. There is the difficulty which besets the modern physicist for whom there can be no measurement of time or space which has more than relative validity. The one leads idealists to treat time and space as 'forms of perception', irremovable contact lenses which inevitably affect our vision so that we cannot be sure that we see things as they are. The other brings doubts whether our scientific investigations give knowledge of a real world revealed to us through our sense impressions.[1]

We are not now concerned with either of these discussions. The idealist argument is based on the assumption that the aim of philosophy is to find the point of view from which our experience of irrationalities may be explained as the mode in which the intelligible self-consistent reality appears to finite minds. For us philosophy is the attempt to make sense of what actually happens. When apparently we are confronted with irrationalities, before we try to explain them as really being something other than they appear to be, we ask whether they can be understood as playing some part in God's purpose. If physicists are puzzled to find that all their measurements of time and space are relative, it is because they are surprised to find that they must take into account a standing condition for all human search after knowledge. Neither to theologians nor to physicists has God thought fit to give the kind of revelation they feel that they would provide if they were God. Theologians, we saw in my fifth lecture, have had to adjust themselves to the fact that God's truth is not given in forms of sound words uncoloured by the outlook of those who bear witness to His revelation. Just so do physicists have to adjust themselves to the fact that all observations of the natural

[1] See, e.g., M. B. Hesse: *Science and the Human Imagination* (London, 1954), chs. v–viii.

world are relative to the standpoint of the observer. It is equally true of God's revelation of Himself that is given through the sciences as of that which is more strictly the basis of Christian theology that to grasp it we must patiently set side by side our several apprehensions of it, asking what the truth must be if it so appears to men who see it from these various points of view. Of time and space it may be said that 'in so far as scientific language is understood in its own proper context, the structures about which it speaks do exist in external nature, and exist just as surely as chairs and tables and scientists and philosophers exist'.[1]

In thus accepting space and time as objective elements in the constitution of the universe which we are trying to understand, I find myself, as a Gifford lecturer, in the tradition of Alexander and Laird. I have never felt that I really understood how Alexander thought of the space-time which for him, apparently, was the original embryonic form of all existents. It is comparatively easy to think in terms of the physicist's model, to think of the original embryonic form of existence as a stream of energy flowing through space and time, but to think of the union of space and time as, so to speak, the stuff of which the energy is made, passes beyond the limits of my mental capacity.

Alexander was not trying, as I am, to examine the postulate of a Creator. He was examining the universe with a view to discovering whether it gave any indications of immanent deity, and, if so, of what kind. He therefore found it necessary to pursue his analysis to the furthest possible limit, and arrived at space and time as its ultimately irreducible constituents. If we think of the universe as brought into being by a Creator who gives it a relatively independent existence over against Himself, we need not so press our analysis of it beyond what is thinkable. Space and time are not to be thought of as the stuff of which it is made, but as conditioning factors necessary to its having the mode of reality required for the fulfilment of His purpose in creating it.

[1] M. B. Hesse: *Op. cit.*, p. 150.

Returning, then, to the study of the actual nature of the universe, we ask what indications of the mind and will of its Creator we may gain from our experience of it as existing in space and time. Here I have two suggestions to offer.

1. It is commonplace to contrast clock-time and yardstick space with our experience of them as measured in terms of our emotions and interests. In so far as our apprehension of them is based upon the alternation of night and day, the sequence of the seasons, the relative movement of the earth and the heavenly bodies, and the comparison of actual lengths measured on the earth's surface, it has objectivity in the sense that 'the structures of which it speaks do exist in external nature'. But in so far as it is an objectivity of sheer successiveness or extension, it is devoid of significance for our understanding of the meaning of things. On the other hand, periods which feel short because of interest or long because of boredom may be filled with significance, but the estimates of their length are private and subjective.

There is, however, a third way in which we have experience of space and time, a way which is patient of a kind of measurement that involves quality as well as quantity, combining significance with objectivity. Questions of space and time may be relevant to value judgments on both things and events. In such cases the scale by which they are to be measured is not reckoned in seconds, minutes, inches or yards, but by asking how far in occasion or place, in duration or scale, what exists or happens approximates to what is right and proper.

This can most easily be illustrated in the sphere of the arts. Not long ago the music critic of *The Times*, in his account of a concert, criticized Sir Thomas Beecham for having taken a certain work too fast. A few days later there appeared in the correspondence columns a letter from Sir Thomas rebutting the charge and quoting in evidence statistics showing the times taken by various famous conductors for the performance of the same work. Logically his argument was an appeal to the authority of a consensus of experts. Possibly the critic had been so inspired and enraptured by what he heard that his 'psychological time' was shorter than the 'real time'. But what was the 'real time'? Whilst for statistical purposes, or for the purpose of fitting it into a programme of the 'right' length, it might be reckoned in terms of so many minutes, what really mattered can only be described in some such phrase as 'the time required to produce the right effect'.

As with time, so with space. The subjects and the style of execution which are right for miniatures would be wrong for a large canvas or a wall fresco. Beautiful as is the west front of Wells Cathedral, it gives the impression that the masters of that particular style of architecture could not exhibit the perfection of their art when working on so large a scale. Its beauty is the beauty of each several tier; the tiers are simply laid one upon another and do not together compose a unity of the whole. In Beverley Minster one finds the perfection that is lacking at Wells. It strikes one as being the size of building ideally suited to the style.

As with the arts, so with the whole of existence in this created universe. To begin with, time and space provide the conditions in which everything that occurs in the creative process has its being. So long as they are simply this, conditions of existence measurable in successiveness and extension, they are colourless, comparatively without significance. But as conditions whose now or then, here or there, more or less, become important for the existence or happening of things and events of value, they become measurable in terms of their adequacy to the worth of their contents, and as such immeasurably more significant. They make possible, for example, the acute remark of a writer on the spiritual life, that one form of sloth is to do a thing before its proper time.[1]

If we now set this way of thinking of space and time in the context of our general postulate of creation, we shall think of them as conditions devised by God to characterize the mode of

[1] L. Scupoli: *The Spiritual Combat* (E. Tr. W. H. Hutchings, London, 1913), ch. xx.

reality He wills to give to the universe. Whilst for our statistical and practical purposes we finite creatures, living within this universe, can measure their extension and successiveness in feet and inches, in minutes and seconds, we shall think of their most significant measurement as being in terms of their adequacy for the fulfilment of God's creative purpose. What we can learn of the nature of that purpose we have still to inquire. On the question of their limits, all we can say is that we must be content to believe that there have been, are, and will be that much space and time as are required for its fulfilment.

There emerges from this discussion a point of importance about the nature of definition. We can attempt to define a thing in one of two ways, either by an analysis of its constituent elements, or by a description of its function. We follow the first method when we define water as H_2O, the second when we say that a chair is a thing to sit on and a pen is a thing to write with, no matter whether the one is made of wood and canvas, upholstery, or tubular metal, the other of goose quill, wood and steel, or plastic and gold. In so far as I have been able to follow the researches of scientists in such an account of them as is given by Miss Hesse in the book I have already referred to, the former method, while it may increase our ability to harness the forces of nature to our own ends, takes us further and further away from understanding the things and events of the world we have to live in. What I wrote nearly twenty years ago still seems to me to be true:

> When we try to study the universe by scientific method, for a while it seems to respond encouragingly to our inquiries, but when we push these inquiries further in an attempt to grasp its fundamental nature, it seems to slip through our fingers and elude us. It is, I believe, true to say that so far as we are seeking to know enough about it to be able to control it, it is responsive to us. It is when we seek to answer the question of what it is in itself, that we are baffled.[1]

[1] *Towards a Christian Philosophy* (London, 1942), p. 171.

I will therefore make no further apology for being unable to explain space and time as constituent elements of the universe arrived at by analysing it with a view to discovering what it is made of. Our starting-point will be the thought of them as conditions devised by God to characterize the mode of reality He wills to give His creation. What, then, is analogous to the definition of chairs and pens as things to sit on and write with?

2. 'Time', Bergson is reported to have said, 'is what prevents things from happening together'.[1] Certainly, so far as material bodies are concerned, this is true of time and space in conjunction: no two bodies can occupy the same space at the same time.

A few minutes ago I was speaking of the fact that we human beings, who exist as self-conscious persons individually responsible for running our own lives, have appeared at a comparatively late stage in the evolutionary process. Each of us comes into existence as the self-conscious subject of the experiences which are his because he is the self-consciousness of that particular body. This applies to characteristics we tend to call spiritual no less than to those we call physical. A man may have artistic gifts or the mind of a mathematician; in so far as either of these have been inherited from his forbears, they have come through his being the self-consciousness of the body born of his father and mother. That body was conceived through the union of genes in his mother's womb at a particular time and place, and no matter how far back he may trace through countless generations of ancestors the career of the specks of germ-plasm which ultimately combined to form his body, they can never have coincided in time and place with those which have gone to the making of anyone else. From the time of his birth influences have been pouring in upon him from father and mother, from brothers and sisters and uncles and aunts and cousins, from nurses and teachers, from people he has met and friends he has made, from books he has read, things he has heard, places he has visited, sights he has

[1] Quoted by F. H. Brabant in Rawlinson: *Essays on the Trinity and Incarnation* (London, 1928), p. 347.

seen. All these have contributed to the content of his selfhood, and they have come to him through his being the self-conscious subject of the experiences of the body in which he was born. He is uniquely individual because the fabric of his selfhood is woven of experiences mediated through a body conditioned by space and time.

This selfhood, this self-conscious personality, is not something which a man possesses fully formed from birth. It is true of the creation of each man, as of the creative process as a whole, that he grows into his true self as he receives himself from God, for creation is the giving and receiving of increasing fullness and richness of being. In the next lecture we shall be considering in more detail the growth of human selfhood. I want now to concentrate attention on the one point, the contribution of space and time to the creation of man as this may be learned from empirical observation of what has actually taken place. Looking back from our human standpoint over the whole evolutionary process up to date, we see its conditioning by space and time to be a device which has secured the individualizing of persons when they shall come into existence as self-conscious subjects of bodily experience.

III

We have seen that the creative process, while it is a process in which it is impossible to draw lines to mark precisely where one stage passes over into the next, is one in which there do come into existence genuinely new kinds of creature. Bearing this in mind, if we now ask what are the specific characteristics which distinguish creatures at the human stage from those which came before, I would say that to be human is to be the individualized subject of self-conscious, intelligent, purposive life.

The self of which each one of us is conscious is the self of which the content is provided by his bodily inheritance and experience. We grow into this self-consciousness at some time after our physical birth. When we become aware of ourselves we are already, as physical organisms, going concerns with some capacity of sensation and habits of reaction to stimuli. A little baby, lying on his back in his cot, may play with his toes and smile at his mother: it will be some years before he is fully aware of what it means to say that the toes are his toes and the face the face of his mother. Man is a gregarious creature. I am not biologist enough to know whether our pre-human ancestors ran about in herds: it is enough for my purpose that we are born into families and come to know ourselves as members of the family circle. I do not myself believe that our awareness of the existence of other persons is a matter of inference from observing that other bodies resemble our own in appearance and behave in a similar manner. When we first have any consciousness of ourselves, before we are capable of any mental activity which could reasonably be called drawing an inference, we are conscious of ourselves as in relation to others. The selves of which we become conscious are the selves individualized through their consciousness being consciousness of the experiences mediated through the particular bodies, bodies which have been behaving gregariously prior to this individualization of self-consciousness.

At what stage it begins to be possible to credit a particular creature with purposive activity I cannot say. This is the kind of point for which we have to distinguish questions of principle from questions of empirical matter of fact, a distinction of which the importance will appear more than once in later lectures. We can say in principle that in so far as a creature is capable of consciously making up his mind to a course of action and acting upon it, to that extent he is a human being. To what extent this or that particular creature has this capacity is a question of empirical fact which it may be very difficult, if not impossible, to answer.

A grown man, visiting a strange city, and feeling hungry with the approach of his accustomed meal-time, will look about him, choose the restaurant he thinks most likely to give him the kind of food he wants, make up his mind and go in. We do not credit a baby, taking his first meal at his mother's breast, with any such prior process of ratiocination. He is moved by some spirit of the race working in him and impelling him to act in accordance with its habits, as millions of babies have done before him and millions more will do after. In so far as there is anything purposive in the action, the purpose is not that of the individual baby but of the Creator who, at this stage of His creative process, has given to the creatures habits of behaviour which by promoting the survival of the individual contribute to the preservation of the race.

Let me again quote from what I have written before:

> 'Why does a hen sit on her eggs?' 'Maternal instinct, aiming at the propagation of the species', says one school. 'Nonsense', says the other; 'it is because a local inflammation on the underside of the hen is soothed by contact with the smooth warm surface of the eggs. Irritate a capon with red pepper, and it will sit just as well as any hen. It is nothing but reaction to stimulus, just like a dog's reaction to the scent of food'.
>
> But the fact remains that the result of this correspondence between maternal inflammation and the soothing power of the eggs does issue in the chickens. It looks as though each school of thought had got hold of one side of the truth; as though what the fact reveals is an order of events which, regarded from the outside, bear all the marks of being both mechanistic and purposive, but cannot be ascribed to any particular purposer. The hen's action does fulfil the purpose of race preservation, but the hen is innocent of aiming at any such thing.[1]

If in such cases we are to recognize anything purposive at all, it seems to me that the postulate of the Creator is more reasonable than the mythology which ascribes the purpose either to the individual creature or to the race in general or to Nature with a capital N.

But if not with purposes of their own, can we in any sense and to any extent think of creatures at the pre-human stage as endowed with awareness of what they are doing, with intelligence? In the one creative process a baby turning to his mother's

[1] *Towards a Christian Philosophy*, p. 71.

breast is at a stage somewhere between the attraction of iron filings to a magnet and a man turning into a restaurant. We may surely credit him with some consciousness of attraction and satisfaction, or of effort and frustration. Moreover, there is a difference between being born as a human baby and being born as a kitten or a puppy dog. But we need not now pause to consider the exact nature or extent of their respective feelings or thoughts; such questions of empirical fact may be left to professional psychologists.[1] My immediate point is this. For the baby to become a man he must become a creature who as an individual is able to compare different possible courses of action, weigh them against one another, and choose between them.

This gives us the clue to the right way of distinguishing between the spiritual and the material. Once again we must give up the attempt to define our terms by asking what things are made of. Incalculable confusion has been caused by contrasting spirit with matter as though they were composed of different kinds of stuff, speaking of man as though he was a combination of a soul made of spirit-stuff with a body made of matter-stuff, imagining that if the physical universe be essentially of the nature of energy it is therefore somehow more spiritual than it would be if it were matter-in-motion. All this confusion is avoided if we draw the distinction in terms of function, if we define matter as that which is moved by forces acting upon or through it and spirit as that which expresses itself in conscious, intelligent, purposive action.

On any theory of creation God the Creator must be thought of as wholly spiritual. Whatever exists owes its existence to, and is maintained in existence by, His conscious intelligent will. In His creative activity He is communicating to the universe a measure of the reality which in its perfection exists in Himself alone. Our scientific study of His activity is the study of it at what I have called the receiving end, study of the process wherein

[1] But see below, Lecture X, pp. 219 ff. And cp. Jacquetta Hawkes: *Man on Earth* (London), 1954, pp. 53–5.

the universe receives such increasing measure of His reality as He wills to give it. If the process begins with energy energizing in space and time, it is no more spiritual because it is energy than are the bodies we can touch and see into which it becomes organized. In so far as it has no will of its own, but functions in passive conformity to the will of its Creator, it is material. As it receives organization into perceptible bodies, and perceptible bodies receive the capacity of being also percipient, of feeling the attractions and repulsions which move them this way and that, the process approaches the stage at which it will be possible to say that there exist on earth created spiritual beings. When at last they appear, we have men and women, creatures who in their self-conscious intelligent purposive mode of existence are individual through being the self-consciousnesses of their different bodies. It is as we become individualized into this kind of creature that we may rightly be called persons.

It follows from this that between creatures there can be three kinds of relationship. At the material stage of existence relationships are mutually impersonal, as when a book lies on a table. When a man deliberately puts a book on a table, the relation is one-sidedly personal, personal on the side of the man, impersonal on that of the book and the table. Between persons relations are mutually personal whenever men speak or act together in ways which engage the conscious attention and intelligence of all concerned. Between God and His creatures there can only be two of these three. There can be no mutually impersonal relationships, for the activity of God is wholly and fully personal. But when He gives its existence and its mode of reality to energy which energizes according to His will without any consciousness of its own, the relationship is one-sidedly personal: personal on the side of God, impersonal on that of the creature. When He brings His creation to the stage at which there are men who have a mode of reality in which they can respond to Him in obedience or rebellion, in worship or blasphemy, then there can be mutually personal relationships between creatures and God.

It would be difficult to exaggerate the importance for theology of recognizing the existence of one-sidedly personal relations between God and created beings. Neglect of it, for example, has often bedevilled discussion of sacramental religion. But this, with other similar subjects, belongs to my second series of lectures. What we must take note of here is the complication involved in our use of the words spiritual and material.

I have defined matter as that which is moved by forces acting upon or through it. But when the material forces are controlled by and express the will of a spiritual being, they may themselves in a sense be said to be spiritual. In this sense of the word, it does not mean that there is any exercise of spiritual or personal consciousness on the part of the creatures concerned; it means that they become the vehicles of the spiritual activity of the spiritual beings who make or take them for this purpose. They can be viewed, as it were, in two aspects. In themselves material, they are charged with spirituality by the context in which they are used and the use that is made of them.

To one who believes that the universe is God's creation, all the things that we commonly call material are in this sense spiritual. He will have a reverence for nature, for natural resources, for tools and for machines. As embodiments of God's creative purpose they are not to be exploited for selfish ends but to be used for His glory. But this use of the word spiritual is carefully to be distinguished from that in which it is only to be applied to creatures who are themselves centres of self-conscious, intelligent, purposive life, who are, in ordinary language, not things but persons.

We men and women are as yet, however, still in process of being created into persons. When we start on our lives as babies whose movements express the habit of the race working through the physical organisms of our bodies, we behave as creatures who are still at the material stage of the creative process. But because we are born as human babies and not as kittens or puppy dogs, God has in store for us a further development in which He will give and we may receive the power each to take charge of the physical organism through which he has come into existence as a unique individual self—to take charge of it and spiritualize it by making it the embodiment of his own self-conscious, intelligent, purposive life. This will be the subject of my next lecture. What needs now to be said is that throughout our earthly life God's relationship to us is of a mixed character. In so far as we continue to behave materially, it can only be one-sidedly personal. In so far as we can respond to Him as persons, it can be mutually so.

LECTURE VIII

Freedom

I

THIS lecture, in position at the centre of Part II, is the centre-piece of the whole series. I have chosen the title 'For Faith and Freedom' because I believe that recognition of the importance of freedom is the clue which points the way towards making sense of all things, and that the finding and following of this clue is a matter of reasonable faith. In my fifth lecture I have tried to explain what I mean by reasonable faith, and have said what I can in justification of it. Now, in order to make good my position, I must give as careful an account as I can of what I mean by freedom, and of its origin, nature and prospects as I see them. For, as Mr. Weldon has pointed out, 'freedom' has long been 'a word used merely to arouse emotion'. ' "Promotion of freedom" and "restriction of freedom" are significant and useful phrases', he remarks, 'but they are also difficult and complicated to analyse'.[1]

I first approached the subject in my sixth lecture, when I asked you to consider our experience of what I called 'freedom at its best, i.e. when, fully conscious of what we are doing, we make up our minds to do something and do it; when the explanation of why we have done it will be given in terms of the end we were aiming at'.[2] I then went on to argue that this experience is not to be explained away as really being something else in disguise, that it implies the existence of two orders of events, the purposive and the causal, and that the purposive order implies a realm of genuine contingency which is intelligible to us through our experience of deliberately created chance.

[1] *The Vocabulary of Politics*, pp. 69, 159.

[2] Above, p. 136.

For the exercise of freedom in purposive activity the causal order is as necessary as is a realm of contingency. If I am to be able to decide between this source of action and that, not only must it be open to me to do either one thing or the other, but the decision must be taken in a world in which I can weigh the consequences likely to follow in either case. The exercise of freedom is hampered by contingency in the field where certainty is required as much as by the reverse. I can decide to make myself a cup of tea because I can depend upon the stove to boil the kettle and the milk to come fresh out of the refrigerator. My freedom to plan journeys between Oxford and Glasgow may be limited by having to take into account such contingent events as strikes or snowstorms.

Whether or no the 'causal sequence of things' is correctly described by the use of the word mechanical is for our present purpose irrelevant. What matters is that it should be dependable, that events in it should be predictable. There have been pious Christians who have shuddered at hearing reports of progress in scientific research which widens the field within which events are discovered to belong to the causal order. It has seemed to them that the widening of the field of the causally determined involves a narrowing of scope for the exercise of freedom. Some Christian apologists have gone so far as to hail the advent of the quantum theory in strains which imply that to substitute indeterminacy for dependable causality in the world of physics would make it easier to believe in divine and human freedom. This is surely mistaken. Since for human beings the exercise of freedom requires a world of dependable causality, the wider the field of the causally dependable, the greater our power of control over the events of the actual world we live in. So far from stunting it, scientific research may promote our growth in freedom by increasing our power of control. Progress in meteorology and radiophony have greatly increased our freedom of navigation by sea and air, and the study of psychology enables doctors to bring healing to mind as well as to body.

Mistaken as it may be for pious Christians to shudder at any widening of the field of the causally dependable, we must recognize that their underlying motive is probably fear lest that field should be on the way to being widened to include all reality, leaving no place for any real freedom either human or divine, requiring us to explain away our apparent experience of freedom as illusory. Enthusiastic materialists have indeed cherished hopes of being able to arrive at this conclusion. They stand at the opposite pole to those Christian apologists who cherish the thought of universal indeterminacy. Both seek to dispel the mystery of our experience by an undue simplification. Our problem is to make sense of a universe in which the occurrence of events is apparently due to the interaction of causation, purpose and chance. It is not to be solved simply by the elimination of any one of these.

Moreover, the notion that belief in God would be strengthened by an extension of the scope of indeterminacy in the created universe has its roots in a persistence of the deistic idea of creation.[1] It presupposes the conception of the universe as a machine set in motion by its maker who then stands aside and only interferes from time to time when it fails to be working properly. The sciences are thought to study the independent working of the machine; belief in God comes from His revelation of Himself in His interferences, in events which do not fall within the causal sequence of things. God, as it has been said, is to be looked for in the gaps, i.e. the gaps in scientific knowledge. Hence shudders at tidings of the gaps being narrowed; hence rejoicing at rumours of indeterminacy in the stronghold of determinism.

The postulate we are examining has nothing to do with this idea of creation. For us, to think of the universe as God's creation means that He, who gives to it its existence, its various modes of behaviour, and its increasing richness and fullness of being, is continually active and revealing Himself in and through them all. Our method is to start from the empirical end of observing

[1] See above, Lecture VI, p. 126.

what actually exists and happens, to look for clues which may help us to see what is His will and purpose in it all. *Prima facie* our experience presents us with the interaction of causation, purpose and chance. Is it possible that as contributing to God's purpose they can be intelligibly related to one another, each really being itself? Or must we, in order to make sense of the whole, explain one or other of them as really being something else in disguise?

The point we have reached so far is that our experience of freedom, if in reality it is what we feel it to be, implies the existence of all three: it is the experience of purposive agents exercising their freedom of choice on a stage where causation and contingency both have parts to play. We must now examine this experience more closely in order to see whether it can really be what it seems.

The first thing to notice is that we use the word freedom in two quite different senses which are to be distinguished by asking with what they are contrasted. In the one sense freedom is explained by reference to the distinction between spirit and matter as those two words were defined in my last lecture.[1] I then said that creatures should be thought of as material in so far as their behaviour is a passive functioning in accordance with forces acting on or through them, and spiritual in so far as it is the expression of their having made up their minds to do this or that. We use the word freedom to describe this ability of the spiritual being to act on purpose as contrasted with the inability of the material thing to do more than respond willy nilly to stimuli. I shall speak of this freedom as freedom (*a*).

The spiritual being, free in the sense of being able to choose between different possible courses of action, may find that when he has made his choice he is unable to carry out his intention. The hindrance may come from some source external to himself, or from some internal weakness of character. Whatever the nature of the obstacle, it would be quite a natural use of the

[1] Above, pp. 164 ff.

words free and freedom to say that on account of it the man is not free to do what he wants to do, that his freedom is restricted or possibly non-existent. When the words are used in this way it is taken for granted that the subject of discourse is a creature endowed with freedom (*a*). Freedom is not being contrasted with the natural state of material things but with the state of persons in slavery. I shall speak of freedom in this sense as freedom (*b*).

This distinction between the two uses of the word is crucial to the development of my theme.

The assertion by some idealists that their brand of determinism is compatible with freedom rests upon an equivocal use of the word which confuses the two. Their determinism springs from the fundamental principle that only what is rational can be allowed to be real. 'Rational', for them, does not mean falling within the causal sequence of things, but explicable either as self-authenticating in its goodness or as done for a good purpose. Whatever is apparently due to chance cannot really be so, for all apparent irrationalities must really be something else in disguise. What, then, is to be said to the plain man who is convinced that he is a free being and imagines that his freedom implies a realm of genuine contingency? He is shown (and shown correctly, as we shall shortly see) that freedom (*b*) is compatible with determinism of the idealist kind; that indeed freedom (*b*) will only reach its perfection when it arrives at the state of idealist determinism; that since this is the only kind of freedom that a wise man would think it worth while to be concerned about, and it needs no realm of contingency, he was foolish to be arguing for the existence of contingency in the supposed interests of freedom. This argument is an intellectual conjuring trick in which the plain man is entertained by a display of sleight of mind. He is distracted from his concern about freedom (*a*) by the suggestion that freedom (*b*) is the only kind of freedom he can really want. 'No one *wishes* to be free from the compulsion of common sense and a fixed purpose'.[1] For the trick to be successful he must

[1] C. J. Shebbeare: *Problems of Providence* (London, 1929), p. 89.

fail to notice that while he has been under the spell of the suggestion the one has been substituted for the other.

From this it is clear that if the distinction between the two kinds of freedom is crucial for the development of my theme, the crux of the matter is the question of the distinct existence of freedom (*a*). This is denied both by the materialist for whom whatever exists must fall within the causal sequence of things, and by the idealist for whom the only possible kind of freedom is freedom (*b*). Yet it is the kind of freedom which the plain man thinks he has before the materialist and idealist philosophers get to work on him, and as often as not goes on believing he has in spite of them. Can we, on the hypothesis of the doctrine of creation, give an account of it such that it can be seen to fit in with the rest of our experience so as to make sense?

Freedom (*a*) apparently comes into existence at a certain stage in the creative process. Certain organisms, when they have arrived at a certain kind of complexity of constitution, find themselves conscious not only of being the subjects of the experiences that come to them through their bodies, but also able to choose between different courses of action in a world of causation, contingency and purpose. From the point of view of either materialism or idealism the element of contingency is an intolerable, an impossible irrationality; and things become worse when these creatures apparently use their freedom (*a*) to introduce fresh irrationalities by their stupidities and sins. Neither they nor their world can really be what they seem.

Now in studying the creative process we are studying (to use Collingwood's phrase) a process of scientifically knowable change. Collingwood, it will be remembered, contrasted our modern conviction that this is possible with the Renaissance and ancient Greek notion that only what will, so to speak, stand still to be looked at can be scientifically studied. The objection to contingency on the part of materialists and idealists seems to me to spring from their persistence in the outlook of the Renaissance and Ancient Greece. Here the postulate of creation may help to emancipate us from the shackles of bygone ages and help us to think more fully as men of our own time.

If there is scientifically knowable change, its phases cannot all be knowable in precisely the same way as objects of knowledge were held to be knowable before. When the object of our study is a process of development, we cannot at any moment take a cross section of it, isolate it from what went before and what will come after, make it stand still to be looked at, and then think that what we are looking at is the thing we set out to study. We set out to study an ongoing process; if we have arrested it in order to study it, what we have before us is a dead specimen, not the living reality. Let us grant to the idealist that ultimately only what is rational can be real, and that the criteria of rationality are non-contradiction and self-authenticating goodness. These must characterize the eternal Being whose existence we postulate in order to be able to evaluate what exists and happens in this world of space and time, and, being eternal, He can be said (if one may use the phrase without impropriety) to stand still to be looked at. But to assume that these same criteria can be applied as tests of what may be held to be real within creation is to beg the question raised by the discovery that within creation there can be scientifically knowable change. This is what we do if, taking a cross-section of the creative process at some one moment, arresting its development, we examine the dead specimen exposed to our view, find ourselves contemplating irrationalities, and conclude that they cannot really be what they seem.

I have argued, and am arguing, for the recognition of irrational elements as having a real existence in the created universe, as existing (to use the phrase quoted earlier from Dr. Hesse) 'just as surely as chairs and tables and scientists and philosophers exist'.[1] For the idealist distinction between degrees of reality I would substitute a distinction between modes of reality, contrasting the absolute rationality of God-in-Himself in His eternal perfect

[1] Above, Lecture VII, p. 156.

being with the incomplete rationality of the mode of reality which He gives to His creation.

This is no mere verbal change. When it is said that within creation chairs, tables, scientists and philosophers have a greater degree of reality than such irrationalities as evil and contingency, it is implied that these latter are to be explained by finding the point of view from which it can be seen that they are not what they seem, that they are the modes in which things with a higher degree of reality appear *prima facie* to our finite minds. The puzzle they present is one which is to be solved by thinking. In contrasting the reality of God in His eternal being with that which He gives to His creation, in saying that the created reality is such as to admit of the existence within it of irrationalities to be reckoned with as no less real than more rational elements, I am in effect denying that these, as they stand, can satisfactorily be explained by any process of thinking about them. It is not that we have to see that they are really something else in disguise; they themselves have actually to become something else in order to become intelligible.

The created universe is an ongoing process in space and time. That is the fundamental characteristic of its mode of reality. Within this mode of reality creatures and circumstances change with changing times and places, and in changing may pass through irrational phases. These may be such that it is no good trying to find a point of view from which, *as they stand*, they can be seen to be rationally explicable. To demand this, and to complain that if it cannot be done, they cannot be what they seem, comes from failure to grasp the methodology of scientifically knowable change. Phases in a process must be studied in their context; some of them need themselves to be changed in order to become intelligible, their explanation must be sought in terms of the whole process in which they occur. And since we ourselves are living our lives as part of God's creative process, it may be that in our experience there will be things and events for the understanding of which we shall have to wait until the changes have been made.

I shall have more to say about this later. I want now to try to show how on the postulate of creation we can make sense of our actual experience of freedom, with all its irrational implications of contingency as well as of cause.

II

When the idealist says that if freedom is to be worth having it must be freedom (*b*), he is telling the truth. I am only concerned to argue for the reality of freedom (*a*) because I believe it to be a necessary presupposition of the existence within the created universe of freedom (*b*), for freedom (*b*) is the ability to carry out decisions which are made in virtue of our being creatures possessed of freedom (*a*).

Our actual experience is of freedom (*b*) in a very imperfect form. Not only is our control of the natural world, of events which occur in the causal sequence of things, very imperfect; we are hampered by defects of character, we may be the slaves of our passions or bound by the chains of our sins. I have already spoken of how progress in scientific research may increase our freedom by increasing our ability to control the forces of nature. I must now say something about our parallel need of increase in the ability to control ourselves.

It is a fact of experience that the more a man grows in goodness of character with its accompanying self-control, the more dependable and predictable he becomes in his actions. There has stuck in my mind an incident from a story which I read as a child. It was a story about the persecution of Christians in the early years of the Christian Church. The scene was set in the Roman Empire somewhere in the Balkans. Among those arrested for their faith were a husband and wife who were taken apart to be examined separately and persuaded, if necessary by torture, to sacrifice to the heathen gods. For a while the wife was left alone while her husband was being worked upon. Then her examiners came and told her that she might as well give in, do as she was bidden, and offer the incense prescribed; her husband had already done so, and it would save time and trouble for all if they need not apply to her the tortures under which he had given way. She indignantly replied that she would do nothing of the sort, that she knew they were lying because she knew her husband too well to believe he would ever do anything of the sort.

This kind of dependability is quite different from that of the causal sequence about which we were thinking a few moments ago, so different indeed that it deserves to be called wholly other. It is the same difference as that between the behaviour of a coin in the air and the behaviour of the sharper who has provided for the tossing a coin with two heads.[1] The one belongs to an order of events which we observe from the outside, the other to an order of which we have a deeper understanding because we know it, so to speak, from the inside. There is all the difference in the world between not getting drunk because one is locked in a room with no possibility of egress to obtain intoxicating liquor, and not getting drunk because one is the kind of person who does not do that kind of thing.[2]

When we reflect upon our actual experience of imperfect freedom we find it to involve the apparent paradox that its perfecting would mean its development into the idealist's determinism, into St. Augustine's *non posse peccare*. The appearance of paradox is due to failure to distinguish between can't-because-won't and can't-because-prevented-by-factors-external-to-oneself. The extent of the difference between them becomes clear when we realize that the limiting case of the one is the perfection of freedom, of the other its complete absence.

[1] See above, Lecture VI, pp. 138, 142

[2] I am assuming a case in which the maintenance of sobriety is due to strength of character and not to the inhibiting effect of psychological factors falling within the causal sequences. Cp. the distinction between rationalizations and genuine decisions referred to in Lecture VI, p. 137.

Now think again of the whole sweep of the creative process; look at freedom as it comes into existence and develops in its spatio-temporal setting. It first appears as a characteristic of self-conscious creatures individualized through being the subjects of experiences that come through particular bodies. When such creatures cease to be moved entirely by a combination of external forces acting upon them and inherited habits of the species working through them, when they begin consciously to choose between different open possibilities of action, they have reached the stage in the evolutionary process at which creatures are endowed with freedom (*a*). In itself, as the idealists remind us, freedom (*a*) is not only irrational but worthless. We do not, however, isolate it and seek to evaluate it in itself; we think of it as a phase in an ongoing process of scientifically knowable change. Indeed, by the time that we become aware of it it is already developing into something further. It comes into our consciousness as involved in our firsthand experience of freedom (*b*) in its present imperfect condition. Here irrationalities multiply: contingency opens the door to stupidities and sins. But consciousness of the imperfection of our freedom enables us to form an idea of what it might be to have it perfected, and this prevents us from dismissing it as worthless. 'If only', a man might say, 'If only I could completely control the world as now I can control it in part; if only I were free from the sloth, the cowardice, the selfishness, from all that in me holds me back from being always at my best. . . . !' We know ourselves to be such that we can only find our own perfection in a life in which, freed from sins, stupidities and all irrationality, we of our own free will will inevitably express ourselves in acts of self-authenticating goodness.

Our understanding of the universe is that of finite minds who can only look at it from the point of view of their position within it. We have discovered it to be a process in which we exist at a stage in which it is given to us not only to live by the exercise of freedom (*b*), but also to reflect upon it with minds that can look before as well as after. We look back upon stages in which the whole creation appears to have moved in accordance with the causal sequence of things. We look forward to a stage in which there shall be creatures who realize their full potentialities as persons. We look back upon stages which conformed to the positivists' canon of rationality. We look forward to a consummation which will conform to that of the idealists. We ourselves come into existence and live our lives at a stage which is honeycombed with irrationalities, a stage transitional between the rationality of the past and of the future.

A few minutes ago I was saying that if we take seriously the conception of scientifically knowable change, we have to regard the objects of our study as themselves passing through phases of change, at any moment of their existence only explicable in the light of their past and their future. This is true of ourselves when, as now, we are the objects of our own study. What I am maintaining is that a man is to a large extent an irrational creature set in a world containing other irrationalities, that he and his world will both have to be changed in order to become intelligible in themselves. It is no good thinking that we can dissolve away these irrationalities by finding a point of view from which they can be seen to be something else in disguise. We have to accept them as what they are, and we can only make sense of them if we treat them as transitional phases in a purposive order, irrationalities allowed to exist for the contribution they can make towards the achievement of a rational end. In the creative process contingency, freedom, stupidities and sins play a part analogous to that of tossing up in the world of sport. Fair play is the rational and intelligible end to which tossing up is contributory. Can we discern anything analogous in our present situation which will throw light on its irrationality?

Put together three observations that I have made in reflecting on the actual nature of the universe. (i) To be spatio-temporal is the fundamental characteristic of its mode of reality, and this keeps bodies apart; (ii) creatures capable of exercising freedom come into existence as self-consciousnesses individualized through being the subjects of experiences mediated through particular bodies; (iii) the existence at this stage of imperfect freedom suggests the possibility of a further stage in which it shall exist in perfection. May we not conclude that our present condition, with all its irrationalities, is a phase incidental to the creation of individualized free persons? For this purpose the genuineness of the two factors, of the individuality and of the freedom, is equally important. The freedom must be genuine freedom, and it must be possessed and exercised individually by genuine persons. Tossing up is our answer to the question: 'How shall we ensure fair play in our method of starting games?' If without irreverence we may imagine God asking Himself: 'How shall I enable creatures individualized as the consciousnesses of bodies, creatures which at present are behaving in accordance with the causal sequence of things—how shall I enable some of these to grow into genuinely free persons?', we may go on to imagine His answer to be: 'I will give their universe a mode of reality which will admit of the existence of the irrationalities necessary to provide the opportunities they need'.

Behaviourism has been described as a psychology based on the idea that for a scientific understanding of human nature the ideal observer would look down on the earth from a star as an entomologist contemplates a colony of ants. Imagine such an observer confronted *per impossible* with three objects of contemplation: a colony of ants, a community of human beings on earth, and a company of the blessed saints in heaven. I suspect that among the ants and the saints he would find an orderliness in glaring contrast to the confused muddle prevailing among ourselves. But his external standpoint, so far from giving him a better knowledge of his objects of study, would prevent him from understanding what is going on. He would not be able to see that the orderliness of the ants is due to each creature being moved willy-nilly in accordance with the co-ordinated habits of the race, while the orderliness of the city of God is due to the harmonious free co-operation of its citizens. The truth in behaviourism, and its value to the advertising profession, come from the fact that we begin our lives behaving like ants, and to a large extent continue to behave likewise in adult life. Its inadequacy lies in its failure to recognize that this life is our opportunity to grow into something different, into human beings and possibly into saints. The irrationalities of the present condition of our universe, the muddle and confusion with which we are surrounded, of which we are part, and to which we contribute, are incidental to our being created out of ants into saints.

Theories inadequate to cover a whole field may nevertheless have great value if, based on accurate observation of a part, they call our attention to factors commonly overlooked. Behaviourism may not satisfy us as a complete account of human activity, but we should be grateful to it for the light it throws upon our origin. So, too, with the pragmatism of William James. As I said at the outset, its espousal by F. C. S. Schiller led to his having to play a very lone hand in the Oxford of my youth.[1] His contemporaries in the sub-faculty of philosophy could only see its inadequacy as an account of what is meant by truth, and he himself, campaigning with the enthusiasm of the pioneer, was blinded to the limitation of the scope within which it embodied true insight. What I now want to suggest is that the pragmatism of James and Schiller and the instrumentalism of John Dewey call attention to a factor of real importance in the nature of things, but are misstated as theories of the nature of all truth. These thinkers had sensed the inadequacy of the classical and renaissance idea of the knowable for the science of knowable change; they realized that we cannot make sense of a changing universe by expecting it to stand still to be looked at, that we are often confronted by situations such that whatever meaning they have is in the first place a meaning for action which must be taken before they will become patient of rational definition and explanation. What explanation is possible at the moment is explanation of the

[1] Above, Lecture I, p. 4.

action to be taken in order to achieve a rational end. Things must be changed in deed in order to become transparent to thought.

To look out on the universe at any moment in its history is like looking at a jigsaw puzzle turned out from its box on the table and partly put together. We believe that there is a picture to be discovered, but the pieces have to be put together before it can be seen. Meanwhile we have to do our best to find it out by study of the pieces before us and the fragments already assembled, for we have no finished copy on the lid of the box. In the present state of the universe its irrationalities are as real a part of its nature as are its jumbled pieces a real part of the puzzle.

From all these considerations it seems to me reasonable to draw two conclusions.

1. The universe, as it presents itself to us for our study, is more intelligible on the hypothesis of creation than in terms of either the materialist or the idealist metaphysic. Neither of these two have any room for the recognition of the irrationalities of our experience as really being what they are. By adopting a methodology suitable to a science of knowable change, and taking a hint from the pragmatists without subscribing to their whole theory of knowledge, we can accept them as phases incidental to the working out of a process, making sense as contributory to the achievement of a rational and intelligible end. We may believe and hope that in the long run the end will give satisfaction to both materialist and idealist—these two, like behaviourists and pragmatists, do good service by calling attention to real elements within the whole. From the materialists we learn to welcome the dependableness that obtains in the causal sequence of things, to respect the truth that nature can only be conquered by being obeyed. The idealist reminds us that we shall not find satisfaction for our minds until we pass beyond the acknowledgment of brute fact to the recognition of self-authenticating goodness. The truths for which both stand fit together and make sense in a universe which expresses the will of One who in Himself and in His creative purpose as a whole satisfies our canons of self-

authenticating goodness, and for that purpose has given to His creation a mode of reality which includes the dependable regularity of the causal sequence.

2. The irrationalities which disrupt the orderliness of the creative process, which make it impossible to account for everything that happens either as falling within the causal sequence or as intelligible on grounds of inherent goodness, occur as incidental to the development of the exercise of personal freedom by finite creatures. It looks as though the bringing into existence of finite persons who shall be genuinely free is what the whole process has been leading up to. When we think of the process as expressing the will of its Creator we can use personal language and say that it looks as though this is what the process has been aiming at. My central thesis in these lectures is that to see the will to create genuinely free finite persons as the determining factor in our understanding of God's creative activity is the master clue to making sense of the whole.

Neither in revelation nor in creation is it for us to dictate to our Creator His method of action. Our part is to take as given what He has done and does and to try to understand it. Nevertheless, we can assert without irreverence or impropriety that God Himself could not give effect to this intention except by giving to His created universe a mode of reality which admits the existence of these irrationalities. If the finite creature is to be genuinely free as an individual person, his perfected freedom must be the expression of a character formed by the exercise of choice in a field of contingencies. A good man is not one who will go through the motions of goodness as a clockwork toy, when wound up, will go through the motions prescribed by its manufacturer. To demand that God should be able to make good men by some other method than that on which He is actually engaged, by some method more or less analogous to that of the manufacturer of clockwork toys, is like demanding that He should be able to make square circles.

Our part is to take as given what God has done and is doing and to try to understand it. When we study the universe of our experience we find it to be an ongoing process in space and time which up to date has issued in the existence of creatures who are growing in the exercise of freedom as responsible individual persons. I submit that, quite apart from any belief in God, quite apart from any hypothesis of creation, the facts of our experience should be enough to make us recognize the promotion of freedom as the end towards which the process is tending. This seems to me to be the conclusion to which one would have to come if seeking, like C. H. Waddington and J. S. Huxley, to construct on purely humanist lines an 'evolutionary ethic'.[1] But whether, at our human stage in the process, we could live up to the requirements of this ethic the events of this century make one very doubtful. Fascist Italy and Nazi Germany have not been alone in demonstrating the power of forces which tend to dehumanize the individual man and reduce him to the status of a cog in the social, industrial or political machine, assimilating him to the clockwork toy, returning him to that condition out of which we Christians believe that God is seeking to create us into something more. This is one of the meeting places for natural and Christian theology,[2] a point from which we look forward to the transition from the first series of my lectures to the second. A striking feature of the Gospel records is our Lord's respect for human freedom, the distinction implied in His ministry between human beings and creatures at the sub-human stages of the creative process. 'He had no scruple about imposing His will upon loaves, storms and fig-trees, but with Peter and Judas it was different. The only kind of obedience He would have from them was a free response which could not be imposed, but must be won'.[3] Consistent with this is His revelation of God's care for each individual man and woman, the hairs of whose heads are all numbered. Natural theology may teach us

[1] C. H. Waddington: *Science and Ethics* (London, 1942); J. S. Huxley: *Evolutionary Ethics* (Oxford, 1943).

[2] See above, Lecture IV, p. 92.

[3] From my *The Doctrine of the Atonement*, p. 80.

of the value to be set upon individual human freedom as implied in the direction taken by the evolutionary process; it may be that only devotion which springs from roots in Christian theology will enable us to live up to its demands.

We have so far been examining our two kinds of freedom mainly in relation to the question of what they are freedom from. We still have to ask what our freedom is freedom for. Confining ourselves to our present proper concern with natural theology, we can look for an answer in the implications of two factors we have already considered.

1. The evolutionary process, through which we are being created into individualized free persons, brings us into existence as selves whose self-consciousness is from first to last consciousness of self in relation to others. For any one of us our growth in freedom (*b*) may be hampered not only by our own stupidity and sinfulness, not only by forces of nature which as yet mankind is not able to understand and control, but also by the deliberate actions of other men and women at cross purposes with ourselves. I have argued that our present experience of imperfect freedom is such that from it we can grasp the nature of the perfect freedom to which we aspire. It must be freedom for unimpeded activity giving full expression to what we ourselves freely will. This can only be if we are living in a community in which the wills of all its members are united in harmonious co-operation towards a common end. We can only make sense of our present experience of freedom if we treat ourselves as in transition from the orderly behaviour of the ants in their colony to the orderly behaviour of the citizens of the City of God.

If to think of God's will to create free persons be the master-clue to our understanding of ourselves and our universe, we cannot stop short at the individualized freedom of ourselves in our present condition. When from the observation of what actually exists and happens we try to get some idea of what God is aiming at in the creation of it all, the answer will be a community of persons, each in the perfection of his freedom making his contribution to the common life.

2. We are in transition from can't-because-prevented-by-factors-external-to-oneself to can't-because-won't. It is a commonplace of ethical experience that certain lines of conduct give increasing self-control while others dissolve it away. The husband whose wife could rely on his integrity is at the opposite pole to a man who could be described as the slave of his passions. There is a dependableness about both, but one is the dependableness of advance towards the perfection of freedom, the other of its loss, of relapse into the kind of predictability proper to sub-human behaviour. The study of this contrast gives a clue for one of the puzzles presented in my third lecture, that of the variety of moral codes prevalent among men at different times and places.[1] It suggests that for moral evaluation the fundamental criterion is whether or no a course of action promotes or retards growth in self-control. Moral theory may have to develop by the method of trial and error as indicated in my sixth lecture;[2] we now have a basis on which to compare different experiments. It is, I think, true to say that in the circles which Mr. Urmson would regard as enlightened, the actions approved (whether or no consciously chosen for this reason) will be found to satisfy this criterion. Man has been experimenting with his freedom long enough for his experience to have taught him that the courses of action which promote it are those which subserve the values we commonly approve as moral or virtuous.

The word 'subserve' introduces a further consideration which points towards a clue for another of my puzzles. Our transition through freedom (*a*) to freedom (*b*) involves first our individualization as initiating centres of personal action, and then the development of our personality into the perfection of its freedom. The first phase is the emancipation of ourselves from constriction within the conditioned-reflex behaviour pattern of our sub-human origin. So we begin to become selves. But what are we

[1] Above, Lecture III, pp. 58 ff. [2] Above, Lecture VI, pp. 129 ff.

becoming selves for? To play our several parts in making our contributions to the common life of the City of God. Now one thing which experience has taught us in the sphere of moral experiment is that what unites men in harmonious co-operation is joint devotion to some end beyond themselves. In the first phase of our development our energies are directed towards the distinction of ourselves from others, towards the assertion of our independence. But if we are to move onwards through the second phase we have, as it were, to go into reverse, to seek to find some end for which to live, to turn from self-creation and ask what the self has been created for. It is one of the paradoxes of human experience that growth in selfhood comes by forgetfulness of self. 'When we pass from words to facts we are faced with a truth which, though paradoxical in words, is a commonplace in experience. Only that will satisfy man which is not sought because it will satisfy. What he needs is a cause objectively existent and greater than himself to which he can devote himself because, no matter what may become of him, its victory must be secured. Anyone who has ever played football knows by experience something of the truth of this, or at least has caught a glimpse of what that experience might be, could he conquer himself sufficiently to enter into it'.[1] Such self-forgetfulness will minister to the growth of true community when devotion to the ends pursued is shared by various pursuers.

So we move on from the evaluation of acts to the evaluation of their ends. It was necessary to distinguish between the self-assertive character of acts proper to the first phase of our development and the self-giving character of those proper to the second. Now, among the causes to which we can devote ourselves in this second phase we have to distinguish between ends which will unite in fellowship those who pursue them in common and ends which will produce hostility between those who pursue them in competition.

This throws some light on the puzzle of the apparent contrast

[1] From my *Towards a Christian Philosophy*, p. 119.

between devotion to persons and to things.[1] If there are ends such that man's growth in freedom and selfhood is promoted by self-forgetful devotion to them, their maintenance as objects of devotion is for the benefit of all. The judge who administers impartial justice, the examiner who upholds the standard of the examination, these and others like them are not subordinating care for persons to care for things of lesser worth; they are maintaining standards essential to the personal welfare of all men, including those who have to suffer in the process.

What, then, is our freedom for? The summary answer, which needs a great deal of elaboration for which there is now no time, is that it is for the pursuit of those ends which give promise of uniting men in fellowship as citizens of the City of God. If we want to make sense of the universe of our experience we must think of it not only as the matrix of our individualized personal existence, but also as the environment in which we are given opportunities of growing in the exercise of our freedom towards a perfection which can only be ours as citizens of that city. We must remember that when we use the phrase 'make sense', we must give its full force to the word 'make'. There are things in this universe of space and time which will only make sense when they have been made into some thing other than at present they are: they must be changed in deed in order to become transparent to thought. We can only make sense of the universe if we treat it as a challenge to action as well as to thought.

III

Hitherto in this lecture I have had to carry on most of my discussion in somewhat general, if not abstract, terms. It will help to make clear what I have been trying to say if I end by drawing out some of its implications for practice as these affect parents, ministers of religion, teachers in schools and universities,

[1] Above, Lecture III, p. 48.

leaders of youth clubs—all who are engaged in education or pastoral care.

Our task is to be fellow-workers with God, helping His children to grow up into the perfection of their personal freedom. This means helping them to grow up into men and women who will shoulder the responsibility for their own decisions and actions. Often we shall be tempted to take the easier road of making up their minds for them: only too often they themselves will be our chief tempters. Our first duty is to remember that God is not content to create clockwork toys; He is not even content to create animals which function according to the habits of the race working through them. His will is to create real persons, and to this end we must follow His example in respecting and promoting the growth of the freedom with which He endows them.

Those entrusted to our care are in need of such knowledge and virtue as will set them free from all that hinders them from being and acting as their best selves, whether the hindrances spring from external circumstances or from their own weakness and sinfulness. Now growth in knowledge and virtue does not come without the disciplining of the kind of freedom we have to begin with—what I have called freedom (*a*). Freedom has to be both fostered and trained. Over and over again we have to be asking the question: 'Is this particular person, at this particular moment, in need of being constrained to conform, so that he may learn what it feels like to behave in the right way? Or does he need to be left free to make up his own mind, to learn to take responsibility, even at the cost of making a mess of things?'

Because of this necessity of seeing in each particular case in each particular moment what kind of treatment is required, education is an art rather than a science. The same is true of all pastoral care. There is a scientific aspect: observation of what actually happens leads to the generalization that human beings have to pass on from freedom (*a*) to growth in freedom (*b*); that there comes a time when self-assertion must be exchanged for self-surrender; that in the first phase the besetting temptation is simply to let oneself go with the herd and never become a man, in the second to continue to behave like the allegedly typical Englishman, 'the self-made man who worships his maker'; that there are two opposite types of arrested development, each relevant to its own phase. Such generalizations are of prime importance for the education of the teacher, but to discern in the light of them the need of a particular pupil at a particular moment is a matter of aesthetic perception.

Consider now the case of a man who has passed from the first phase into the second. In order to get as clear an instance as possible of what I have in mind, let him be a man whose vocation it is to be an artist, a man who knows in his inmost being that if he is to be true to himself he must be true to his calling, must spend himself in seeking to express in the medium of his art, in shapes or colours or words or sounds, that which it is given to him to express. He knows that for him the central temptation, the central sin, is to produce what he knows is trash because it will bring him popularity and wealth. He may be sorely tempted: it may be that the threat to his artistic integrity comes from no selfish desire for popularity and wealth, but from his duty to provide for the wife and children whom he has undertaken to support. Where shall he look for the understanding sympathy in his struggle if not to his parish priest and fellow Christians? Heaven help him if they take the line that so long as he does not get drunk or misbehave himself with women, God does not care what kind of pictures he paints. If he is helped to keep true at the centre, to see that his struggle to be true to his double vocation as artist and as husband and father is for him (to anticipate the language of next year's course of lectures) his sharing in the cross of Christ, there is hope that his conduct in matters of drink and sex may be brought into line. But if he goes to pieces at the centre, he goes completely.

An artist is a man with gifts that make him responsible for making a definite kind of contribution to the common life.

There are other men and women marked out for particular vocations, in medicine, scientific research, education, politics or otherwise. But most of us are not troubled by the question of how to find scope for the exercise of our special gifts: our problem is that of making our very average abilities suffice to support ourselves and those dependent on us. It sounds well to exhort undergraduates to view their choice of a career as a matter of vocation. How can one do it when one knows that the choice before so many of them will lie between different dull and uninspiring jobs that happen at the moment to be on the books of the University Appointments Board?

If we look on the universe as the creation of our Creator who is creating us into citizens of His City, the artists and the rest of us have this in common, that our life here on earth is the opportunity of finding and doing His work in His world, and so fulfilling His aim in His creation of ourselves. It matters little whether we have gifts that make us responsible for making outstanding contributions, or whether our responsibility is simply that of being the best parents, neighbours, citizens that we can be in the humdrum circumstances that fall to our lot. This is God's world, in which God's work is waiting to be found and done. It is waiting, not only in potentialities of artistic creation as yet unactualized, but in every situation where good can be made to triumph over evil, where truth can dispel error, where beauty can replace ugliness, where love can conquer hate. It is enough that we have in common the conviction that the freedom we have been given to run our own lives is to be used in the giving of ourselves to the finding and doing of God's will.

LECTURE IX

Evil

I

IN these lectures we are trying to discover how we can make sense of the universe we live in and the lives we have to live in it. In this first series we are trying to see how far we can get without taking into account the special witness of the Christian revelation. Our aim is to look with open eyes on all that actually exists and happens. Inevitably one who is a Christian will see what he sees with Christian eyes: his interpretations cannot but be coloured to some extent by his beliefs. All he can do is to make open confession of his standpoint and leave it to his hearers to discount what they think fit.

Working on these lines I have suggested that we can best make sense of things if we view the universe as the creation of a Creator whose aim is the production of a community of finite persons characterized by the goodness which is the expression of perfect freedom. To take this aim as the key to understanding all things enables us to accept the irrationalities we experience as really being what they are, as material needing to be worked upon in order to make sense. In the course of my argument I have once or twice referred to evil as among the irrationalities we have to deal with. But for the most part I have hitherto ignored it and concentrated attention on the search for indications that the creative process is directed towards an intelligible end, an end which will satisfy our demand for logical consistency and self-authenticating goodness.

This postponement of attention to evil has been deliberate. In all our attempts at thinking it is, I believe, a sound principle to seek first to grasp the nature of the ideally perfect. It is only by reference to the perfect that the imperfect can be understood. It is only when we know what we mean by 'straight' that we can understand what is meant by 'crooked'.

At first sight this may seem to contradict the method which allegedly I have been trying to follow throughout. I have claimed to be trying to observe and interpret what actually exists and happens. Am I now deserting to the camp of the idealists, asserting that we ought not to start from the evidence of what actually is, but from our idea of what ought to be?

I do not think so. Let me remind you of what I said in my second lecture, of how all our quest for objectivity is a matter of interaction between evidence and categories.[1] Now it often happens that our categories are not only modified, they actually come to us through our experience of the evidence. Our experience of the imperfect gives us our idea of the perfect. We had an instance of this in the last lecture when we saw that our experience of imperfect freedom gives us the idea of what perfect freedom would be.[2] Somehow or other we are so made that in our experience of the imperfect it makes itself known to us as being imperfect and brings with it an apprehension of the perfection it fails to reach, a perfection which we do not experience but aspire after. I am not now denying—indeed, I wish to assert—that our idea of the perfect, of the ideal, must be grounded in our experience of the actual: it must be the kind of perfection towards which the actually existing imperfection points. What I am saying is that, when we have grasped it, it becomes the criterion by which we judge of approximations towards it. Then it throws back light upon them; indeed it is only in that light that we can really begin to understand them.

Two illustrations may help to make my meaning clear. Every human act is a response to the circumstances of a situation. To be perfect it must both be the right act in the sense of being that which objectively the situation demands, and also be done from the right motive. One has heard misguided preachers maintain

[1] Above, Lecture II, pp. 32 ff.   [2] Above, Lecture VIII, p. 178.

that whereas the religion of the Old Testament paid attention to the first, for the Christian all that matters is the second; and sometimes moral theologians are tempted to err in the opposite direction. Both mistakes come from failure first to grasp in its fullness the nature of that towards which we should aspire. Again, love in its perfection is the devotion of the whole personality, of feelings, mind and will. Only when we have seen this do we realize that to be defective in any one of the three is to be imperfect. It may be that, since our acts are more immediately under our control than our feelings, we have to give our first attention to the question of what we will. But we can never be *content* with acting correctly towards our neighbour while our feelings lag behind: we shall know ourselves to be unprofitable servants.

I make, therefore, no apology for having prefaced any attempt to deal with the subject of evil by an attempt to envisage the good end towards which the whole creative process moves. It may be that the universe as we know it is deeply infected with evil, that our experience is experience of a mixture of good and evil. But the evil is only known to be evil in contrast with the good: we can only discuss it profitably if we see it in the light of the good with which it is to be contrasted. We must begin our study of evil by trying to determine more closely what we mean by good.

Fundamentally, as I have already said, the word should be used to denote that which justifies its own existence.[1] When once we have been bitten by the desire to know the nature of things, the desire which has given birth to the sciences and philosophy, there can be no end to the quest short of the discovery that the universe is such that we are content, and more than content, to accept it as being what it is. It must be self-authenticating in its goodness. Nothing less than this will make sense.

But who are we, that we should set up to be judges of what is self-authenticating in its goodness? I need not again go over all that I have said in my second, fourth and fifth lectures in refutation of the scepticism of existentialists and so-called biblical

[1] Above, Lecture II, p. 37.

theologians. God's ways may not be as our ways or His thoughts as our thoughts. But if we are to think at all, we must have faith enough to affirm what He has thought fit to reveal of His ways and thoughts to men of our day and generation, leaving it to our successors to correct our errors in the light of what more He may reveal to them. Later on I hope to show that for us who are Christians and accept the biblical revelation God has revealed Himself as willing to submit His truth to our judgment, that He requires us to use our reason to sift and criticize what is offered for our acceptance as true. That belongs to next year's course. Here and now I take my stand on the ground that to think at all implies the attempt to make sense of the available evidence, criticizing it by the canons of consistency and self-authenticating goodness.

We must once again face the fact that the position I wish to maintain is based upon an act of faith.[1] I cannot demonstratively prove that to think of the universe as existing to produce a community of finite persons living together in the perfection of freedom must so satisfy the human mind as to make it rest content without further question. I can only say that it is a conception which would satisfy me, and express the faith that in this I have an apprehension of the truth. Moreover, it is a conception which involves a multitude of component elements, each of them subject to the same condition. The perfection of freedom, as I envisage it in the life of the city of God, involves on the part of its citizens such characteristics as honesty, unselfishness and self-control. My respect for each of these, as for all other qualities commonly called virtues, rests upon a similar act of faith that they are truly admirable. The word 'admirable' reminds us that it is not only in the sphere of ethics that we deal with matters incapable of demonstrative proof. *De gustibus nil disputandum* does not mean that in the arts there are no objective standards to be recognized; it means that their recognition rests on something other than argument by logical demonstration.

[1] See Lecture VI, p. 129.

Further, our presence here, our entry upon an inquiry in accordance with the terms of Lord Gifford's will, implies that we regard knowledge of the truth as good. Once more, it would surely be generally agreed that to enjoy good health of body and mind, and to live in conditions which make for healthy growth and the exercise of one's powers, are good things, things which, when we come across them, do not make us ask why on earth they should be so.

Here, then, we have four fields in which we recognize values that are potentially self-authenticating. We rest content in the contemplation of virtuous action, of knowledge of truth, of excellence in art, of healthy living. There is, however, a certain difference between the first three and the fourth. For each of the first three our partial and imperfect apprehensions postulate the existence of a standard of perfection which is absolute and eternal. Here on earth, at our present stage in the creative process, the standards which claim our devotion are foreshadowings of the goodness, the truth and the beauty enjoyed by its citizens in the City of God. In that city there will doubtless be what corresponds to bodily health, to good housing, and to all that the American Prayer Book calls the 'comforts and conveniences of life'. But this correspondence will be a correspondence in the provision of means necessary to the enjoyment of the others. In this world, in order to be and to express ourselves, we need bodies appropriate to the conditions of this world, and we call 'good' that which makes for the welfare of these bodies in these conditions. When we cherish the faith that in 'the life of the world to come' we shall still be ourselves and able to express ourselves, we imply that we shall be embodied in bodies appropriate to the conditions of that world. But of what those bodies would be like, or what would contribute to their welfare, we have no idea. We do not think of those bodies as being the perfection of our present bodies in the same way that we think of the perfection of virtue, of truth or of beauty as being the perfection of our present apprehensions of them.

This difference is connected with the difference we noted in the seventh lecture between the exercise of reason at the sub-human and human stages in creation.[1] We share with the animals the use of our reason to secure means to our bodily welfare, but we also apprehend ideals which demand our devotion and the surrender of ourselves in their service. There is a direct kinship between these ideals and their perfections in the city of God which does not obtain between the satisfactions of our bodily needs and whatever corresponds to them in that city.

Nevertheless, the recognition of this difference must not lead us to underestimate the importance of bodily welfare in this world of space and time. We must keep in our list of goods the enjoyment of good health in body and mind, and the conditions which make for it. There are four, not three, fields in which evil is to be recognized by its contrast with what is good. Hence four kinds of evil: ignorance and error in contrast with truth and the knowledge of it; ugliness, dullness, squalor and vulgarity in contrast with beauty; wickedness and weakness in contrast with virtue; sickness and suffering in contrast with health and happiness.

In the course of the creative process, as it discovers itself to our observation, the third of these—wickedness and moral failure in general—could only come into existence at the human stage. Not until there are creatures responsible for deciding whether to do this or that can there be any moral choice: both wickedness and moral weakness are characteristics of persons endowed with freedom (*a*) but deficient in freedom (*b*).

What of the other three? It is difficult to determine in what sense one can speak of ignorance and ugliness existing as evils at the sub-human stages. Ignorance is only an evil when it is a deficiency in a mind capable of knowledge. Possibly we should recognize approximations to this in animal life. We may see no reason for thinking that magnets and iron filings have awareness of their mutual attraction: its absence is no evil. But when in

[1] Above, Lecture VII, pp. 161 ff.

pursuit or escape an animal misjudges its distance and misses its aim, there is a deficiency of knowledge which can rightly be called error. To speak of ugliness implies a spectator to whose eyes it would appear ugly; how, then, can we speak of ugliness in a universe in which there are as yet no persons capable of forming aesthetic judgments? If, as I believe, such judgments, now that we are here and can make them, claim objective validity, we can reasonably say that the undiscovered ugliness was there, offensive to the eyes of God if not of man. That there is pain, both physical and mental, in the animal world seems to me undeniable. When we have done our utmost to minimize our impression of it by pointing to differences in sensitiveness between animals and men, enough remains to demand recognition as an evil within creation.

So there exist in the universe four kinds of evil. Ugliness may have been the first to appear: it may have been there in the eyes of God before the existence of any creature whose eyes it could offend. Ignorance and suffering appear with the coming of creatures capable of moving and feeling, wickedness and moral weakness with man. All these have somehow to be fitted in with the rest of our experience if we are to make sense of the whole.

II

Underlying the whole postulate of creation is a baffling mystery which we can only avoid by failing to think deeply enough to be brought face to face with it.[1] Similarly, it is only at a superficial level of thought that the problem of evil can be held to discredit belief in creation by God. Whether the philosopher be atheist or Christian, he is living in a universe in which he has to try to make sense not only of the mystery of the relation of time to eternity, but also of the problem of the co-existence of good and evil.

[1] Above, Lecture VI, p. 133.

This latter problem is twofold. We have to consider (i) the nature of the relation between good and evil as co-existing in one universe, and (ii) the so-called problem of the origin of evil: how (if it is not to be explained away as illusory and unreal) the evil has got into an otherwise good universe. In both cases our ultimate explanation must be in terms of goodness: only what is good makes sense by justifying its own existence.

The first question is that of the relation between good and evil. We are familiar with three theories, each of which has its own difficulties.

(*a*) There is the hypothesis that what we regard as evil is not really what we take it to be. This theory finds expression in a number of religions of which Christian Science is probably the best known to us. The underlying philosophy is an idealism of the kind that seeks to explain away irrationalities by finding a point of view from which they can be seen either to be unreal or to be something else in disguise, that 'nothing is evil but thinking makes it so'.

This theory has obtained a footing in the thought of some would-be orthodox Christian apologists. Their starting-point is the Thomist tradition in which goodness is equated with being and evil is defined as the privation of goodness. From this it might seem to follow that since evil is essentially negative and unreal, however troublesome it may be to us in practice, we need not trouble our philosophical minds about it any further. The intellectual problem is solved when we see that what we call evil is privation of goodness and goodness alone is real.

This theory sometimes claims to be based on the principle that in God his *esse* (His being) and his *essentia* (His goodness) are one. Hence any diminution of His goodness would be a diminution of His being. The created universe, it is argued, and we ourselves within it, only exist in so far as we draw our being from God our Creator; in so far as we and our universe are deficient in goodness we are deficient in being.

This argument is open to criticism on three counts. (i) It does not take seriously enough the principle that in God *esse* and *essentia* are one. (ii) It is inconsistent with a genuine doctrine of creation. (iii) It implies univocal predication when speaking of Creator and created.

(i) In thinking of God as Creator we think of Him as personal. His goodness is the goodness of His personal character which finds expression in His will to create. This is all included in the *essentia* which is one with His *esse*. We cannot seek to solve our earthly problems by considering the relation between His being and His goodness. If our starting-point is the inextricable interfusion of God's being and His personal character, our ultimate explanation of all things will have to be in terms of His will. To seek to go beyond the attempt to discover His intention implies the notion that there is something in His *esse* which fails to find full expression in His *essentia*.

(ii) I have more than once distinguished the postulate of creation from theories which try to show how God and the universe are related to one another in some metaphysical system inclusive of both. The argument in question seems to belong to the latter school of thought in so far as it takes what is held to be a necessity of God's own being and treats it as prescribing conditions to which both He and His creation must conform.

(iii) It is commonly agreed that in trying to gain from our experience of creation an understanding of its Creator we cannot argue univocally from the one to the other. Whatever we predicate must be predicated analogically. Surely the same principle must hold in the opposite direction. It does not necessarily follow that because in God diminution of goodness would imply diminution of being, the same would be true of His creatures.

I have argued that all human thinking implies an act of faith that in the long run whatever exists and happens makes for good. I have also maintained that we only know evil by contrast with a logically prior conception of good. But the evil which we thus know is not adequately described in negative terms as the absence of good or deficiency in goodness. We do, of course, experience evils of this kind in all four fields: would-be works of art which are just dull; essays by pupils deficient in knowledge of their subject; physical, mental and moral inertia manifesting lack of vigour. But these are not all. No account of evil can be complete which fails to recognize instances that are definitely positive in character, not merely deficient in, but antagonistic to their relative goods: discords which clash and jar, errors which wreak havoc, cancers which destroy and crimes which corrupt. To attempt to explain these away as illusory, as unreal or as goodness disguised, is to trifle with them. We cannot in this way make sense of these awkward elements in the universe of our experience.

(*b*) If we cannot thus explain away our evils, can we solve our problem by undermining the distinction between good and evil? Is this, perhaps, one of those ideas commonly taken for granted which philosophers exist to question? We remember that just as Christian Science is the religious expression of certain idealist metaphysics, there are philosophies which find expression in pantheistic religions, philosophies in which whatever exists and happens is the manifestation of an ultimate reality which is neutral, 'beyond good and evil'.

If this be so, we are back in the universe of the materialist, the universe in which the acknowledgment of brute fact is not only an obligatory task in our thinking, but also its final end, the universe in which we discover that in the long run nothing has any meaning at all, in which the last word lies with Amaryllis, Neaera and the dictators.

(*c*) Besides Christian Science which makes too little of brute fact and pantheism which makes too much of it, there are religions which have their philosophic basis in dualism. For them the ultimate reality is an eternal strife between the opposing principles of good and evil. To my mind there is more to be said for this view than for pantheism. In religion it can nourish a healthy combativeness on the side of the good principle, and its philosophy is an honest recognition of the antinomy which gives rise to our problem. It does not acquiesce in a solution which is no solution. It leaves the question open. It is thus a challenge to further inquiry rather than a position with which we can be content.

Our problem is the co-existence of good and evil in one universe. We have been considering three conceivable ways of thinking of the relation between them. Logically, I suppose, there might be a fourth, the opposite of the first, the theory that evil alone is real, that what we call good is either an illusion or is evil in disguise. As the other three find expression in different religions, so Ophites and Satanists might be held to show that this theory also has to be reckoned with. But it need not detain us long. While dualism leaves the question open, a fundamental pessimism joins with pantheism in rendering all attempts at thinking ultimately futile.

These four conceivable ways of relating good and evil seem to me to exhaust the logical possibilities so long as we insist that everything that exists and happens in this world of time and space must *as it stands* be capable of rational explanation. Of them, only the first makes any show of achieving this, and it does so by denying that evil is what we experience it to be. It is the inability to account for it in any of these ways which drives us to make a fresh start, to consider it as one of the irrationalities which can and do exist in the mode of reality which God gives to the created universe, irrationalities which must be changed in fact in order to become transparent to thought.

If it is indeed one of these irrationalities, then we need not be surprised that we can give no rational description of it as it stands. There can no more be a rational description of an irrational existent than there can be a definition, a *logos*, of a square circle. If there is to be any rational explanation of it, it must be on the basis of its acceptance as a passing phase in an ongoing process in which it is incidental to the achievement of a rational end.

That rational end, I have suggested, is the creation of a community of persons whose perfection is the perfection of finite individual freedom. It is for the development of individuality that the creative process is spatio-temporal. It is for the development of finite freedom that it contains the irrational element of contingency. Can we account for the existence of evil by thinking of it as contributory to the genesis, development, and perfection of that freedom?

Once again our thinking must start from our idea of the perfection towards which our experience of imperfection points. Only by the light reflected back from the goal towards which we press can we understand where we are or whence we have come. That goal is a state of being in which, as finite individual persons, we are united by devotion to the service of ideals we hold in common, ideals which are no idols of our own creation but objective realities which demand our allegiance. We must so share in knowledge of truth and intelligent appreciation of beauty that where our apprehensions of them differ through the individuality of our different approaches, each will welcome the enrichment of his mind by what he learns from others. This can only be if in each and all there is that perfection of virtuous character wherein all the virtues are fused in the perfecting of the love or charity of I Corinthians xiii.

This perfection must be in each and all, and in each and all it must be the perfection of finite individual freedom, of that can't-because-won't which differs *toto coelo* from the behaviour of creatures moved by forces acting on or through them. It seems to me that the only possibility of giving a rational account of the existence of evil in the world of our experience lies in the hypothesis that the determination to create genuinely free persons is at the heart of God's creative purpose. I do not see that we can 'justify the ways of God to man' unless we hold that such creation of freedom is a creative end that needs no further justification, and can then go on to find grounds for believing that the evils which actually exist can be accounted for as incidental to its achievement.

Let us begin with wickedness or sin. This, as we have seen, is a form of evil which could only appear at the human stage in the creative process. Only when there are created beings who can distinguish between moral good and evil, between right and wrong, and are capable of doing what they know to be wrong, can there be moral evil; and only when they think of such action as disobedience to God will they use religious language and speak of it as sin. For our practical purpose of living, this form of evil, the latest to appear in the temporal process, is the hard core of the whole problem, but it provides the least difficulty for our present intellectual inquiry.

Whereas the other evils, ignorance, ugliness, and suffering, are things which happen to us; our own wickedness is a corruption of our inmost selves, and is the great obstacle to our getting rid of the others. For these reasons it is the hard core of our practical problem. Moreover, that it is the most serious form of evil is implied by the thought of those for whom the contemplation of the other evils makes it difficult, if not impossible, to believe in God.[1] But if we can believe that the aim of creation is the production of persons whose goodness is the perfection of freedom, it makes sense to regard their permission to be wicked in the course of their making as incidental to the achievement of that purpose. And if at times we are appalled by the depths to which, in the history of this world, wickedness has been allowed to descend, and the extent to which it has been allowed to prevail, I can see no light in the darkness except by taking these depths and this extent as the measure of the value set by God upon the created freedom being genuinely free.

I have pictured creation as a process analogous to teaching, a process of giving and receiving, the created universe developing as it receives increasing fullness and richness of being from its

[1] On this, see my *Christian Faith and Practice*, p. 35.

Creator.[1] At the human stage the analogy becomes closer: when man's growth is growth in spiritual personality, and God stands to man in a combination of one-sidedly and mutually personal relationships,[2] the bringing of the creatures to their perfection becomes a process of education. An earthly father has a certain amount of control over the circumstances which condition his children's lives. As we have seen, he has constantly to be asking himself: 'Is this particular person, at this particular moment, in need of being constrained to conform . . .? Or does he need to be left free to make up his own mind, to learn to take responsibility, even at the cost of making a mess of things?' We may without irreverence think of God's creative treatment of man as answering this same question, and from the extent to which he takes the latter alternative gauge the intensity of his care for freedom.

To pursue the analogy further. Since the earthly father has some power of control over the circumstances which condition his children's lives, here too there is a mixed relationship, in part mutually personal, and in part one-sidedly. In his exercise of one-sidedly personal control, during the years when they have to do as they are told, and the details of their lives are for the most part arranged for them, the good father will have in view the development of his children's personalities, his aim will be to promote their growth in true freedom. On the postulate of creation the Creator's power of control over the circumstances which condition the lives of His creatures is absolute. The earthly father has to do his best within the limits prescribed by such factors as his income, the requirements of his daily work, the neighbourhood in which he dwells, and the laws of his country respecting education and national service. For much of all this he has no personal responsibility; he has to take it as it comes. But the Creator is personally responsible for the whole setting of His creatures' lives. They, if human beings, only draw their breath, think their thoughts, and move their limbs by

[1] Above, Lecture VII, p. 152. [2] Above, Lecture VII, p. 165.

making use of the power with which He endows them; the universe which is the matrix and the conditioning environment of their existence as persons, equally owes its existence and its nature to what it has received and continues to receive from Him. Often an earthly father, when planning for the upbringing of his sons and daughters, may have wished in their interest that he could alter the conditions within which he must make his plans. How can there be anything analogous in the mind of the Creator, seeing that every detail in the circumstances conditioning every one of His creatures owes its existence to and draws its being from Himself?

We have seen that to think of God creating is to think of Him as suspending the absoluteness of His impassibility: in relation to His creatures we both speak and think of Him in sentences in which He is the subject of verbs in the passive voice.[1] This reaches its climax in His relation to us human beings. He allows Himself to be blasphemed and sinned against. We may be able to account for this by saying that it is the measure of His determination to endow us with genuine freedom. Can we on these lines also account for other evils besides the wickedness of ourselves and our fellow men and women? Can we find rest for our minds by regarding the ignorance and error, the ugliness, the suffering which torture and disfigure creation at both the human and pre-human stages as incidental to the creating of ourselves into free persons?

To a certain extent I think we can. Our inquiry began as an attempt to make sense of the actual universe, examining what exists and happens with a view to discovering what, if anything, it is achieving. We have found it to be a process which has led to our coming into existence as individualized centres of consciousness in a world in which the combination of contingency with dependable causation gives us the environment we need for growth in freedom. This growth requires occasions through which we may learn to make up our own minds, to take responsi-

[1] Above, Lecture VII, p. 152.

bility for our actions, even at the cost of making a mess of things, occasions when God knows that the treatment we need is to be (as St. Paul puts it) 'in a strait betwixt two'. This could not be except in a world in which we can suffer from ignorance and make mistakes.

I was once in retreat at Mirfield when the late Father Fitzgerald, C.R., was the conductor. In one of his addresses he spoke of a general under whom he had served as a chaplain in the war of 1914–18. There were three things, he said, for which he was to be remembered: he was a great soldier, he was a great Christian, and he was a great gambler. 'Padre', he used to say, 'you ought to gamble. Everyone ought to gamble. All life is a gamble, and when there's nothing doing gambling is the best way to keep your hand in for living'. An exaggeration, perhaps, but there is truth in it. We should always be suspicious of expositions of divine guidance which imply that if we were sufficiently pious we should never have to make decisions and act in circumstances which involve taking a leap in the dark. We come into existence as creatures moved hither and thither by the inherited habits and customs of our race. We must not let our religion become an excuse for refusing the responsibility of becoming selves. If we are asked 'Why on earth did you do that?' we must be prepared to explain the grounds on which we made the decision for which we take responsibility. It is not unreasonable to suppose that for the creation of genuinely free persons there is needed a world in which they can grow up amidst ignorance and error. Possibly we may also account for ugliness on the ground that, starting as we do, we need to be trained in aesthetic appreciation. God will no more be content with a parrot-like expression of conventional judgments in art than He will with a mechanical going through the right motions in morals. In the perfection of created freedom a man's acts must be his own acts and his judgments his own judgments.

Human suffering, apart from what is due to human wickedness, would seem to come from our living amidst the interaction of causation and contingency. Here it becomes most difficult to believe that everything that happens makes for good. On the postulate of creation as I have tried to present it we cannot take refuge in a deistic view which would relieve God of responsibility for what goes on in the universe after He had wound it up and set it going. We have to think of Him as intimately concerned with every detail of its happenings. Perhaps we have here reached the limit of explanation possible to purely natural theology, the point at which our right conclusion is to confess an agnosticism well expressed by an earlier Gifford lecturer:

> I might be challenged, 'Would I maintain that such things could exist in a just universe?' I am not going to answer the challenge, but to point out what I hold an absurd implication in it. Am I, an elderly gentleman almost tied to his arm-chair, to be asked to dictate the limits of heroism and suffering necessary to develop and elicit the true reality of finite spirits?[1]

I think this is probably so, and that for further light we have to turn to the Christian interpretation of those events in the history of this world which for Christians are in a special sense revelatory. Natural theology has brought us to the point where we can see that the universe will only make sense if everything that exists and happens contributes to the creation of a community of finite persons perfected in the exercise of freedom. It contains irrationalities which can only be accounted for on the postulate that it is the creation of a Creator who gives it a mode of reality in which they can play their part as incidental to the fulfilment of His purpose. Among these irrationalities are various evils: in some cases we can form some idea of how they may play their part, but others leave us asking for further light.

There are, however, a few more things that can be said. We must not forget that the evils occur in a world of scientifically knowable change in which what meaning they have may be in the first place a meaning for action. We must get to work on the jig-saw if we are to see the picture. It often seems to be taken for

[1] B. Bosanquet: *The Value and Destiny of the Individual* (London, 1913), p. 157.

granted by religious people that the natural world, as it is given to us unaffected by human intervention, is more directly revelatory of God than are the actions of men and women. We think we are more likely to see His beauty in landscapes and sunsets if we get away from streets and factory chimneys, to hear His voice in thunderstorms than in the roar of aeroplanes. Storms and earthquakes are referred to in insurance policies as acts of God.

Years ago, in the days of the silent cinema, I saw a film in which the villains were a gang of Chinese thugs in San Francisco. The beauteous heroine had been seized and taken to their underground lair, where she was at the mercy of the lustful leader of the gang. In a flash back one saw the hero vainly searching, beating his brow and tearing his hair as he failed to obtain entrance to the den. All expostulations and entreaties having failed, and the heroine being about to suffer what was described as a fate worse than death, the villain was called away for a moment on some pretext. Slipping off the bed on to her knees by its side, she turned to prayer. Sentence by sentence the words of the 'Our Father' appeared on the silent screen. At the petition 'Thy will be done on earth' there came the great San Francisco earthquake of 1906, and amidst scenes of ruin the hero rescued the heroine and the villains were destroyed.

If this cinema theology were the true natural theology we should have to hold that God is more fully revealed in the earthquake than in the response of those who took up the work of rescue and healing. That is not how we see God revealing Himself to us in His creation. If the history of creation is the history of the universe receiving from God in increasing measure the fullness of being which He wills to give, we shall expect man to be the creature in which God can be most fully revealed. But because for man to be the image of God his goodness must be the expression of his freedom, he who is capable of the most sublime revelation is also capable of its most blasphemous disfigurement. It is the measure of our failure that we so easily fall into thinking that nature is more likely to be the image of God if left untouched by man. We should rather think of it as material put into our hands by God which we are to use in such a way as to bring out its revelatory powers.

The tendency to see God in nature as it stands, and attempts to find a rational explanation of evil as it actually exists, are relics of the classical and renaissance outlook, the outlook which demands that the creative process shall arrest its development, shall stand still and present to its would-be knower a cross section of itself which can be logically defined. Neither it, nor we (who are part of it) are of this kind. The universe is in the making, and we have come into existence at a stage in the process at which we are made by God to have a hand in the making of it. The natural world, over which by progress in scientific research we extend our control, and the circumstances of our own lives as they come to us from day to day, are raw material put into our hands for us to make of them what we will. As they come to us they may be as shapeless, as devoid of meaning, as a casual lump of clay in the eyes of a sculptor. Or, like some block of rough-hewn stone, they may already suggest to the expert the treatment by which their latent possibilities for good can be revealed. Only in retrospect, when the work has been done, will it be possible to understand how it has come about and to appreciate the materials that have been used.

Can this throw some further light on the subject of human pain? We are all familiar with the apologia for pain which points out how much that is most valuable in human character, patience, for example, and fortitude, is bred and born and raised by the endurance of pain. It is not always sufficiently remarked that whether or no the pain will have this good issue depends on how it is taken. The real problem of pain is not presented by pain endured heroically in a noble cause. We must bear in mind those for whom neither to themselves nor to those around them can their acute or long-drawn-out agony appear to serve any useful end, and, worst of all, those who perish embittered and resentful, a curse to themselves and to others.

Here the problems of pain and of moral evil are interfused and need to be kept distinct. If we are asking for a rational explanation of the pain which serves no useful end or is the source of further evil, we are pursuing a will-o'-the-wisp. Pain is one of those irrationalities of which no rational explanation can be given until it is rendered intelligible by the use that is made of it. If that use is not made, it is no good wasting our time trying to explain it.[1] The question to be asked is why God has put it in the power of His creatures to decide between use and misuse. Again we are driven back to find our ultimate explanation in terms of God's care for freedom. Again we have to confess agnosticism when we are asked how in detail the unused suffering can be related to the intelligible end.

If this be so in the case of human pain, it is even more so when we turn our minds back to the evils existing in the pre-human stages of the creative process. I have already expressed my conviction that we cannot explain these away on the ground that where there are no human spectators we need not bother our heads about ugliness and squalor, and that pain may be a negligible quantity in the absence of human sensibility. One may admire the ingenuity displayed in the successive phases of the story of a liver fluke as told by Sir Charles Sherrington in the last of his Gifford Lectures,[2] but one cannot help asking how such things can fit in with the purpose of creation as I have been trying to expound it. A Christian of simple faith and no philosophical pretensions may put the question in the form of asking how God could have made creatures like this, or how He could allow them to behave like this. We have translated his question into asking what part they can play in a process which expresses God's will to create a community of free finite persons, but I doubt whether by doing so we have come much nearer to giving a satisfactory answer to it. We have made some advance by discovering the lines on which the answer must be sought. It does

[1] *I.e.*, in terms of the kind of explanation with which we are now concerned.
[2] Sir Charles Sherrington: *Man on His Nature* (Pelican Edition, 1955), p. 272.

make a difference that we give up trying to find a point of view from which it can be seen that whatever exists or happens is as it stands explicable as revelatory of God; that we think of it as a phase in a process contributing material to be used towards the fulfilment of His purpose. We may now know the question to be asked, but in its details much of the answer remains obscure.

III

In discussing the problem of the co-existence of good and evil in one universe, we have approached the second of my two questions. If evil is neither to be explained away, nor accepted as one constituent in an eternal dualism, how are we to account for its having come to play the part it plays in the creative process?

If what is desired is a quasi-historical account of the actual event or events in which an otherwise good process first suffered infection by evil, the only possible answer is that no such account can be given. That is the kind of question which requires evidence of a kind we have not got, about which the best we can do is to frame a Platonic myth.[1] History there cannot be: the myth can only be 'like the truth' in the sense of being in accordance with what by now we have discovered to be the nature of things.

Here, as always, our starting-point must be the world of our actual experience. For myths, as for theories and doctrines, the content must be the criterion of the source. That we men are sinful is not a deduction from an assumed historical event in the Garden of Eden of which the historicity is guaranteed by its source. Our sinfulness is the fact of experience from which we start. Just as the problems of time and eternity and of good and evil remain problems whether or no we believe in God, so the fact that we are sinful remains true whether or no there is any historical truth in the story of Adam and Eve. The extent to

[1] Above, Lecture VI, p. 121.

which it is 'like the truth' depends upon the extent to which it is in accordance with what we know of the interaction of good and evil.

In one respect it is, to say the least, inadequate. It rings true to our experience of meeting and yielding to temptation. It is a myth which may be taken as truly picturing the way in which moral evil originates at the human stage of the creative process, picturing it as seen from the receiving end, from the point of view of those who are tempted and fall. So far, so good. But it has nothing to say about whatever evils had infected creation in the pre-human stages, or of how they can be explained and justified by reference to God's creative purpose.

I have argued that moral evil, or sin, is the easiest kind of evil to justify in this way because it can be directly related to God's will to create persons perfected through the exercise of genuine freedom. It is not surprising that the framers of modern myths carry their imagination back beyond the observable origins of the creative process and picture it as consequent upon a prior rebellion of a creature or creatures endowed with personal freedom.[1] From those that I have read I have not been able to gain any clear idea of what kind of creatures they were that are held to have rebelled or 'fallen', and I am profoundly sceptical of attempts that have been made to give the myths a historical colouring by quasi-scientific correlations of stages in evolution with parallels in their moral rehabilitation. To my mind, if we are to have myths of this kind at all, there is more to be said for the traditional story of fallen angels who still persist as devils. On this I cannot do better than quote from Dr. C. C. J. Webb:

> The problem of the suffering of the lower animals is the most difficult part of the problem of pain. When it was usual to regard such suffering as always due to the results of the fall of man . . . the fact of animal suffering was considered to be due to human sin, and so we might pass on to the problem of human sin. Nor can we in any case hold this view, since we have every reason

[1] E.g., C. W. Formby: *The Unveiling of the Fall* (London, 1923); N. P. Williams: *The Ideas of the Fall and of Original Sin* (London, 1927); P. Green: *The Pre-Mundane Fall* (London, 1944).

to suppose that animal suffering existed ages before the appearance of man upon the earth. We are not, indeed, debarred . . . from the conjecture that this pre-human suffering might yet be traceable to an evil, though not a human, will; for such a conjecture cannot be ruled out of court because it has in the past been presented in a mythological shape in which we cannot accept it. . . . It is worthy of notice that *some* of the difficulties which are commonly felt in approaching the problem are certainly due to an assumption which we are nowadays too apt to make without hesitation, that moral evil can exist only in human wills, and that the environment of humanity must be attributed wholly, if at all, to God. The very ancient and widely-held view that the world, as we know it, is depraved through the activity of an evil will or wills antecedent to the appearance of man in it, is often hardly considered as worthy of serious consideration. Yet many thinkers have found themselves unable to dispense with it. Plato . . . Mill. . . . For my part I cannot doubt that an ultimate unity is required alike by religion and by philosophy. But that morally evil *human* wills exist, we know; that they affect injuriously the environment of other persons we also know. No new difficulty is added by the thought that superhuman evil wills exist and have injuriously affected the environment of humanity as a whole. And this supposition would go some way towards explaining why it is hard to regard nature as altogether good.[1]

Ever since I first read this passage forty years ago it has remained in my mind as making more sense than its rivals. Even so it leaves much that is obscure. Attempts to work out its implications in detail, to describe the original creation of the angels, to picture the circumstances of their rebellion and transformation into devils, to trace the connection between these events and the creation of this actual universe which we are trying to understand—all such attempts, however 'like the truth' they may be in the Platonic sense, leave us without conviction that they give any record of what actually occurred.

What, then, does it all come to? Our setting out to make sense of the universe has brought us up against the problem of evil, and the problem of evil gives us the sharpest reminder of what is our situation throughout. We start from our actual experience. We try to observe it carefully and to describe it accurately, seeking to avoid pitfalls by paying attention to ques-

[1] C. C. J. Webb: *Problems in the Relation of God and Man* (London, 1911), p. 268.

tions of logic and epistemology. All this is with a view to working out its implications. We come to see ourselves as creatures existing at a certain stage in an evolutionary process in which we are given the opportunity of growing in freedom as individualized persons. To make sense of this whole process we postulate an eternal Creator who is creating us into a community of persons perfected in their freedom. To a certain extent we can see how the evils we encounter and the evils which we harbour in ourselves can contribute to this creation of our freedom, but we look out from the sphere of our immediate experience in which we can see this more or less clearly, peering into a world around where there is much that is obscure.

What are we to do? We must go on peering. We need make no apology for being unable to answer all the questions that puzzle us. Philosophy is a quest, and so long as we go on peering we may be most philosophical when we confess ourselves baffled. What we can see, we see by the rays of what light we have got, and our only hope of being able to see more lies in our allowing those rays to penetrate further into the surrounding obscurity.

This year I have been doing what I can to see by the light of natural theology, and have got as far as I can. One thing, however, remains to be said. We must not forget the lesson we have learned from the pragmatists. The light we have got is light by which we must live as well as look, and it may be that by the action we take this or that opaque object in the surrounding darkness may be changed so as to become transparent to thought. It may be that to have learned something of the nature of true freedom, and that we are created to grow in it, will give us light enough to walk by, and that to walk by it is the way to the solution of our puzzle.

We need make no apology for being unable to solve all the questions that puzzle us. It is a clear implication of our Lord's prayer in the garden of Gethsemane that the problem of evil was one which in His earthly ministry He was content to leave veiled in obscurity, and that at the point at which we have found ourselves most baffled. We seemed to see our way towards making sense of the universe and of our lives within it by deriving it all from God's will to create freedom. But we had to acknowledge a good deal of evil of which we could not see why its occurrence should be necessary for the achievement of this end. If He whom we believe to have been God incarnate could not see clearly why His death was necessary to the fulfilment of God's purpose, why should we be surprised when in this life we find that we too have to walk by faith and not by sight? 'It is enough for the disciple that he be as his master, and the servant as his Lord.'

Appended Note

Towards the end of the eighth lecture I was saying that education is an art rather than a science in that the kind of question involved is whether a particular pupil at a particular moment is more in need of discipline or of independence, of sympathy or of severity. To this may be added considerations drawn from the statement near the beginning of this ninth lecture, that 'our idea of the perfect, of the ideal, must be grounded in our experience of the actual: it must be the kind of perfection towards which the actually existing imperfection points'.

If this be so, there may be two opposite errors in educational theory and practice. The one is to start out with a fixed idea of perfection, a stereotype of character to which all children and pupils must be made to conform irrespective of their various idiosyncrasies. The other is that each individual should be allowed to develop along his own lines without correction or discipline. It may be that the traditional educational practice of the Victorian age tended towards the former error, and that in reaction against it some Edwardians went too far in the direction of the latter.

The upshot of what I have been urging in these lectures would seem to be this. The universe reveals its Creator to be aiming at the production of a community of persons who grow in freedom by devoting themselves to the pursuit of ends of eternal value. These ends are of various kinds, demanding various kinds of service for which in turn are appropriate various types of character or capacity. The task of the teacher, therefore, is not only to discern what kind of treatment a pupil may need at this or that moment of his career, but also towards what type of perfection he should be encouraged and trained to aspire, this being 'the kind of perfection towards which the actually existing imperfection points'. Thus doubly it is a matter of aesthetic perception rather than the application of a scientific rule.

LECTURE X

Prospect

I

I HAVE been arguing that we can best make sense of things by thinking in terms of creation. If this be so, there are certain corollaries that call for attention.

To think in terms of creation is to seek for the explanation of whatever exists and happens by asking how it can be seen to fit in with, or, if necessary, be changed to be made to fit in with, the Creator's purpose. We have to observe and study what exists and happens in order to learn from the course of events what it has to teach us of the nature of that purpose. Looking back over the scene in the light of what we have learned of the purpose we gain a deeper understanding of its inner meaning. But whatever understanding we may arrive at, whether of the whole or of its parts in detail, so long as our ultimate explanation is sought for in terms of purpose, we are thinking of the Creator as personal. Let there be no mistake about this. The word 'purpose' has no meaning except what it derives from our experience of being able, as persons, to make up our minds and take decisions. How comes it that this is so often overlooked, with so much resulting confusion?

It is due to the combination of a number of factors. There is, first, the natural reluctance of our minds to accept the real existence of irrational elements in this world of space and time, to adjust our categories to deal with scientifically knowable change. We take it for granted that what is rational and dependable is 'more real' than what is wayward and chancy. Secondly, our direct experience of the personal is of persons in process of creation, at the stage of transition through freedom (*a*) and freedom (*b*) at which we are all still wayward and chancy. It is in two impersonal realms, in those of the 'causal sequence of things' and of the logical consistency exemplified in mathematics, that we seem to find the dependableness, the order, the rationality so woefully lacking in our own lives. It is an easy step to the assumption that one or other of these realms is 'more real' than the world of our consciously personal activities, 'to speak as though what appears to be a man's own decisions and purposive acts are *really* effects of the interaction of 'inhibitions' and 'complexes' and other similar abstractions which we regard as more real than human volition'.[1] As what appears to be a tailor's shop in Oxford or Glasgow may be an outlet for the sale of the wares of a manufacturer of cloth in Leeds, so what appears to be a man or a woman may be an outlet for eruptions from the system of complexes. So much for ourselves. Passing from the microcosm to the macrocosm it is again an easy step to assume that all our interplay of personal life is tragedy or comedy played by strolling players who come and go upon a stage provided by the interaction of more real impersonal forces.

But, thirdly, there is the discovery that, quite apart from conscious human volition, things happen which can only be understood in the light of the ends to which they contribute. Attempts to account for them by reference solely to the causal sequence of things are clearly inadequate: indeed, the causal sequence itself seems to be adapted to the achievement of ends. There must be a purposiveness working itself out both through the system of complexes which finds expression in human behaviour and in the principle of creativity which informs the evolutionary process.

Consider first the psychological form of this hypothesis. We come into existence as persons when we become conscious of ourselves as individuals endowed with freedom (*a*), when we know in ourselves what it is to be sources of purposive action. As we look back over the earlier history of what has gone to our

[1] *Towards a Christian Philosophy*, p. 23.

making, we note the appearance of living creatures who as individuals respond to stimuli with varying degrees of approximation to our condition. When we see a dog showing evident signs of joy at the presence of his master and rendering an obedience that looks as though he felt honoured to receive his commands, we credit him with something more like our own purposive self-consciousness than we attribute to iron filings responding to the attraction of a magnet. As our mind travels down the scale of degrees from the dog who is a member of a human family, though the dogs of Pavlov's experiments and the bluebottle fly who can't rather than won't keep away from the joint of meat, to the iron filings, we attribute less and less of purposiveness to the creatures concerned: they become less and less analogous to ourselves, more and more analogous to the filings.

When we come into existence as persons we become conscious of ourselves as already going concerns, including the characteristics and powers of the preceding stages in our ancestry. What we feel as hunger and thirst and the desire for sexual satisfaction is the way in which we are conscious of physical relationships which at bottom are analogous to the attraction of the filings to the magnet. By the time we become aware of them they have become organized into a system of forces working in and through us, subject matter for the researches of psychologists.

We only really know by experience what is meant by purposive action in so far as we take all this as raw material for our creation and direct it in accordance with our ends. Since 'nature is conquered by being obeyed' the value of psychological research lies in the contribution it can make to the effective control of the material for the making of ourselves. When we use language which speaks of the behaviour of dogs, flies, or other creatures down to iron filings as being purposive, we are personifying them after the analogy of ourselves. In varying degrees there may be truth in this; but I find it hard to believe that anything like a system of psychological complexes can rightly be treated as more analogous to the dog or to ourselves than to the filings.

The puzzle presented to us by the universe is this. We only know purpose as originating in the will of a self-conscious person. Yet events which cannot be attributed to any known person happen in such a way as to look purposive to the observer. To my mind the attempt to solve this puzzle by invoking a generalized immanent spirit of purposiveness is as unconvincing a piece of mythology as the panpsychism which regards the universe as made up of a multitude of more or less personified monads.[1]

On the cosmic scale, those who put their faith in an immanent purposive spirit of creativity seem to me to manifest an essentially similar confusion of thought.[2] I can understand the materialist for whom everything happens in a causal sequence in which consciousness and self-consciousness with their ideas of purposiveness occur as epiphenomena. I can understand the idealist for whom the sequence of events expresses the purpose of the eternal Absolute Being in process of self-realization. But the notion of an immanent impersonal purposiveness is a bastard mythology, the illicit offspring of a union between rationality and personality in which neither party has had the courage to get properly married to the other.

While frankly aware of its difficulties, I submit that a genuine doctrine of creation is more able than its rivals—whether materialist, idealist or purposive-impersonal—to assimilate the actual facts of our experience. For the psychologist it means that the forces at work in our personality at the subconscious and unconscious levels exhibit in their behaviour the habits given to them by their Creator as modified by the action of creatures to whom He has given freedom to work with or against Him. They are not to be revered as more real than the conscious personality of the man or woman in whom, by some such method

[1] Above, Lecture VII, p. 154.

[2] E.g., Miss Jacquetta Hawkes, in the last chapter of her *Man on Earth* (London, 1954). Miss Hawkes' understanding of the evolutionary process as a whole is very much akin to my own, but we part company in our beliefs about what makes it move.

as deep analysis, they are discovered. On the contrary. The ultimate reality is God, the Creator of the raw material out of which He is creating men and women into a community of fully self-conscious persons each perfected in the exercise of freedom. In so far as they grow towards this end, selecting, rejecting, disciplining and developing what is given in the available material and weaving it into the selfhood of their conscious personalities, they receive a fuller measure of the reality which God is giving them according to His method of creation.

If this be so, if all our being is what in less or greater degree we draw from God, then the perfection to which we aspire will be that in which we receive our fullest measure of reality. The more we become fully self-conscious persons, in conscious control of our thoughts, words and deeds, entering into and enjoying personal relations with others like ourselves, the more we approach the fullness of created reality. And God Himself, in so far as for natural theology He reveals Himself in His creation, reveals Himself as personal in that the more fully He gives of His reality to His creatures the more personal they become.

If ever there were a myth that needed to be exploded as not being 'like the truth' it is the myth that the impersonal is more real than the personal, that it is more philosophical to speak in impersonal terms, to speak of systems of complexes, of a spirit of creativity, of a deiform universe, of the trend of evolution, of nature with a capital N, than of God creating men and women to be in personal relations with one another and with Himself. Philosophy is the attempt to make sense of the universe of our experience by examining to the best of our ability what actually exists and happens. If as a result we find that the nearer we approach an apprehension of what is ultimately real, the more we need the language of persons and personal relationships to describe it, we must claim for philosophy the right to follow whither the argument leads. When the philosopher means God let him say God, and not go hunting about for some periphrastic impersonal phrase because he thinks it will sound more philosophical.

I am not, I repeat, unaware of the difficulties involved. These difficulties spring from the fundamental mystery of our being, and beset all attempts to make sense of our universe or describe the relation of time to eternity.[1] It is true that to stop short at the thought of God creating the universe, to say that it is futile to attempt to go further and discover the metaphysical system in which creator and created are mutually related, that further inquiry must take the form of trying to enter into and understand the mind, will and purpose of the Creator—it is true that this involves what John Laird with apparent good reason has called an impossibility.

> There is no possibility of effective partnership or of grounded dependence between a changeless and a changing existent. The implications of this statement are quite general and apply to the relation between a divine unchanging over-world and a secular changing under-world as much as to any other reputed instance.[2]

We are in a dilemma. On the one horn we can only achieve the logical neatness of a materialist or an idealist metaphysic either by pretending that things are not what they are or by the mythology of impersonal purposiveness. On the other, if we postulate an eternally perfect reality which somehow or other is in relation to a developing universe in process of creation, we have to accept Laird's challenge. In spite of the seriousness of this challenge I believe this second choice to be the right one because it is the more able to accept as being what they are the things and events which as philosophers we set out to try to understand. And if, as I have tried to show, the facts suggest that we should think of the eternal perfect reality as personal, as the Creator who abides unmoved while guiding His universe through its changes, this does somewhat ease the necessity of confessing that all our thinking has to end in the acknowledgment of mystery. It is

[1] See above, Lectures III, p. 68; VI, pp. 133 ff.
[2] *Theism and Cosmology* (London, 1940), p. 163.

when we think of God as God, instead of as some 'power not ourselves', that we can credibly think of Him as willing to express His omnipotence in giving to His creation an independence which involves for Himself a relative passibility. It is as philosophers philosophizing, not as turning aside to adopt some other role, that we are 'lost in wonder, love and praise'.

But if so, if the end of our natural theology is the acknowledgment of God as personal, then the door is opened to other elements in traditional Christian faith. So long as it was thought to be more philosophical to speak impersonally of powers not ourselves that make for righteousness than of God creating, calling, commanding, punishing and forgiving, to speak of angels seemed to betoken a naïvely mythological imagery: they, too, had to be depersonalized if a religious man wished to philosophize about his religion. But if men and women are more real than the psychological complexes which go to their making, if all that is sub-personal is created by God as material for the creation of persons, if in God Himself is eternally the fullness of personal life, then to think of the company of heaven as including created personal spirits is a mythology more 'like the truth' in the Platonic sense than to think of it as a ballet of bloodless categories or other impersonal abstractions. If I go on to think that my idea of angels is like the truth in a sense more than the Platonic, that it gives me a picture of them as they actually exist, I pass beyond what can claim the warrant of natural theology. But so long as I bear that in mind, it is with a clear conscience that as a philosopher I can keep the feast of Michaelmas and lift up my heart to join with angels and archangels in the worship of God. My imagination will be based on thinking in terms which are more like the truth than are any others that are open to me.

The second corollary follows from what was said in the seventh lecture about the meaning of the words material and spiritual.[1] If this created universe has the reality which God gives it for the purpose of creating a community of finite good persons;

[1] Lecture VII, pp. 164 ff.

if the material world (i.e., those elements in creation which constitute the causal sequence) be the matrix for the production of free persons and the continuing environment for their exercise of and growth in freedom; if man be not a composite being, a soul made of spirit-stuff encased in a body made of matter-stuff, but a growing unity of ensouled body or embodied soul, a creature growing in self-conscious, intelligent purposive selfhood as the subject of the experiences mediated through his bodily life, then true religion cannot be 'escapist' either in the intellectual sense of condemning matter as evil or explaining it away as unreal, or in the practical sense of attempting to 'seek those things that are above' by getting out of our bodily life.

I do not wish to deny that God calls some men and women to the 'religious life' in the narrower sense of those words, as members, for example, of a contemplative order. This is a special vocation. A healthy university can carry a certain proportion of athletes who 'barely make the grade' in their examinations, and of scholars who cannot tell one end of an oar from the other: their contribution to the common life keeps up the general standard both of work and play. So the presence among us of those who concentrate their attention on the life of prayer inspires and strengthens the prayer-life of us all.[1] But for most of us the degree of our spirituality is not to be measured by the extent to which we extricate ourselves from our bodily life, but by that to which we make that bodily life the vehicle of our spiritual purpose.

We come into existence as self-conscious subjects of the experiences mediated through our bodily life. Our bodies are the media through which we not only become our individual selves, but also express ourselves. Through them, in this world of space and time, we play our part in the ongoing process of

[1] I have a vivid recollection of a discussion group in which one member was maintaining that contemplative orders were out of place in the Christian Church; true Christian faith must find expression in active benevolence. There was a pause, broken by the voice of Dr. Clement Webb: 'I cannot believe that the world would have been better if Keats had been a philanthropist.'

its creation. For our growth in true freedom we need opportunities to forget ourselves in the pursuit of ends that make self-authenticating claims on our devotion.[1] If these ends may be summed up in the familiar triad: truth, beauty, goodness, we have to remember that in this world their pursuit must take the form of working for their actualization in things and events in space and time. Neither scholar nor scientist can effectively serve the cause of truth without uttering words in lectures or putting pen to paper for publication in pamphlets, periodicals or books. The artist must strive to embody what he has to express in colours, shapes or sounds. And since the aim of creation can only be fulfilled in a community of persons united through their common devotion to these ends, whatever makes for social welfare and the promotion of brotherhood among men will have its contribution to make. In the industrialized society of our present-day world, when the economic foundations of our common life can only be secured through methods of mass-production and conveyor-belts, the efficient conduct of such operations by men versed in their technicalities may be as spiritual an activity as teaching in a Sunday School.

To grow spiritually, to grow in freedom (*b*), is to grow in our power to make the material the vehicle and expression of our spiritual purpose. The degree of our spirituality is to be measured by the quality of our life in the flesh. Matter is to be wrestled with as matter, in order that its potentiality as vehicle of the spiritual may be realized. Scientific research, the pursuit of art and learning, industry, commerce, finance, politics and many other similar activities are to be viewed as occasions for the service of God in His creative purpose. In our thinking and teaching about religion we need to beware of the tendency to imagine that God is chiefly (if not only) interested in what a man does in his spare time.

Thirdly, there is something to be said on the difficult subject of providence. Its difficulty is well known. To speak of a situa-

[1] Above, Lecture VIII, p. 203.

tion as 'providentially meant' surely implies that it has been brought about by the overruling power of an omnipotent and omniscient God who 'ordereth all things both in heaven and earth'. How, then, can there be any genuine contingency, any sphere of operation for created freedom?

Once again we are face to face with the fundamental mystery of our being, the mystery of the relation of time to eternity, the mystery which underlies Laird's challenge and produces an antinomy not only in any adequate doctrine of God but in any attempt to make sense of our experience which does not stop short of probing the ultimate questions.[1] Once again, as we seek to peer into the baffling mystery, we must be guided by what rays of light shine forth from our study of God's actual revelation of His purpose and method in creation.

In any case the postulate of creation involves a limitation of God's impassibility. In relation to His creatures He can be spoken of in the passive voice, can be said to be obeyed or disobeyed, loved or hated, worshipped or blasphemed. What we have to try to discover from the evidence provided by the actual nature of His creation are the lines on which He has thought fit to assume this limitation. I have tried to show how this evidence favours the view that God's aim is the creation of finite beings endowed with freedom, and that He has given to the created universe the mode of reality required for this purpose. If it be argued that to admit the existence of this mode of reality would be inconsistent with His omniscience, it may be replied that to deny Him the power to create free finite beings would equally be inconsistent with His omnipotence. Confronted by this choice it seems to me reasonable to stand by the evidence and to hold that the limitations He assumes are those relevant to creating the conditions required by His central purpose.

Turning again to that evidence we may note three points: (i) the existence of an order of causal sequence in which whatever purposiveness there may be expresses the will of the Creator or

[1] Above, Lecture VI, p. 133.

of other personal beings, (ii) the existence of men and women whose decisions and actions constitute a purposive order maintaining itself in a world where their ignorance and inadequate control of the forces of nature involve an element of contingency, and (iii) the occurrence of irrationalities which have to be changed in order to become intelligible. I want to suggest two things. First, in thinking of God's providence in general we must think of Him as exercising His control over His universe in accordance with the ways in which He has actually revealed Himself as doing so. If it is His will to entrust certain of His creatures with responsibility for deciding the course of events in the history of His universe, we must think of Him as acting in ways which will respect their freedom and promote their growth in it.[1] Secondly, when in particular we are inquiring whether any situation can usefully be described as 'providentially meant' we have to remember that in the first instance the meaning may be a meaning for action.[2] It may be that the situation is an irrationality such that no intelligible explanation can be given of it as it stands. Only if the right action be taken will the result become transparent to thought.

This much, at any rate, is relevant to our present discussion as a corollary of the postulate of creation. What more I have to say on the subject of providence belongs to next year's series of lectures.[3]

II

The evidence suggests that the aim of the creative process is to be a community of persons perfected in that goodness which is the expression of perfect freedom. This aim is as yet very far from being attained. We may well ask what prospect there is of its ever being reached and, if so, whether from the actual nature of the universe we can gain any indication of when, where, or how.

[1] See above, Lecture VIII, p. 184. [2] See above, Lecture VIII, p. 181.
[3] See also my *Towards a Christian Philosophy*, ch. vi.

These questions concern the destinies both of individual persons and of the universe as a whole. It follows from the argument of my seventh and eighth lectures that we cannot ignore the former and content ourselves with the vision of an earthly paradise to be enjoyed by our successors at some dim distant future date. At first sight such a prospect might seem to embody the Christian ideal of humility and self-abnegation: how, it might be asked, could this better be expressed than in the devoting of one's life to the attainment of a bliss which only others will enjoy?

We have already had occasion to notice that as a matter of fact practice based on this theory is most characteristic of those who have no faith in the Christian revelation of God's love and care for every individual man and woman.[1] The point now to be stressed is that whether we are considering Christian theology or (as at present) natural theology in general, our primary task is to try to discover what God reveals Himself to be being and doing. Its effect upon ourselves is a secondary question: we start at the wrong end if we argue from what we think will be good for us.

Without drawing on the Christian revelation of God's loving care for His creatures, there is in the nature of the universe as we have been studying it evidence that its Creator must be thought of as having a care for the perfection of individual human selves. The evolutionary process, conditioned by its spatio-temporal character to be an individualizing process, issues in the production of individualized self-conscious persons growing in selfhood through the exercise of freedom. With this individuality of personal selfhood there comes a uniqueness of individual value. Whereas at the sub-human level the individual creature (unless adopted to share in human society) may be regarded as an interchangeable organ for keeping alive the species from generation to generation, a man has it in him to become a person whose value lies in the uniqueness of the combination of qualities in himself. Here in this life, from our experience of our imperfection, we gain some idea of what our perfection might be, and it

[1] Above, Lecture VIII, p. 184.

is clear that if the whole process which has gone to our making is to come to a successful conclusion, this will mean the perfection of ourselves as ourselves and not as merging in a oneness in which our own selfhood is absorbed and lost. No one of us has as yet reached this perfection.

We are trying to make sense of what actually happens. It surely makes nonsense of the whole creative process if we think that through countless ages it moves towards the production of a certain kind of creature, and then, when at last such creatures appear, leaves the making of them incomplete. Some kind of belief in the continuance of personal life after death seems to me to be necessary to make sense of what in the past has gone to the production of us human beings in our present condition. It will not be on this earth in space and time that we shall know what it is to enjoy to the full the glorious liberty of the children of God.

We have pictured the evolutionary process as God communicating to His creation in increasing measure the fullness and richness of being which He wills to give it, and bringing it to the stage at which He is interested in the growth of individual persons. Now I am arguing that this interest must be thought of as continuing beyond their life in the sphere in which they are open to our observation as material which we are trying to understand. This raises a whole host of questions. Are all men and women to pass on through death to this further stage of growth? If not, on what grounds is the selection to be made? Is this world, this whole universe, only of importance as a crucible for the manufacture and extraction of immortal souls? Is it of no concern to God whether we make of the earth's surface a garden or leave it to be a squalid patch of weeds? Are all attempts to fashion our social life after the pattern of the City of God a utopian distraction from our true task of preparing ourselves for the life of the world to come?

These are questions to which, in our present state of knowledge, it seems to me impossible to give an answer. There are, of course, those who, having no belief in God or life after death, pin their faith on the prospect of a far-off age when by progress in the sciences, the arts, and increasingly enlightened humanitarianism, peace and harmony will prevail among men and women enjoying a high degree of civilized culture in an earthly paradise. Their picture, as I have just tried to show, ignores the individualizing character of the evolutionary process. Moreover, so far as we can understand a world of space and time in which inevitably things change and pass, it is difficult, if not impossible, to imagine it reaching a state of perfection which will exhibit such self-authenticating goodness that in it we find the goal of our intellectual quest, that both of itself and of the process which has led up to it we shall cease to ask why they should be so. On the other hand, it is in and among the things of this world that we learn to discriminate between those of less and greater value. We may see this, perhaps, most clearly in the sphere of the arts, where things of eternal worth find embodiment in sounds and shapes and colours. But not only in the arts. Where a machine is intelligently designed and accurately and well made so as efficiently to perform a function useful to human civilization; where a school or a college, an industrial undertaking or a municipality is organized and conducted so as both to provide a good life for those within it and to work for the benefit of the larger community to which it belongs—here and elsewhere within creation we have to recognize things which cannot be treated merely as means towards the manufacture of immortal souls. They may have their part to play in that process, but meanwhile they demand our interest and respect as being good in themselves for what they are here and now. We cannot join the Utopians, but neither can we fly to the opposite pole and ally ourselves with those fanatics who care for none of these things. In increasing measure God is communicating to His creation fullness and richness of being: if here and there He enables it to produce, in such measure as is possible under conditions of space and time, things which embody and manifest eternal values, it is for us to share His interest and His delight in them.

Whatever there may be of this nature is seldom, if ever, free from imperfections of its own, and exists in a world in which there is much evil, much that God can take no delight in. What prospect is there of such growth in what is good at the expense of what is evil that the time will come when God shall look upon the whole of His creation and see that it is good? And what will it be like if it is still this spatio-temporal universe, with this world of men and women in it?

I can see no way of answering such questions. Responsible philosophers and theologians must leave them to the writers of science fiction. When we are dealing with events of the present and the past, observation and historical study can give us material for the exercise of our minds. We can reflect upon what has been and what is going on; we can try to discover whether there is any meaning or purpose in it. We may reasonably discuss what is likely to happen in what may be called the foreseeable future. But when we try to look ahead into the more distant reaches of things to come, we enter into the realm where Platonic myths are the order of the day. If the writers of Genesis had to deal in this way with the lost but potentially recoverable history of the past, how can we expect to be better placed in respect to the as yet undecided contingencies of the future? Those of us who have grown up in the apparently permanent security of the horse-drawn Victorian era, who have passed from a scientific outlook based on Newtonian physics through the relativity of Einstein to the dawning of the atomic age, will be the last to attempt dogmatically to define the limits of what changes may lie ahead.

Once again we must take it that the immediate meaning of things as they are is a meaning for action, for action which must be taken if the pattern of things to come is to be disclosed. If we have discovered that we are made for growth in freedom, and that this growth comes by devotion to those ends of eternal value which can be embodied and expressed in things of earth, we have light enough to walk by, walking in the faith that by so doing we may be opening doors to fuller knowledge and deeper understanding for thinkers yet unborn.

III

In my third lecture I tried to set before you some of the puzzles which to my mind demand the attention of a Gifford lecturer. I mentioned (i) the apparent absence of logical consistency among principles of right action, (ii) the question of the ultimate destiny of those who live and die with no belief in God, (iii) the variety of moral codes acknowledged at different times and in different places, (iv) the difficulty of explaining one's acceptance of positions which, while coherent and intelligible in themselves, appear incompatible when looked at together, (v) speculation concerning the probable future history of this world, and (vi) the mystery of the relation of time to eternity. It is now time to look back over the course as a whole and ask whether I have been able to throw any light on these puzzles.

Already in this lecture I have said as much as I can about the last two of them. The first, third and fourth are variations on a single theme, the necessity of recognizing in this universe the existence of irrational elements which have to be changed in fact in order to become intelligible to thought. It is in order to make sense of a universe which contains these elements that I have been led to the postulate of a creative activity which demands for its study the methodology of a science of knowable change. When in this way we try to study the actual process of creation, observed (as I have put it) 'at the receiving end',[1] we find that we ourselves are in the midst of it, that among the irrationalities are the various forms of evil, and that our creation into persons is coincident with the tackling of them as among the things which have to be changed. One form of evil is ignorance and error. I suggested

[1] Lecture VII, p. 153.

in my fifth lecture that the history of human thought is the history of God making Himself known to man through minds conditioned by the outlook of their time and place.[1] If we set this in the context of all that I have said later about the will to create genuinely free persons as being central to God's purpose, we can, I think, begin to see how the illogicalities we took note of may fall into place as incidental to that purpose.

There remains my second puzzle which was stated in the form of a question about the ultimate destiny of those who live and die with no belief in God. In so far as it questioned the consistency of traditional Christian teaching about the ground of our hope of a future life with God's revelation of Himself in Jesus Christ, it belongs to next year's course of lectures. But it will be in order here to say something on the general question whether different men and women may rightly be thought of as on the way to different destinies.

I have been arguing that our hope of a future life is grounded in the conviction that the creative process would make nonsense of itself if it stopped short of fulfilling the end for which it has been individualizing human beings as persons. Our individualization is due to our coming into existence as the self-conscious subjects of experiences mediated through particular bodies. When we are born, our individualization *as persons* is far from complete; indeed, it is only beginning. For a long time we are for the most part creatures moved by the inherited habits of the race working through us. We have to become persons by taking charge of the running of our own lives.

If we come into existence, and continue to exist, as the self-conscious subjects of the experiences mediated through our bodies, what ground have we for thinking that when these bodies perish we shall be able to go on existing without them, each of us as himself or herself? That is the form in which we have to pose the question of the possibility of continued life after death.

[1] Lecture V, p. 115.

To begin with, the body is not only the means of our individualization; it is our bond of unity. As self-conscious subjects we find ourselves drawn in different directions by different instincts, passions, interests and ideals, so much so that sometimes (to quote what I have written before) 'when the day is done, and we look back over it, and see this creature dragged hither and thither by this interest and that, we may well ask 'Which of these things is the real I? Am I really anyone at all?'[1] The only bond of connection between the various selves that I have shown myself to be in the course of the day is the fact that in all of them I have been the subject of the experiences that have come to me through my body, and responsible for the actions done in that body. What ground can I have for hoping that with the disintegration of the body that holds together what there is of me on earth, I shall not be disintegrated with it, shall be able to hold myself together as a self by some independent inner principle of coherence?

It seems to me reasonable to think of this life as giving us the opportunity to develop such an inner principle of coherence. Let it be granted that to begin with, as the self-conscious subjects of the experiences of our bodies, we are, each of us, an uncoordinated tangle of heterogeneous impulses, instincts, interests and what not. We are here for the purpose of growing in freedom, and this growth comes by devotion to those ends whose service brings increase of self-control. This achievement of self-control is a unifying activity. It involves the subordination of some of our passions, desires and interests to the requirements of those which we make central and dominant; it implies the development of a personality with a definite character of its own.

It is true of our bodies that their growth depends on their receiving sustenance from the world around. If we have good food and drink and breathe good air we are healthy; without these, or if they are bad, we are weakly, or sick, or we die. So, too, with the inner life of our self-conscious, personal selves. In

[1] *The Doctrine of the Trinity*, p. 184.

literature and the other arts we are accustomed to discriminate between works of enduring value and what I may, perhaps, describe as ephemeral trash. If, as I have earlier suggested, the enduring works are the embodiment in things of earth of eternal values, is it fantastic to suppose that the man who nourishes his mind on what is of eternity thereby helps to create a self which is not entirely dependent on the body but shares to some extent in the eternity on which it feeds? If there is anything in this suggestion, it cannot be limited to the sphere of the arts, or of the things of the mind in the narrower sense of that phrase. It would clearly be absurd to regard immortality as a prerogative of aesthetic or intellectual prowess. In the whole conduct of life there is the same distinction to be recognized between what is ephemeral and what of eternal import. 'There came a certain poor widow, and she threw in two mites, which make a farthing.'[1] There, surely, we see a comparable laying hold on eternal life.

Here, then, are three grounds on which we may base the hope of a future life: the creative process requires it for its fulfilment and provides us with opportunities both for self-unification and for nourishing our growing selves on elements of eternal value. This suggests that all are not moving alike to the same destiny. If our hope depends on our making use of our opportunities, the more convinced we are that to make us genuinely free is at the heart of God's creative purpose, the more we have to reckon with the fact that we may throw away our opportunities, may either dissipate our selfhood in wayward pursuit of ephemeral trivialities or take some evil interest to be the principle of our self-unification.

This seems to me to be as far as we can get as a matter of natural theology, if that term is taken to mean the study of the universe in general without taking into account the evidence provided by the Christian revelation. But this use of the term, though taken for granted in the days when Lord Gifford made his will, is no longer adequate. I have argued in my fourth and

[1] St. Mark xii. 42.

fifth lectures that what I call the Christian revelation should not be thought of as a system of divinely communicated truths to be accepted on authority as a complement to what we can learn by our own study of what actually exists and happens. It comes by taking certain events in the history of the world as of unique and supreme significance for our understanding of all things. This involves, indeed, the seeing of these events with the eye of faith. But so do all attempts at making sense of the universe of our experience. For the Christian to try to interpret it with the historic Christ as his key to its understanding is as much a matter of natural theology as for a Marxist to take as his key the interplay of economic forces.

In my second lecture I spoke much of how human thought progresses by the interaction of categories and evidence. Sometimes the categories have to be revised; sometimes the evidence has to be reconsidered. If all goes well, the result is a gain on both sides: as the categories grow in comprehensiveness and accuracy there comes deeper insight into and fuller understanding of the reality underlying the evidence. If God reveals Himself both in general in His creative activity as a whole and in particular in His redemptive activity in Christ, then we may expect a similar mutual benefit to come from seeking to relate to one another the general and the particular. In this part of my course we have been studying the general. I have been trying to show that this study gives us reason to believe that the universe springs from and expresses the creative will of God, and that we can find a meaning and purpose for our own lives by thinking of them as given us for growth in freedom. This study of God's revelation of Himself in general gives us the categories with which in my second series of lectures we shall approach the evidence for what Christians believe to be His revelation of Himself in particular.

INDEX

FOR FAITH AND FREEDOM

THE GIFFORD LECTURES, 1955—1957
IN THE UNIVERSITY OF GLASGOW

VOL. II

CHRISTIAN THEOLOGY

CONTENTS

PART III
CHRISTIAN THEOLOGY: FOR FAITH AND FREEDOM

Part III

CHRISTIAN THEOLOGY: FOR FAITH AND FREEDOM

LECTURE I

The Bible

LET me begin by recalling from my first series of lectures some salient points which I must be allowed to presuppose in entering upon my second.

I have argued that the mode of distinguishing between natural and revealed theology which was generally taken for granted when Lord Gifford made his will half a century ago can no longer be maintained. All man's discovery of truth is by the interaction of divine revelation and human reason. If the Christian is to claim that his faith is in some special sense derived from revelation, this must mean that, within the wider area of what is revealed to us through our study of the universe in general, there are certain elements of unique and supreme significance for our understanding of the whole. God does not give this special revelation in words conveying information about matters too high for scrutiny by human reason, forms of words to be accepted in unquestioning faith like official *communiqués* issued after a secret meeting of heads of governments. He gives it by doing certain particular things in the history of the world and inspiring certain men to see the significance of certain events as acts of God. So far as the logic of the process is concerned, the method by which one man argues from the universe in general to the existence, the *esse*, of God is the same as that by which another argues from these particular events to His nature, His *essentia*. Thus all theology which has any truth in it is to that extent both natural and revealed. Christian theology should be thought of as a specific form of natural theology, differentiated by its seeing in certain events particular acts of God of unique and supreme significance for our understanding of everything.

In the remainder of my last year's lectures I was trying to see how far we can go towards an understanding of the universe and of our own lives while confining ourselves to the study of natural theology in general, that is, by reflection upon the nature of the universe in general without taking into account the Christian estimate of the significance of certain events within it. I concluded that we can best make sense of it by thinking of it as a process expressing the will of a Creator to bring into existence a community of finite free persons, and that most light is shed on many of its dark mysteries, on its containing such irrationalities as contingency and evil, by postulating at the heart of His creative will the determination to give His creatures genuine freedom. My aim in this second course of lectures is to expound as best I can the special form of natural theology which is Christian theology, to try to show how the Christian interpretation of certain events in the history of this world fits in with, illuminates and carries further what understanding of the universe and of our lives we have already gained.

In my fourth and fifth lectures last year I have argued that for Christians to attempt to find the unchanging *depositum fidei* in a form of sound words is to pursue a will-o'-the-wisp, that our proper starting-point is not the apostolic *kerygma* but that to which the apostolic *kerygma* bore witness. 'Christ gave His life; it is for Christians to discern the doctrine.' I have described the history of human thought as God seeking to make Himself known to man through minds inevitably conditioned by the forms of thought and linguistic usage of their age and culture. This conditioning has to be taken into account in our study of the books of the Bible just as much as in that of the conciliar creeds, the patristic writings, and the works of scholastic and Reformation divines. We have to learn all we can about their authors' ways of thinking and linguistic self-expression in order to discover in what way their insight into truth was coloured by this outlook and to what extent there was miscolouring which needs to be discounted. We ourselves have to think and speak as twentieth-century Western Europeans, in terms of the thought and language of our time and place. As we study the writings of the past the question we have always to be asking is: what must the truth have been and be if men who thought and spoke as they did saw it and spoke of it like that?

It is towards the acceptance of this principle in our study of the Bible that the trend of theology, as I tried to describe it in my opening lecture last year, has been moving. But we have not as yet seen our way through to its full adoption in such a way as to provide us with a positive basis for theological and devotional exposition. A constant subject of discussion among academic theologians is the prevalence of so-called fundamentalism, the fact that among university students, including theological students, many who are most deeply and sincerely Christian nourish their religion on a use of the Bible to which the progress made by scholars in its literary and historical criticism is apparently quite irrelevant. Attempts to meet the situation are made by exponents of what they call biblical theology. These are scholars who are well versed in the critical study of the provenance, date and historical value of the various books of the Bible, who endorse its methods and accept its results, but hold that all such studies are concerned with details in the structure of a book which as a whole exists to set forth in words the truths which for his soul's health a man must accept and believe.

It would be uncharitable to call this biblical theology a policy of appeasement. I would rather describe it as resting in a half-way house towards the radical reconstruction of our way of using the Bible which I believe to be required of us. Its value lies in its reminder that a theology which is wholly concerned with antiquarian research into questions of the historical origin, date and value of documents is only propaedeutic to the study of theology proper. In this it marks an advance on the academic theology of my early youth. But it is not satisfactory as a solution of the problem it raises. It shares with genuine fundamentalism the disadvantage that different exponents of biblical theology proclaim different, and often conflicting, versions of what the Bible is given us to teach. Compare, for example, the biblical theologies of Karl Barth, Emil Brunner, Anders Nygren and Lionel Thornton. The claim to let the Bible interpret itself turns out on examination to rest upon what I have called the method of eclectic quotation, the choice of certain passages to control the interpretation of the rest.

How are we to decide between differing rival biblical theologies? The only possible way is by submitting them to the arbitrament of our reason, laying them alongside, looking at them together, and asking which best fits in to make sense with all our experience of life. What I now want to argue is that we shall make no real progress so long as, in seeking for the right interpretation of the Bible, we think of it as a self-consistent manual of doctrinal information. The problem we have to face is extremely complicated. I am profoundly conscious of it as one to which I have as yet found no completely satisfactory solution. All I can do is to make some suggestions about the road I believe we should follow in the search for one.

Let me first try to explain what I mean by the complicated nature of the problem. There are three distinct factors to be reckoned with.

1. We have inherited from our ancestors a *mystique* about the Bible as though in itself and of itself it were possessed of a certain sacrosanctity. This may be symbolized by the fact that from my upbringing as a child I still feel uncomfortable when I see other books put down on top of a Bible. In those days this *mystique* manifested itself in the generally accepted idea that somehow or other there was a religious value in the sheer fact of knowing the contents of the Bible: to a large extent this provided the substance of so-called religious education.

Christopher stared at her. He was not prepared for a religious aspect in Miss Mullen's remarkable young cousin.

'Do you teach in Sunday Schools?' He tried to keep the incredulity out of his voice, but Francie caught the tone.

'You're very polite! I suppose you think I know nothing at all, but I can tell you I could say down all the judges of Israel or the journeyings of St. Paul this minute, and that's more than you could do!'

'By Jove, it is!' answered Christopher.[1]

From Sunday Schools to universities. Until after I left Oxford for New York in 1925 it was still necessary for candidates for the degree of B.A. to pass the 'Examination in Holy Scripture', commonly known as 'Divvers'. All that was required of them was to show knowledge of the contents of the Gospels of *St. Matthew* and *St. John* and the *Acts of the Apostles*: they were not to be asked questions which would involve their use of commentaries or discussion of the significance of what they read in the text. I remember an occasion when I was one of the examiners. We had asked for a comparison of the raising of Jairus' daughter in *St. Matthew* with that of Lazarus in *St. John*. A candidate whose paper as a whole showed her to be a girl of deep Christian piety, quite unaware of the possible implications of her answer, wrote: 'In the case of Lazarus, who belonged to a poor family in the country, our Lord delayed three days and went at His ease. In the case of the daughter of Jairus, who was a wealthy and influential ruler of the Jews in the city, He lost no time and went at once.' Every detail correct, and therefore full marks.

We have long ago ceased to be satisfied with this kind of 'religious education'. We have passed through the arid period in which we sought to nourish the soul by discussing questions of origin, authorship, date and significance as sources for historical reconstruction. When we come to think about it, we see that this period also was governed by the same Bible *mystique*; we may have substituted historical study of the biblical material for sheer knowledge of the biblical text, but in both cases what made it 'religious' education was the fact that its subject-matter was the Bible. We have passed through the arid stage of historical study to the realization that if education is to be in truth religious

[1] Somerville and Ross: *The Real Charlotte* (World's Classics Edition), p. 195.

education it must be education in the saving truths of God's revelation of Himself to man. But we still tend to think of the Bible as in itself and of itself the original source from which we are to quarry these truths, as a manual in which they are set forth in words for our acceptance.

The late Professor J. A. Smith used to tell a story of a Scottish village in which there was a division in the Kirk on account of 'they wearifu' rabbits'. All held themselves bound by the decree in Acts xv which prohibits eating meat with the blood in it, but whereas a laxer party would allow one, when buying a rabbit, to accept the salesman's word for it that it had been shot and not snared, the stricter party insisted that each must investigate and verify the matter for himself before the animal could be eaten. We may laugh at this story, and dismiss it as of no importance for serious theology: it is absurd, ludicrously absurd, to lay such stress on a single text, and that text one clause in a decree only directly relevant to the circumstances of its own time. But what is there in this that is different in principle from the assumption of many serious theologians that we are to be bound by the teaching of this or that passage in Holy Writ? In an earlier lecture I have referred to Dr. R. S. Franks' selection for this purpose of St. Peter's sermons in the early chapters of *Acts*.[1] In a recent book by Dr. Ernest Best[2] it seems to be taken for granted *passim* that when we have discovered precisely what St. Paul meant by the words he used, this must be determinative for our theology. An even clearer instance of the persistence of the Bible *mystique* is the following passage from a pamphlet written by the late official lecturer of the Church of England Central Council for Moral Welfare:

> In Genesis i God is described as 'making man in our image'. In v. 2 this is clarified: 'Male and female created he them, and he called *them* Adam (Man).' There is set out the fact that the basic sociological unit of humanity is not *that*

[1] Vol. I, p. 86.
[2] E. Best: *One Body in Christ* (London, 1955).

man and *that woman* but the man-woman nexus. Thus we are confronted with a relational unit as the foundation element in the structure of human society.[1]

In this quotation it is clearly implied that for a particular point in connection with the Christian doctrine of man the foundation on which all else is to be built is to be secured by asking what 'the Bible says'.

We are all of us under the influence of this *mystique*. Both as theologians and as preachers, both in the lecture-room and in the pulpit, we feel we have solid ground under our feet, and can commend what we have to say to our hearers, if we can quote some biblical passage as the underlying substance of our teaching of doctrine or words of exhortation. I am not at the moment concerned to assert that this is wrong, or that we should abandon the practice. I am calling attention to its prevalence as one of the factors in our present situation, pointing out that it comes to us as an inheritance from an age when our fathers could take biblical statements on trust in a manner which is impossible for us, and suggesting that we need to examine ourselves and our habits with a view to making sure that we know what we are doing.

2. A second factor in the situation is the unfortunate fact that in the history of Christianity reliance on biblical authority has been productive of evil as well as of good. As an Englishman profoundly ignorant of Scottish history, I have no right to express any opinion about the rights and wrongs of the seventeenth-century struggles in this country. But no one can read Scott's *Old Mortality* without being convinced that many horrible deeds sprang from reliance on biblical authority. There is evidence that at an earlier date the torturers of the Inquisition believed themselves to be acting in obedience to such texts as 'Compel them to come in', and that to-day some devout members of the Dutch Reformed Church in South Africa hold themselves bound to direct their racial policy in accordance with

[1] Hugh C. Warner: *The Theological Issues of Contraception* (London, 1953).

God's curse on the children of Ham.[1] Before we can accept the Bible as the ultimate source of authority for belief and practice we must take into account the empirical fact of its power for evil as well as for good.

3. Nevertheless, we have also to take into account the fact that the Bible produces good as well as evil. In it men find not only words that bring them comfort, help and encouragement from God, but also the revelation of God in Christ which comes home to them as saving truth. Some two years ago Mr. Wilfred Pickles, in a broadcast given from some institution for the blind, was heard to ask one of those round him what gave him the greatest abhorrence. The blind man replied: 'The thought of children being brought up without being taught the Christian faith.' He went on to say that every day he and his wife opened the Bible at random at three places, and never failed to receive help and guidance. This kind of testimony could be multiplied indefinitely from the experience of those who regularly read their Bibles in the course of their devotion; and the two words 'at random' are not, in fact, as superstitious as they may sound at first hearing. For those of us who are clergy of the Church of England our daily portions are prescribed by the Prayer Book lectionary, and what we shall find each morning and evening is as much something 'given' as if we opened the book 'at random'.

To this testimony of Christian believers, of whom it may be said that they find in the Bible what they are looking for, must be added the testimony of missionaries from overseas. There is no gainsaying the evidence which tells of non-Christian men and women who have been moved to Christian faith through reading of God's righteousness and love as set forth in the Old and New Testaments.

[1] 'Differences divided the conference into three groups: (*a*) those who believed in a righteous separation in the Church based on the Scriptures; (*b*) those who practised such separation for expediency; (*c*) those who were convinced that separation in the Church was wrong and stood condemned according to Scripture. Resolution unanimously passed: This conference places on record its gratitude to God for the one common ground which we possess in Holy Writ.' From the report of a conference of church leaders held in Pretoria in November, 1953. Geneva: *Ecumenical Press Service*, Jan. 15th, 1954, p. 10.

A book with a *mystique* that still has power over us in spite of having lost its foundations, a book which empirical evidence shows to have power both for evil and for good. These are factors to be taken into account as we try to find a way of thinking about and reading the Bible which shall inhibit its power for evil and secure its power for good on more trustworthy foundations. The task is further complicated by the fact that our foundations must provide for both the theological and the devotional use of the Bible. It might be comparatively easy to provide for the former without the latter, to say no more, for example, than that, if we accept the Bible as bearing witness to God's redemptive activity in history and His education of His people in knowledge of Himself culminating in His revelation of Himself in Jesus Christ, we have enough on which to build our dogmatic theology. But this would be of little use to those who are not theologians and whose need is to be able to turn to the Bible for the nourishment of their spiritual life. In recent years I have become acutely conscious of this problem. For a quarter of a century, as successively a member of two Cathedral chapters, I have taken part in daily public worship according to the Prayer Book of the Church of England. Over and over again, as I have myself read, or have heard others read, the portions of Scripture appointed for the day, I have found myself asking: 'What on earth can we—I, the professional theologian, and these fellow-worshippers in the congregation who have no such pretensions—what can we be expected to draw from these passages for the sustenance of our souls?'

This, it seems to me, is the problem as it confronts us to-day. Whether in the present state of our knowledge it is possible to arrive at a satisfactory solution, I do not know. I offer what follows as a contribution towards that end, in the hope that discovery of its inadequacies may stimulate others to more successful attempts.

II

To begin with I suggest that we should give up thinking and speaking about the Bible as though in itself or of itself it were the ultimate source of authority for any doctrinal statement in matters of faith or morals. As one who has been a professional teacher of theology for forty-three years I now publicly declare my hope that no pupil of mine will ever be guilty of using the expression: 'The Bible says . . .' Ninety-nine times out of a hundred, when that expression is used, it means that the speaker has found some passage which he quotes as authority for the position he is maintaining, regardless of the fact that those who disagree with him may find others which support their views. In the hundredth case its use may be more deserving of respect: it may be based on a study of the Bible as a whole, and the words may be intended to mean that what is being said is in accordance with what Dr. S. C. Carpenter has called the 'Bible view of life'. Even so the phrase is misleading, and its use is to be discouraged.

It is misleading because it implies the ascription to the Bible of an ultimate authority which cannot rightly be credited to anything within this created universe. More than once in my last year's course of lectures I had to urge our acceptance of the kind of revelation which requires us to be content with walking by faith and not by sight.[1] I have argued that false ideas of revelation spring from inattention to this condition of our earthly pilgrimage, from demanding of our Creator that He shall give us the kind of revelation which will relieve us of this necessity. From the roots of this thorn or thistle tree come many fruits which men mistake for grapes or figs but which are really poisonous berries. Among them is the notion that somewhere within creation is to be found a source of ultimate authority which in truth is only to be found in the living God Himself.

This notion appears in different forms in different traditions of Christian thought. The largest single body of Christians seeks to

[1] Vol. I, Part I, iv, v.

invest the Bishop of Rome, as Vicar of Christ, with this kind of authority. Elsewhere in Christendom there is in some circles a tendency to set the Bible and the Church in opposition, as though they were rival authorities, between which a man must choose, to one or other of which he must pledge his allegiance. On the one hand it is insisted that the Church is founded on the Bible; it derives its title to be the Church from the Bible in much the same way that a municipality or a college may derive its claim to its possessions or its authority from some title-deeds, charters or statutes. Carried to its logical conclusion, this leads to a fundamentalist type of biblical theology; its *reductio ad absurdum* may be seen in some publications of the British Israelites, where the Bible shares with the Great Pyramid in having the same kind of ultimate authority that a lawyer ascribes to an Act of Parliament. On the other hand it is asserted that the Church is prior to the Bible. The Bible, it is said, is written from faith to faith, and the faith from which it is written is that of the Church. The Church of the Old Testament produced the books of the Old Testament and determined its canon; the New Israel took this over from the Old as part of its inheritance and added to it the canon of the New Testament. Under the guidance of the Holy Spirit the Church was the author of the Bible, and is therefore its authoritative interpreter. To be rightly understood the Bible must be read in the light of the traditions of the Church. The nemesis of this point of view is a tendency to seek to solve every question that may arise by reference to precedents in the past, forgetting that the maxim *quod ubique, quod semper, quod ab omnibus* must include reference to the insights of piety and scholarship in the present and the future. This mention of the insights of piety and scholarship remind us of yet more rival claims, of modernists who pin their faith on the researches of scholars and of pietists who invest with absolute authority the so-called 'inner light'.

I have maintained in last year's course of lectures that nowhere within creation is there to be found any attempted statement of truth which is not coloured, and possibly miscoloured, by the outlook of its authors. Those who seek to set up as rival ultimate authorities the words of the Bible, the judgments of the Pope, the decrees of Church Councils or the utterances of saints or scholars, all agree in arguing from the same false premise. In the course of the last half-century we have seen theologians rescued from the thought that when we say 'God' we mean simply the immanent spirit of the evolutionary process. He is the Creator to whose will that process owes its existence, in whose sustaining, redeeming and fostering care lies its hope of perfection. It is a poor thing to have emancipated our conception of God from constriction by so-called laws of nature only to re-enslave Him in our minds to the written word, the ecclesiastical institution or the private judgments of human beings, be they saints or scholars. We must think of Him as standing behind them and working through them all, using their tensions and conflicts in order that by their interaction He may lead us onward into fuller knowledge of Himself and conformity to His will. It is by these tensions and conflicts that He keeps our minds alive and growing. It is not His will that once and for all we should settle the general question of priority between the Bible, the Church and the inner light, and then put it comfortably out of our minds. His purpose in creation is not to surround Himself in heaven with the type of functionary whose mind can only be held together by red tape. He has so arranged things that the question we have always to ask, and have to ask over and over again as times and circumstances change, is this: On this occasion, in respect of the issue now before us, where is for us here and now the word of God? Is it to be found in the *prima facie* meaning of the text of Scripture, in the tradition of the Church, in the conscience of contemporary piety, or in the judgment of current scholarship?[1]

Our present concern is with the Bible, and for the moment we may ignore the Church, the Pope, the saints and the scholars. What difference will it make in our approach to the Bible if we

[1] In these last two paragraphs I have been largely reproducing part of a lecture on *Biblical Theology and the Sovereignty of God* given at Wesley House, Cambridge, in 1946 and published by the Cambridge University Press in 1947.

think of it, not as having ultimate authority in and of itself, but as being an organ through which the living God may reveal Himself to us? It will be necessary to consider separately what this will mean for the theological and for the devotional use of the Bible. And we must ask whether it is enough to say 'an organ'; should we not say 'the organ'?

Much that I have said in earlier lectures has prepared the way for considering the theological question, and provides the answer to the issue between 'an organ' and 'the organ'.[1] I have maintained that Christian faith springs from the recognition in Jesus Christ of God at work in His creation and that this comes to us from His disciples who, with minds conditioned by their spiritual ancestry, saw in Him the fulfilment of God's promises given to His people through the prophets of the Old Testament. Their insight, and that of the prophets before them, is not to be regarded as some kind of unique miraculous mental endowment. It is of the same order as the *flair* for diagnosis which distinguishes one doctor from another, as the gifts of insight which are given to some men and not to others in all the arts and sciences. We who accept their testimony do so because, when we understand what they are trying to say, it fits in so as to make sense with what else we think we know of our life in this universe.

Next there is the fact that whether we are dealing with the disciples of Christ, with the prophets of the Old Testament, or with any other characters in or writers of Holy Scripture, whatever they said or did or wrote is conditioned and coloured by the fact that they were men who saw with the eyes, thought with the thought-forms, and spoke or wrote in the linguistic usage of their age and culture. If we are rightly to understand the books of the Bible we need all the help that scholarly research can give us towards discovering how its authors and characters felt, thought, and expressed themselves. This is preliminary to our asking what is for us the vital question: What must the truth have

[1] See especially Vol. I, Part I, iv, v.

been and be if men who thought and spoke as they did put it like that?

For, thirdly, the real object of our study is not what this or that other human being thought or said, but what God has been seeking to reveal of Himself through the medium of their minds. Seeing Jesus Christ through the eyes of the disciples, recognizing in Him the Messiah who revolutionized the conception of messiahship, Christians came to see that He could not have been and done what they were convinced He had been and done if He had been anything less than God incarnate. The *depositum fidei* is not to be found in any form of words, but in the acknowledgment of what God has *done* in the history of this world. 'Christ gave His life; it is for Christians to discern the doctrine.'

For us Christians the revelation of God in Christ is the climax of the biblical revelation. It provides for what was to follow and throws light on what had gone before. It provides for what was to follow in that the whole subsequent history of Christian theology is the history of Christians trying to think out its implications in the thought-forms of their various times and places. We shall be concerned with this in later lectures. We have now to ask how far the light it sheds on what went before will help us towards deciding how to think about the Bible.

The history of human thought is the history of God seeking to make Himself known to us through human minds conditioned by their outlook, seeking to reveal Himself in the nature of the universe in general, and with supreme significance in the series of events which have their climax in the figure of Jesus Christ. On this hypothesis there will be an interaction between our studies of the Old and of the New Testament. What evidence we have for knowing anything about Christ comes to us from the New Testament, and comes through the minds of Jews conditioned by their standing in traditions of thought for which our evidence comes from the Old Testament. Jesus Christ was 'born of the Jews': we can only grow in understanding His mind and the mind of His disciples by learning to understand the

Jewish outlook at the beginning of our era. In this sense the study of the Old Testament is a necessary preliminary to the study of the New. But since the ultimate aim of our study is to learn what God is seeking to reveal to us of Himself, there is a sense in which the reverse is the case. It is only by the light of the revelation of God in Christ that we can sift the true from the false in the ideas of God which were held by men, Jews as well as Gentiles, before His coming. In this sense the study of the New Testament is a necessary preliminary to the understanding of the Old.

How, then, are we to proceed? First there must come what are traditionally called lower and higher criticism, attempts to secure the true text of what was originally written and to determine the date, authorship and relation to one another of the various documents. Building on this foundation we must next aim at exegesis, that is, at grasping as accurately as possible what at the time the writings meant in the minds of their authors and of those who read or heard them. Then, and only then, are we ready for the vital question: What must be the truth which has been striving to make itself known to us through the minds of these men and their writings?

While still at the stage of exegesis we can be learning what ideas of God and His activity, of the nature of the universe and of men, were held by the biblical writers at different times and in different circumstances in the history of Israel and the early days of the Christian Church. But if we are to compare them with a view to determining their relative truth and adequacy, we need a standard of comparison. So far as the Bible is concerned, this is provided by the revelation of God in Christ. But to say this is to bring back into our consideration the forward-looking aspect of that revelation. The only understanding of the revelation of God in Christ which we can use as a standard of comparison is that which comes to us as Western European theologians of the twentieth century, thinking and speaking as men of our own age and culture as we look back over the intervening centuries of Christian thought and seek to grasp its implications.

Once again we are driven back to faith in the living God as the link between past, present and future. He has been seeking to make Himself known through the events of Israel's history and His incarnation in Christ, through the insights of prophets and apostles, of scholars and saints. Still He is seeking to make Himself known through our minds, as we study their testimony to what He has done in the past and scan the world of to-day for evidence of what He is doing now. We dare to put down what we think we see because we believe that through our successors in the future He will lead men on to sift the false from the true.

In the chapter entitled 'The Time of the Church' in his *Royal Priesthood*[1] Professor Torrance says of the story of the healing of the paralytic in St. Mark ii and parallels:

> The account clearly intends us to see the theological significance of the fact that forgiveness of sins and resurrection of the body belong together as two parts of a whole. . . . The Marcan narrative, written for the use of the Church, intends us in the light of the two moments, the moment of forgiveness and the moment of miraculous healing, to see also the relation between the moment of the crucifixion of Jesus and the moment of His resurrection, the time of the Gospel of the Cross and the time of the resurrection of the body.
>
> The supernatural life of Christ flows into the Church giving it a new relation to space and time as we know them in our fallen world. To describe that Paul uses the words *oikodome* and *auxesis* where he thinks of the flow of the Church's new life as against the stream of decay and of the structure of the Church as erected downwards from the coping stone (Eph. ii. 20 f.; iv. 15 f.; Col. ii. 19).

Similarly in *The Dominion of Christ*[2] Dr. Thornton prefaces his exposition of New Testament theology with phrases like 'the apostolic writers have no doubt'. I personally doubt whether the ideas attributed to the evangelists and St. Paul in these books ever entered their minds, and 'the narrative intends us to see' is the same kind of improper mode of expression as 'The Bible says'.

[1] Edinburgh, 1955, pp. 47, 49. [2] London, 1952, e.g., p. 4.

If Torrance and Thornton are right in their theological understanding of the Scriptures, it would be more in keeping with God's method of revelation to say that in this twentieth century the Holy Spirit, who inspired the biblical writers to put down what they saw in the terms of their own thought and language, has now inspired these scholars to open our eyes to points hitherto unnoticed by human minds. If they are not, it will be for others, now or later, to produce more convincing expositions.

For theology the Bible is an organ of divine revelation in that it is the record of God educating our spiritual ancestors in knowledge of Himself. It should be noted that to say this is not to say that in the Old Testament we can trace a steady chronological advance in apprehension of truth and correction of error. In the days of my youth this view was popular among those who wished to commend the Bible as a manual of so-called 'progressive revelation'. But further study of the documents has shown that it is impossible to establish any such correlation between their dates and their insights—which is what we should expect, for in no field of study does human knowledge progress by steady chronological advance. The revelatory value of passages in Old Testament documents is not to be judged by whether they occur in earlier or later documents, but by their consistency with the revelation of God in Christ.

Even so, so long as what we are looking for is a manual of information about the nature of God, the Bible for us can never pass on from being *an* organ to being *the* organ of revelation. It would be difficult, if not impossible, to prove that in the Bible there is teaching about the nature of God and His will for man to which no parallel can be found elsewhere. One remembers with what sense of shock Major Yeats Brown discovered in sacred writings from India teaching which he had been brought up to believe to be uniquely revealed in the Bible.[1]

It seems to me that the only ground on which we can claim uniqueness for the biblical revelation is that to which I called

[1] See F. C. Yeats-Brown: *Bengal Lancer* (London, 1930).

attention in my fourth and fifth lectures last year. If we can believe that in the series of events which make up the history of Israel, culminating in the coming of Christ and issuing in the life of the Christian Church, God was actively at work within His creation, rescuing it from its infection by evil by a mighty act of deliverance, wrought out once for all and of universal significance, then we can speak of the Bible as *the* organ of divine revelation because it is the book through which we learn of this that God has done. The emphasis must be on the word 'done'. The evidence for these events comes to us through the minds of men whose account of them, and reflections upon them, were coloured by their outlook. When we have discounted this, asking our perennial question: 'what must the truth have been, if they saw it like that?', can we agree about the meaning of the whole story, that 'God was in Christ reconciling the world to Himself'? If so, then their thoughts and our thoughts may approximate in varying degrees to an understanding of what is implied by what God has done. That He has done it is the standing truth, the *depositum fidei* to which the Bible bears witness.

I speak as one who believes that we can accept the Bible as in this sense containing the *depositum fidei* of genuine revelation. As I have said more than once, this is something that I cannot prove. If I wish to commend the belief to others, all I can do is try to explain what I see and how I see it in the hope that they may be led to see it too. This is what I shall be attempting in the rest of this course of lectures. But first I must finish what I have to say about the way in which we can read the Bible.

The hypothesis these lectures attempt to expound is as follows. God reveals Himself in the universe of His creation, and within that creation in a special series of historical events. In both cases what He gives is material for study which we have to try to understand with such minds as we have got. He does not provide us with ready-made statements of what we are to believe, but inspires certain men with gifts of insight through which they are able to make advances in understanding and open the eyes of others to see what they have seen. This is part and parcel of His method of creating free finite persons, and is the means by which progress is made in every department of human activity, in the arts and the sciences, in all the spread of civilization. Among those so gifted were the prophets and apostles who saw God at work in the history of Israel and the Person of Jesus Christ. Through their writings our eyes are opened to see what they saw. But we see it through the eyes of men whom to-day the living God is inspiring to disentangle what He was seeking to reveal from possible miscolouring due to their ways of seeing, thinking and speaking. We are only interested in what they thought and said and wrote in so far as through it we can grasp what to-day He is seeking to reveal to us through their minds.

Christian theology is the study of certain things that God has done in the history of this world for which the primary source of evidence is the Bible. There are many beliefs about God which Christians share with the adherents of other faiths, such as that He is one, is the Creator of the universe, is good. Specifically Christian doctrines are those derived from the acceptance of Jesus Christ as God incarnate rescuing His creation from its infection by evil. Christian theology is not the exposition of statements taken on trust because they are what 'the Bible says'; it is the working out of the implications of certain acts of God to which the Bible bears witness.

So much for the Bible as it is to be read for the study of theology. Whether what I have said can be maintained must be judged by the use to be made of it in the lectures to follow. Now I must say something about the more difficult question of what may be called the devotional use of the Bible.

III

This question is difficult enough if we are only to think of the devotional use of the Bible by the scholarly theologian. The difficulty is increased when we take into account, as we must do, the needs of others as well.

Let us first consider the professional theologian. I may as well put what I have to say in the first person, for I am speaking of what is for me a practical problem which I am trying to see my way through. Now that I have come to the conclusion that for the purposes of theological study I must read the Bible in the way that I have been describing, how am I to look for spiritual nourishment in the passages that I read, or hear others read, in the course of Morning and Evening Prayer in our Cathedral church?

It seems to me that I must start from the fundamental principle that God Himself is the active source of all revelation. I am not listening to hear what the Bible says, but what God is seeking to say to me through its words. God is the one and only God there is, the Creator of the universe. He is the Creator whose method and purpose in creation, whose concern for our growth in true freedom we were learning about last year. He is the God whom we believe to have been incarnate in Jesus Christ, the same yesterday, to-day and for ever. This is how I must try to think of Him who is seeking to speak to me through the words that are being read.

Let us suppose that I am meditating while the choir is singing the twentieth psalm. I have learned from the commentaries that in all probability this was originally meant to express thoughts appropriate to a ceremony in which a king was offering sacrifice to God before going out to battle. The king brings and offers the materials for the sacrifice. The priest takes them, and in the first five verses invokes God's blessing on the king in the coming fight. Then as the fire consumes the offering, the king bursts into a pæan of confident anticipation of success through God's blessing on his arms. When I have thus put the psalm in its historical setting, and remember how I have learned from Plato that God is not to be bribed by offerings to grant earthly favours, and how the whole gospel story confirms this teaching, what is there of spiritual nourishment to be drawn from this psalm?

Or, again, suppose what is being read is the story of Samuel hewing Agag in pieces before the Lord in Gilgal, in 1 Samuel xv. In the story as told, Saul's sparing of Agag is clearly meant to be regarded as sinful and Samuel's savagery as doing God's work. Can I really agree with the writer in this? Should I not rather hear the authentic voice of God in the words of Elisha to the King of Israel in 2 Kings vi. 22: 'Thou shalt not smite them. Wouldest thou smite those whom thou hast taken captive with thy sword and with thy bow?'

This second passage is the easier to deal with. If God be the God of righteousness, the fundamental act of faith for man is to do what he honestly believes to be right and trust God to support him in it.[1] He may be mistaken about what is right and what is wrong. He may need further education in learning what kinds of things God does and does not like objectively to have done. But the condition of receiving further light is fidelity to the light he already has: we must not judge Samuel by standards illuminated by nearly two thousand years of Christian faith. If the choice before him, as he saw it, was between loyalty and disloyalty to God, he was right to obey what we must regard as his erring conscience. We learn to acknowledge the paradox that if a man does what he honestly believes to be right God will approve his doing the kind of thing that God does not like to see done.

So much, perhaps, we may see for ourselves. But in the seeing of it it makes a real difference if we think of ourselves as in communion with the God revealed to us in Christ, looking back with Him over His education of our spiritual ancestors. He takes us to share in the memory of His delight at seeing one of His people come so far in understanding and seeking to do His will; He reminds us of how we should be thankful for the fuller light that He has given us since those days, and that still His fundamental

[1] Vol. I, pp. 106 ff. and 145 ff.

demand upon us is that we should seek to be equally sincere in trying to do what we honestly believe to be His will.

So too with the twentieth psalm. We may not be able to be confident that our earthly aims are also God's ('nevertheless, not my will but thine be done'); we may have learned that we must not seek to win God's favour by gifts. But we can share in God's rejoicing at the sight of any earthly ruler acknowledging that he exercises his authority as himself subject to God. Only so long as this is so can earthly rulers be taught to grow in understanding how God and His will are to be thought of and sought: a lesson of which the world is in need to-day as much as ever. We are reminded that for all of us, whether or no we are rulers of others, acknowledgment of responsibility to God is another fundamental requirement of Christian living, parallel to Samuel's obedience to his conscience.

It may be objected that to read the Bible in this way is not really to be reading it at all. Instead of listening to what it has to say to us, submitting our minds to its authority, we shall be reading back into it meanings that spring from our own minds. There is, of course, danger of this. We must be constantly on our guard against it. But the true safeguard is to put our trust in the living God of to-day, submitting ourselves to His guidance so that what we find in the Bible may not be a reflection of our own subjective ideas, but what He opens our eyes to see. Here the Bible comes back into its own. For whether or no our minds are truly guided by the *testimonium Spiritus sancti internum* will depend on how far we think of the God whom we trust to guide us as the God made known to us through the theological study of the biblical revelation of which I have just been speaking. How this may work out will, I hope, become clear as my theme develops. What I am now doing is taking my stand on three principles: that the only ultimate source of authority is God Himself; that the Bible is at best the most significant organ of His self-revelation; and that what I said last year about the pursuit of objectivity, in the second and fifth lectures of Part I, is relevant to our study of it.

There remains the question whether this way of reading the Bible can be of any help to the Christian who is not a theologian. I do not for a moment wish to deny that God does at times speak through the Bible to men and women who read it without any theological preparation. As I have already said, the evidence of missionaries to this effect is incontrovertible. But most of us do not approach the Bible with minds so unprepared. Our Christian faith does not first come to us by our coming across the Bible and reading it on our own. Faith in God and in His revelation of Himself in Christ are things which we take over from the Christian community, and we turn to the Bible expecting to find what we have been encouraged to look for. If at present the average Christian believer would not be likely to approach the Bible along the lines I have suggested, if he would be inclined to say that to ask him to do so is asking something beyond his powers, the answer may be that this is because the church as a whole has not yet adopted this as the normal and natural way of looking for God's revelation and brought him up to look for it in this way. In the whole body of the Church the task of the theologians is to seek to set forward our understanding of the mysteries of our faith. If their studies lead them to conclusions with implications for practice, they must themselves try to live by them and commend them to others. Then it is for parochial clergy and ministers and religious teachers to pass them on to their flocks and pupils. I do not despair of the time coming when to learn the Christian faith will be to learn of the God revealed to us in Christ in such a way that the simplest Christian will go to the Bible expecting to hear God speak to him in the way that I have been trying to describe.

LECTURE II

God

I

LET me now take for granted four principles which I have sought to establish in earlier lectures.

1. The history of human thought is the history of God making Himself known to men through the minds of men.

2. The men through whose minds God has been (and is) making Himself known are men whose apprehensions are conditioned by their outlook. As a result, the history of human thought proceeds by what I have called the interaction of categories and evidence, meaning by 'categories', in this context, the presuppositions which condition a man's outlook, and by 'evidence' the objective facts which he is seeking to understand.

3. The Christian claim to a special revelation is the claim that a certain series of events in the history of the world is of unique and supreme significance for our understanding of the universe as a whole and of the meaning and purpose of our lives within it; an understanding which has to grow by the same interaction of categories and evidence. This claim presupposes that the God who is giving the special revelation in these events is the same God who is making Himself known through the universe in general.

4. In the method which I am following in these lectures, the conclusions we have drawn from consideration of the nature of the universe in general give us the categories with which we approach the study of the events alleged to contain the special revelation. We have to remember that, in this case, when we say 'events' we mean events as seen by what last year I called the eye of faith.[1] The witness of a succession of men who have seen the

[1] Vol. I, Part I, iv, v.

happenings as having this significance is itself a succession of events, part of the evidence we have to examine.

In Part I of last year's lectures I tried to elucidate the categories in general with which, as Western European thinkers of the twentieth century, we approach the study of the universe as a whole. In Part II I argued that it throws light on the mysteries of our existence to adopt the postulate of creation. Given that postulate, I went on to ask what we can learn from the actual nature of the universe of the mind and will of its Creator, and of His purpose in creating it. I propose now to treat the Christian claim to a special revelation, given in and through the events to which the Bible bears witness, in the same way in which last year I treated the idea of creation. That is to say, I shall be asking whether to postulate it will enable us to go further in making sense of the universe of our experience and in understanding the will and purpose of the Creator.

We are to take into account fresh evidence beyond that which we considered last year, scrutinizing it in the light of the categories which now possess our minds. We must begin by reminding ourselves of what these categories presuppose, remembering that in this lecture our aim is to ask what more we can learn about God.

I argued last year that we can only justify spending time in trying to think about the nature of things if we make an act of faith that whatever exists and happens fits into a pattern that makes sense, and that to make sense means to be such that we are content to have it so and cease to ask why it should be so. We can best make sense of the universe by treating it as expressing the will and purpose of an eternal personal Creator who must Himself be self-authenticating in His goodness, i.e., be such that we cease to ask why He should be what He is and rejoice to give Him our worship and adoration. As it lies open to our observation, creation is a process which issues in the existence of individualized self-conscious persons, and the irrationalities which it contains are due to God giving it the mode of reality required to make possible a community of such persons perfected through the exercise of freedom.

This summary of last year's argument should make it clear that the position arrived at has been reached as a matter of purely natural theology and is not based on any considerations drawn from religion or religious experience. It may be that to speak of the will and purpose of God is to use religious language, but it is language to which I have been driven by observing the actual nature of the evolutionary process and finding that it looks as though it were aiming at the production of this community of persons perfected through the exercise of freedom. We have now to take into account evidence provided by men who do not pretend to be detached and impartial observers of the course of events; to ask how far their seeing with the eye of religious faith either obscures and distorts, or sharpens and improves, their vision.

However much the detached observer may find himself using religious language, speaking of God in personal terms, he is not himself being religious until he seeks to enter himself into personal relations with the God of whom he has thus been speaking. Here, as on a previous occasion, I can best define what I mean by religion in words quoted from Professor Hocking and Dr. Clement Webb: 'A conversation of the self with reality as an assertion of kinship with the controlling energies of the world', and 'It is, I think, true from the start that what men have sought in religion is always communication with that which is supposed or suspected to possess within itself the secret of our life and of our surroundings, and therefore to exert over us and them a mysterious power which we shall do well to enlist upon our side'.[1] We have in our minds such knowledge of God as we have been able to draw from His revelation of Himself through creation in general. Thus equipped we are to ask how far this knowledge can be enriched by the study of what has

[1] References in my *Towards a Christian Philosophy* (London, 1942), p. 44.

been revealed to those who have sought to know Him by the way of religion.

But first we must consider an implication of the statement that the history of human thought is the history of God seeking to make Himself known to men through the minds of men. It will be remembered that we were driven into this use of religious language, into speaking of God, because we had found ourselves using such phrases as 'the truth struggling to make itself known', and reflected that verbs like 'struggling' imply a personal subject.[1] Now, whether we think of God seeking, or of the truth struggling, to make themselves known, or simply of men striving to discover the truth or to know God, we may well ask why there should be this seeking, struggling, or striving at all. Why should one aspect of the creative process be the requirement of this long drawn-out, and sometimes painful, effort in order that the truth may be fully and clearly known in the minds of men?

That this is so is one piece of the evidence that creation has been infected by evil at some stage anterior to the coming of man with his potentiality of wickedness and sin. On this general question I have now nothing of substance to add to what I said last year. The question we have to ask is how the actual kinds of evil which we experience can be related to God's central purpose to create us into genuinely free persons. 'It is not unreasonable to suppose that for the creation of genuinely free persons there is needed a world in which they can grow up amidst ignorance and error. Possibly we may also account for ugliness on the ground that, starting as we do, we need to be trained in aesthetic appreciation. God will no more be content with a parrot-like expression of conventional judgments in art than He will with a mechanical going through the right motions in morals. In the perfection of created freedom a man's acts must be his own acts and his judgments his own judgments.'[2] However that may be, my point at the present moment is this. If in general the history

[1] Vol. I, Part I, p. 115.
[2] Vol. I, p. 207. On the general question see pp. 212 ff.

of human thought is the history of the clarification of ideas in the minds of men through interaction of categories and evidence, and if we may think of this as the history of God making Himself known to man, we shall expect to find that what is true of the history of human thought in general is also true of that particular way of thinking, of seeking knowledge of God, which I have called religious. If we are to examine the Christian claim that the Bible bears witness to a self-revelation of God which is of supreme significance for our understanding of Him and of all things, we must set that witness in the context of the history of human religion in general. If the history of human thought is the history of men being forced to revise their notions, of their emancipation from false presuppositions which miscolour what they are trying to see, we shall expect this to be as true of their religious thought as of their secular.

II

'A conversation of the self with reality . . . with the controlling energies of the world.' 'Communication with that which is supposed or suspected to contain within itself the secret of our life and of our surroundings, and therefore to exert over us and them a mysterious power which we shall do well to enlist upon our side.' The manner of a man's approach to a power with a view to enlisting its support will naturally be governed by what he thinks its nature to be. Accordingly, from the start religious beliefs and practices have been coloured by what men thought to be the nature of the power or powers with which they had to reckon. They found themselves subject to forces sometimes helpful and sometimes destructive. If one were to speak in personal terms one might say sometimes beneficent, sometimes malevolent. Inquirers who have sought to track down the sources of religion along quite different lines are agreed that originally human ideas of God have this ambivalent character. It runs through all the various forms of religion which Dr. E. O. James has examined in evidence from Crete, Egypt, India and elsewhere[1]; it characterizes the *libido* which for Jung takes the place of God as the fundamental driving force with which men have to do.[2]

Not religion alone, but both religion and science derive from the efforts of men to enlist on our side the mysterious powers which pervade the universe. When to-day we seek to extend our control over the forces of nature by researches enabling us to turn to our own use the energies latent in fissile materials, we are in the direct line of development from those who in earlier times practised what we should now call magic. We may differ from them in that we have a better informed and more intelligent understanding of how these forces work, but essentially we, like them, are seeking how we may impose our will on objects which we treat not as persons but as things. Very early, if not from the start, there were also attempts to approach these mysterious powers in a more personal manner, to seek the favour of the friendly and to propitiate the hostile. This often took forms which we should now regard as superstitious. In so far as it is possible to distinguish the two approaches in the attitude of our primitive ancestors, we may say that our science has developed from their magic and our religion from their superstition. To investigate the former of these developments is the work of the historians of science. Our concern is with the latter.

The history of human thought is the history of God making Himself known in the minds of men through the interaction of categories and evidence. The history of religion begins with men seeking to enter into personal relations with powers that are thought of as alternating between friendliness and hostility. We have to take into account a further factor which came to our notice last year: the contribution to progress in knowledge made by men gifted with a *flair* for seeing truths to which others are

[1] E. O. James: *The Concept of Deity* (London, 1950). Cp. the following passage from Karen Blixen: *Out of Africa*: 'The Natives . . . had preserved a knowledge that was lost to us by our first parents; Africa, amongst the continents, will teach it to you: that God and the Devil are one'. (Penguin Edition, 1954, p. 27.)

[2] Jung: *Psychology of the Unconscious* (E. Tr., London, 1922).

blind until their eyes are opened by those who have this gift.[1] On the hypothesis that the whole process is God at work making Himself known, we shall have to think of all instances of this *flair* as gifts of God, as gifts of insight enabling men to make progress in the observation of new evidence and in whatever revision of categories is necessary for its assimilation. When we compare the history of the emancipation of religion from superstition with that of science from magic, we shall expect to find in it parallels to such names as Copernicus, Newton and Einstein. Here we must be careful. We must avoid making the mistake of thinking that the Christian claim to a special revelation rests on the belief that the Bible is a manual of unique statements of truths about the eternal nature of God made by men gifted with a *flair* for grasping them. We need make no claim for such uniqueness when, in looking back over the history of our religion, we ask at what points our spiritual ancestors were manifestly being led out of darkness into light.

From the period covered by the Old Testament I take for consideration four points in the doctrine of God: that He is one, that He is the Creator of all things, that He is good, and that the Israelites are His chosen people.

1. His researches into the origins of religion have led Dr. E. O. James to doubt the development of 'anything in the nature of a genuine monotheism' in primitive society. 'That such a belief ever existed at the threshold of religion, as Fr. Schmidt and his followers have endeavoured to maintain, is highly improbable.' There may have been belief in some kind of a Supreme Being behind and above the powers for good or evil with which men have to do, but it is with these several powers that men seek to communicate in their religion. 'To be effective gods must be ritually accessible, efficacious, and responsive to man through the established technique of a cultus. Therefore, while the Supreme Being stands alone, head and shoulders above all secondary figures—animistic spirits, lesser divinities, deified ghosts, totems,

[1] Vol. I, pp. 98 ff.

and so on—he never holds the field in primitive society to the exclusion of all other gods.'[1]

If this be so, then the significant feature in Jewish monotheism is not so much the assertion that there is one Supreme Being as that it is directly with this Supreme Being that in his religion man has to do. This is the point of the preposition in the first commandment: 'Thou shalt have none other gods *before* Me', of the destruction of Aaron's golden calf in Exodus xxxii, and of the relentless warfare against the cult of the Canaanitish Baals.

It may be that the full significance of this was not realized until well after the time of Moses, that to begin with the Jahweh whom the Israelites were to worship to the exclusion of all other deities was the Thunder God of Sinai and not the one Supreme Being, Lord of all Creation. If so, the worship of this Jehovah was a stage in the pilgrimage of the Israelites towards a fuller faith. We are not now concerned to trace historically the dates at which, or the channels through which, different prophets or other teachers became possessed of this or that detail in the doctrine of God. Our subject is the significance of their beliefs as they were woven into the structure of Jewish faith at the time of the coming of Christ.

2. It is with belief in Jahweh as the sole and only Creator of all things in heaven and earth—a belief which Gilson finds in Exodus iii,[2] which appears in Amos and finds full expression in *Second Isaiah*—that we have monotheism in the ordinary sense of the word. In so far as this is a doctrine concerning the unifying principle which we must postulate if we are to find an intelligible interpretation of experience, it is not peculiar to the biblical teaching. It is the form in which Hebrew thought, thinking in the dramatic, personal language which is natural to religion, expressed what was put in more abstract terms by the philosophically-minded Greeks. As Dr. Elmslie has put it:

> For the prophetic faith *God* meant what the word ought to mean—the only Source and Sustainer of absolutely all that exists. . . . The Prophets freely spoke of God as *Jehovah* because the ancient name denoted in their minds not a

[1] *Op. cit.*, p. 28.
[2] E. Gilson: *The Spirit of Mediaeval Philosophy* (London, 1936), pp. 51 ff.

national Deity, but the only God there is, whom Israel should revere. If the Prophets had known the term Ultimate Reality, they would surely have used it in their anxiety to emphasize how profoundly their sense of Deity differed from the utmost men had hitherto meant by 'a God'.[1]

Nevertheless, if the argument of my first course of lectures be sound, in thinking in these personal terms, and speaking of creation by a Creator, the Hebrews were being used by God to make Himself more truly known to mankind.

3. It was by the combination of the doctrine of creation with that of the goodness of God that our spiritual ancestors took the step which is for us both the most inspiring and the most embarrassing. How decisive a break it was with more primitive religion, and how embarrassing it was destined to become they were probably unaware—possibly because of the piecemeal way in which they moved from the adoption of one belief to that of another without sitting back to philosophize after the Greek manner on the result of holding them all together. By the guidance of theologians who are expert in Old Testament studies we can trace the moralizing of the idea of God's holiness and the parallel extension of Jahweh's lordship into that of the sole Creator. Each by itself was a coherent advance in reasonable thinking. It is when they are put together that trouble comes.

The belief in God's goodness had an importance both negative and positive. Negatively it marked the decisive break with the past in that religion is no longer to be concerned with the effort to get in touch with, to make friends with or propitiate, whatever mysterious supernatural powers may be at work in the universe, good or bad, benevolent or maleficent. Positively it meant that henceforward men were to treat their apprehensions of moral obligation as being for them the revelation of the mind and will of God. When Nathan told David the story of the rich man seizing the poor man's ewe lamb, when Elijah rebuked Ahab for the murder of Naboth, they prepared the way for the 'thus saith the Lord' of prophets such as Amos, Micah, Hosea and Isaiah.

[1] W. A. L. Elmslie: *How Came our Faith* (Cambridge, 1948), p. 369.

In the history of our faith this is the point at which the line was crossed between superstition and the beginnings of reasonable religion. God is no longer a mysterious being, so 'wholly other' that His incalculable will may be whatever results from casting lots or getting a wizard to peep and mutter. The fundamental act of faith is for a man to ask himself what in his heart of hearts he honestly believes to be right and then trust God to support him in trying to live up to it. It may be that he will turn out to have been mistaken. If so, the important point is that to have been mistaken in his moral judgment is to have been mistaken in his theology too. In morals as in the sciences, in metaphysics and in aesthetics, God's education of man in knowledge of Himself comes by man learning to recognize his mistakes and revise his ideas.[1] I make this reference to the sciences, metaphysics, and aesthetics because clearly the principle involved cannot be confined to the sphere of morals alone. To the Christian believer all human apprehension of truth is man by the use of his reason laying hold on what God is revealing; it is God making Himself known in the minds of men in so far as those minds are permitted by the conditions of their age and outlook to recognize Him.

This step forward from superstition to the beginning of reasonable religion is indeed inspiring. But when combined with belief in the unity of God as the sole and only source and creator of all that exists, it brings with it acute embarrassment, for it brings religious thought face to face with the problem of evil. So long as in their religion men were seeking to communicate with mysterious powers which manifested themselves indifferently as helpful or harmful, beneficent or malevolent, there was no need to ask how evil could have come to exist as it does in the creation of God who is good. Their position was not without difficulties of its own. Whether or no we believe in God there remains for the philosopher the unresolved problem of the co-existence of good and evil in one universe.[2] In her broadcast

[1] See above, p. 23; also Vol. I, pp. 106 ff., 145 ff.

[2] See Vol. I, pp. 198 ff.

talks Mrs. Margaret Knight was apparently unaware of the seriousness of this difficulty for the non-theistic philosopher, but she rightly reminded us of that which besets all who follow in the footsteps of those who lifted religion over the threshold into the realm of reasonable faith.[1] What more I have to say about this must be left till the next lecture, where at last we shall find what we may claim to be the unique and distinctive element in the biblical revelation. The point we have now reached is that God is no longer to be thought of as equally manifest in all the mysterious forces at work in the universe with which man has to do. His faithful worshipper must be prepared to find Him in some and not in others; indeed, to take sides with Him in antagonism to powers of evil.

4. This belief that the God who is the creator of all things visible and invisible is nevertheless to be found revealed in some rather than others is carried a stage further in the conviction that He has chosen the children of Israel to be in a special sense His own people, and that the events of their history are acts of God in some way distinguishable from His activity in creation in general. 'I will take you to me for a people, and I will be to you a God: and ye shall know that I am Jehovah your God, which bringeth you out from under the burdens of the Egyptians.'[2] Paradox upon paradox! We first become aware of the universe by experiencing it as a multitude of things and events. In trying to make sense of them by discovering how they can be seen to fit into a coherent pattern we are led to postulate an eternal Creator, and to look for our ultimate explanation in terms of His will. Now we find that those in whose religious tradition we stand think of Him as revealed in what is good as against what is evil, as doing particular things as well as responsible for all things in general. The question we have to ask is whether these apparent paradoxes are aids to our fundamental quest for a faith which will make sense of our experience, whether the beliefs involved

[1] M. Knight: *Morals without Religion* (London, 1955).
[2] Exod. vi. 7.

can be accepted as evidence of God making Himself more truly known in the minds of men. Before we set ourselves to tackle this question we must add the witness of the New Testament to that of the Old. We must have before us the whole biblical doctrine of God.

III

The outstanding contribution of the New Testament is belief in the godhead of Jesus Christ and of the Holy Spirit, with the consequent doctrine of the Trinity. The beliefs about Christ and the Spirit will have to be treated in more detail in later lectures. Our present concern is with the Christian doctrine of God as a whole.

Here, as throughout, we have carefully to remind ourselves of what we are doing, of the nature of our inquiry. For us the writers of the New Testament, and the men and women of whom and for whom they wrote, are witnesses to the truth which is seeking to make itself known to us through their minds. We are only interested in what they were consciously aware of thinking and believing in so far as it is for us a guide to what the truth about God must be. As we study the Christianity of the New Testament and of the Fathers we see the truth about God forcing its way into minds only partly prepared to receive it, minds in which existing categories have to be revised in order to assimilate the new evidence.

Jesus Christ was born into a Jewish family. He and His disciples, from whom the books of the New Testament come to us, grew up thinking of God as the one and only God, the Creator of the universe, the good God who had called the Israelites to be His chosen people. They also believed that while for the time being, for some mysterious purpose of His own, God allowed His people to be ruled by an alien invader, in His own good time He would intervene in history for their rescue. This was the creed of Judaism at the time of the coming of Christ, and the original Christian creed was that Jewish creed enriched by the conviction that this coming of Christ had been the fulfilment of the promise of divine intervention. The original Christian preaching, preached to their fellow Jews by Jews who had come to this faith in Christ, proclaimed Him as fulfilling their expectations of a divine Deliverer. When the Church went on to preach its gospel to the gentile world, it could not appeal to any such expectation in the minds of its hearers. Indeed, it was only too likely that the whole notion of a chosen people to whom God had made such a promise would be dismissed as a phantasy-figment of Jewish imagination. But there was alive in Hellenistic thought the idea of the Logos as the divine agent in creation. The Jesus who had been presented to the Jews as the incarnation of their expected Messiah could be presented to Gentiles as the incarnation of the Logos.[1]

To what extent to begin with, in consciously formulated theology, either Jewish or Gentile, Christians would have thought of Jesus as in the full sense God incarnate, it is impossible to determine. What is certain is that at Nicaea in A.D. 325 the Church decided that henceforward there could be no place in Christian thought for belief in a divine Being of equivocal status intermediate between Creator and creation.

During those first centuries, while preaching Christ as the incarnation of the Messiah and the Logos, the Church also bore witness to its conviction that as a result of His coming, and by His gift, it had experience of a new quality of life which it called life in the Spirit. At Constantinople, fifty-six years after the Council of Nicaea, it was decided that just as Christ is to be thought of as God personally incarnate in Jesus of Nazareth, so the Holy Spirit is to be thought of as God personally active in human lives.

Looking back we can see that what was going on, unrealized at the time by those who were taking part in the discussions, was a revision of the idea of unity. Greek thought reached its logical

[1] On this, see the illuminating contrast between the opening verses of St. Mark and St. John in C. H. Dodd: *The Interpretation of the Fourth Gospel* (Cambridge, 1953), p. 8.

development in neo-platonism, where the ultimate reality is the One in which all inner differentiations are absorbed. 'Even intellect has still a certain duality, because, though intelligence and intelligible are the same, that which thinks distinguishes itself from the object of thought. Beyond thought and the being which, while identical with it, is distinguishable in apprehension, is the absolute unity that is simply identical with itself. This is other than all being and is the cause of it.'[1] The goal of religion is a mystical absorption of the soul into a unity with the One in which all personal distinction is lost. There was no such thought of an impersonal mystic union in the Hebrew tradition: the highest bliss to which man could aspire on earth and hope to enjoy in eternity was that of personal communion with God. But in thinking of God as personal, the Jews thought of Him as unipersonal. Christianity began as a trinitarian religion with a unitarian theology.

When we grasp this point we can understand the controversies which led to the formation of the creeds of Nicaea and Constantinople. The Christian faith was this, that God had made Himself known to His people in Jesus Christ who had been crucified and risen from the dead, and in the Holy Spirit who bound them together in fellowship and was their guide. As heirs to Jewish religion and Greek philosophy it was impossible for them to be other than monotheistic. But on neither side did the idea of unity with which they had to work admit of essential inner differentiation. Hence the various experiments at explaining the new evidence to which the Christians bore witness in terms of the categories of thought with which they were equipped. For modalistic monarchians Christ and the Spirit were different modes in which the essentially unipersonal God had appeared in manifesting Himself to men. For subordinationists the divinity of Christ and the Spirit was theirs by derivation from the essential godhead of the Father; the unity was kept by making the Father the ultimately one God. But the main body of Christians insisted

[1] T. Whittaker: *The Neo-Platonists* (Cambridge, 1918), pp. 54, 103–4.

on bearing witness to their faith in the reality of the godhead of Christ and of the Spirit; it could not be satisfied with any explanation which compromised on this. The result was the formulation of the faith in creeds which, in terms of the categories of thought with which they were working, were a confession of contradictory beliefs—a fact which found clearest expression in the *Quicunque Vult*.

We can, I repeat, now see what needed to be done. Instead of treating the Father as the real one God and ascribing divinity to the Son and the Spirit either as modes of the Father's appearance, or as in some way given a share in the Father's godhead, it was necessary to put in the place of the unipersonal God of the Old Testament and the original Christian theology the tripersonal God who has His being as a unity in and through His tripersonality. There was needed a revision of the category of unity, the concept of the ultimate reality as essentially internally differentiated.

The Christian Church did not come to the doctrine of the Trinity by importing metaphysical speculation into an originally simple faith. The historical sequence was the reverse of this. The doctrine came by Christians, in defiance of contemporary metaphysics, insisting on bearing witness to what they believed to be empirical evidence of God acting on earth in Christ and in the Holy Spirit.

With the Christian doctrine of the Trinity we have come a long way from the beginning of the history of religion in efforts to communicate with whatever powers may be at work in the universe, friendly or hostile, good or evil. We have come along a road leading to the kind of idea of God that natural theology has taught us we must believe in if we are to be able to make sense of the universe of our experience: 'an eternal personal Creator Who must Himself be self-authenticating in His goodness'.[1] The connection between His goodness and the teaching of the Hebrew prophets has been made clear enough; something

[1] Above, p. 27.

further must be said about that between the doctrines of the Trinity and of creation.

I have argued that in order to make sense of the universe as it actually exists we have to think of it as brought into being by the will of the Creator, that our ultimate explanations must be in terms of His purpose, and that this implies thinking of Him as personal. Now to think of God as Creator in the true sense of the word involves acknowledging the fundamental and inescapable antinomy confronting all human thought: we have to think of God-in-Himself as impassible and of God-in-relation-to-creation as passible.[1] But we cannot think of God-in-Himself as unipersonal, for to be personal is to be living in personal relationship, and where God is all in all there is nothing and no one for Him to be related to. It is not for nothing that unitarian theology tends to be associated with cosmologies of the Greek rather than of the Hebrew type, to mean by 'creation' the activity of a demiurge imposing form on co-existent matter, rather than of 'the only Source and Sustainer of absolutely all that exists'.[2] The Hebrew prophets, it is true, thought of God in this way and thought of him as unipersonal, but that was because they did not ask philosophical questions and so become aware of the difficulty involved in their belief. Looking back we can see, as they could not, that the doctrine of the Trinity was required by their doctrine of creation.

More than once I have drawn a distinction between the doctrine of the creation and an idealist metaphysic wherein the universe of our experience is the mode in which the eternal God manifests Himself to Himself in forms of space and time.[3] Now consider the following passages from the closing pages of Professor Pringle-Pattison's Aberdeen Gifford Lectures for 1913:

> The accidents of language have combined with the ingrained materialism of our ordinary thinking to make the doctrine of the Trinity a supra-rational mystery concerning the inner constitution of a transcendent Godhead, instead

[1] Vol. I, pp. 68, 152. [2] Above, p. 33. [3] E.g., Vol. I, pp. 143 ff.

of the profoundest, and therefore the most intelligible, attempt to express the indwelling of God in man. . . .

For a metaphysic which has emancipated itself from physical categories, the ultimate conception of God is not that of a pre-existent Creator, but, as it is for religion, that of the eternal Redeemer of the world. This perpetual process is the very life of God, in which, besides the effort and the pain, He tastes, we must believe, the joy of victory won.[1]

On the general question of Pringle-Pattison's philosophical idealism I need only remind you of what I said last year: that it seems to me to dispose too easily of the stubborn reality of such irrationalities as contingency, freedom and evil. My present concern is with his misunderstanding of Christian theology. This betrays itself at two points: the use of the words 'supra-rational mystery' and the insertion of the epithet 'pre-existent' before Creator.

Take the second point first. It is true that when we are thinking and speaking in the temporal terms that come most naturally to us, we express God's transcendence over His creation as His pre-existence. Pringle-Pattison's strictures may be deserved by those who follow Oscar Cullmann in refusing to go deeper and think out what is involved.[2] But just as the Christian Church found itself unable to rest content with New Testament phrases about the pre-existence of Christ and was driven on by the logic of the facts to coin the timeless *homoousion*, so the Christian thinker is driven to realize that what is involved by his ordinary religious language is the antinomy required to give substance to all his judgments of value.[3] To believe in the Creator is to believe in One who here and now maintains all things in their existence, who in His eternal perfection is both in Himself impassible and in relation to His creation passible. The attempt to get behind the acknowledgment of this mystery entails the explaining away of stubborn elements in our experience. Therefore it is reasonable to try another line of approach, to acknowledge the mystery and seek for light in it by ascribing its own existence to the will of

[1] *The Idea of God* (Oxford, 1917), pp. 410, 412.
[2] See Vol. I, pp. 77 ff., and below, pp. 83, 4.
[3] Vol. I, pp. 132 ff.

the Creator. This is not to think of the ultimate reality as irrational, but as a rational Being who for a rational purpose wills to bring into existence a created universe, and to give it a mode of reality which admits of the existence of irrationalities.

To think of the ultimate reality as the Creator in whose will is to be found the ultimate explanation of all things is to think of Him as personal. The Creator who in creating creates the antinomy by voluntarily limiting His impassibility and entering into relations with the created universe, must in Himself be a rational Being who can conceive and give effect to a rational purpose. To think of the unity of God as the unity of a life in which are unified personal distinctions is the logical consequence of acknowledging the existence of irrationalities in the mode of reality characteristic of the universe that in our philosophy we are seeking to understand.

It was not by following any such line of thought that the Christian Church came to formulate the doctrine of the Trinity in its creed. In its historical origin that doctrine was an attempt to give theological expression to the idea of God implied in its religious practice. In their worship the Christians addressed both to Christ and to the Spirit a devotion which could only rightly be addressed to God. They had either to change their practice or to find some answer to charges of polytheism or idolatry. What they did was to assert as an article of faith a doctrine of Trinity in Unity which made nonsense according to contemporary categories of rational thought. Of them in their own time Pringle-Pattison's words would indeed be true: they made the doctrine of the Trinity 'a supra-rational mystery concerning the inner constitution of a Transcendent Godhead'.

Why did they do this? They were not philosophers philosophizing, but witnesses testifying to what they believed to be facts. The more they reflected upon the evidence of what Christ and the Spirit had actually been and done, and still were being and doing, in the history of this world, the more convinced they became that in each case they had to do with God. They could not give up their belief that there was only one God. But neither could they be false to the witness they had to bear. Let the philosophers make of it what they could.

We are now trying to take up this challenge in terms, not of third, fourth or fifth, but of twentieth-century European thought. In later lectures we shall have to examine for ourselves the evidence for their beliefs about Christ and the Spirit. The point I want to make now is this. Let us assume for the moment that they were right, that they provided philosophy with reliable evidence that has to be taken into account in our attempt to make sense of the universe. Then, if this be so, the incident illustrates the nature of revelation as I have been trying to expound it throughout these lectures.

The history of human thought is the history of God making Himself known to men through minds conditioned by the circumstances of their time and place. He reveals Himself in what He does and by inspiring men to grasp the significance of events as His acts. This grasping of significance is a matter of interaction between categories and evidence, and what I have now described as being inspired by God is what earlier on I have called being gifted with a *flair* for diagnosis.[1] The witness that the Christians bore to Christ and the Spirit was evidence of their interpretation of certain historical events. There lay behind it a series of other interpretations of events, each involving, in the continued process of interaction, the reconsideration of existing categories. There had been the interpretation of Israel's history as that of the Chosen People of God; there had been the revision of the idea of messiahship in the minds of those Jews who accepted Jesus of Nazareth as Messiah. Now they gave evidence about what they took to be God's revelation of Himself which would not fit in with the idea of unity presupposed in the monotheism of their time.

I have traced elsewhere the course of the revision of the idea of

[1] Vol. I, pp. 98 ff.

unity necessitated by the evidence they brought, and will not go over that ground again now.[1] I believe we can now see that, so far from its being a 'supra-rational mystery', the idea of unity implied in the doctrine of the Trinity is the only one we can reasonably entertain when thinking about God. To this may now be added the argument of these lectures, that natural theology leads us to postulate a Creator within whom are personal differentiations. If this be so, it casts some light on the relation between God's revelation of Himself through natural theology and through the witness of those who testify to what they have learnt in the practice of the Christian religion. It is well known how once there was an astronomer who deduced from his calculations that there must be a comet in a quarter of the heavens where none had been observed. The inventor of a more powerful telescope was able to say: 'Yes, I have seen it: there it is'. In attempting to make sense of the universe of our experience, we are led by natural theology to postulate a Creator of a certain kind. When from their religious experience men draw conclusions inconsistent with what we have been led to believe the truth must be, we have to examine afresh the relative value of their testimony and of our reasoning. But when their witness dovetails into the position to which our argument has led us, then it is reasonable to believe that the interaction of categories and evidence has borne fruit of value both for the pursuit of philosophy and for the practice of religion.

One further point. If the history of human thought be the history of God making Himself known in the minds of men, it has both a negative and a positive aspect. Deeper and fuller grasp of the truth is only achieved at the cost of stripping away presuppositions which miscolour our apprehension of it. This is as true of our understanding the Christian revelation as of the history of human thought in general. What God has done in Christ stands for ever as the enduring *depositum fidei* of the

[1] *The Doctrine of the Trinity* (London, 1943); *Journal of Theological Studies*, Vol. V, Pt. i, April 1964, p.49.

revelation. Our understanding of it grows as we learn to discount the miscolourings of our predecessors, leaving it to those who shall follow us to discount our own. We shall find reason to think that we in our time, after nearly two thousand years of Christian history, may be only beginning to know what Christianity really is.

LECTURE III

God and Evil

I

A YEAR ago we were considering some of the problems presented by the existence of evil to natural theology in general, apart from the Christian revelation.[1] The analysis of our experience showed that we have to recognize the reality within creation of four kinds of evil: ignorance, ugliness, wickedness and suffering. I then argued that if we are to be able to make sense of all these, it must be on the ground that somehow or other each is incidental to the Creator's central purpose to create a community of persons endowed with genuine freedom. I made some suggestions about this, but had to conclude that 'we look out from the sphere of our immediate experience in which we can see this more or less clearly, peering into a world around in which there is much that is obscure'. We have now added one point of detail to last year's statement of the problem, that the evil of ignorance is manifested in the fact that the history of human thought is the history of men struggling for rescue from webs of erroneous presuppositions which miscolour their apprehensions of truth.[2]

This year we have to ask how far the witness of the Christian revelation fits in with these conclusions of natural theology in general, and whether it can carry us any further towards an understanding of the mystery of evil. But first there is something more to be said about the relative insistence of the problem on the minds of Christians and non-Christians, of those who profess belief in God and those who do not.

At the risk of being tedious, let me repeat once again my reasons for holding that we can only ignore the problem at the

[1] Vol. I, Lecture IX. [2] Above, pp. 29 ff.

cost of abating the rigour of our thinking. We set out to try to make sense of the universe, of what we experience as actually existing and happening in this world of space and time. In order to make sense, everything that exists and happens must somehow or other be fitted into a pattern that approves itself to our minds as good, as such that we are content to have it so and question it no further. Among the things that are to be fitted in are the various kinds of evil. We cannot hope to dispose of them by finding a point of view from which they may be seen to be either unreal or good in disguise. Unless we can find some other way of fitting them in we have to admit that it is impossible to make sense of the universe, an admission which hamstrings all inquiry after truth, and leaves scientists to be the tools of existentialist dictators. To ignore this dilemma betrays insufficiently rigorous thinking.

If we compare the development of Greek philosophical thought from the Ionians to Socrates and Plato with that of Hebrew religious thought from early polytheism to the prophetic faith, we find that both leave to their successors the heritage of this dilemma. The difference between the secular philosopher and the Christian believer is that the latter, because of the nature of his belief in God, feels the pressure of it the more acutely. We are often reminded of how it weighed upon the mind of St. Augustine,[1] and I have a vivid recollection of an evening I once spent in Albany, New York, at the house of the late Archdeacon Guy Purdy. He had invited me to spend with him the four hours or so which I had to wait between trains, and had asked in some three or four of the neighbouring clergy to meet me. The talk turned on this problem of evil. We exercised our ingenuity in trying to find ways of approach which might lead, if not to the solving of it, at least to the easing of the burden. Now one of us, and now another, would make a suggestion, which was seized upon and examined, its inadequacy discovered and exposed. When towards midnight I had to leave for the station we

[1] E.g., in M. Knight, *op. cit.*, doubtless referring to *De Ordine* I.

confessed ourselves still baffled and unsatisfied. I came away encouraged by the thought that in no gathering of students of philosophy, or of any other subject, had I ever found a more rigorous refusal to be satisfied with anything that would cover over or evade the issue than in this group of my brother clergy. From that day to this I have found it difficult to restrain my impatience whenever I hear it said that Christians cherish the comfort of blindness to the problem of evil. The truth is that of all men they feel it most acutely and are troubled by it most deeply, because from the nature of their faith in God they are jealous for His honour. The secular philosopher, while forced to confess that he can give no satisfactory explanation of the co-existence of good and evil in one universe, can coolly and dispassionately put the matter aside as one on which reasonable men must maintain an attitude of suspended judgment. He cannot, it is true, be entirely unconcerned about the fundamental question on which the value of all his thinking turns, the question whether it is possible to make sense of the universe. But the act of faith on which all thinking is based obtrudes itself more insistently on the mind when the faith is consciously acknowledged as faith in God.

It is not surprising, therefore, that when we study the history of Christian thought we see repeated efforts by Christian thinkers to relieve God of any responsibility for the evils which infect His creation. We saw last year that in secular thought there are three lines along which a solution of the problem is pursued: (*a*) the explanation away of evil as unreal; (*b*) the explanation away of the distinction between good and evil as unreal; and (*c*) the acknowledgment of an eternal dualism.[1] Of these three hypotheses, which between them apparently exhaust the possible ways of accounting for the co-existence of good and evil, two at least appear, clad in religious garb, in Christian attempts to justify the ways of God to man.

(*a*) I said last year what I have to say about this hypothesis as

[1] Vol. I, pp. 199 ff.

it appears in traditional Thomist theology. Its persistence in spite of its inadequacy is evidence of the continued uneasiness produced in the Christian mind by the existence of the problem. Until the holes in it are discovered, it appears to swimmers struggling in a sea of doubt as a raft on which they may climb and rest in safety.

(*b*) The attempt to solve the problem of evil by explaining away the distinction between good and evil can take either of two forms. One is the hypothesis that the ultimate reality is, in Nietzsche's phrase, 'Beyond good and evil'. God, if there be a god, must be thought of as neutral, equally manifested in what we think good and what we think bad. The other is to maintain that while the distinction may be a real one for God as well as for man, we men in our blindness are incapable of drawing it in a way that would be valid for Him. Here we see through a glass darkly. When we know even as we are known we shall find that our distinctions were mistaken, and that what we thought to be the problem of evil was really no problem at all.

The Christian cannot avail himself of the first of these expedients. To do so would bring no advance in understanding; it would be a reversion to the primitive religion out of which his ancestors were led by the Hebrew prophets. He would resolve the difficulty inherent in his Christian faith by ceasing to be a Christian. Nor would he be in any better case if he tried to make use of the second. As I have already argued, God's revelation of Himself in judgments of value is on a par with that in judgments of fact. It is true that all our judgments are provisional, subject to revision by those who will be able to dispel our miscolouring. But unless we are willing to put our trust in what it has been given to us to see, we have no faith in such revelation as God has thought fit to give us. To hold that I am to be prepared to wake up in the next world and discover that I had been mistaken in rating unselfishness above selfishness and honesty above low cunning is to make nonsense of any claim that the Bible bears witness to God's revelation of Himself.[1]

[1] See Vol. I, pp. 106 ff., 145 ff.; above, p. 34; and below, p. 180. Also my *Doctrine of the Atonement*, pp. 143 ff.

In spite of all this, some Christian theologians try to deal with the problem of evil on these lines. A recent instance is to be found in Bishop Anders Nygren's commentary on Romans ix. 14–29. To the suggestion that God has acted unjustly St. Paul replies: 'Nay, but, O man, who art thou that repliest against God? Shall the thing formed say to him that formed it, Why didst thou make me thus? Or hath not the potter right over the clay, from the same clay to make one part a vessel unto honour, and another a vessel unto dishonour?' At first sight that certainly looks as though St. Paul were denying the validity of any of our moral judgments, were saying that good and evil are whatever God says they are, that we simply have to take what He gives and ask no questions. But, as Sanday and Headlam point out, this passage is part of a sustained argument which does not reach its conclusion until the end of Chapter xi. The sequence of thought is that while, in virtue of being our Creator, God might have taken that line, as a matter of fact He has not done so, but has enabled us to see that His rejection of the Jews was incidental to His beneficent purpose of saving all mankind. The three chapters are a carefully worked out theodicy. Bishop Nygren, however, ignoring the bearing of the whole argument on our understanding of its first step, writes as follows:

> The question asked comes quite close to the traditional issue in theodicy. It is of particular interest to see how Paul, by his answer, completely rejects the issue. Otherwise we should have expected that, when the question was raised, he would have presented an array of arguments to defend the righteousness of God. But there is not a trace of that in Paul. We get the impression that the problem of theodicy does not even exist for him—and that for good reasons. For there is a basic fault in all that concerns theodicy: it measures God by human standards. But when man sets out to judge God's dealings by man's own standards, the results cannot be other than the conclusion that God's goodness is faulty.[1]

In view of much that I have said in earlier lectures I need not linger now to expose the confusion of thought displayed in these last few lines, or their inconsistency with the revelation that God

[1] A. Nygren: *Commentary on Romans* (London, 1952), p. 365.

has actually thought fit to give us. I have quoted them to illustrate the pressure of the problem of evil on Christian minds. It is a counsel of despair to seek to escape from the need of a theodicy by denying its legitimacy.

(*c*) I have said that of the three possible ways of explaining the relation between good and evil, 'two at least appear in Christian attempts to justify the ways of God to man'. I said 'at least' because of the third, the acknowledgment of an ultimate dualism, I have not found a clear instance to present from modern theological writing. If there were such a theology it would, I suppose, take the form of a modernized version of second-century marcionism or third-century manichaeism. The Christian Church rejected both the manichaean attribution of the evil in creation to a source independent of God and Marcion's antithesis between the good God of the New Testament and the tyrannical creator God of the Old. Under the pressure of the problem of evil Christians are always subject to the temptation to be false to their monotheism by seeking relief along these lines, and of late years in some religious teaching there has been a christocentric emphasis so excessive as to imply, if thought out to its logical conclusion, a theology of this kind—teaching reflected in the reported saying of a learner: 'If Jesus had been God, there would not have been any Crucifixion'. But so far as I know responsible Christian theologians have avoided committing themselves to this position by drawing out these implications. In his explicit revival of such dualism H. G. Wells opened his preface with the statement that his belief 'is not orthodox Christianity; it is not, indeed, Christianity at all'.[1]

I have said enough to show how persistently the Christian mind is troubled by the problem of evil, what strenuous efforts it has made, and continues to make, to struggle with it. In so doing I have indicated various lines along which solutions have been sought. Let it be clearly understood that in what follows I do not claim to have found the solution we are all seeking. We

[1] H. G. Wells: *God the Invisible King* (London, 1917), p. ix.

are still in the position of men peering into a world in which much is obscure, asking to what extent the rays of the light that is given us will enable our mental eyes to penetrate the surrounding darkness. But I want to suggest that from the Christian revelation there shine out certain rays of light of which full advantage has not hitherto been taken. It is as though to Christian thinkers, thinking along lines traditional in human thinking, there speaks the revelation of the love of God: 'And yet shew I unto you a more excellent way'.

II

'It is not surprising', I have said, 'that when we study the history of Christian thought we see repeated efforts by Christian thinkers to relieve God of responsibility for the evils which infect His creation'. That God must be relieved of this responsibility is the presupposition common to all the attempts we have considered. If evil can be dismissed as unreal or explained away as good in disguise; if our value judgments are of no value towards the knowledge of what is good and what evil in the judgment of God, and to think that they are is arrogant impiety; if on a dualist theory the existence of evil is to be traced to some source independent of God—could conclusions be established along any one of these lines of thought, God would be relieved of all responsibility for the existence of evil in His creation. No longer would there be any difficulty in thinking of Him as both omnipotent and good. That, for believers in God, this must be the aim of their search in all attempts to find a solution of the problem of evil seems so self-evident as not to be open to question. It is not surprising that Christian thinkers should think along the lines traditional in human thinking, should make this their goal. Yet it is this presupposition which the revelation of God to which the Bible bears witness not only questions but denies.

Consider once again the nature of this revelation. It comes to us in the words in which the biblical writers set down their interpretation of events in the history of this world. We become convinced of the truth of their interpretation in so far as, when we read or hear their words, our eyes are opened to see the events through their eyes and we say: 'Now I see it for myself, and see that it is so'.[1] But in coming to see that it is so we see it with a difference. We see it as Western Europeans of the twentieth century, and what we see we see as the answer to our question: 'What must the truth have been and be if men who thought and spoke as they did wrote of it like that?'

In succeeding lectures we shall be considering some of the points which to-day we see with a difference. For the moment I want to concentrate attention on the central core of the biblical testimony, 'the belief that in Jesus Christ we see God at work in the history of this world, personally incarnate for the purpose of rescuing His creation from the evil with which it had become infected'.[2] I believe myself that this is the true interpretation of the facts, a truth of which, after scrutinizing the evidence, a natural theologian of to-day is justified in saying: 'Now that I see it for myself I see it to be so'. My reasons for this belief are irrelevant for our present purpose and must be deferred till the next lecture. Right or wrong, it is undoubtedly the central affirmation of the Christian creed. For the time being we must content ourselves with treating it as a hypothesis as we try to draw out its implications and ask what would be their bearing on our thought about the relation of God to evil.

In the history of Christian theology there have been many so-called theories of the Atonement, attempts to determine the meaning to be given to St. Paul's words: 'God was in Christ reconciling the world to Himself'. If, as we have seen, one form of evil is ignorance and error, and the history of human thought is the history of God making Himself known in the minds of men, stripping off successive layers of misconception which hinder them from grasping His truth, this forms part of God's rescuing activity. Already, in the sphere of revelation in general,

[1] See Vol. I, p. 104. [2] Vol. I, p. 82.

of what we can learn of God from observation of what has been going on in the universe, we find activity which may be called redemptive. Man's quest for the knowledge of God is met by such words as 'He that hath seen Me hath seen the Father'.

Some expositions of the Atonement have tended to speak as though this were the whole of it, as though man's only need were for knowledge and Christ's whole work could be summed up as revelation. This is true not only of those with an over-intellectualist emphasis, such as Rashdall ascribes to Clement of Alexandria,[1] but of the 'moral influence' theory which Rashdall himself favours. In this the explanation of the Atonement is that the revelation in Christ of the nature and depth of the love of God wins men back to penitence and obedience on the principle that 'man needs must love the highest when he sees it'. As William Temple has put it: 'We cannot go on wounding One who accepts our wounds like that'.[2]

So far as it goes this is true. But it is not the whole truth. I have argued this at length elsewhere and will not go over all the ground again.[3] For our present purpose it is enough to call attention to one point. The moral influence theory assumes that when a man has committed a sin, all that needs to be put right is the state of his soul. It ignores the fact that the sinful act may have let loose in the world's history forces of evil which will continue to work havoc long after the sinner himself has repented and been forgiven. This can most clearly be seen when the sin takes the form of the injury of one man by another. If as a result the injured man becomes embittered and revengeful, there is no telling how far the ensuing corruption may not spread. If God's creation is to be rescued from evil, not only must we men be rescued from our intellectual and aesthetic blindness and our moral sinfulness; somehow or other the forces for evil set in

[1] 'With him the chief purpose of the incarnation is the communication of knowledge—fuller knowledge of the truth about God and human life than the world had ever known before.' H. Rashdall: *The Idea of Atonement in Christian Theology* (London, 1919), p. 214. See also below, p. 227.

[2] *The Faith and Modern Thought* (London, 1910), p. 135.

[3] See *The Doctrine of the Atonement* (London, 1951).

motion by our sinful acts which have passed beyond our control, the objectively existent sources of corruption which we have brought into existence, must be taken in hand and deprived of their power of spreading further evil.

Somehow or other. I use these words because, apart from those which are inadequate through failing to face this problem, theories of the Atonement are attempts to explain the action taken by God to secure this end. The Christian gospel is the proclamation that somehow or other through the incarnation, ministry, crucifixion, resurrection and ascension of Jesus Christ, this has been done: 'God was in Christ reconciling the world to Himself'. All start from this, but vary in their attempted explanations of the somehow or other.

We are not now concerned with these various explanations but with that which all are trying to explain, the belief that in virtue of what God has done in Christ the power of evil to corrupt God's creation has been met and overcome. Indeed, our present concern is narrowed down to one point, to the use of the word 'done' in the statement that the Christian gospel is the proclamation of what God has *done*.

Consider this in the light of all that I have said about the nature of the biblical revelation. To us Christians the Bible is a medium of revelation because it bears witness to events in which we recognize the rescuing activity of God. The enduring substance of the revelation, the *depositum fidei* is what God has *done*. 'Christ gave His life, it is for Christians to discern the doctrine.' God seeks to make Himself known in our minds by stripping off successive layers of misconceptions which hinder us from grasping the significance of the evidence He has provided for us in what He has done. To accept the biblical revelation is to take the biblical witness to what God has done as the basis for our thought about what He is. What must God be like if He has thus revealed Himself in His action? In the last lecture I was arguing that acceptance of the revelation drove those who thought about it to acknowledge internal differentiations in the unity of God.[1] This revision of the idea of unity was an instance of God stripping off a layer of misconception. I am arguing now that our thinking about His redemptive activity should lead us to see that He is seeking to free us from the misconception that He must be relieved of responsibility for the existence of evil.

Over and over again I find myself driven to the conclusion that to accept the revelation which God has actually thought fit to give us requires a revision of the presuppositions with which we start our thinking. It is so with the idea of revelation itself. We have to be content with a revelation which is not the kind of revelation we think we would have given if we had been God. It is so with the idea of the divine unity. And it is so with the idea that if God be wholly good He cannot be responsible for the existence of evil in His creation. No one of us left to himself would dare to make such an assertion. It sounds like self-contradictory nonsense, and blasphemous at that. Yet to preach the Christian gospel is to preach that in His actions God has revealed Himself as claiming this responsibility.

Just as we have found that evil, and other irrationalities, are obstacles to thought which cannot be removed by thinking, which have to be changed in deed in order to become transparent to thought, so the Christian gospel is the proclamation that God has not regarded the evil in His creation as something which can be cured either by the communication of some explanatory truth or by the issue of a decree bidding the evil become good or be gone. It has been revealed to us that for God Himself evil had become such that it could not be remedied by any kind of word in any ordinary sense of the word 'word'. Deeds, not words, were called for. Something had to be done. God took upon Himself the doing of it, made Himself responsible for casting out the evil which He had allowed to enter in.

To say that God has made Himself responsible for remedying what has gone wrong is not, of course, the same as to say that

[1] Above, pp. 38 ff.

He has made Himself responsible for its going wrong. But to divorce the two implies a dualism inconsistent with a genuine doctrine of creation. In traditional Christian apologetic a distinction is drawn between what God does and what He permits. This distinction only throws the question a stage further back. It does not dispose of the question of God's responsibility for having permitted evil to become what it is. How can it help to say that by the nature of His redemptive activity God has revealed Himself as claiming to be held responsible?

We begin to see some light on the mystery when we put together two conclusions reached in last year's lectures: (i) that ultimate explanations must be in terms of the Creator's personal will, and (ii) that the clue to understanding His will is to see it as a will to create persons endowed with genuine freedom.

(i) We find it difficult to take seriously the conclusion I reached in my final lecture last year: that we think most philosophically and most truly about the nature of ultimate reality when we think in terms of personal will, when our analogies are drawn from our experience, admittedly imperfect as it is, of personal life rather than from the behaviour of impersonal forces, logical abstractions, or linguistic habits.[1] I have noticed, for example, in some Reformed theologians a curious combination of the statement that we know nothing about God except through the revelation in Christ with an acceptance as a fundamental principle of an idea of the sovereignty of God which is not derived from that revelation but is an *a priori* notion, taken for granted and unquestioned. My contention is that instead of arguing that God must behave in accordance with our idea of sovereignty we must learn from His revelation what for Him the exercise of sovereignty actually entails. To do otherwise is to seek our ultimate explanation not in terms of His personal will but of some impersonal abstract idea of sovereignty to which He has to conform. Once more we shall be trying to fit God into a metaphysical system which shall explain His relation to the

[1] Vol. I, pp. 218 ff.

universe, an attempt which we have seen to be inconsistent with belief in Him as Creator.[1]

I do not say—note this carefully—that our ideas of sovereignty are of no value in our attempts to think about God. That would be to fall into the error for which I was criticizing Bishop Nygren a few minutes ago. What I am maintaining is that we must always be prepared to revise our categories in the light of fresh evidence, that if the historic Christ be fresh evidence for our knowledge of God we must ask what is its bearing on our thought about His sovereignty.

Our natural theology has driven us to postulate a sovereign Creator and to think of Him as personal and good. By 'good' we mean such that the more we learn to know Him, the more content we are that He should be what He is—and more than content: 'lost in wonder, love and praise'. We have learnt to see that the essential character of this goodness is love of the kind made manifest in Jesus Christ, in whom we see 'what love might be, hath been, indeed, and is'. We are to ask how far this revelation will cast light on His exercising His sovereignty in such a way as to allow the evils in creation to be what they actually are.

The parable of the labourers in the vineyard[2] provides an illuminating illustration of the way in which our existing categories both help us to understand the revelation and are modified in the understanding. At first hearing it seems unjust that those who had borne the burden and heat of the day should be given no greater reward than those who had been hired at the eleventh hour. How can the ruler of the universe be just if this is how he exercises his sovereignty? But think of it like this. Imagine yourself to be a Christian who for many years has been trying to live a Christian life, saying your prayers, going to church, living a disciplined life which involves the denial to yourself of many pleasures and indulgences. Imagine yourself, being such a one, to be thinking about and praying for a friend who has no belief

[1] Vol. I, pp. 135, 143 ff.

[2] St. Matt. xx. 1–16.

in God, for whom life has been a series of opportunities for enjoying the things that you, because of your Christianity, have had to do without. Whatever your Christianity may have cost you, for the privilege and joy that have come to you through faith in Christ it has been well worth while, and you cannot help praying that your friend may come to share these too. Now suppose that while you are praying there comes into your mind a questioning thought: would it not be unjust and unfair for your friend by a conversion late in life to be admitted to share equally with yourself the joys and privileges that are yours through bearing the burden and heat of the day for forty years or more? It comes into your mind, but it is a thought you cannot think. You cannot think it because, if you really love your friend, you are linked with him in a relationship in which such questions are not asked. Just or not, fair or not, you *want* him to have the best that can be hoped for, in this world and the next. The parable opens our eyes to catch a glimpse of a world in which such questions have no place, for all its inhabitants are linked together in such bonds of love.

Our world is not like that. We cannot love like that, except fitfully and here and there. How, then, is it that we can have a glimpse of an understanding of what such a world would be? Because, as we have noticed before, when our eyes are opened our experience of imperfection reveals to us the perfection to which we can aspire.[1] At our present stage in the creative process, the stage at which it is only fitfully and here and there that we can love like this, it is usually, if not always, through feelings rooted in the sexual character of our human nature. From the experience of what it is sometimes given to us to feel in connection with those to whom we are physically attracted we can form some idea of a world in which we could care for all men as now we care for him or her. It is from our experience of *eros* that we begin really to understand what is meant by *agape*.

[1] Vol. I, p. 193.

Hear a Christian bearing witness to what he learns from the revelation of God in Christ:

> It is no happy guess of mine that *God is Love*. This strange figure on the Cross shows me love—thus and thus God loves me. In that depth and breadth and length, God loves the world.[1]

Now add to this another element integral to the Christian idea of God, that we think of Him as our Father. In its Christian setting this must be clearly distinguished from apparent parallels wherein to think of God's relation to the world after the analogy of human parenthood takes the place of the Christian doctrine of creation. Neither in the Old Testament nor in the New were Israelites thought of as sons of God in a sense analogous to that in which they were sons of Abraham. It was not in virtue of their physical origin, but of God having called them into a covenant-relationship as His chosen people. The analogy was not with the initial act of procreation but with the enduring relationship of the head of a family to its members as their ruler and protector. Already in Old Testament times fathers knew what it was to feel affection for their children as well as to govern, provide for and protect them. This enriched their thought of how God cares for His people. For us Christians the relationship between our Lord on earth and the Father in heaven, as we can learn about it from the gospel record, is the pattern for all our thought about fatherhood and sonship in heaven and on earth.

We are to think of the Creator as one who thinks and feels like that kind of a father and loves like Christ. This is what we learn if we accept the Christian interpretation of the events which form the substance of the biblical revelation.

(ii) We now go back to what we learnt about the Creator from the manner of His creation, that we can best make sense of it on the hypothesis that His purpose is to create a community of persons endowed with genuine freedom. His omniscience tells him that He can no more produce such persons ready made than

[1] L. Menzies: *Retreat Addresses of Edward Keble Talbot* (London, 1953), p. 133.

He can make a square circle: if He is not to deny His omnipotence by admitting that their creation is beyond Him, He must devise a method through which they can be brought into existence. From the harmony of His omniscience and omnipotence there issues the spatio-temporal process, the mechanism for the individualization of persons and the sphere for their growth in freedom.

Consider further what is implied by saying that our ultimate explanations are to be in terms of God's personal will. We need not assume, as sometimes seems to be supposed, that we have to choose between two alternatives: either to think of God as arbitrarily determining truth and values so that for us the words 'God is good' can have no intelligible meaning, or to hold that He is determined by some factor external to Himself, by some rationality which prevents Him from making square circles or some moral force which ensures that God cannot lie. When we postulate God the Creator as the ultimate term in our search for an explanation of the universe, we think of Him as the God who makes Himself known to us as He opens the eyes of our minds to understand His manner of working. When we think of Him as rational and good we do not think of Him as a characterless Being conforming to standards external to Himself, but as expressing His own essential character, as expressing that which He is. This is what is meant by saying that in God *esse* and *essentia* are one.[1]

We think of God as willing to create a community of finite beings whose goodness shall be the goodness of genuinely free persons. His essential character, the *essentia* which is one with His *esse*, is love of the kind revealed to us in Christ, and the word Father best suggests to our minds the nature of His concern for His creatures. Is it possible that when we think of God like this we can think of Him allowing to exist in His creation the evils of our actual experience?

Last year I suggested that we can go some way towards finding this possible if we think of the endowing of His creatures with

[1] See Vol. I, pp. 199 ff.

genuine freedom as central to the Creator's purpose.[1] The Christian revelation dovetails into this hypothesis of natural theology with its message that the God who has willed to create genuinely free beings has taken upon Himself the responsibility for whatever evil such creation may entail. To quote from my earlier work on this subject:

> . . . There is nothing unphilosophical in speaking of the evil in creation presenting a practical problem to God. In religious language, there is nothing irreverent in asking how, in the pre-Christian era of this world's history, the problem of its evil must have appeared to God as a problem for action.
>
> As God surveyed the world, He would see that the evolutionary process of His creation had reached the stage at which, in human beings, endowed as they were with the freedom He had given them to enable them to grow into persons, evil had taken on the form of immorality and sin. How could this world be rescued from its evil without infringement of the creaturely freedom that was essential to the creation of persons? Sin could not be ignored or connived at by the God of righteousness; sinners could not be abandoned by the God of love. . . .
>
> If we accept the Bible as the record of God's revelation of Himself, we must not shrink from the belief that He has Himself claimed the ultimate responsibility for the evil in His creation. If we seek to excuse Him by the invention of some theory which will account for it otherwise, we must expect to receive His rebuke: 'Get thee behind me, Satan: thou savourest not the things that be of God, but those that be of men'.[2]

I have spoken of the Christian revelation as dovetailing into a hypothesis of natural theology. We must not forget that logically both have the same character. The one is the interpretation by human reason of the appearance of human beings and their history in the evolutionary process; the other is the interpretation by human reason of the appearance within that history of the events to which the Bible bears witness. Those of us to whom the latter, equally with the former, approves itself as apprehension of truth, do find in it some further light on the dark mystery of evil. We still have to walk more by faith than by sight. But light shines into the darkness from the faith that the mystery we seek to fathom springs from the intensity of our Creator's care for

[1] Vol. I, pp. 203 ff. [2] *The Doctrine of the Atonement*, pp. 69, 77

our freedom. Whether we walk by the path of philosophy, of theology or of religion, we draw nearer to our goal when we think of the ultimate reality not as It but as Him of whom the prophet wrote: 'He said, Surely they are My people . . . so He was their Saviour, in all their affliction He was afflicted'.[1]

III

Here, if this Christian faith be true, we have discovered the sense in which the Bible is unique as a medium of God's self-revelation. It does not come from its writers having been inspired to surpass all other men in moral and spiritual insight, but from the fact that the events to which they bore witness were those in which God was surmounting the difficulties inherent in His will to create genuinely free beings. If in theological language we call this His redemptive, as distinct from His creative, activity, we must be careful not to press the distinction so as to think of it as an afterthought, a remedy devised to recover from 'a divine fiasco'.[2] The will to create persons endowed with genuine freedom includes within it the will to remedy their misuse of it in such a way as not to set aside but to set forward their growth in true freedom. The Christian gospel is the proclamation that actually, in the history of this world, God has been at work, and is still at work, doing this. We are not to proclaim this gospel either as derived from a divinely guaranteed manual of doctrinal information or as a theory issuing from the minds of men specially endowed with religious genius. We are to proclaim it as the true interpretation of a series of events, starting with the story of Abraham, continuing in that of the children of Israel, culminating in the coming of Christ and issuing in the history of the Christian Church. If we want to commend it to others we have to do what we do in all spheres of discussion: we have to explain how we see the evidence and ask, 'Cannot you see it for yourselves?'[3]

[1] Isa. lxiii. 8, 9.
[2] Robert Bridges: *The Testament of Beauty*, I, 476.
[3] See Vol. I, p. 104.

In saying this I am not intending in any way to undervalue the extent to which the Bible comes to us as the witness of men gifted with inspired insight into the truths of God. It may be that the uniqueness of their witness is in part due to the Hebrew race having been such as to produce men apt to receive such gifts of insight; and that this underlies the enduring value of the Bible as an aid to devotion. What I am denying is that the uniqueness with which I am now concerned in this lecture was a uniqueness in their bodily, mental or spiritual characteristics. It was the uniqueness of that to which they bore witness. Their insights were inevitably coloured by the outlook of their age and culture. We have to do our best to understand and allow for the colouring, asking what the truth must have been, and be, if they wrote of it like that. We grasp the true uniqueness of the Christian revelation when as a result we say, 'Yes, now we see for ourselves that this is the story of God rescuing His creation from evil'.

This is a uniqueness which does not require us to shut our eyes to the truth and the value of God's revelation of Himself in other ways and through other channels. Undoubtedly the Christian creed has in its content certain standing truths about God, as that He is the Creator of the universe whose essential nature is love. Moreover, if the Christian is asked on what grounds he believes in these truths, he will reply that they are implied by his acknowledgment of Jesus Christ as God incarnate. They are thus, for him, part and parcel of the biblical revelation. But they are not the specifically biblical, the specifically Christian, element in that revelation; and if in Greek, Persian, Indian, or Chinese writings, or anywhere else, he finds teaching which bears witness to such truths, he will welcome it as coming from the one true God who reveals Himself at sundry times in divers manners as and when and where He will. In order to maintain the uniqueness of the biblical revelation it is not necessary to assert that men who have never heard of Christ are on that account unable to hold and teach truths about God through which men may live lives pleasing to Him. That a certain streak of history embodies the unrepeated and unrepeatable acts of God for the rescue of His creation from evil is the specifically Christian content of the revelation, the gospel which we hold in trust to proclaim to all mankind.

More than once last year I distinguished the Christian doctrine of creation from the metaphysic of absolute idealism. On one occasion also I remarked that the time would come when we would be able to estimate the value of its contribution.[1] That time has now come. The account of the Christian gospel which I have been giving in this lecture brings out its similarity to the idealist teaching. In both the centre of interest is the activity of God manifesting Himself in the transforming of evil into good. When one sees this one can understand how it was that half a century ago this philosophy was widely welcomed by Christians as rightly interpreting their faith, that when I was ordained, a book prescribed to be read by candidates for ordination in the diocese of Winchester in the year 1913 was Pringle-Pattison's Gifford Lectures on *The Idea of God in Recent Philosophy*. Both then and now, to think of the ultimate reality as God transforming evil into good is more akin to Christian faith than to think of it as a meaningless interplay of impersonal forces inexplicably giving birth to human beings and human society.[2] Indeed, when I reflect upon what I believe to be the gist of the biblical revelation, that it tells of God claiming responsibility for having allowed the existence of evil and taking upon Himself to overcome it, I have to ask myself wherein this differs from what the idealists were saying.

As I have repeatedly reminded you, sooner or later all human thought comes up against the fundamental antinomy: how can we make sense of the universe and our own existence, seeing that to do so requires the acknowledgment of both their reality and God's perfection?[3] Where all have to acknowledge mystery which neither I nor you nor any creed, philosophy, or school of

[1] Vol. I, p. 39.
[2] On this see also *The Doctrine of the Trinity*, pp. 124 ff.
[3] Vol. I, pp. 68, 133.

thought can claim to have dispelled, it ill becomes us to dismiss with scorn any of those who have wrestled profoundly with its problems. For reasons that I have given I think that the Christian doctrine of creation enables us to maintain a truer estimate of the reality of certain elements in our experience than does the idealist metaphysic, and that the Christian doctrine of God, which enables us to seek our ultimate explanations in terms of His personal will, throws some light on the difficulty which that metaphysic was devised to surmount. But to these idealists, as to pragmatists and behaviourists,[1] although we cannot go all the way with them, we owe a debt of gratitude for their contribution to our understanding of the nature of the mystery with which we have to deal.

[1] Vol. I, pp. 180 ff.

LECTURE IV

Christ

I

'GOD was in Christ, reconciling the world unto himself.' For us Christians these words of St. Paul give the central affirmation of our faith. But in themselves they are not enough. They do not necessarily express the uniqueness which we see in the manifestation of God in Jesus of Nazareth. They might be consistent with the recognition of God as working in him in a fuller degree, but after the same manner, as in other inspired men. I have tried to describe the uniqueness we believe in by saying that 'in Jesus Christ we see God at work in the history of this world, personally incarnate for the purpose of rescuing His creation from the evil with which it has become infected'. This is intended to be a statement in language of to-day of what our fourth-century ancestors meant when they wrote 'Very God of very God who . . . was made man'. We are now to treat this belief as a postulate, asking how it will fit in with the rest of our experience and help towards making sense of the whole. We must inquire how it fits into the biblical witness to God's redemptive activity, and how it affects the fitting of that witness into our thought about His creation.

Our starting point is the New Testament witness to the earthly ministry of Jesus Christ. In my opening lecture last year I pointed out that for historical study the New Testament is primarily evidence of what the original Christians believed about our Lord. We have to ask what the truth about Him must have been, and be, if men with their ways of thinking and speaking wrote of Him as they did.

The first Christians were Palestinian Jews of the first century B.C. and A.D. Although they wrote in Greek, their ways of thinking were Hebraic and the background of their thought was the Old Testament. They believed that the Messiah promised by God to His people through His prophets had come in the person of Jesus of Nazareth, that He had been crucified, had risen from the dead, had ascended into heaven, and had sent His Spirit to possess His followers until He should return as Judge at the end of the world. It looks as though to begin with they thought of Him as absent in heaven and sending down the Spirit to keep them in touch with Him; but before the end of the New Testament period they believed Him to be personally present with them, 'unseen but ever near'. They were the true Israel, the inheritors of God's promises to His chosen people. And somehow or other, through His death and resurrection, the Messiah had brought them forgiveness of their sins and reconciliation to God. United to one another through their union with the risen and ascended Lord in the Spirit, they were a fellowship of forgiven sinners.

The gospels are evidence for the earthly life of Jesus as seen by men who had this belief and looked back on it from that point of view. They enable us to see that in their recognition of Him as Messiah they were accepting His own belief about Himself, though far from understanding all that it meant to Him. Before His coming, some Jews had looked for a 'Son of David' who should rally God's people, drive out the Roman invaders, and, from the centre of His kingdom at Jerusalem, rule the earth in God's name. Others looked for the intervention of a supernatural 'Son of Man' who should take up God's elect to reign in heaven and bring this earth to an end. Yet others thought that God would intervene Himself and be his own Messiah. Jesus was born as truly man in the Davidic line; He thought of Himself as the 'Son of Man', come on earth for the establishment of God's kingdom; but he interpreted messiahship as a call to exercise a saving ministry, to pass through suffering, death, resurrection and ascension to His work as Judge. Whether or no during His earthly ministry He thought of Himself as actually

God the evidence is insufficient to determine. The conception of messiahship provided the means whereby on earth He could and did claim a unique status in relation to God and man. It may be that a genuine incarnation involved that in His human mind He claimed no more than this. The developed doctrine is not simply concerned with what He thought of Himself while on earth, or what His disciples thought of Him, but with what He was. The truth may be that He could not have been what He and they believed without having been more. The history of the doctrine of the Incarnation in the first four centuries is the history of the Church discovering that Jesus could not have been God's Messiah and done God's saving work without Himself being God.

That Jesus Christ was a unique figure in history, being God personally incarnate, is the belief that gives the Christian creed its specific character. It is the ground of the claim of Christianity to be the true religion for all mankind. Much confusion of thought, springing from false ideas of the nature of revelation, has been caused by failure to grasp this point. We are not to claim that the Bible is a collection of saving truths transmitted from God through men inspired to be His spokesmen, truths which must be accepted as substitutes for whatever we may have learned of God from other sources. We are not to claim that our religion is supreme because it comes to us from men who had a monopoly of insight into spiritual truths. The only claim we can rightly make—and, if we are to be true to our faith, it is the claim we must make—is that once for all in history, in Palestine some two thousand years ago, God did something which is of significance not only for all mankind but for His whole creation.

For Christians the understanding of the earthly life and work of Christ as the gospel is the supreme instance of the truth that God gives His revelation by doing things and inspiring men to see their significance. But if this be so, in this instance as elsewhere, however much men may be inspired, their seeing is coloured by the circumstances of their outlook. Our Lord's disciples, Palestinian Jews of the first century, became the first Christians by seeing in Jesus the promised Messiah. The explicit recognition of Him as God was the offspring of the marriage of Jewish religious with Greek philosophical insight in the minds of those who were the heirs of both cultures. Before we go on to that we must consider further what the acceptance of Him as Messiah meant when the Gospel first was preached.

That first preaching is found in the early chapters of the Book of *Acts*. In Chapter ii St. Peter is represented as preaching the first Christian sermon to a number of Jews in Jerusalem on the day of Pentecost. He makes three points: (i) The crucified, risen, ascended Jesus is the promised Messiah (vv. 22–36); (ii) He has fulfilled prophecy by the gift of the Holy Spirit to His disciples (vv. 14–21, 33); (iii) The most important effect of His work is the forgiveness of their sins (v. 38). The first of these points is our present subject in general; the second will be the subject of my next lecture; we must now pay particular attention to the third. It is not actually mentioned in the sermon itself, but in St. Peter's response to the question 'What shall we do?' it is put in the forefront of the benefits to be received by those who are baptized into the messianic community: 'Repent, and be baptized every one of you, in the name of Jesus Christ, for the remission of sins'. This is repeated in the second sermon that we hear of: 'Repent ye therefore, and be converted, that your sins may be blotted out' (iii. 19). And again, when testifying before the High Priest and the Sanhedrin: 'Peter and the other Apostles answered and said: The God of our fathers raised up Jesus, whom ye slew and hanged on a tree. Him hath God exalted with His right hand to be a Prince and a Saviour, for to give repentance to Israel, and forgiveness of sins' (v. 29–31). A fundamental characteristic of the Christian Church from its beginning was to be a fellowship of forgiven sinners. That this had been the central aim of Jesus in His messiahship, and that through His life, death, resurrection and ascension it had come to pass, is the answer of St. Peter and the Apostles to the question: 'What think ye of Christ?'

This poses two questions. (i) Were they right about what had been Jesus' aim? (ii) Were they right in believing that He had achieved it?

(i) To accept as correct their understanding of Jesus' aim enables us to fit the gospel story into its historical context. It is not difficult to account for His rejection by the Jewish people as a whole: to the High Priests and the Sanhedrin, to the great bulk of Sadducees, Pharisees and Zealots He showed none of the expected signs of 'restoring the Kingdom to Israel'.[1] What needs to be explained is His acceptance by the little band for whom St. Peter spoke when he said: 'Thou art the Christ, the Son of the living God'.[2] When we read the Old Testament as the record of God seeking to make Himself known in the minds of men, we see Him seeking to teach His people that of all forms of evil their own sinfulness is the most serious, and that it is an evil of which they cannot cure themselves. We see the witness borne to this by the development of sacrificial worship in post-exilic Judaism. Looking back, we see the Old Testament as bringing God's people to the point of realizing that their fundamental need was rescue from their own sinfulness. But we also see that at the time only a few did as a matter of fact realize that this was what God was seeking to teach them. Among these few our Lord found those who had ears to hear, because He spoke to their condition.

During the past six or seven years I have been impressed by the fact that a number of older men, men of experience in various professions, have come forward to seek for ordination to the ministry of the Church impelled by a common motive. The world, they feel, is in a terrible mess. They want to do something to help. What they are doing at present, and efforts in other directions, good and valuable as they may be in themselves, appear to them to be superficial compared with ministering the gospel of Christ. That alone goes to the root of the trouble, men's need to be rescued from themselves. They may be few compared with those who put their faith in scientific research or

[1] Acts i. 6. [2] St. Matt. xvi. 16.

economic organization. But they do exist now. And they did exist then. St. Paul was clearly one of them. From among such men came our Lord's disciples and the Christian Church.

Whether or no, both then and now, such men are right in their judgment is one of the basic questions on which depends the truth of the Christian faith. It is the kind of judgment which one cannot confirm by demonstrative proof. All one can do is to explain how one sees the matter and say 'Cannot you see it for yourself?' By way of such explanation I would urge two things.

First I suggest that as we consider the state of the world to-day, we ask ourselves what difference it would make to the problems we have to face if in the relations between nations, races and classes we could eliminate such factors as national, racial and class pride, ambition, envy and greed. Only a blind fanatic could maintain that this is all that is required. If all the doctors in the world became perfect exponents of the absolute virtues of Moral Rearmament there would still be need of medical research to discover the cause and cure of cancer. Similarly there are industrial, sociological, economic, political and other problems which can only be solved through study of them by those with the necessary technical training and skill. But can anyone doubt the difference it would make to their prospects of success if such factors as those which I have mentioned could be eliminated? Then, if we are honest with ourselves as we look into our own hearts, we cannot deny that in our own lives, and in our relations with our fellow men and women, there are working those same forces which wreak havoc on the larger scale. To deal with these is to go to the root of our troubles. So long as they are ignored and left to fester our civilization, for all our efforts, bears within it the seeds of its decay.

Let us, secondly, see how this judgment fits in with what we have learnt of the actual nature of the universe as God's creation. It is the process through which He is bringing into existence a community of persons whose goodness is to be the goodness of genuinely free beings. From this point of view, of all the kinds of evil which beset them, the most serious is that which corrupts their own innermost nature and hampers them in their efforts to deal with the others.[1] The Christian gospel proclaims that in His redemptive activity God has gone straight to the heart of the problem and set in motion a creative process which is to work from the centre outwards.

If this, as we look back on it, is our interpretation of what God was doing when He came in Christ to reconcile the world unto Himself, would it not have appeared to our Lord's disciples, as they looked on it in the circumstances of their time, precisely as we find them bearing witness to it in the New Testament? Can we go further and find any answer to the question how it appeared to our Lord Himself?

This raises the difficult question of the nature of His human consciousness which we shall have to consider later. For the moment I must be content to point out that, according to what evidence we have, He thought of Himself as Messiah, He would not be the kind of Messiah most people expected, He called on would-be citizens of His kingdom to repent, He claimed to have authority to forgive sins, and He spoke of His impending passion and death as the means whereby that forgiveness should be made effectual.

(ii) The first Christian preachers urged their hearers to be baptized in the name of Jesus Christ unto the remission of their sins. They invited them, that is, to join the fellowship of forgiven sinners. The whole of the New Testament is written out of the consciousness of belonging to this fellowship, written by men conscious that somehow or other through Christ they are reconciled to God. 'I live', says St. Paul, 'yet not I, but Christ liveth in me'. 'Heirs of God, and joint-heirs with Christ.' 'Ye have received the Spirit of adoption, whereby ye cry Abba, Father.' St. John expresses the same consciousness by the use of the phrase 'eternal life'. To their testimony can be added that of countless men and women in all ages of the Church's history. One and all

[1] Vol. I, p. 204.

they ascribe their forgiveness and their reconciliation to the work of Christ.

Here we must carefully distinguish between two questions: (*a*) of their consciousness, and (*b*) of the objective fact of that of which they feel themselves to be conscious.[1] Of their consciousness of being forgiven and reconciled there can be no doubt; but we cannot regard this as the specifically Christian element in our faith any more than we can ascribe the revelatory character of the Bible to the nature of the Hebrew consciousness. We must be prepared both to welcome whatever revelation of Himself God may give through men of other faiths, and to recognize as genuine the consciousness of being reconciled to God in men in whose minds it has no relation to the cross of Christ. The specifically Christian element in our faith is the belief that somehow or other, as objective fact, it is through what Christ has done that this forgiveness and reconciliation are available, ready and waiting for all who repent.

I am not going to argue for this belief here. I have said what I have to say in support of it elsewhere.[2] In doing so, I have maintained that we can only justify the belief if we think of what was done as having been done by God Himself, God taking the necessary action to rescue His creation from evil in such a way as to set forward His central purpose of perfecting men in freedom. What I am maintaining here—in accordance with what I have been saying throughout these lectures about the nature of revelation—is that, if this be the truth of the matter, it would have appeared to our Lord and His disciples, thinking, speaking and writing in the forms of thought and language of their time and place, as we find it set down in the pages of the New Testament. To Him it appeared as God's work to be done, a work which could not be accomplished by words alone but must be wrought out in very deed by the way of the cross; to them it appeared as the fulfilment in Him of the promises of God.

[1] On this distinction see L. S. Thornton: *The Common Life in the Body of Christ* (London, n.d.), pp. 82–4.

[2] In *The Doctrine of the Atonement*. See especially p. 83.

The revelation of Himself which God gave in Christ required for its understanding a revision of existing ideas of godhead, of manhood and of unity. I have already spoken of the last of these;[1] I must now say something about the others.

It seems to me that within the New Testament period Christians were already, in practice, adopting an attitude towards Christ which implied the recognition of Him as God. This went beyond, but was a development from the relationship which had grown up during His earthly life. To quote from Dr. Easton:

> His closest disciples must have experienced in Him a sense of aloofness and of mystery. Dibelius has put it perfectly: 'If we search for a term that will express this unique relation between the disciples and the Master, we probably should not speak of a mystic bond . . . we should rather use the word numinous, as Rudolf Otto does, because here an apprehension of the Divine is dominant, which releases awe and self-surrender as in an act of worship.' And he goes on to say that, whatever criticism may teach about Mk. 10. 32: 'And Jesus was going before them and they were terrified, and they that followed were afraid', this verse expresses profoundly a fact of history. 'Here an intuitive apprehension of the truth struggles to find expression; it attempts to make men realize the zone of silence that lay between the Holy One and His disciples. . . . The movement that Jesus initiated had a *personal* significance, and discipleship had a *personal* emphasis. Even in Jesus' lifetime the disciples were personal believers.'
>
> All of this is profoundly true. And, when it is remembered, the so-called 'mythical' sections in the tradition cease to be a problem. In so far as they picture a Divine Being walking in the midst of men, who partly pierce His imperfect disguise, these stories at the most simply heighten the impression that the Jesus of history actually produced.[2]

I think it is doubtful whether these first Christians thought out the theological implications of their religious belief and practice. But sooner or later this was bound to come, and the early attempts at it were well summarized by Dr. H. M. Gwatkin when he wrote: ' "If He suffered", said the Ebionites, "He was not divine". "If He was divine", answered the Docetists, "His sufferings were unreal" '.[3] The discussions in which the Church

[1] Above, Lecture II, pp. 38 ff.

[2] B. S. Easton: *The Gospel before the Gospels* (New York, 1928), p. 161.

[3] *Studies of Arianism* (Cambridge, 1906), p. 6.

was engaged up to the Council of Nicaea in A.D. 325 can best be understood if one thinks of them as Christians trying to fit the new evidence provided by Christ into their existing categories of godhead and manhood. It was generally presupposed that God, being eternally perfect, is eternally unchanging, is (to use the technical term) impassible, while men are subject to change and to suffering, are passible. If Christ had been one He could not at the same time have been the other. Hence adoptionist monarchians, following the Ebionites, thought of Him as a man who on account of His super-excellent virtue had been adopted by God to share in His divinity; modalistic monarchians followed the docetists in treating the gospels as the record of a theophany rather than an incarnation.

These discussions took place in the Hellenistic world where the Hebrew-Christian faith was being examined in the light of its inheritance of Greek philosophic thought. Here attempts had been made to solve the problem of creation by theories of intermediary beings, through whose interposition it might be possible to think of passible creation as derived from God without any derogation from His impassibility. Could the Christian problem be solved by thinking of Christ, under the title of Logos, as the archetypal intermediary?

On the fringes of the growing and learning church were various schools of gnostics. I remember as a young man, more than forty years ago, reading a statement in a textbook that the gnostics were men who put knowledge above faith. Now for some years I have come to see that that, in terms of our present-day ways of thinking and use of language,[1] is the opposite of the truth. What the gnostics were trying to do was to fit the evidence provided by the Christians into a framework of myths based on a dualist metaphysic, myths accepted with the kind of faith that we should describe as fundamentalist. Meanwhile the Christians insisted that their responsibility was to bear true witness to what they believed to be the empirical facts, whether or no the

[1] See Vol. I, pp. 8, 9.

philosophers and theologians could make them fit into any metaphysical scheme. Through Christ there had been opened up to them a new quality of life, life in union with God and one another in the fellowship of forgiven sinners. In view of what He had done for them, and what He was to them, they could not think of Him as anything less than God. Yet He who had done that and was this was the crucified, risen, ascended Jesus of Nazareth, the genuine humanity of whose earthly life was clear from the evidence of those who had known Him.

When at Nicaea the word *homoousion* ('of one substance with the Father') was adopted to express the Christian faith, it marked the end of the period in which Christ could be thought of as God's intermediary in His work of creation. The Hebrew doctrine of direct creation by God had triumphed over Greek and Hellenistic theories seeking to evade the antinomy involved in the idea of creation by postulating an intermediary or intermediaries who should link the world to God without linking God to the world. Henceforward there was no room in Christian thought for any being of intermediate status between Creator and created. How then could Jesus Christ be thought of as both God and man?

This was the problem which engaged the mind of the Church in the so-called christological discussions between Nicaea in 325 and Chalcedon in 451. Again, as with the doctrine of God, the result was the formulation of the faith in words which in terms of the categories of thought with which they were working, were a confession of contradictory beliefs. In this the Chalcedonian Definition is parallel to the *Quicunque Vult.*[1]

II

Once again we are brought face to face with the fundamental problem confronting all human thought. How are we to make sense of the universe of our experience? We have first to postulate its creation by God, and then to acknowledge the antinomy

[1] See above, p. 40.

between the impassibility of God-in-Himself and the passibility of God-in-relation-to-creation. These technical terms of theology are best understood by seeing that their root meaning is preserved in the grammatical distinction between active and passive verbs. As God-in-Himself, the eternal Source of all being, God cannot be the subject of a verb in the passive voice, for there is nothing other than Himself by which He can be acted upon. But in creation He wills to bring into existence a universe to which He gives a relative independence. He can then be spoken of as the subject of verbs which express its relation to Him; when among His creatures there are persons whom He endows with freedom He can be said to be obeyed or disobeyed, loved or hated. In speaking of Him in the passive voice we assert a limitation of His impassibility. In creating the universe he creates the antinomy.

This was implicit in the monotheism that came to the Christians as their inheritance from Judaism. Jews did not raise the philosophical questions involved in their faith; and during the first four centuries of our era Christians had not grasped the fundamental issue. They had rightly acknowledged the truth of the Greek conception of the timeless eternity of God, and of the impassibility of God-in-Himself. But while occupied with the question whether they could think of Christ as God in the same sense as the Father, they had not faced the fact that the Hebrew-Christian doctrine of creation involves an antinomy in the conception of God which the Greeks avoided or evaded by theories which enabled them to contrast God as impassible *simpliciter* with creatures as passible. Because they took this contrast for granted they found themselves in difficulty in the fifth century when the christological question came to the fore. Nestorius rightly saw that the christology which ultimately found expression in the Definition of Chalcedon, was inconsistent with this conception of God.

I argued last year that the philosophical attempt to make sense of the universe drives us to this antinomy in our thought of God. It is not the product of obscurantist faith, but of thinking deeply enough to uncover the underlying mystery of our existence. So far this year I have been urging that in what they say of God as Creator the biblical writers bear witness to this same God who reveals Himself to us in the actual world of our experience. What I now want to add is that in their witness to Him as Redeemer we can recognize the working of one and the same God. We should not think of Christ as a combination of impassible God with passible man. The Creator, who in His creative activity accepts a certain limitation of His impassibility, for the purpose of its fulfilment accepts the further limitation incidental to His redemptive activity.

According to the Christian gospel this further limitation took the form of being, in the words of the Creed, 'made man'. For the theologians of the fifth century to be a man was to be a *hypostasis* of human *ousia*, that is to say, an individual being characterized by the qualities which constitute human nature. Their problem was to explain how One who as God was a *hypostasis* of divine *ousia* characterized by the qualities of impassible divine nature could also be characterized by those of passible human nature. What they did was to adopt a formula according to which One who as God was a *hypostasis* of divine *ousia* assumed the characteristics of human nature without becoming a human *hypostasis*.

We to-day, when we want to define what we mean by human beings, do not try to do so in terms of *ousia*, nature and *hypostasis*. Our task is not to try to think in the categories of our forefathers, but to re-examine the evidence they had before them in accordance with our own way of thinking.[1]

Creation for us is a process in which a stream of energy is organized into different kinds of creatures. Human beings come into existence as the conscious subjects of experiences mediated through bodies distinct in space and time. To be a man is to be living as the conscious subject of such experiences. In our own

[1] The following paragraphs summarize conclusions arrived at in Vol. I, Lectures VI-VIII.

experience of manhood we know ourselves to be very imperfect specimens of what a man might be. We are in process of being created into persons perfected in the possession and exercise of freedom.

The whole creative process is one in which in increasing measure, from the richness of His own being, God is communicating to His creatures the fullness of their created reality. Each of us comes into existence as the potentiality of a fully free individual person. To begin with we have little or no reality of this kind. We do not act as persons, but behave in accordance with inherited or environmental factors working in or on us. In order to become established in our reality as persons we have to accept the responsibilities attaching to the gift of individual freedom which God wills to give us. His making this gift depend on our willing to accept it is one element in the limitation of His impassibility involved in His will to create genuinely free persons. Throughout our earthly life our status in reality as individual persons is a matter of degree. In fifth-century terminology, we are not by nature hypostases but are in process of being hypostatized.

If, then, to be a man is to be the subject of experiences mediated through a body in space and time, what will it mean to say that in Jesus of Nazareth God was made man? It will mean that He entered upon the experience of living as the subject of such experiences. This could only be if it was done at some particular time and place in the history of this world. Christian belief is that that is what was done in Palestine not quite two thousand years ago.

As I have said so often, this is the kind of belief of which we can give no demonstrative proof. All we can do is to set down our interpretation of the evidence as we see it, asking: 'Cannot you see it too?' In this case the primary evidence is that of the witnesses to the earthly life of Christ whose testimony is set down in the Gospels. To this is added the evidence of those from St. Paul onwards who have borne witness to His continued power in their own lives and in the shaping of world history. I will content myself with quoting from two men of our own time. Father H. H. Kelly had not only himself spent some years in Japan, but through the Society of the Sacred Mission was in touch with the work of the Church throughout the world. I remember hearing him, when speaking of the gospel records of the earthly life of Christ, say that He was unique in that He had 'burst the bounds of self'. He went on to explain this epigrammatic phrase as meaning that whereas all other characters in history made a limited appeal to men of particular racial, national, professional or cultural affinities, in the Christ of the gospels men and women of all races, tongues, colours and kindred found their ideal. To this I would add the following passage from Dr. Charles E. Raven:

> Yet when, with the aid of the exact scrutiny of the documents, of full allowance for the characteristics of the narrative and the personal equation of the authors, of historical research and psychological analogy, we try to reduce this impression to a scheme of ethics, the attempt fails; the casket of moral theology only contains a selection of its dry bones, its life breaks out of the tomb. And if we try to produce a biography of the Teacher, the result is not more successful, as the countless 'lives' of Christ bear witness. Most of them have two qualities in common, their ingenuity and their inadequacy. They are composed with obvious scholarship, sympathy, earnestness; and yet vary indefinitely and often to the verge of contradiction. They set out to describe Jesus; they end by describing only a religious projection of their author. If they are the work of those rare students who have acquired knowledge without forfeiting imagination and freshness, like Dr. Glover or Dr. Schweitzer, they are often arresting and beautiful; but their subject will not, as our cousins say, 'stay put'; their categories cannot enclose Him. No other character (except God!) could be described honestly in such divers fashion; no other character so obviously transcends his interpreters. Such criticism of them is necessarily subjective, and may be wholly mistaken; but if a personal confession is permitted it would be this. I have learnt much from many, indeed, from most 'lives' of Jesus, and envy the knowledge, sincerity, versatility and insight of their authors. Each of them helps me to appreciate elements in Him which might otherwise be lost. But none of them in the least satisfies me as doing full justice to Him; and when I try to balance one against another, I see merely their incompatibility. Yet when I study the New Testament carefully, trying

not to shirk or explain away apparent contradictions, or to neglect any sound strand of evidence, the result, although it defeats my powers of analysis, satisfies my deepest intuitions. How the same Person could call the missionary Pharisee 'a child of Gehenna', and yet warn with the threat of the same Gehenna him who should call his brother 'thou fool'; how He could at once cleanse the Temple and say 'Do not stand up against the evil'; how He could both refuse and on another occasion promise thrones to His followers—these, like the problem of His teaching about the Second Coming or the meaning of the bitter cry upon the Cross, exercise the ingenuity of those who would make of Jesus a pacifist, or a 'Die-hard', a dreamer, or a Rotarian, a social reformer, a mystic, or an Apocalyptist. It is abundantly necessary so to attempt to classify and rationalize; each one of us must do it to the best of his ability, and each must help his fellows; but I confess that though there are times when I glimpse the meaning of Him and reach out to understanding of the paradox of goodness and severity, the systematizing of it all eludes the grasp. I can see and explain aspects; if I set them out they look contradictory: yet beneath the surface contrast they fill me with a sense of congruity and of completeness; if I cannot fully understand, at least I want to worship. That such confession is mere obscurantism will be the obvious verdict. So be it. Let the critic wrestle as I have tried to do with the problem. He may attain its solution: I can merely 'follow after', with mind lagging behind spirit.[1]

The more we Christians ponder over the records of that earthly life, the more we find ourselves driven to the conclusion that this was the life of no ordinary man, that it was the life of One for whom we can find no place in our thought short of acknowledging Him as God. In this we retrace in our minds the path which was followed by our fathers in the faith in the first four centuries of our era, reviewing in terms of our categories of thought the evidence which they assessed in theirs. On this I would make two further remarks.

The adoption of the word *homoousion* at Nicaea marked the realization by the Church of the philosophical implications of the faith originally expressed in the religious terms of thought and language natural to the Jews. In the New Testament early attempts to express the conviction that Jesus was no ordinary man but must be thought and spoken of as divine asserted His pre-existence. But when once the Greeks have raised the ques-

[1] *The Creator Spirit* (London, 1927), pp. 234–6.

tions which did not trouble the Hebrews, it becomes impossible to think of the relation between time and eternity as such that a period of some thirty years in time can be inserted into an infinitely long period of the same sort of time called eternity. We may have to continue to picture it so in the imaginative language of religious devotion. But for strict theological thinking it is clearly an advance to have substituted the statement of a standing truth for an extension fore and aft of time into eternity. The revelation is given in a certain series of events which all take place in time, from Bethlehem to Olivet. These are open to human observation. When we say *homoousion* we pass on from talking about before and after, and simply say that in these events we recognize the human life of One who is, in the fullest sense of the word, God.

In their attempt to explain this belief in the fifth century theologians spoke of Christ as assuming the characteristics of human nature without a human *hypostasis*. They were not intending in any way to minimize the reality of His humanity. They were attempting, while safeguarding that, to express the conviction that He was no ordinary man, that there was and is an essential difference between Him and the rest of us. Here they had their finger on a real point, and in the terms of their thought and language probably found the best expression of it that they could. We to-day, if we want to express the same faith in our own terms, would not speak of Him as being without the kind of *hypostasis* which each one of us has. To what extent any one of us has such a *hypostasis* is a matter of degree: we are in process of hypostatization. We should state the difference between Him and us the other way round. To be human is to be the conscious subject of experiences mediated through a body in space and time. That is common to us and to Him. But whereas at the conception of each one of us there was an absolutely new beginning, the beginning of a process which, if all went well might ultimately issue in the existence of a human *hypostasis*, He was unique in that His conception was the entry upon the experience of human life of One who was and is fully hypostatized as a Person in the Blessed Trinity. To the Christian believer His was the only human life that has ever been lived which had at its centre a fully real *hypostasis*. The mistake we make is to take our own humanity as the standard and measure His manhood by ours. We ought rather to measure ours by His, for His humanity, so far from being less real than ours, was more so. Indeed, we shall find grounds for believing that we only become truly and fully human selves in so far as we find our selves in Him.[1]

III

God who limits His impassibility in creating limits it further in entering upon the experience of life as the conscious subject of experience mediated through a body in space and time. This is the Christian faith, the doctrine of the Incarnation. It is not mythology in the sense of being a story whose only value to the theologian and philosopher is as symbolizing truths in some other order of greater reality, whether that be thought of as impersonal forces, abstract ideas, or existentialist piety.[2] It is sober fact, of the highest kind of reality attainable by our minds here on earth. I shall be arguing later that in the personal communion with God made open to us through that divine activity we reach our highest level of reality in living as well as in thinking.

'What think ye of Christ?' Answers to this question are attempts to account for certain actual events in the history of this world. Reflection upon them led our forefathers to say 'Two natures in one Person'. It leads us to express what is essentially the same interpretation as God experiencing life under human conditions. We may be able to dispel some of their difficulties by seeing that creation involves divine passibility and that our humanity is not by nature hypostatized. But it would be foolish to imagine that for us the doctrine has now no difficulties. What we have done is to transfer them into the sphere of consciousness. If anything, they are sharpened. In the Chalcedonian formula

[1] Below, Lecture IX, p. 198. [2] Vol. I, pp. 218 ff.

consciousness is treated as one of the qualities of a nature. It is asserted that in Christ were united divine nature with divine consciousness and human nature with human consciousness. In their acceptance of the formula the Fathers were like the Jews whose faith in God as Creator was untroubled by questions of its effect on His impassibility. When such questions have been raised they must be faced. We cannot evade them by saying that we must confine our thought either within the religious categories of the Hebrews or the ontological categories of fifth- or thirteenth-century Christian theologians.

I have argued that to be human is to be living as the conscious subject of experiences mediated through a particular body at a particular time and place. I have represented Christian faith as the belief that in Jesus Christ we see God experiencing life in this way. How can this be compatible with the thought of Him as God omniscient and omnipotent? Once again we have to acknowledge mystery. Where there is evidence that our categories cannot assimilate we have to choose between denying the evidence and revising the categories. Where we cannot deny the evidence or see just how the categories should be revised, we have to suspend judgment, that is, in other words, acknowledge mystery. In this case the evidence is that our Lord was subject to these limitations[1] and that, nevertheless, we cannot account for what He was and did by thinking of Him as anything less than God.

Theologians are familiar with attempts to deal with this problem by the use of the word *kenosis*. This is the Greek noun corresponding to the verb used by St. Paul in Philippians ii. 7, which, literally translated, could mean that He 'emptied Himself'. I am attracted by the suggestion that the use of the verb in this passage may have been suggested to St. Paul by a recollection of the Hebrew of Isaiah liii. 12: 'He hath poured out his soul unto death'.[2] The mystery now before us is essentially one and the

[1] E.g., St. Mark vi. 5; xiii. 32; St. Luke ii. 52.
[2] See, e.g., L. S. Thornton: *The Dominion of Christ* (London, 1952), p. 95.

same with that which throughout we have found confronting us in all our attempts to make sense of the universe of our experience. Given the reality in some sense of the time-process, we are driven to the postulate of a Creator who is personal in His activity. This produces the antinomy between God-in-Himself and God-in-relation to creation. It is this same antinomy which reappears between Christ as God-in-Himself and as God-incarnate. We are face to face with the fundamental questions: Can the time process be real? Can the Eternal create? Can the Eternal live a human life? Who are we to say that He cannot, to deny the evidence that He does the one and has done the other? I have suggested that it throws some light on the mystery if we seek for our ultimate explanation in terms of God's personal will.[1] To connect Philippians ii. 6 with Isaiah liii. 12 keeps us moving within this frame of reference.

There is one thing more to be said. When we think of Christ as limiting His impassibility to the extent of living as the conscious subject of human experience we must beware of the mistake of measuring His humanity by ours. We must not, for example, think of His knowledge of the Father's will as subject to limitations due to our imperfection and sinfulness. Do we realize how much the faith of which He spoke as necessary to the working of miracles may depend upon the possession of a knowledge we have not got, knowledge arising from such utter dedication of Himself to the one end of finding and doing the Father's will, from such perfect communion with the Father in the Spirit, that he can *know* it to be the Father's will that this person at this time shall be healed of his disease, that He Himself shall not be drowned in a storm on the Sea of Galilee before He has accomplished His work at Jerusalem? If we are to think of Him as thinking within the limits bounding human consciousness, we must be careful to remember that throughout His growth from infancy to manhood His mind was a human mind charac-

[1] Vol. I, p. 223.

terized by the perfection relevant to each stage of growth and continuously in communion with the Father in the Spirit.

Other questions abound. If our Lord was perfect in His manhood at each stage of growth, if He had, in the colloquial sense of the words, no 'lower nature', how, it may be asked, could He really know what it is to be tempted? This question too easily takes for granted that all temptation comes from what St. James calls one's own lusts.[1] No doubt some do. But not necessarily all. It argues no such lustfulness that a man who has a piece of work to do, the preparation of a lecture or a sermon, for example, should feel the attraction of a novel in an armchair. In a world infected with evil temptation comes from without as well as from within. The sharpness of our Lord's rebuke to St. Peter in St. Matthew xvi. 23 suggests that He was as aware of the attractiveness of less exacting ideas of messiahship as is any lecturer of that of novels and armchairs. If at first sight the evidence that Jesus Christ was 'tempted like as we are, yet without sin' seems inconsistent with our *a priori* notion of what is possible, further reflection may lead us to revise the notion in the light of the evidence and conclude that in such a world as this the conflict between duty and pleasure is an essential element in the experience of human life.

We come now to the crux of this lecture. I have maintained that God gives His revelation by doing things and inspiring men to see the significance of what He does, that the Bible is in a special sense revelatory because it bears witness to His redemptive activity which is the key to our understanding of the whole. I have shown how our grasping of the significance of God's action is a process with a history in which in each age men's understanding is conditioned by the outlook of their time and place. I have been arguing that our understanding of the Bible as revelatory depends upon our recognition of Jesus Christ as God personally at work in the history of this world, that to know what is truly of God in the Old Testament, in other teachings

[1] St. James i. 14.

ancient and modern, and in successive expositions of Christian faith, we have to ask how far they are consistent with God's revelation of Himself in Christ. What of the criterion itself? If in Jesus Christ God was genuinely 'made man', lived, thought and taught as the subject of the experiences mediated through a body born of the Jews in Palestine not quite two thousand years ago, must we not regard His teaching as conditioned by the outlook of His time and place and racial origin? Must we not be asking, as we read His recorded sayings, 'What must the truth have been and be if one who thought and spoke as He did put it like that?'

I have already in part answered this question by doing this very thing, by suggesting that our belief in Jesus as God incarnate may have appeared in His mind as no more than a conviction of messiahship. For the rest, I would say that the true answer to the question is that He answers it Himself. The more we ponder over His sayings, the more completely, in doing so, we treat them as directly relevant to the particular situations He was in, as expressing the reaction to them of one with the mind of a Palestinian Jew of that age, the more we find ourselves driven with Fr. Kelly and Dr. Raven to acknowledge One who has 'burst the bounds of self'.

In saying this we must be careful not to interpret that phrase in such a way as to minimize the reality of our Lord's manhood. If to be human is to be living as the subject of experiences mediated through a body in a particular time and place, we must not think of the sayings of Jesus as *ex cathedra* utterances of a spectator of all time and all existence. On the other hand, we have no experience enabling us to know the extent to which perfect self-dedication to the finding and doing of God's will, in a life of unbroken communion with God in the unity of the Spirit, would enable a man to deal with his own particular circumstances in such a way as to reveal principles of universal relevance.

I have described the history of Christian thought as the history of the growth of our understanding of the revelation of God in

Christ. I have pointed out that this history has both a negative and a positive side, the discovery and stripping off of mis-colourings and the deepening grasp of what is truly implied. We can now see that this process is concerned with what Jesus both did and said. The more we are enabled by critical and historical study to see the meaning of His sayings in direct relation to the particular circumstances of His earthly life, the more clear becomes their relevance by analogy to very different events in other times and places. It is not necessary to think that at the time when the words were spoken these implications were consciously present in His mind. Of His words, no less than of His deeds, it may be said: 'Christ gave His life, it is for Christians to discern the doctrine.'

Appended Note

I have said nothing in this lecture about our Lord's birth from a virgin or His bodily resurrection, both of which form part of what is in general believed among Christians. This has been deliberate. I have aimed at concentrating attention on what I hold to be the central core of Christian belief about Jesus, that He has shown Himself to be such that we cannot think of Him as anything less than God living a human life. This conviction is drawn from that part of His revelation of Himself which is open to our inspection, between His birth and His burial. I have argued that if it be true, it implies a certain difference between Him and us: that whereas for each one of us our conception is the absolute beginning of a potential new *hypostasis*, for Him it was the entry upon the experience of human life by the eternal second *Hypostasis* in the Blessed Trinity. I shall be arguing later that there is a similar difference in respect of resurrection.[1]

There is a certain amount of evidence to the effect that the body of His earthly life was conceived without the agency of a human father, and after His burial was mysteriously transformed to be the organ of His risen and ascended ministry. This evidence

[1] Below, Lecture IX, p. 196.

has been collected, tabulated, sifted and discussed to such an extent that no further progress is likely to be made by that kind of so-called historical investigation. To my mind it is as good as one can reasonably expect historical evidence to be, and one who holds the belief about our Lord which I have been advocating is justified in accepting it at its face value, as I do.

If it be asked whether the doctrine of the virgin birth and the bodily resurrection of Christ are necessary to that of the incarnation, we must be careful to keep apart two distinct questions: (*a*) whether objectively this was necessary in order that God should be made man; and (*b*) whether subjectively it is necessary that a man should hold these beliefs about His conception and resurrection in order to believe that He was God incarnate.

(*a*) The only possible answer to this question is that we do not know. To be able to prescribe the conditions necessary for God to enter upon the experience of life as man we should require exhaustive knowledge in detail of what it means to be God and of what it means to be man.

(*b*) The only possible answer to this question is 'No'. There are men who combine a genuine belief in Jesus Christ as God incarnate in the fullest sense of the words with a disbelief in the traditional account of the peculiar circumstances of His birth and resurrection. When men are actually doing a thing, it is no good saying that it cannot be done.

What we need here is a sense of proportion, to realize that questions about the mode of God's entry upon and passing from His earthly life are secondary to belief in the fact of His having lived it. When in this way we think of these doctrines as concerned with God's entry upon and passing from the experience of life as man on earth we cease to be surprised that they are the points at which we find mystery. We are confronting another aspect of what throughout we have found to be the fundamental mystery of human thought, the relation of the temporal to the eternal. We try to make sense of the things of this world and have to postulate its eternal Creator. We try to make sense of the events of Christ's life and have to postulate its being the life in space and time of eternal God. In both cases it is at what, for want of any better phrase, I may call the points of contact between time and eternity that *omnia abeunt in mysterium*.

LECTURE V

The Holy Spirit

I

AT Nicaea in the year 325 the Christians explicitly asserted their belief that Jesus Christ was and is God in the full sense of the word. At Chalcedon in 451 they made equally clear their belief that the life He had lived on earth was a genuinely human life. Almost midway between these two dates, at Constantinople in 381, the doctrine of the Trinity was made complete by the recognition of the Holy Spirit as the co-equal Third Person in the godhead. Our ultimate aim is to discover how this element of doctrine fits in with the rest of the Christian faith, and whether it will help us to make sense of the universe of our experience. We must begin by considering its history, remembering that, if it be true, it comes to us from God as He seeks to make Himself known to us through minds conditioned by the circumstances of their outlook.

God gives His revelation by doing things and inspiring men to see their significance. He reveals Himself as Creator in the universe as it is studied by scientists, historians, artists and philosophers. He reveals Himself as Redeemer through those events to which the Bible bears witness. If we look to the New Testament for the historical origin of the Christian doctrine of the Holy Spirit we shall not simply ask what this or that writer or speaker said about it. In order to interpret their evidence we need to understand their minds. For this purpose we must learn all that we can from biblical scholars about the contemporary meaning of words like *ruach*, *nephesh* and *pneuma*. But all this is preparatory to asking what, so far as we can see, was actually being done, and what the truth must have been and be if men who thought and spoke as they did put it like that.

For two reasons, one general and one particular, our starting-point will be the outlook of the primitive Christian Church. It is my thesis in general that the revelation which forms the substance of Christian theology is given in a series of events which is still going on. We trace it back approximately to the call of Abraham; we see its climax in the coming of Christ; we follow its continuance in all that issues from Him in the history of His Church. Among the revelatory events to which the Bible bears witness, the history of the New Testament Church must be included as equally significant with what went before. Secondly, I pointed out in my first lecture last year that primarily the New Testament is evidence for what was in the minds of the members of that Church. The gospels give us the picture of Christ as seen through their eyes. It is no good our thinking that by our methods of critical analysis we can isolate earlier passages of greater evidential value to be the basis of our reconstructed history. 'The starting-point for the historical study of Christian theology is the faith of the Church as set forth in the books of the New Testament.'[1]

According to the evidence provided by these witnesses the presence of the Spirit in the Church was a noticeable phenomenon. 'Received ye the Spirit by the works of the Law, or by the hearing of faith?' says St. Paul to the Galatians[2]—a question without sense in an argument without point, unless there were something definite and noticeable to which they would know that he was referring. In Acts viii. 17–19, in the account of the visit of St. Peter and St. John to Samaria, we read: 'Then laid they their hands on them, and they received the Holy Ghost. And when Simon saw that through laying on of the Apostles' hands the Holy Ghost was given, he offered them money, saying, Give me also this power, that on whomsoever I lay hands, he may receive the Holy Ghost.' Two chapters further on, in x. 44, 45, in Cornelius' house at Caesarea: 'While Peter yet spake these words, the Holy Ghost fell on all them which heard the

[1] Vol. I, p. 20. [2] Gal. iii. 2.

word. And they of the circumcision which believed were astonished, as many as came with Peter, because that on the Gentiles also was poured out the gift of the Holy Ghost.'

What was it of which St. Paul was reminding his Galatian converts? What was it that Simon Magus saw in Samaria, and the Jewish Christians, who had come with St. Peter, in Caesarea? In this last case we are given an answer to the question: 'For they heard them speak with tongues and magnify God'. This takes our thought back from chapters viii and x of *Acts* to the account of the first coming of the Spirit to the Christian community on the day of Pentecost in chapter ii. Just precisely what happened on that occasion it is impossible now to determine. We cannot say for certain how far the account comes from those who were themselves present, or to what extent the story had grown before it reached the shape in which it appears in *Acts*.[1] Even supposing that it comes substantially from those on whom the Spirit came, the most we can say is that they spoke of an experience which, as they looked back on it, they could only describe as the hearing of the sound of a mighty rushing wind and the vision of tongues of flame. What was noticed by others was that they spoke with tongues in praise of God.

Whatever the facts, there is no doubt of the interpretation put upon them. These outward phenomena were evidence that the Spirit had been sent to His followers on earth from His Father in Heaven by the crucified, risen and ascended Christ (Acts ii. 32–36), in fulfilment of Joel's prophecy concerning the messianic age (ii. 16 ff.), and of the promises of the Lord Himself (i. 5, 8). Through this they were bound together in what here is simply called 'the fellowship' (ii. 42), but is more explicitly described by St. Paul as 'the fellowship of the Holy Spirit'.[2] Christianity began as the faith of a body of men and women who believed themselves to be the messianic community, the heirs to the promises of God to His chosen people, united to one another and

[1] See, e.g., the discussion in J. G. Davies: *The Spirit, The Church and the Sacraments* (London, 1954), pp. 26–31.

[2] 2 Cor. xiii. 14.

to their risen, ascended Lord by His gift of the Spirit. It was to the body corporate that the Spirit was given, in order to constitute them the messianic community, the new and true Israel. In the name of Christ they were to preach the gospel of God's promise of forgiveness to all who should repent, and baptize them into the fellowship of forgiven sinners which was the fellowship of the Spirit.

In the next lecture we shall be considering further the bearing of this on the origin and nature of the Christian Church. Our present concern is with the doctrine of the Holy Spirit.

A rushing mighty wind, tongues of flame and speaking with tongues in praise of God are given as noticeable outward phenomena at Pentecost. The last of these is explicitly mentioned in the case of Cornelius and his household, and the presence of the other two may be meant to be implied by the phrase 'the Holy Ghost fell on them *as on us*' in xi. 15. Something of the same kind is mentioned in connection with St. Paul's baptism of Ephesian converts in Acts xix. 6. All this suggests that it was probably some kind of ecstatic behaviour which aroused the admiration and envy of Simon Magus in Samaria. I remember hearing Dr. Burton Easton remark that in all probability the ecstatic leaps and shouts of converts as they emerged from the baptismal waters were to the earliest Christians the convincing evidence of the gift of the Spirit.

Are we to conclude that this was what St. Paul had in mind in his question to the Galatians? And what are we to make of it for our own belief?

Forget, for the moment, St. Paul. Remember that what we have to ask is what the truth must have been, and be, if men who thought as they did put it like that. Our concern is not with what the New Testament Christians thought about it. That is important as a matter of exegesis, and a scholarly exegesis is a necessary preliminary to any sound interpretation of the evidence. But what we want to know is what was actually going on, whether or no they realized it at the time.

To discover this we have to take into account some further evidence hitherto unmentioned, evidence concerned with what they were and did rather than with what they thought about it. I refer to the change wrought in the disciples themselves. According to the order of events given in *Acts* the turning point of the story was the coming of the Spirit on the day of Pentecost. The Fourth Gospel suggests that there may have been no such interval of time as is presupposed in *Acts* between Christ's resurrection, ascension and gift of the Spirit. The point is irrelevant for our present purpose. What we have to notice is the contrast between the disciples before and the disciples after a certain event regarded as the gift of the Spirit by the risen Lord. It makes no difference whether the change came early or late. If in discussing it I make use of the account in *Acts* it is because its extension in time, like a slow-motion film, enables one to see some details more clearly.

The two words which most succinctly describe this change are insight and initiative. In the last lecture I was maintaining that for Christ His messiahship meant the giving of Himself to bring men rescue from their sinfulness, and that from the start the Christian gospel was the message that this freedom had been won. In spite of all that I then said about His disciples following Him because in this He appealed to what they were aware of as their deepest need, the evidence shows that throughout His earthly ministry they continued unable to see in it the fulfilment of His messianic work. St. Peter's acknowledgment of His messiahship is coupled with such misunderstanding of its nature that Christ rebukes him as the mouthpiece of Satan and not of God. 'How is it', he asks more than once, 'that ye do not understand?' When in the end He puts up no fight but allows Himself to be arrested, 'they all forsook Him and fled'. Still less had they grasped the truth that they were called to be sharing in His work of reconciliation, seeing the world as He saw it and going out in His name to carry on His work. When by His resurrection their faith was restored that after all this 'had been He who should redeem Israel', they were still asking such questions as 'Lord, wilt

Thou at this time restore again the kingdom to Israel?'[1] They were without insight into the meaning of His work, without initiative to go and carry it on. All they could do was to wait about from one appearance of the risen Lord to another, hoping to be told something more of His plans.

Contrast the picture of these same men as given by the author of *Acts* after their pentecostal experience: St. Peter preaching the gospel of God's forgiveness as the central content of the Christian faith, and saying to the cripple, 'In the name of Jesus Christ of Nazareth, rise up and walk'.[2]

Whether we follow the Lucan or the Johannine time-scheme, this change in the disciples seems to me to be an undoubted fact of history which we have to interpret. If we are to take all the evidence into account, we have to include the fact that its coming is associated with certain ecstatic phenomena regarded as marking the coming of the Spirit from the risen, ascended Christ. What is to be our understanding of the evidence as a whole?

Let us now go back to St. Paul. In *Acts* we have a narrative of events compiled from such evidence as its author has been able to collect. He gives us this two-sided picture of men seeing visions, hearing sounds, and uttering strange cries in praise of God, while at the same time they are undergoing an inward spiritual change of the significance of which neither they nor he seem to be fully aware. In turning from *Acts* to the Pauline epistles we turn from the narrator of other men's stories to one who gives us the result of his reflection upon events of which he has had personal experience. In I Corinthians xiv he shows clearly that he knows all about such behaviour as 'speaking with tongues', but for evidence of the working of the Spirit regards it as of less importance than intelligible speech. To this negative judgment on irrational phenomena he adds, in I Corinthians xii and Galatians v. 22 ff., a commendation of socially valuable activities and the practice of virtue as positive marks of the

[1] St. Matt. xvi. 16, 23; St. Mark viii. 21; xiv. 50; St. Luke xxiv. 21; Acts i. 6.
[2] This summarizes a fuller account in *The Doctrine of the Trinity*, pp. 44 ff.

Spirit's presence. In all this St. Paul is in agreement with the author of the first Johannine epistle who in iv. 1–3 bids his readers test all alleged spirit-messages by their consistency with the revelation of God in Christ. The content is to be the criterion of the source.[1]

Like St. Paul the Johannine writer was a thinker rather than a narrator. We may surely take these two as representing the considered judgment of the New Testament Church on the kind of events depicted in the narrative of *Acts*. Their verdict, I suggest, would be this. They would not deny either the occurrence of the ecstatic phenomena or their significance as evidence of possession by some supernatural spirit. But the proof that He who was at work in them was none other than the Holy Spirit of God was not to be found in these accompaniments of His presence; it lay in the fact that both in what they said and what they did they showed an intelligent and intelligible grasp of the revelation of God in Christ, that (to use a Pauline phrase) they 'had the mind of Christ'.[2] It may be that the enlightenment of the eyes of their mind to see themselves as the messianic community, the new Israel, the fellowship of forgiven sinners charged with the proclamation of the message of God's forgiveness—it may be that this enlightenment came to them accompanied by visions and sounds which moved them to ecstatic behaviour; it may be that at their baptism into the fellowship new converts were often similarly moved to ecstatic cries and leaps; it may be that there had been events of this kind which St. Paul recalled to the memory of the Galatians. But the tenour of the epistle taken as a whole makes it clear that this could only have been a part, indeed, a minor part, of what he had in mind. He addresses the Galatians as men who by their faith in Christ are in a special sense sons of God, sharing by adoption in the sonship which is Christ's by nature. Awareness of this sonship is the mark of their membership in the Christian community. He exhorts them to stand fast in the liberty which they enjoy in that fellowship of

[1] See Vol. I, p. 91. [2] 1 Cor. ii. 16.

forgiven sinners. All their experience of a new quality of life, their realization of what it is to be (in language he uses elsewhere) 'new creatures'[1] must be included in what St. Paul means when he asks about their receiving of the Spirit.

If, then, the starting-point for the historical study of Christian theology is the faith of the Church as set forth in the books of the New Testament, the origin of the doctrine of the Spirit must be looked for in the faith of the first Christians that they had been constituted the New Israel by the gift of the Spirit from their crucified, risen and ascended Lord. By baptism into their number the new convert found himself sharing in the life of a community which saw the point of Christ's ministry from a new angle. In this fellowship of forgiven sinners he found a psychological release that issued in what St. Paul calls the 'fruit of the Spirit'. This Christian community, this new Israel, came into existence as the fellowship of the Holy Spirit.

While this may be the starting-point for the historical study of the doctrine, we want to know more than that. We want to know how far the doctrine tells the truth about God. We have seen that the doctrine sprang from the first Christians interpreting their experience as the fulfilment of Joel's prophecy and the promise of Christ. We must look back to the story of Christ's earthly life as they present it to us in the gospel records, asking what light this may throw upon the question before us.

II

'As they present it to us.' More than once I have spoken of the change in the study of the gospels between my youth and the present time, of how we have given up trying to isolate primitive strata uncoloured by the outlook of worshippers in the early Church and now treat the whole as giving us Christ's ministry as, looking back, they saw it.[2] We who to-day are Christians are so because we share their understanding of what with them

[1] 2 Cor. v. 17. [2] Especially in Vol. I, Lecture I.

we believe to be historical facts. We who are Christian theologians have to turn our critical eye on their beliefs and ours, asking how much has to be discounted as miscolouring of the evidence, and what deeper insight we may be given into what that evidence reveals.

Here let me emphasize the importance of a principle I have already mentioned in passing, that in the study of the evidence for what our Lord said and did we should begin by relating each instance to its particular circumstances. We are not to take His sayings out of their historical context and treat them as celestial *ex cathedra* pronouncements applicable to all times and places. On the contrary, by the use of our historical imagination, disciplined and controlled by all that we can learn of the circumstances of the time from professional historians, we are to put ourselves back into His context, try to see His actual situation as he saw it, and understand what He said and did as His response to it. It is this narrowing down of their immediate reference which gives His words and deeds their widest application. When we grasp the principle involved on the one particular occasion we can see its analogous implications for other and quite different circumstances.

Consider St. Luke xii. 11, 12. By this time it had become clear to our Lord—as is reflected in St. John xv. 20–24—that persistence in His messianic claims will involve persecution for Himself and His followers. He is thinking and speaking of what will happen to them when He is gone, and says: 'When they bring you unto the synagogues, and unto magistrates, and powers, take ye no thought how or what thing ye shall answer, or what ye shall say: for the Holy Spirit shall teach you in the same hour what ye ought to say'. To understand this passage we have to take it in connection with St. John xvi. 7 and St. Matthew xii. 22–32.

Whether or no the Fourth Gospel contains *ipsissima verba* of Christ, I have no doubt that over and over again it rightly expresses His thoughts as He lived His human life on earth.[1] St.

[1] On this, see my *And Was Made Man* (London, 1928), Ch. viii.

Matthew xii. 22–32 shows how during that life He thought of Himself as doing His rescuing work by the guidance and power of the Spirit. 'I don't mind what you say about me', He says, 'but don't you dare to blaspheme against the Spirit that is working in me, for it is none other than the Holy Spirit of God'. The gospel picture of Christ is the picture of One who saw this world as His heavenly Father's world in which the Father's work was waiting to be found and done; who saw it and found it and did it by the guidance and power of the Spirit who was the *vinculum*, the bond of union, of Him on earth with the Father in heaven. I have shown elsewhere how, given belief in the godhead of Christ, the doctrine of the Trinity comes by projecting this relationship into eternity, thinking away from it elements incidental to the spatio-temporal character of the human life.[1] The point to notice now is that in St. John xvi Christ's promise to His disciples is that life on earth is to be for them what it has been for Him, the finding and doing of the Father's work by the guidance and power of the Spirit. They are to pass from second-hand dependence on His presence in the flesh to first-hand sharing in His way of life. Verse 7: 'It is expedient for you that I go away; for if I go not away, the Paraclete will not come unto you; but if I depart, I will send him unto you' gives utterance to His realization that the time is coming when His presence in the flesh will be more of a hindrance than a help to their gaining the insight into the Father's will and the initiative to go and do it which He wills to share with them.

Returning to St. Luke xii. 11, 12, we see this as falling within the general promise that His disciples are to be taken to share in His way of life. At the moment He happens to be thinking of occasions when they will be put on trial for their discipleship. They are not to lie awake at night trying to make up answers to accusations they have not yet heard: they are to trust to being able, when they hear the speech for the prosecution, to be able to see in it what reply it demands, and they are to be able to do

[1] In *The Doctrine of the Trinity, passim.*

this because they are Spirit-guided men. From narrowing down the immediate reference of the saying to these particular occasions we see how wide are its implications. For His disciples, as for Himself, life is to be a series of opportunities of seeing in every situation what the Father wants done.

All this is our interpretation of what was actually going on as it is revealed to us through the records of how the first Christians felt and thought about it at the time. They were a body of men and women bound together in devotion to their crucified, risen and ascended Lord whom they believed to have constituted them the messianic community by sending them His Spirit in fulfilment of God's promises to His people made through such prophets as Joel. Doubtless they thought of the Spirit in much the same way as the writer of *Judges* thought of the spirit of Jahweh coming on Samson, or as Ezekiel thought of God's Spirit as taking him up to hear voices or reanimating dead bones: that is to say, as a kind of power or effluence through which a unipersonal God worked His will on earth and not as a distinct Person in a triune godhead. Interpreting all that had come to them in terms of the Old Testament background of their thought, they believed that as the messianic community, the remnant of the old Israel which was now the new and true Israel, God had bound them to Himself by a new covenant replacing the old covenant of Sinai. The essence of this new covenant relationship was that by the act of God in Christ they were cleansed from their sins and reconciled to God, and charged with the proclamation of God's love and forgiveness to draw others into the fellowship. In the context of all this way of thinking they put down recollections of what Christ had said about the Spirit as working in Himself and to be given to His followers.

From that day to this Christian theology has been engaged in discovering the significance of what had happened to those men. In *The Doctrine of the Trinity* I have written of its implications for the doctrine of God and will not go over that ground again now. I want now to speak of the working of the Spirit in creation rather than of His place in the inner life of God.

I have traced back the origin of the Christian doctrine of the Spirit to the interpretation by St. Peter and St. Paul of the experience and behaviour of the first Christians. They ascribed this to their receipt of the gift of His Spirit from Christ. Our first question is whether this witnesses to the coming of something genuinely new in human history.

I believe that it does, and that the evidence of the newness lies in their ascription of the coming of the Spirit to the gift of Christ. Once again we are driven back to face the central affirmation of Christian faith, that in Jesus Christ we see God Himself personally entering upon the experience of life as man on earth. If this be true, His coming was an event unique in history, something which had never happened before. Whatever took its beginning from it shared in its newness. In His human life He was united to the Father in heaven by the Spirit through whom with His human eyes and strength He found and did the Father's will. The New Testament is written by men who use different metaphors and images to testify to their conviction that they are enjoying a new kind of life: they have been 'born again', they are 'in Christ', they are 'members of the body of Christ'. 'If any man be in Christ, he is a new creature: old things are put away, behold, all things are become new.' Whatever they may have thought about it, the evidence seems to me to show that the meaning of the newness of which they were conscious was that they had been taken by Christ to share in His outlook and His way of life.

This was, however, only the beginning—the beginning of a process which has been continuing ever since and is still going on. I have distinguished between the two modes of God's self-revelation: the revelation of His creative activity which we receive through study of the universe in general, and the revelation of His redemptive activity given in the events to which the Bible bears witness. In both His method is the same: He reveals

Himself by doing things and inspiring men to grasp the significance of what He does. When considering revelation in general, I have shown how in this inspiring of men to grasp the significance of His doings, God acts in a way which expresses His determination to create them into persons endowed with genuine freedom. He allows their outlook to be conditioned by their circumstances, and waits for growth in understanding to come through men gifted with a *flair* for diagnosis. What we have now to notice is that His method is the same in His redemptive as in His creative self-revelation. The new thing in Christian theology, as compared with natural theology in general, is not only that Christians interpret everything by the light of the recognition of God in Christ, but that they are inspired by the Spirit who comes to them from God through Christ. If I may put it so, they are inspired by the Spirit who sees as God sees when looking out from inside human life, who has perfect knowledge of the mind of Christ. But He allows their reception of His inspiration to be conditioned and coloured by their outlook; He lets growth in understanding come by stripping off various layers of miscolouring of what men see, so that we are still in process of discovering what Christianity really is.

As we look back over the early history of Christian theology we see developments in the doctrine of the Spirit which are of importance for our thought. It began with the recognition of the Spirit as inspiring the Christian fellowship, moving its members to ecstatic behaviour, illuminating their minds with understanding of Christ, and strengthening their wills in the practice of virtue. From this have issued two divergent lines of thought, which both persist to-day. In the one, the recognition of what I have called newness is exaggerated into an assertion of wholly-otherness. There are passages in theologians of the catholic tradition which imply that the Church has an exclusive claim to the indwelling of the Holy Spirit, and there are protestant theologians for whom all natural theology not based on biblical sources is a ploughing of sands of error. The other, which I believe to be the true one—I shall have more to say about it in the next lecture—goes the opposite way. It fully recognizes the distinctive newness of the gift of the Spirit through Christ to His Church, but (to use a colloquialism) it regards this as giving to Christians an 'inside knowledge' of the Spirit which enables them to recognize His working elsewhere.

We can trace the extension of this line of thought into three expanding spheres. First, like Christ Himself in His earthly life, the Church hears the voice of the Spirit speaking through the prophets of the Old Testament. This finds expression in the Niceno-Constantinopolitan creed of 381, when to the affirmation of faith in the Holy Spirit as Lord and Giver of life are added the words 'who spake by the prophets'. Meanwhile, the coming of the original Jewish-Christian Church into the Gentile world had brought it into contact with the traditions of Greek, Roman and oriental thought. In Clement of Alexandria and others we find appreciation of apprehensions of truth by Greek philosophers. I have a strong suspicion that Origen's most valuable contribution to the doctrine of the Trinity, the interpretation of sonship as 'eternal generation', was an enrichment of Christian thought from the neoplatonism of his youth.[1] I am not, of course, suggesting that these fathers themselves thought of this as being guided by the Spirit to recognize His work in extra-biblical spheres; indeed, some of them attempted to account for what they found by a theory of Mosaic influence through documents that had perished.[2] But that, I submit, is what was going on. Thirdly, there was explicit reference to the working of the Spirit at what we should now call the sub-human stages of the creative process. In both the so-called Apostles' and the Nicene Creeds

[1] This suspicion was engendered by reading the following description of Plotinus' cosmology: 'The One produces universal Mind, or Intellect that is one with the Intelligible. Intellect produces the soul of the whole. This produces all other existences, but without itself lapsing. Nothing within the series of the three intelligible principles can be said to lapse in production. . . . The order throughout, both for the intelligible causes and for the visible universe, is a logical order of causation, not an order in time. All the producing causes and their effects in every grade always existed and always will exist.' T. Whittaker: *The Neo-Platonists* (Cambridge, 1918), p. 55.

[2] Clem. Al. *Str.* I, xv, 72–4; II, v, 1; V, xiv, 94–5.

the conception of Christ's body in the womb of His virgin mother is ascribed to the Holy Spirit, and in the development of sacramental doctrine it is by the operation of the Holy Spirit that the material elements become the vehicle of God's spiritual energy.

I have pictured creation as a process in which in increasing measure God is communicating fullness and richness of being to a spatio-temporal stream of energy. This last extension of the doctrine of the Spirit shows how Christians believe that God is not only at work as the Giver of what creation needs for its growth but also within creation, enabling it to receive what is given. More than once last year we were faced by the question of what makes the evolutionary process move. I maintained that to think of it as due to the will of its personal Creator is more reasonable than the panpsychism implicit in Whitehead's metaphysic and other similar mythologies.[1] We have now reached the point at which Christian theology articulates further this conclusion of natural theology. It is by the Holy Spirit that grass grows and trees bring forth leaves and flowers and fruit, that birds fly and fishes swim, that engines turn and trains and cars and aeroplanes go on their way. All is in keeping with God's revelation of Himself in Jesus Christ. He came as a little baby, putting Himself into the hands of men to do what they would with Him. We men being what we are, we crucified Him. When we remember how He let us do that, we begin to understand how He lets us mishandle Him in His creation. St. Paul said of the Jews that if they had known what they were doing, they would not have crucified the Lord of glory. We do well to remember that as by advance in scientific research and technology we increase our control over the forces of nature, the secret of the energy we control is that it is God the Holy Spirit putting Himself into our hands.[2]

In saying this, I am quite frankly using the language of Christian faith, speaking from within the community of those who interpret

[1] Vol. I, pp. 154, 163, 221. [2] Cp. Vol. I, pp. 115, 159.

all that goes on in the universe by the light of the revelation of God in Christ. The Christian thinks of himself as one of God's creatures to whom in some way or other God has reached out and called him into the fellowship of the Christian Church. As he reflects on the progress of his spiritual life, he sees this as one of those processes which can be viewed from either end: from below he is growing up into his true self, from above God is giving to him his true self, through Christ in him, the hope of glory. He knows within him that God is at work from both ends. He could never have heard and responded to God's call to Christian faith had not God the Holy Spirit opened his ears to hear the call, enlightened his understanding, and given strength to his will. He knows that in every decision he makes for God, every step he takes towards God, God the Holy Spirit is the source of his ability to decide and to act. In his interpretation of the evolutionary process he is explaining the unknown from the known, interpreting the universal creation by the light of his own inside knowledge of what it is to be a creature.

If we then ask whence the Christian derives this understanding of his own nature, we have to retrace our steps to the study of the New Testament which occupied the earlier part of this lecture. We saw then that the coming of Christ issued in the constitution of a fellowship of men and women the secret of whose life was to be the seeking, finding and doing of the Father's work in the Father's world as the earthly body of the ascended Son in the guidance and strength of the Spirit. That was how it all began, and still to-day it is by his baptism into that fellowship, by his coming to share in its experience and its outlook, that the individual Christian comes to his understanding both of his own life and of all God's creation.

'Our Christian faith does not first come to us by our coming across the Bible and reading it on our own. Faith in God and in His revelation of Himself in Christ are things which we take over from the Christian community.'[1] For the non-Christian

[1] Above, p. 25.

world all we can do is to explain how we see things from within this community and affirm our conviction that this outlook gives us the right perspective.[1] But how do we see things among ourselves?

When we think of the doctrine of the Holy Spirit as concerned with God at work within creation we have to remember what was said last year about the two kinds of relation between God and His creatures,[2] and that in the doctrine of the Trinity what is true of the godhead as a whole is true of each Person. Thus we think of the Spirit as working differently in the sub-human, material stages of evolution and in ourselves. In so far as we are persons, He will only possess and influence us in ways consistent with the promotion of our growth in freedom, our growth into our true selves. If, as I have argued earlier,[3] this involves our making the truth our own by exposing misleading presuppositions and winning deeper insight, we shall not be surprised to find that in taking of the things of Christ and showing them unto us the Spirit, working within minds conditioned by the outlook of their age and culture, is continually opening our eyes to see where our categories are in need of revision in order that we may understand more fully the significance of what God has done.

III

To the whole question of the doctrine of the Holy Spirit I know of no better introduction than the following passage quoted from a French theologian:

> Throughout the New Testament, the Christian revelation will be found to keep the same character which it had at its beginning. The mystery of the Son of God will remain the luminous centre of the whole faith, and of the doctrine of the Trinity in particular. If the heavenly Father is more intimately known, it is because He is revealed in the Son. If the Christians understand better than the Jews the close union with the heavenly Father which it is ours to enter upon here on earth and to consummate hereafter, it is because they share in the unique sonship of Jesus, because they have access by Him to the Father.

[1] Vol. I, p. 104. [2] Vol. I, pp. 165 ff., 205 ff. [3] Above, p. 29.

If, in accordance with the Saviour's teaching, they believe in a Holy Spirit, personally distinct from the Father and the Son, they have not been able to grasp and hold fast to the assurance of His personality except by estimating it, so to speak, by the analogy of that other divine Person who has appeared to them in Christ.

Jesus was not only the revealer who, from His full knowledge of the Father, was the first who was able to tell us of His secrets. He was also the Son, who only has appeared to us, and in His appearing has shown us the Father and brought us to knowledge of the 'other Paraclete', the Holy Spirit. The reader must not be surprised if study of the doctrine of the Trinity is mainly occupied with the doctrine of the Son. It is in and through the doctrine of the Son that the origin of the doctrine of the Trinity will become most clear to us, since it was by this light that it was first perceived.[1]

As I have already said, I am not in these lectures concerned with the doctrine of the Spirit as an element in trinitarian theology, but as illuminating our understanding of God's way of revealing Himself to man. From this point of view, to accept the Council of Constantinople's affirmation of the godhead of the Spirit means that we regard the Spirit who opens our eyes to discover truth as God Himself equally with the Son who has lived as man on earth and with our Father in heaven. I want now to look back again to the New Testament evidence, and to end this lecture with some speculative suggestions about its interpretation.

We have seen that according to that evidence the coming of the Spirit was marked by certain outward phenomena which accompanied an inward spiritual transformation, that at first the outward phenomena bulked largest as evidence of the Spirit's presence, but that in the considered judgment of the New Testament Church the inward change was what was most important.

When we take into consideration the Gospels as well as the Acts and Epistles we add to the evidence of outward phenomena the accounts of the appearance of the Spirit as a dove and the hearing of a voice from heaven at the time of Christ's baptism.

Between thirty and forty years ago I was watching a perfor-

[1] Translated from J. Lebreton: *Les Origines du Dogme de la Trinité* (Paris, 1910), pp. xxii, xxiii.

mance of a nativity play in the parish of St. Barnabas at Oxford. It ended with a glance into the future, a soliloquy by St. Mary standing in the shadow of the cross, in which she used the words: 'When thou didst lie, a little babe, unconscious in my arms'. At the time I was much occupied with problems of kenotic christology, and these words struck me with special force as showing how they are implied in the language of orthodox piety. If as a babe our Lord had lain *unconscious* in His mother's arms, He must have grown through all the stages of growing consciousness to know Himself as child, as boy, as man. There must have been a time in the growth of His human mind when He came to know Himself as Messiah.

It seems probable that in the Gospel narrative the account of His baptism marks the critical moment at which this conviction became a certainty. In the earliest account, that of St. Mark, on which the other two are based, the hearing of the voice and the vision of the dove are clearly recorded as experiences, not of the whole company but of Christ Himself. The call to special sonship and the special anointing by the Spirit meant to Him a call to messiahship, and He went away into the wilderness to ponder over this certain conviction of His office in silent communion with His Father. There He put from Him the temptations to adopt conceptions of messiahship such as were common among His contemporaries but were not in accordance with the divine will.[1]

If we may assume that this was so, and that the suggestion that the dove and the voice were apparent to St. John and others was due to later elaboration of the original story, the event falls into line with what we read in *Acts* about the disciples on the day of Pentecost and possibly about Cornelius too. In each case it was the recipient of the Spirit who experienced the visual and auditory sensations. It seems reasonable to conclude that while the most important coming and activity of the Spirit were inward and invisible, quickening the human body and mind for the service of the divine vocation, the outward sensible manifestations were a means of bringing home to the conscious human mind at the time the conviction of God's action.

[1] *And Was Made Man* (London, 1928), p. 63. See also pp. 146, 152.

These three events all share in the uniqueness of the coming of Christ; they were once-for-all beginnings in the history of Christianity. Christ's baptism was the beginning of His messianic ministry; Pentecost the constitution of the messianic community; Cornelius its opening to include all races of mankind. We need not be surprised either at the occurrence of the abnormal phenomena that are said to have accompanied such novel and unexpected divine action, or at the recurrence of similar experiences from time to time in the history of the Church. It needed the vision of the Lord on the road to Damascus to bring about the conversion of St. Paul. But already in New Testament times the Church was learning, not only to distinguish between ecstatic phenomena which come from God and those which do not, but also to regard those which do as exceptional gifts not generally necessary to the Christian life.

For the regular routine conduct of the Church's life something is needed to fill the part played by these ecstatic phenomena in exceptional cases, to bring home to the conscious human mind the conviction of God's inward action. What I want to suggest is that as the Church settled down to its work, with a long history before it, the sacraments were found to make permanent provision for what at the beginning took special and exceptional form. When we try to look at the matter from the point of view of the recipient of the gift, may we not say that to him the touch of the baptismal water, the laying of hands on his head, or the reception of the eucharistic species take the place of the dove and the voice at Christ's baptism, the pentecostal mighty wind and tongues of fire? 'An outward and visible sign of an inward and spiritual grace, given unto us . . . as a means whereby we receive the same and a pledge to assure us thereof.'

LECTURE VI

The Christian Church

I

CHRISTIANITY began as the faith of Christ's disciples who believed themselves to have been constituted God's messianic community, the new and true Israel, by the gift of the Spirit from their ascended Lord. It seems probable that to begin with they thought of Christ as absent in heaven above the clouds, that the Spirit had been sent to bind them together as His people, to be the link between the Lord in heaven and His people on earth, until He should return in judgment to claim them as the true Israel. Meanwhile they were to preach the gospel, make as many converts as they could, and baptize them into the fellowship of the chosen people.

The Christian Church began as a Jewish sect. Many years ago I was helped to understand its relation to official Judaism by considering the position in the Church of England of an organization called the Church Socialist League. This was composed of members of the Church of England who in the sphere of economics were agreed that the means of production and distribution of consumer goods should be publicly owned. In any parish in which there was a branch of the League its members would attend the regular services and make their communions at the parish church; they would come together to the altar for corporate League communions and hold intercession services to pray for the furtherance of the cause; they would also have their own meetings at which they would hear speakers and read and discuss papers confirming them in their economic and political convictions. Doubtless they would have held that if their fellow churchmen rightly understood the meaning of the gospel they would see that it implied acceptance of socialism in economics and politics. Just so the original Christians, firm in the conviction that true understanding of Judaism implied acceptance of the Christian faith, continued to take part in the worship of the Temple in Jerusalem and of synagogues elsewhere, as well as holding their own meetings for prayer, for the baptism of converts, and for eucharistic worship.

To be a member of the Church Socialist League one had to be a member of the Church of England. Now suppose that in Penzance or Penrith the local branch found many sympathizers among Baptists and Congregationalists, and began to admit them to membership on the ground that this true understanding of the gospel was of more importance than their ecclesiastical allegiance. It is easy to see how when the news reached the head office in London the fat would be in the fire, how letters and emissaries would be sent down to condemn the unconstitutional action and bring the unruly branch into line. It was a crisis of this kind which was provoked by reports reaching Jerusalem of St. Paul admitting uncircumcised Gentiles as Christians.

The endorsement of St. Paul's action was the first of three major developments in the life of the Church which came within the New Testament period. The second, for which it paved the way, was the separation of the Christian Church from official Judaism, evidenced by the Johannine use of the term 'the Jews'. The third was the realization that Christ was not to be thought of as absent above the clouds but was spiritually present with them, 'unseen yet ever near'.

A parallel may be drawn between the dawning of this realization and the earlier recognition of Christ as messiah. He had been with His disciples as friend and teacher for some time before St. Peter was moved to express their faith: 'Thou art the Christ, the Son of the living God'. So again it took time for them to realize that His ascension had not meant His absenting Himself from them. To what extent this may have come through their experience in 'the breaking of bread', a fruit of their obedience to His command: 'Do this in remembrance of Me', it is impossible to determine.[1] All suggestions in this field are hypothetical reconstruction of possible history. What is certain is that in both Pauline and Johannine writings Christ is spoken of as present here and now with His people: the Church is His body; He is the vine of which its members are the branches.[2] Already, before the close of the New Testament period, the Church has the characteristic described by Sir Ernest Barker:

> The community is in no sense a transcendent being which stands above the individual and determines his being and his duties in terms of its own higher nature.... A common content of many minds does not involve a common mind—at any rate when we are thinking *sub specie humanitatis* and dealing with the sphere of our transitory human groups. (The conception of a Church in which there is an indwelling Spirit of God belongs to a different plane of thought. But we only confuse thought, with sad and tragic results, when we take what belongs to one plane and transfer it to another and different plane.) ...
>
> The Christian conception of a Church goes further than this. God has not simply left a Word in custody with a Church, which is thereby made unique, in virtue of the unique character of its common substance, among all other forms or varieties of community. He Himself remains in the Church, and His Spirit dwells perenially in its members. In the community of the Church there *is* a Being which transcends the members, and yet is immanent in them. Here we may speak of an organism, as St. Paul did.[3]

So Christianity began as the faith of a body of men and women conscious of being the messianic community, the new and true Israel, the inheritor of God's promises to His chosen people charged with the duty of preaching the gospel of God's forgiveness ready and waiting for all who would repent of their sin, and accept the crucified, risen, ascended Lord Jesus Christ as messiah, baptizing into the fellowship those who responded to the preaching. The question is sometimes asked whether it was a man's faith or his baptism which made him a member of the Church. This is the kind of question to which no direct answer

[1] See, e.g., A. E. J. Rawlinson in Bell and Deissmann: *Mysterium Christi* (London, 1930).

[2] Rom. xii. 5; 1 Cor. xii. 12–27. See also 2 Cor. xiii. 5; Gal. ii. 20; St. John xiv. 20–23; Eph. i. 22, 23; iii. 17–19.

[3] E. Barker: *Essays on Government* (Oxford, 1945), pp. 249, 251.

can be found in the New Testament because the circumstances which give rise to it had not yet arisen. No one, unless driven by his faith, would have thought of joining, or remaining in, that small, despised, persecuted, poverty-stricken sect; if anyone had the faith, he would seek to be baptized into the fellowship. The question of the relation to the Church and to one another of the baptized unfaithful and the faithful unbaptized was one which would emerge later. It is no good asking what St. Paul or the Church of New Testament times thought or said about it.

The idea that Christianity began as the faith of a number of individual followers of Jesus who afterwards banded themselves together to form the Church is now dead as a matter of history. The messianic background of the gospel story makes it clear that in His calling and training of the twelve Apostles Christ had in mind the constitution of the messianic community.[1] Great difference of opinion remains on whether He gave the Church any definite internal structure: whether in particular He gave the Apostles any definite position in regard to jurisdiction or the ministry of word and sacraments, whether in the New Testament Church there was any office corresponding to the later episcopate from which that episcopate is descended by a sequence of consecrations.

It would take me too far afield to go into all the evidence on these points which is differently interpreted by different historians. I must simply set down the conclusions I have come to after giving what study I can to the subject.

First, I think we may take it as certain that Christ intended to constitute the messianic community as a continuing earthly body. By the new covenant in His blood He established the Church as the true Israel, an earthly body charged with the preaching of the gospel and administration of the sacraments. It was to grow and spread by converting men to penitence and faith, baptizing them into the fellowship of forgiven sinners, building them up in Christian faith, and maintaining their spiritual life by the

[1] Vol. I, pp. 18 ff.

sacrament of His body and blood. In this sense the universal Church was prior to the local churches.

Secondly, I think we may take it as certain that Christ called and trained the twelve Apostles to be the leaders of His Church, and entrusted it to their guidance and care. This involved something more than the responsibility of preaching the word as those who had been the companions of His ministry and His chosen witnesses—a responsibility which in the nature of things could not be handed on to successors. It involved also responsibility for what we call jurisdiction, including both the general government of the Church, the ordering of its sacramental and liturgical life, and its spiritual discipline. But I am not convinced that Christ constituted the Apostles His representatives and authorized them to pass on that representative character to others in such a way that He could not repudiate actions which they or their successors might claim to do in His name, or that He abrogated His right to raise up, call and commission others to do His work if they or their officially appointed successors should be unfaithful. Neither am I convinced that the later episcopate is adequately accounted for either by the theory of the elevation of chairmen of colleges of presbyters or by the settlement in local charge of dioceses of men who from the start had been specifically appointed as representatives and successors of the Apostles. In those days, when quite possibly most Christians looked for the return of Christ in their own lifetime or soon after, why should we expect the organization of the Church to proceed everywhere on the same lines? Why should we treat the evidence for the enthronement of leading presbyters and the evidence for the consecration of apostolic men as rival accounts of the same events, one of which must be preferred to the other? It seems to me most reasonable to conclude that what from the second century onwards became the standard method of providing for the continuance of the ministry was standardization in accordance with what had been one of various methods in use in the pre-history of different dioceses.

Thirdly, I believe that a false antithesis underlies the question whether the ministry is derived from the Church by the secretion of certain of its members for certain functions, or the Church formed round the ministry by accretion. Whether we are thinking of apostles, apostolic men, and presbyter-bishops or of bishops, priests and deacons, it makes nonsense to set the ministry over against the Church and ask which is prior to, or dependent upon, which. If from the start the messianic community, the Church of the new covenant, was a community with a ministry, each needed the other in order to be itself; if the Church needs the ministry in order to act as the body of Christ on earth, the minister must be acting as minister of the Church if he is to have any claim to be acting in the name of the Lord. If any questions are to be raised about ordinations in non-episcopal churches, parallel questions must be raised about ordinations by *episcopi vagantes*.

II

From the evidence provided by what the New Testament writers thought and said about it we have been trying to discover what the Church in their time actually was. Since then it has had a chequered history, and in the divided Christendom of to-day many different bodies claim on different grounds to be most truly one with that on which, according to *Acts*, the Spirit came at Pentecost. We must take a brief glance at some of the main views of what should be the nature of the unity and continuity of the Church down the ages.

In the literature issued in preparation for the World Conference on Faith and Order held in Edinburgh in 1937 there was a paper by Dr. Karl Barth.[1] As I understand this paper, Dr. Barth maintained that essentially a church is a group of men and women united by common faith in Christ. This faith is not simply agreement in holding certain beliefs about Christ, it is what last

[1] In *Some Prolegomena to the* 1937 *World Conference* (Faith and Order Paper, No. 76), pp. 22 ff. Translated from *Theologische Existenz Heute*, Heft. 27 (München, Chr. Kaiser Verlag), 1935.

year I called fiduciary faith, the acknowledgment of Christ's lordship and the surrender of self to Him. It is, moreover, a gift of the ascended Christ Himself, who gives the Spirit to bind together His followers by faith in Himself. Being in this faith-relationship to Christ is what constitutes a church. Some passages in the paper seem to suggest that at different times, according as their faith comes and goes, the same group of people can be and not be a church. Here on earth the church appears and disappears after the manner of the Cheshire cat.

At first sight there might seem to be little or no unity or continuity in the life of a church which exists in diverse groups of men and women according as from time to time they are possessed by faith of this kind. But no Christian believer can lightly dismiss the theory on this ground. To the Christian there can be no more assuredly objective reality than the risen, ascended Lord Jesus Christ, 'the same yesterday, to-day and for ever'. What more objective ground of unity with the Church in the upper room at Jerusalem could we have than to be united with Christ by the Spirit so that He is the link between that Church and this? Why should we need any further doctrine of the Church beyond that given in this Barthian paper?

The answer is that it is inadequate to the biblical revelation. God's revelation of Himself in His redemptive activity has taken the form of commissioning a body of men and women to be the instrument of His working for the rescue of His creation from all kinds of evil. I shall have more to say about this in a few minutes' time. For the moment it is enough that this Barthian theory, taken by itself as the whole truth of the matter, ignores the results of historical study of the New Testament which shows Christ to have reconstituted the Jewish *ecclesia* as the Christian Church, thereby surely intending it to have a life with some kind of unity and continuity as an earthly body in space and time. Nevertheless, it calls attention to a side of the truth which we neglect at our peril.[1]

[1] See below, Lecture VII, pp. 153 ff.

What does it mean to say that the Church of to-day should be one with the Church of the New Testament? I was once listening to a conversation between a German Lutheran and a French Reformed theologian. The former said: 'The difference between us Lutherans and you Calvinists is this. You think that because the Church in the New Testament was presbyterian, therefore the Church must always be presbyterian. We say that this is misusing the Bible. The Bible is not given to us to be a manual of church order, but as the word of God's grace to sinful man, and in each age and place the Church is competent to adopt whatever order will lead to the most effective preaching of that gospel.' The Calvinist would join with the Lutheran in holding it essential that the Church of to-day should be one in faith with the Church of the New Testament, but would lay greater stress on its also reproducing its order. A catholic theologian would agree with the Calvinist that the Church should be one in order as well as in faith, but he would not be content to think of this oneness as reproduction. Indeed, for him, precise similarity to the order of the New Testament would not be essential. His concern would be for continuity rather than for likeness, that in ministry, membership and faith the Church of to-day should be what the Church of the New Testament has become, remaining the same Church through changes incidental to a continuous process of growth.

Thus the emphasis on different elements has varied in the three main traditions in western Christendom. They hold in common that from the start Christianity was the faith of a body of men and women with an organized corporate life; that to be a Christian was to be sharing in the fellowship of that community; that the Church should be to the world to-day what that Church was to the world of its day; that, indeed, it should be not only like that Church but the same Church. Where they differ is on the relative importance of different elements in sameness.

This is not the time or place to consider the arguments put forward in support of their differing positions. But in the history of their discussion a question has arisen which requires our attention.

I distinguished last year between the intellectual and the fiduciary senses of the word faith.[1] When we say that the Church of to-day should be one in faith with the Church of the New Testament, it is important to make clear which sense of the word we have in mind, whether we simply mean believing as a matter of fact, with all that it implies theologically, that Jesus Christ was the fulfilment of God's messianic promises to His chosen people, or whether we mean the surrender of ourselves to His lordship. I think it would be true to say that in the history of Christian thought protestant theologians have laid greater stress than catholic on faith in this second sense of the word as constitutive of the Church. For the catholic the Church corporately should maintain its oneness in faith down the ages by professing the truth about Christ, thus providing the intellectual basis for the fellowship within which its members are to make the surrender of themselves. So far as faith is concerned, by the maintenance of its creed the Church can still be the Church even though the majority of its members fail to live up to its requirement of surrender. For the protestant this failure destroys something so essential to the being of the Church that what remains no longer deserves the name.

In the sixteenth century this question came to a head. Reformers felt that the corruption in the existing catholic church had reached such a pitch that it would be blasphemous to speak of it as the body of Christ.

> If we shall allow them for the true Church of God that appear to be of the visible or actual Church, consisting of the ordinary succession of bishops, then shall we make Christ which is an innocent lamb without spot and in whom is found no guile, to be the head of ungodly and disobedient members, which thing is as impossible as to make God to be the author, original and cause of all evil.[2]

Turning to the New Testament, these Reformers found there

[1] Vol. I, pp. 105 ff.

[2] *Miscellaneous Writings and Letters of Cranmer* (Parker Society, 1846), p. 18.

that the Church is sometimes spoken of as the body of Christ, the heir to God's promises to Israel, and sometimes as an organized body of men and women.

> M. More will not understand that the Church is sometimes taken for the elect only; which have the law of God written in their hearts—and that the Church is sometimes taken for the common rascal (i.e., mixed multitude) of all that believe whether with the mouth only and carnally without spirit.[1]

To account for this they drew a distinction between the visible and the invisible Church which has troubled protestant theology ever since. I use the word 'troubled' as a result of having spent hours in trying to understand attempted explanations by various protestant theologians of the meaning of the terms and of the relation between them. The nearest I can get to understanding it is to take it as meaning that the 'true' church is the invisible Church consisting of 'the elect . . . which have the law of God written in their hearts', and that what makes a visible Church a 'true' Church is its being an embodiment and expression of the invisible. If this be so, one can see how the doctrine, carried to its logical conclusion, would issue in the Barthian theory that the only kind of unity and continuity required with the Church of the New Testament is that of embodying and expressing the same invisible reality.

I have come to the conclusion that the distinction between the visible and the invisible Church, like the phrase 'justification by faith', is a sixteenth-century formula which now encumbers our attempts at thinking and had better be dropped from our theological vocabulary.[2] The fact that it was based on a false exegesis, reading back into the minds of the New Testament writers a distinction which never occurred to them, does not matter very much. That might be corrected as a matter of biblical scholarship without affecting its value as an insight into the implications of their witness. The real ground for discarding it as no longer useful to us is of another kind.

[1] Tyndale: *Answer to Sir T. More's Dialogue*, p. 113.
[2] Vol. I, pp. 108 ff.

The Reformers were confronted by a paradox at the heart of the Christian life, writ large before their eyes in the contemporary state of the Church. 'I live', says St. Paul, 'yet not I, but Christ liveth in me.' When you come to think of it, this presents in the life of the individual Christian precisely the same problem that Cranmer saw in the life of the Church. Is it not as blasphemous to speak of Christ in me—this so often rebellious and sinful me—as to make Him 'to be the head of ungodly and disobedient members'? One knows how the Reformers wrestled with this problem, how it underlies Luther's 'simul iustus et peccator' and controversies about assurance and predestination. But I am not aware of any theologian who suggested resolving the paradox by the insertion of an invisible me between the visible me and Christ, as was done in the case of the Church. Apparently the two problems were dealt with separately without any realization that essentially they are one and the same.

There is here a real problem for our thought, and we can see that any attempt at its solution must be relevant to the life of the individual Christian as well as to that of the Church. Now Reformation theology belongs to what Collingwood called the Renaissance period of human cosmological thinking, its theologians lived at a time when it was not possible for them to think in terms of scientifically knowable change. Last year I was showing how to do so enlightens our understanding both of the creation of the universe and of our own experience of freedom.[1] I described the difference between the two ways of thinking as follows:

> If there is scientifically knowable change, its phases cannot all be knowable in precisely the same way as objects of knowledge were held to be knowable before. When the object of our study is a process of development, we cannot at any moment take a cross section of it, isolate it from what went before and what will come after, make it stand still to be looked at, and then think that what we are looking at is the thing we set out to study. We set out to study an ongoing process; if we have arrested it in order to study it, what we have before us is a dead specimen, not the living reality.

[1] Vol. I, pp. 125 ff., 173 ff.

In thinking about the universe and human life we found ourselves driven to recognize the reality of irrational elements of which, as they stand, no rational account can be given. If they are to be explained at all, it must be as phases in a process devised or permitted for the purpose of achieving a rational end. It is no good trying to find a point of view from which they can be seen to be intelligible, or to discover a formula which shall give them a logical definition. What meaning they have at the moment is a meaning for action rather than for thought. They have to be changed in order to become intelligible.

There are irrational elements in the universe which we have to accept as devised or permitted by God as incidental to His purpose to create a community of finite free persons. There are irrational elements in ourselves which are incidental to our being created into members of such a community. Neither of the universe in all its details, nor of ourselves, as existing at any one moment of time, is it possible to give a logical definition. It and we have to be changed in fact in order to become intelligible.

What is true of the universe and of ourselves is true also of the Church. The distinction between the visible and the invisible Church came into existence as an attempt to do the impossible, to devise a formula for a logical definition of an illogical phase in a process which only in its completion will be fully intelligible and logically definable. That is why I think we should now be wise to discard it, and address ourselves directly, in terms of the thought of our own time, to the problem it was invented to meet.

The Christian Gospel proclaims God's entry into the history of this world to work from within for the rescue of His creation from evil. He does this at the stage in His creative process at which in human beings evil has taken the form of sin. Living as man among men He wins by His death and resurrection the right to offer full and free forgiveness to all who repent of their sins. By the gift of the Spirit He binds together His followers in the community of forgiven sinners to be His instrument for carrying forward His work of rescue. He binds them together by binding them to Himself so closely that they may be spoken of as the branches of which He is the vine, as members of His body, or as the body of which He is the head—His feet to go on His errands, His mouth to speak His words, His eyes to see what He wants done, His hands to do it.

The question before us is that of the relation of Christ to the Church and its members, the 'I, yet not I but Christ' of Galatians ii. 20. In both respects there is language in the New Testament which implies identification, and language which implies distinction. The Church is not only the vine and the body, it is also the bride of Christ. St. Paul not only says of himself: 'To me to live is Christ', and writes to the Colossians of 'Christ in you, the hope of glory'; he warns the Romans that 'we shall all stand before the judgment seat of Christ'.

I want to suggest that we should think of the relation of Christ to His Church in a manner analogous to that of God to His creation. Last year we thought of creation as a process which can be looked at from either of two ends. From above, it is God communicating in increasing measure the fullness of being which He wills to give to His created universe. From below, it is that universe growing in fullness of being as step by step it becomes capable of receiving it in fuller measure. Within creation God the Holy Spirit is at work, disposing and enabling creatures to receive and grow. But all is conditioned by God's central purpose to create a community of persons endowed with genuine freedom. This requires for the universe a mode of reality in which there can be irrationalities of which no intelligible account can be given as they stand beyond saying that they are phases incidental to a process devised for an intelligible end.

If we think of the Church as the body of Christ in the sense of being His instrument for carrying forward His rescuing work, the Church, like the universe, will be a process with a history in time and space. It will be a process subject to the same condition, in which both the giving of Himself by Christ from above, and the working of the Spirit within the body at the receiving end, will be directed towards the perfecting of human freedom, and patient of whatever limitations are entailed by respect for that end. We shall not be surprised to find the Church, at any one moment in its life, going through a phase in which it defies all attempts to devise a logical formula which will accurately describe its nature.

It is a process which can be looked at from either of both ends. From above it is the crucified, risen, ascended Lord Jesus Christ carrying on His redeeming work in and through His Church. From below it is the community of human beings receiving from Him what it needs for its own growth and for His service.

> The man in Christ, the new creature, is in process of growing up into his true self as Christ, the hope of glory, is formed in him. The Church is in process of growing into the fullness of its true nature as the earthly body of the risen, ascended Lord, as that Lord is giving to it in increasing measure the fullness of the life that is His.
>
> Seen as from above, as Jesus Christ at work in the world, it is one, holy, catholic and apostolic; seen as from below, as the fellowship of forgiven sinners growing up into the perfection that the Lord is giving it, it is divided, very imperfectly holy, too often self-regarding and worldly. Yet it is one and the same process of which these contradictory things are true. . . . So long as the Church is still *in via* we must not be surprised to find that it has a paradoxical character which renders it impatient, as it stands, of logically coherent definition. It must be changed in deed in order to become transparent to thought.[1]

To the trouble caused among protestants by the distinction between the visible and the invisible Church there correspond in catholic and orthodox theology arguments about whether the Church can be said to sin. This is an instance of the way in which what is essentially one and the same question can appear in another guise in a different theological tradition.[2] No one can have much experience of inter-church discussions on questions of faith and order without coming up against the question in this second form. Sooner or later it is sure to be suggested that the first step towards the reunion of Christendom is for the Church

[1] From *The Doctrine of the Atonement*, pp. 98, 99.

[2] See also below, Lecture VII, pp. 143 ff.

to be truly penitent for its sinfulness manifested in its divisions. But in any attempt to issue a joint statement of agreements, clauses on these lines will have to be revised or deleted in order to meet the objections of those who hold that, while its members may be sinners, sin cannot be predicated of the Church itself. Here is one of the points at which deadlock will continue until we cease to conduct our discussions in terms of the thought of a bygone age. When we realize that the Church is Christ and the Spirit at work in and through its members whose perfection in genuine freedom is as central to God's creative and redemptive purpose as is their service of the world in His name, we need no longer be kept apart by disputes arising from attempts to give a logical and coherent description of it in its present condition.

III

We have been considering the historical origin of the Church and its constitution. In both respects, in studying the evidence from the past we have had to ask our persistent question: what must the truth have been and be if men in their circumstances, who thought and spoke as they did, put it like that? This becomes of even greater importance when we pass on to ask for what purpose it exists, when the definition we seek is not in terms of origin or constitution, but of purpose and function.[1] It has been through the study of this question, and from reflecting on the implications of the fact that in its historical origin the Christian Church was the Jewish messianic community, that I have been led to think that after nearly two thousand years of Christian history we may only be beginning to know what Christianity really is.[2]

I have spoken of how, in the case of Christ Himself, our understanding of the Gospel evidence has grown by reading it in the light of contemporary expectations of the Messiah. His interpretation of messiahship was so unlike what His people were looking for that for the most part they were unable to recognize

[1] Vol. I, pp. 159, 164.

[2] Above, p. 46.

in Him the fulfilment of their hopes. Those who accepted Him did so in spite of appearances, with a faith that stood much in need of enlightenment by the gift of the Holy Spirit. Guided by the Spirit we have come to see that to accept Him involved a revolution in the idea of messiahship. He had not come to take His power and reign, either as the monarch of a world-empire ruled in the name of God from Jerusalem, or in a celestial kingdom to which His faithful subjects should be raised out of this realm of space and time. He had come to rescue His creation from the evil which prevented His creatures from growing into the perfection of the freedom that He willed for them. For Him messiahship meant giving Himself to win for His people freedom from the burden of their sins in order that He might have on earth a body through which to work for the rescue of His creatures not only from sin but from all other forms of evil too.

Within the New Testament period the author of the Fourth Gospel is guided by the Spirit to see in this the manifestation of the glory of God. 'The action in which He most fully expressed Himself, namely His self-devotion to death in love for mankind, is the conclusive manifestation of the divine glory . . . in other words, the revelation of the eternal majesty of God in His love for mankind.'[1]

The acceptance of this revolution in the idea of messiahship was an outstanding instance of a revision of categories of human thought due to the coming of new evidence. The Fourth Gospel shows that it is not merely a matter of our idea of messiahship, that it has implications for our thought about God, implications which still to-day we have not fully grasped. His clear exposition of this is one of the many things for which Dr. Donald Baillie is to be remembered.[2] I shall have more to say about it later on. Our concern now is with its implications for our thought about the Church. Put briefly, what I have to urge is that the revolution in the idea of the Messiah involves a corresponding revolution in the idea of the messianic community.

[1] C. H. Dodd: *The Interpretation of the Fourth Gospel* (Cambridge, 1955), p. 207.
[2] See his *God was in Christ* (London, 1948), especially pp. 63 ff.

At the time of the coming of Christ it was generally taken for granted that religion exists for the benefit of the religious people, religious organizations for the benefit of their members. It was not only in Judaism that to be one of the elect was held to give a man a superior status in relation to God, with hopes of eschatological bliss. This was what was offered to their initiates by the various oriental mystery cults which were the live religions in the Gentile world. Inevitably, when the Christian Church came into being, it was taken to be one more body existing for this same purpose.

The first Christian preaching was the proclamation that as a result of what God had done in Christ, forgiveness of their sins was ready and waiting for all who would repent of them.[1] It would be unreasonable to expect St. Peter, when he preached those first sermons, to have thought of this otherwise than as an offer of welcome into a body which, as the new and true messianic Israel, existed to give its members what in the old Israel they had hoped to receive. Membership in the old Israel had been the privilege of the circumcised descendants of Abraham, extended to proselytes who acknowledged their monotheistic faith in the God of Abraham, Isaac and Jacob and were duly circumcised. Membership in the new Israel was offered to those who should repent of their sins, should acknowledge Jesus as the Christ in whom had been fulfilled God's promises to His people through the prophets, and should be baptized into the fellowship. Through the death, resurrection and ascension of Christ, and the gift of the Spirit, there had been accomplished for them what they had sought in the sacrificial worship of the old covenant. From this earliest preaching throughout the New Testament the Church continues to be thought of as the fellowship of forgiven sinners into which men and women are baptized in order to enjoy the privilege of reconciliation with God and the promise of eternal salvation.

Throughout the New Testament. And is this not still largely

[1] Above, pp. 71 ff.

true to-day? Whether one studies theology in the Catholic, the Orthodox, the Lutheran or the Reformed traditions, in all it is apparently taken for granted that the Christian religion exists to promote the salvation of Christians, that the Church exists for the salvation of its members. Many, indeed, would say that in the first place the Church exists for the glory of God. We need not dispute that. But to say it leaves open the question of the way in which God is to be glorified. We can re-phrase our concern by saying that it is with the assumption that the Church will best minister to the glory of God by making the salvation of its members the end for which it exists. How widespread is this assumption may be seen from the way it is taken for granted as the basis of missionary work and of evangelistic campaigns and crusades.

Still to-day, after nearly two thousand years, the Holy Spirit is leading us further into truth by taking of the things of Christ and showing them unto us. What will be the effect of taking seriously the realization that Christ's revolution in the idea of messiahship involves a corresponding revolution in the idea of the messianic community?

If I am right in my understanding of the gospel picture of Christ, there was never a man in the history of this world who was so completely forgetful of self as He was in His devotion to the Father and the finding and doing of the Father's work. I have already referred to the passage in St. Matthew xii where He says in effect: 'I don't mind what you say about Me, but don't you dare to blaspheme against the Spirit that is working in Me'.[1] 'My meat is to do the will of Him that sent Me, and to accomplish His work' sums up the impression produced on the author of the Fourth Gospel. 'Even Christ', writes St. Paul, 'pleased not Himself'. And in the moment of supreme agony there is no thought of self: 'Father, forgive them'.[2] He, the sinless One, gives Himself to cleanse from their sins those through whom He

[1] Above, p. 102.
[2] St. John iv. 34; Rom. xv. 3; St. Luke xxiii. 34.

wills to work for the rescue of His creation from all forms of evil. The form in which the commission He gives them has come down to us is 'As the Father has sent Me, even so send I you'.[1]

The Church is the earthly body through which the crucified, risen, ascended Lord wills to carry on His work of rescue. Professor Torrance has criticized the description of it as the extension of the Incarnation, but rightly understood that phrase is a valuable reminder that the mind and work of the Church militant here on earth are to be patterned on those of its Lord in His incarnate ministry in Palestine, what Torrance calls having the form of a servant, or being under the cross.[2] In that ministry He had come not to judge but to save. United by the Spirit with the Father in heaven, He must in His manhood walk the way of the Cross, caring nothing of what happens to Himself so long as the way is opened for the cleansing of creation from its infection by evil. He opened that way by the sacrifice of Himself through which God's forgiveness is made available for all who repent of their sins.

The making of that sacrifice, the opening of the way, was something which only He could do, which He has done: a once-for-all achievement in virtue of which we live in a redeemed world. What He has entrusted to the Church is the work of harvesting the fruits of the victory He has won. For this He needs a body of men and women enlisted to fight under His banner against sin, the world and the devil, cleansed from their own sins in order that they may be able to forget themselves in sharing in His interest in the rescue and perfecting of His creation. He who in His godhead 'did not count equality with God a thing to be grasped',[3] in His manhood did not think of His sinless perfection as a prize to be enjoyed for Himself but as equipping Him for the doing of God's redemptive work. The first fruits of His sacrifice must be the winning to penitence and discipleship

[1] St. John xx. 21.
[2] T. F. Torrance: *Royal Priesthood* (Edinburgh, 1955), pp. 31, 84–7. [3] Phil. ii. 6.

of those who are to be the members of His Church. Until they have been cleansed and taken by Him to share in His freedom from sin they cannot be used as His agents for the extension of His work. So to begin with the Church was charged with the duty of proclaiming the gospel of forgiveness and baptizing penitent believers into the fellowship of forgiven sinners.

Conditioned as they were by the outlook of their age, both those who preached and those who were converted thought of baptism into the Church as synonymous with inclusion among those to whom God promised eternal salvation. But if Christ's messianic community is to be patterned on Christ's messiahship, if the attitude of the Church to the world is to be that of its Lord in His earthly ministry, this is a confusion of two quite different things. Because faith in Christ as God incarnate and Saviour from sin is required for membership in His Church on earth it does not necessarily follow that without it a man can neither please God in this world nor hope for salvation in the next. The line between those who are and those who are not in the way that leadeth to eternal life cannot be made to coincide with that between those who are and those who are not members of the Church—or even with that between those who do and those who do not consciously believe in Jesus Christ.

In my third lecture last year I spoke of the puzzle presented to Christians by the fact that while we base our own hope of salvation on God's gift to us of faith in Christ we cannot reconcile the thought of His condemnation of others with the belief that He is the God revealed in Christ.[1] I then said that for the solution of this puzzle we might find it necessary to revise assumptions commonly taken for granted in traditional theology. My contention now is that the assumption which chiefly gives rise to it is untrue to the biblical revelation of the Church as the messianic community. The Church corporately should think of its calling and election as a calling and election to forget itself in devotion to God's work of rescuing His creation from evil. To say that

[1] Vol. I, pp. 53 ff.

the individual Christian should think of himself in this way is perhaps no novelty. But to say it of the Church corporately seems to me to challenge so many of the ideas we commonly take for granted that I will end this lecture by putting what I have to say in the form of questions. Are we right in thinking and preaching that to receive God's forgiveness a man must have faith in the sense of consciously accepting Jesus Christ as Saviour? Are we right in thinking it to be God's will and purpose that all men shall be gathered into membership of the Church militant here on earth?

1. In considering the effect on converts of the preaching of the Christian Gospel we saw that we have to distinguish between their consciousness and the objective fact of which they feel themselves to be conscious.[1] Subjectively, the Christian accepts with gratitude and joy the forgiveness which he believes to be ready and waiting for him in virtue of what God has done in Christ. It is ready and waiting because of the once-for-all act of God in history. He has come to know of it through hearing the gospel story which has won him to penitence for all that needs to be forgiven. But what is the evidence that the requisite penitence is only possible in association with hearing and responding to the gospel story?

I have argued that it would be unreasonable to expect Christians in the New Testament period to have thought of the Church otherwise than as the messianic community into which men should come in order to be in the way of salvation. Their immediate task was to convince men that the Messiah had come in the person of Jesus, and to win for Him disciples to be baptized into membership of His earthly body. Interpreting the messianic community by the light of Christ's messiahship, may we not conceive more widely the meeting of penitence with God's forgiveness and reconciliation?

Our natural theology has taught us that God's aim is to create a community of finite free persons, and that to this end He gives

[1] Above, p. 75. See also Vol. I, p. 57.

us a world in which we grow in freedom by losing ourselves in devotion to ends of eternal value.[1] In the fullness of His revelation of Himself in Christ He reveals Himself as the God already made known to us in this natural theology. The infection of His creation by evil had reached its climax in the diversion of men from this self-forgetfulness to other self-regarding ends. In His redemptive work God has struck at the heart of the problem by action through which men are cleansed from their own sinfulness and won back to share in His interests and to be His agents in the rescue of the rest of His creation. To be sharing in His interest in earthly embodiments of beauty and truth and goodness is to be expressing devotion to Himself. It was to set men free from all that hindered them from this devotion that Christ died and rose again.

This gives us our clue in our attempt to see where the line is to be drawn between those who are and those who are not in the way of salvation. What God looks for in a man is that he should be devoting himself to what in God's eyes is worth doing. Imagine a case in which someone who has been living a dissolute and selfish life is kindled by enthusiasm for some worthy cause and moved to devote himself henceforward to its service. This means for him a genuine turning over of a new leaf, and in his new life he loathes his past self and his wasted years. Whatever it is that has moved him by kindling his enthusiasm, it has had nothing to do with any hearing of or responding to the Christian gospel. Yet who can say that he has not had a genuine conversion and brought forth fruits of repentance such that in him the crucified, risen and ascended Lord sees of the travail of his soul and is satisfied?

This is what our natural theology would lead us to expect, and it is confirmed by the biblical revelation. Last year we noticed the epoch-making advance in God's education of His people made by the prophetic principle that the faith that matters is for a man to try to live by what he honestly believes to be true and right.

[1] Vol. I, pp. 186 ff., 231.

'Faith in God . . . means trusting in One who reveals Himself to us in and through our judgments of fact and value.'[1] Now we have seen how this was preparing the way for Christ's interpretation of His messianic ministry as one of self-forgetfulness in care for the rescue of God's creation from all forms of evil.

What advantage, then, hath the Christian? To begin with, as I said in the last lecture, the enjoyment of 'inside knowledge' of what is going on.[2] He knows, as the converted non-Christian does not know, that in this universe of space and time all embodiments of eternal value are manifestations of God in His creation, and that those in whose hearts is kindled enthusiasm for them are being moved by the Holy Spirit. He knows, moreover, that the forgiveness for the past in virtue of which they are free to go forward in the new life is theirs because of the 'full, perfect and sufficient sacrifice, oblation and satisfaction, for the sins of the whole world', made once for all by Christ on the Cross of Calvary. He would thus be able, should they inquire of him, to interpret them to themselves. Meanwhile he has, too, the joy of knowing what it is to be the object of God's love in Christ. This joy, which he looks forward to seeing shared by the others in the world to come, is already given to him while still on earth.

2. To go into all the world and preach the gospel to every creature; to bring all nations into discipleship to Christ, baptizing them and bidding them live according to His teaching: this is what the New Testament Church understood to be the commission given to it by its crucified, risen and ascended Lord.[3] The question now to be asked is whether this necessarily implies that the end to be aimed at is the bringing of all men into membership of the Church militant here on earth. The French theologian, Auguste Sabatier, took the fulfilment of this aim to be the shape of the future envisaged in the Epistle to the Ephesians.[4] All Christian thinkers have not been so optimistic. Some have thought the concern of the Church to be to rescue out of the

[1] Vol. I, pp. 106–7. [2] Above, p. 106.
[3] St. Mark xvi. 15; St. Matt. xxviii. 19, 20.
[4] *The Apostle Paul*, E. Tr., p. 239. Quoted in my *Doctrine of the Atonement*, p. 125.

world those who were not to be left to perish. Those who cannot reconcile this with their belief in God's love and care for all His creatures tend to assume that the method by which His will is to be accomplished will be the incorporation of all men in a world-wide Church. For both schools of thought the practical conclusion is the same, that the concern of the Church may be summed up in the two words evangelism and edification, the conversion of men to faith in Christ and nurturing their Christian life. The Church's interest is in its own expansion and inner spiritual progress.

But if the interest of the Church is to be patterned on that of its Lord in His earthly ministry, will it not have to take a wider outlook than this? Let me refer to two incidents to illustrate what I mean.

A few years ago in a town in the south of England there was a trade union official, a good man who valued his office as giving him opportunity to work for the true welfare of his fellows. He was won to faith in Christ, and became a regular and sincere worshipper in his parish church. Shortly afterwards his vicar said to him that now that he was a member of the Church he ought to undertake some definite work for God, such as taking charge of the church boys' club. Being the conscientious man he was, he threw himself so thoroughly into this new work that he found he had to resign from his trade union activities.

Further north in this island another trade union official was a lay preacher in a Christian church. Not long ago he told me that on the shop floor he made no secret of his Christian profession and ministry, that he found them treated by his fellow workers with respect, and that men who would not think of approaching any of the regular clergy or ministers would come to him for counsel and advice because he was one of themselves. He added, somewhat apologetically, and as one confessing an obvious failure in duty, that it did not often result in their joining the church. I could not help asking him: Was not the Church through him doing its true work? If, for example, someone had been helped to save his marriage from disaster, was not that the kind of thing that Christ wanted to use His Church for, whether or no the man and his wife should be won to effective membership of it?

In an earlier lecture I have spoken of how the parable of the labourers in the vineyard gives us a glimpse of an understanding of God's love for His world as revealed to us in Christ.[1] Is not the true import of the biblical revelation that Christ has commissioned the Church to love the world with a love which is not only to be like his, but actually to be His love expressing itself through His continuing earthly body? When we begin to realize what this will imply for our thought and practice, may it not truly be said that we are only beginning to understand what Christianity really is?

There is more to be said about this later.[2] One final word is necessary here. Throughout this lecture we have been concerned with the Church militant here on earth. We must not forget that this is only part of the whole, that the Church Militant, the Church Expectant and the Church Triumphant are one Church whose members are at different stages in their pilgrimage. It is only with reference to the Church Militant on earth that I wish to raise the question whether it should be aiming at the inclusion of all those who are to be saved for membership of the Church Triumphant in heaven.

[1] Above, pp. 59 ff. [2] Below, pp. 208 ff.

LECTURE VII

Grace

I

THE Christian doctrine of God's grace is a complicated and confusing subject, more so than is always realized. If a man grows up in the catholic tradition of theology, and only reads about it in works written from that standpoint, all is clear and straightforward. Another man, confining himself to expositions by protestant divines, may be equally untroubled. It is when one reads both that the trouble begins. How can the same word mean such different things in different traditions of Christian theology? Is it merely a terminological dispute about the meaning of a word? Or is there some deeper issue at stake?

So far as the use of the English word is concerned, it would be true, I think, to say that in protestant theology its associations are with those of the German *Gnade*, in catholic with those of the Latin *gratia*. Both look back to the Greek *charis* of the New Testament. We will take our start from that.

The background of St. Paul's use of the word is the language of inscriptions commemorating the gifts of emperors or other benefactors. It brings with it a sense of gracious favour bestowed by a sovereign. What St. Paul does is to substitute for a drinking fountain or city charter the specifically Christian content of the benefaction. 'Grace for St. Paul signifies the generous love or gift of God by which in Christ salvation is bestowed on man and a new world of blessings opened.'[1] But, as we have seen, this gift of forgiveness and reconciliation has a dynamic effect in the recipient. 'In this fellowship of forgiven sinners he found a psychological release that issued in what St. Paul calls the "fruit of the Spirit".'[2] Hence

The term 'grace' is also used by St. Paul with reference to the Divine influence or influences which operate from within the Christian nature. The

[1] W. Manson, in Whitley: *The Doctrine of Grace* (London, 1932), p. 43. [2] Above, p. 100.

gracious initiative of God in salvation appears as taking effect in human hearts in immanent fashion and under differentiated forms. . . . It seems best then to say that St. Paul, keeping steadfastly to the original sense of the word, thinks of the grace of God as becoming effectual in various ways, now as giving men a new status, now as conferring various special gifts, now as inspiring to fresh tasks and responsibilities.[1]

For convenience I will call the use of the word for God's gracious activity in giving forgiveness, or a new status, or any spiritual gifts, St. Paul's primary sense; its use for 'the Divine influence or influences which operate from within the Christian nature' his secondary sense.

In the development of catholic theology the predominant emphasis in the use of the word *gratia* came to rest on this second sense. Just how or why this came about it is impossible to determine. It may be connected with the fact that in the New Testament there is a similar ambiguity with regard to the Holy Spirit: there are passages which imply a personally active He, and passages which could be paraphrased as the power of God working within creation.[2] The fact that the doctrine of the Spirit developed along the lines of the He passages may help to explain how what the It passages stood for found a home in the doctrine of grace.

In St. Augustine, St. Paul's twofold use is continued. The word *gratia* expresses both the graciousness of God the giver and the gift of God's power working in man. In its widest reference all God's action, creative as well as redemptive, is gracious; but as a technical term in specifically Christian doctrine, grace is relative to sin. It is (i) God's redemptive activity in Christ, and (ii) the power of God working for his restoration in fallen, sinful man. Where the thought is of God's gracious activity, the emphasis is on the gratuitousness of God's saving work. Carried to its logical conclusion, this would produce an antinomy, a doctrine of predestination inconsistent with the biblical revelation

[1] W. Manson, *op. cit.*, pp. 47, 49.
[2] See my *Doctrine of the Trinity*, pp. 77 ff.

of God as righteous love.[1] Where the thought is of the power of God working in human nature, the problem involved is that of the relation of God's grace to human freedom. To meet this latter problem St. Augustine draws a distinction between the *liberum arbitrium*, with which man is endowed by nature, and the *libertas* which may come as a gift of God's grace in Christ. By his *liberum arbitrium* a man can choose between different acts, but owing to his sinful nature his will is too weak to do what is good. God's grace strengthens the will, enabling it to do the good, and this freedom to do the good is *libertas*. Last year, when analysing our experience of freedom, I distinguished between what I called freedom (*a*) and freedom (*b*).[2] These two distinctions have so much in common that at this point St. Augustine gives a clear instance of the manner in which Christian dovetails into natural theology. But of that more later.

Since grace is God's love in action, the thought of God acting, of St. Paul's primary sense, is never entirely absent in later catholic theology. But in mediaeval scholastic elaborations of the doctrine the thought is more and more of his secondary sense. St. Thomas Aquinas' detailed analysis of grace as *gratis data, gratum faciens, operans, co-operans, praeveniens, subsequens*[3] presupposes this approach. Moreover, increasing attention was being paid to the question of the means whereby the grace of God is received by man. There was a parallel growth, with similar elaboration, in sacramental doctrine. The two lines of thought should not, indeed, be called parallel. They were closely interwoven, and sacraments came commonly to be spoken of as 'means of grace'.

It is, of course, important to distinguish between the intended meaning of theological doctrines and the understanding of them which finds expression in popular religion. Where this is obscured, confusion ensues, and out of the heat of controversy may come curious results. The impression produced on my mind by

[1] On this, see W. Temple: *Nature, Man and God* (London, 1934), pp. 400–3.
[2] Vol. I, pp. 171 ff.
[3] *Summa Theologia*, II, i, 108 ff.

what little I know of the theology of the later Middle Ages and the Reformation is that the divergence between catholic and protestant doctrines of grace is due to something of this kind.

In my youth, brought up as an Anglican, south of the Border, I had always thought of the Reformation as a revolt against religious formalism in the interests of morality, a re-assertion of the teaching of Isaiah i or Amos v. 18–24. It was with surprise that I discovered what doubtless the learned Scots had known all along—that it was something far deeper and more far-reaching than this, a re-assertion of Augustinian anti-pelagianism in which morality is coupled with formalism as the enemy. The antithesis to justification by faith is justification by works, and morality, no less than rites and ceremonies, comes under the heading of works.[1]

There seems little doubt that, whatever may have been the intended meaning of the catholic doctrine of grace and sacraments, what was taught and practised as the Christian religion often expressed a degenerate form of it which provoked a prophetic revolt against formalism, and that this led on to discovery of the danger of pelagianism in emphasis on morality. What was commonly taught and practised was held to imply that a man could earn his salvation by the correct performance of sacramental acts through which grace would work in his soul like medicine in his body. Catholic sacramentalism being by this time largely bound up with the doctrine of grace as God's power working in man, in their revolt against it the Reformers went back to St. Paul's primary sense of the word *charis* and insisted that this was not only the truth but the whole truth.

I take Grace here strictly for the favour of God, as it should be taken—not for a quality of the soul, as is taught by the more recent of our doctors.

We take this term *gratia* in the simplest way, by following the phrase of Scripture, to the effect that Grace is favour, mercy, free kindness of God towards us. The gift is the Holy Spirit Himself, which He pours into the hearts of those on whom He has taken pity. In short, Grace is nothing but the

[1] See, e.g., R. Otto: *Religious Essays* (Oxford, 1931).

pardoning or remission of sin. The gift is the Holy Spirit regenerating and sanctifying our hearts.[1]

In Reformation theology the word grace is no longer used for the regenerating and sanctifying work of God in men's hearts. That is ascribed to the Holy Spirit. Man's part is simply to accept by faith God's promise of forgiveness in Christ. This acceptance of God's promise is the faith that justifies. It is a momentary act. However often it may be repeated, it is on each occasion all or nothing. The Reformers rejected the scholastic doctrine of the development of *fides informis* into *fides caritate formata* because, like the doctrine of grace as something working in man to achieve salvation, it implied for them a trust in work-righteousness as contrasted with the simple acceptance of the once-for-all accomplished gracious activity of God in Christ.

Another aspect of their teaching is the doctrine of imputed righteousness as against all ideas of infused righteousness or infused virtue. To say that the repentant believing sinner is in any sense made righteous reintroduces the notion of salvation achieved by human progress. A man is justified when he accepts the word of God telling him that his sins are covered by the righteousness of Christ.

But what of the act of faith by which the sinner accepts God's forgiveness? Must not that be his own act, so that at least to that extent he co-operates in his justification? Even this element of synergism is excluded, for the sinner's response of faith is itself a gift of the grace of God. Carried to its logical conclusion, as in Calvin's doctrine of double predestination,[2] this brings us up against the same antinomy that threatened St. Augustine.

A further corollary, drawn by some Reformers, is the repudiation of all natural theology. To quote from Professor Hermelink:

The God of the Bible, the God of Jesus Christ, is the unconditionally gracious God. He alone is this . . . and conversely: the God of the Bible is

[1] Quoted from Luther and Melancthon by H. Hermelink in Whitley: *op. cit.*, pp. 179–81.

[2] Institutes (1559), III, xxi.

only known when He is known thus. . . . Where the *sola gratia* is not known or acknowledged, there we have not Christian but heathen knowledge of God.[1]

So much for the way in which the word grace has come to have such different meanings in different theological circles. Is it simply a difference in the use of words? Or does this express some more substantial disagreement? And what, for us, is the truth of the matter?

The more I think about these historic controversies, the more it appears that in both camps the theologians were wrestling with the same baffling problem in the Christian faith. Under the pressure of the circumstances of the time they adopted different expedients in their attempts to frame doctrinal statements about it. But the problem was the same for all, and at bottom all were trying to say the same thing. This can be shown most clearly by setting out in tabular form the three beliefs which all were concerned to maintain:

1. Man's salvation is God's gift, freely given through the crucified and risen Christ.

2. Man's moral responsibility to God is such that we cannot rightly think of his being 'mechanically' or 'physically' saved irrespective of his own personal character.

3. Being God's free gift, salvation is not in any sense earned or received as a reward of his own merit.

How can the second of these be reconciled with the first and third? How can we maintain both that a man's salvation depends on the kind of life he lives and also that it is a free gift of God which must not be thought of as earned by his own merits? In a few minutes we must squarely face this question as a problem for ourselves. But first let us see how it is posed in the two schools of thought that we have been considering.

In catholic theology the evangelical doctrine that salvation is by God's free gift and must not be thought of as earned finds expression in the teaching that God's action in the sacraments is

[1] In Whitley: *op. cit.*, p. 210.

ex opere operato. This phrase is often misunderstood; it is thought that the *operans* is the earthly minister and that God's grace is said to be secured by the right performance of ritual acts, a combination of pelagianism with magic. It may be that this error was indulged in by ignorant catholics who thereby gave ground for attacks on the phrase by protestant critics. But to one who knows from the inside what the phrase is intended to mean it is otherwise. The *operans* is God. 'Sacramental worship is to him a bulwark against pelagianism; it is the kind of worship in which the importance of the human element is at its minimum; what gives their meaning to the services of Baptism and Holy Communion is the belief that it is Christ who in Baptism incorporates the new member into that fellowship of forgiven sinners which is His mystical body on earth, it is Christ who in the Eucharist takes the bread and wine to be His means for continuing the ministry on earth begun at Bethlehem. The important thing about the service he has been attending is not what he was believing, thinking, or feeling like, but what God has done: *ex opere operato*.'[1]

Even when rightly understood this might open the door to carelessness in the matter of moral responsibility. So it has to be balanced by the teaching of requirements in that field.

> What is required of persons to be baptized?
>
> Repentance, whereby they forsake sin; and Faith, whereby they steadfastly believe the promises of God made to them in that Sacrament.
>
> What is required of them who come to the Lord's Supper?
>
> To examine themselves, whether they repent them truly of their former sins, steadfastly purposing to lead a new life; have a lively faith in God's mercy through Christ, with a thankful remembrance of his death; and be in charity with all men.[2]

In protestant theology the substitution of preaching the Word for the administration of sacraments as the central act of worship expresses the personal and ethical character of the Christian

[1] Quoted from address in O. S. Tomkins: *The Third World Conference on Faith and Order* (London, 1953), p. 114.

[2] From the *Catechism* in the Book of Common Prayer.

religion. A preacher addresses a man as a responsible person, calling upon him for an act of decision, for the response of faith. This is balanced by the doctrine that the faith which finds expression in the response is itself the free gift of God. Again, what is most important is what God is doing. Faith to the protestant is *ex opere operato* in the same sense as are sacraments to the catholic.

Underlying all forms of the doctrine of grace there is the problem of reconciling the ethical and personal character of the Christian religion with man's utter dependence on God's free gift of salvation.

II

Let us set this problem in the context of what we have learned of God's way with His creation. We have seen reason to think that His central purpose is to create a community of persons endowed with genuine freedom, that this spatio-temporal universe, with its combination of orderliness and contingency, is both the medium through which they are brought into existence as individualized centres of consciousness and also provides the environment and material for their growth in freedom. The extent of its infection by evil is the measure of His concern to create genuinely free persons. The steps He takes to counteract the evil are such as to set forward, and not to vary, His creative purpose: men are rescued from the chain of their sins by a method which depends on winning their free response and enlisting them to share in His work of ridding His creation from evil in all its various forms.

Once again we are face to face with the fundamental mystery of our existence, a puzzle not peculiar to Christian faith but confronting all who do not stop short of thinking deeply enough to discover it.[1] Our thinking starts as the attempt to make sense of the universe of our experience. Step by step we are led on to the postulate that we are being created into persons destined for

[1] See above, pp. 48, 87. Also Vol. I, p. 133.

perfection in freedom. We who are Christians have faced the issue that any kind of creation involves a voluntary limitation of the divine impassibility, and a consequent antinomy in our doctrine of God.[1] When we embrace this postulate as a matter of faith—when, that is, we take it as the view of the nature of things by which we pledge ourselves to try to live[2]—we begin our Creed by saying that we believe in God Almighty. To anyone who might say that God could not create without ceasing to be God we should reply that we believe His omnipotence to be expressed in His ability not only to create at all but to create free persons, and that we are encouraged to persist in this belief by the fact that it is the postulate required to make sense of what actually exists and happens.

Men and women come into existence at the human stage of the creative process, the stage, that is, at which God wills the development of individualized personal freedom. The process we are trying to understand is one in which we are ourselves involved, in which we have to play our part. It is a process which moves through phases which as they stand are illogical, whose meaning is a meaning for the action that must be taken if they are to be rendered intelligible as contributing to its intelligible end.

Looking out on this process from our position within it, 'What', we must ask, each one of us, 'is our Creator's will for us?' He has given us our freedom (*a*), the opportunity of considering different possible lines of action and choosing between them, in order that we may grow in freedom (*b*), the unimpeded activity of those whose freedom finds expression in devotion to the welfare of the city of God. 'How can I', each one of us must ask, 'how can I, at one and the same time, obey the divine command which bids me develop my individual selfhood, and also acknowledge that my only true way of life is that of complete surrender to the will of God?' He must answer: 'I am God's creature. Whatever being I have I draw from Him as His gift.

[1] Vol. I, pp. 152, 227. [2] Vol. I, p.105.

He is not only giving me what I need to grow into the fullness of being that He wills for me; He is also giving me whatever ability I have to receive and be nourished by what He is giving. Whenever I draw a breath or lift a finger I am making use of the power of the Holy Spirit put at my disposal. "Put at my disposal." Note these words. For this same God has revealed Himself as willing me to use the powers of body and mind which He gives me to make decisions and to take actions for which I am willing to be held responsible. There may be times when He deliberately leaves me to make up my own mind in situations where the issues are not clear. My surrender to His will must take the form of accepting the treatment that He thinks good for me. It is in making my own decision and acting upon it that I shall be most completely surrendered to His will, and in my decision and action His creative power will be most fully expressing itself in my life.'

Except in the reference to the Holy Spirit I have not in this drawn anything from specifically Christian theology. I have expressed what a man might say when speaking from within his experience of creaturehood on the basis of my last year's exposition of natural theology. To be specifically Christian he would have to add that he receives from God not only his existence, his ability to think, decide and act, his responsibility for his decisions and actions, and a world in which he can give effect to his decisions and himself grow by the making and acting on them—not only these, but also the access of fresh freedom and power that comes from sharing in his Lord's victory over the forces of evil. My present point is that, quite apart from this specifically Christian element in our belief, the nature of the universe, at the human stage of the creative process, is such as to involve in the relation between creature and Creator, between man and God, the apparent inconsistency which we have discovered in Christian expositions of the doctrine of grace, both catholic and protestant. It is no good trying to find some point of view from which this inconsistency can be seen to be something else in disguise, or to find some way of stating the doctrine in which it can be explained away. Together with contingency and evil, the paradoxical character of our relationship to God has to be accepted as one of the realities of our present condition, accepted as incidental to God's giving effect to His will to create persons endowed with genuine freedom. On this I would make three further remarks.

1. The apparent contradiction in the doctrine of grace is due to our being at a stage in the creative process at which irrationalities can occur, at which situations can arise which need to be changed in order to become intelligible. In our present condition, self-assertion and self-surrender appear as contradictory terms. We need continually to be reminding ourselves that this is not because of any intrinsic contradictoriness in them. In the life of God, the blessed Trinity, each Person finds His full self-expression in self-giving in responsive love. In the perfected city of God each finite created person will similarly find his full self-expression in the devotion of himself to the welfare of all. We shall reach the fullness of freedom only when we have become such that this contradiction, like that between can't and won't, has disappeared.[1] Meanwhile we, at the receiving end of the process, have to struggle for the reconciliation of the two. God, from His end, gives what we need for our growth in freedom.[2] His manner of giving is adjusted to the needs of creatures for whom there is still this contradiction to be overcome. Thus we see why in the language of traditional theology, both catholic and protestant, grace is relative to sin.

2. Towards the end of my eighth lecture last year I was saying that the task of parents and teachers is to help those entrusted to their care to grow up into men and women who will shoulder the responsibility for their own decisions and actions, that 'over and over again we have to be asking the question: "Is this particular person, at this particular moment, in need of being constrained to conform, so that he may learn what it feels like to behave in the right way? Or does he need to be left free to

[1] Vol. I, pp. 185–8. [2] Vol. I, pp. 152–3.

make up his own mind, to learn to take responsibility, even at the cost of making a mess of things?" ' In the following lecture I suggested that it may help to throw light on the existence of certain kinds of evil to think of God caring for His creatures after the analogy of a father making provision for the upbringing of his sons and daughters.[1] In the third lecture of the present series I was explaining further the sense in which we Christians speak of God as our Father.[2] Now I would ask: is there any father among us who in the exercise of his fatherhood has not had personal experience of precisely that paradoxical relationship to son or daughter which is implied by the Christian doctrine of grace? In our ordinary earthly experience we know what it is to want to encourage our children's growth in individual selfhood and freedom, standing by to do what we can to retrieve the errors which we deliberately leave them free to make. God has revealed Himself as caring for us in this way. In the thought of His fatherhood lies the clue to our understanding the operation of His grace.

3. It will help us to carry further this attempt to think of God's grace by analogy from our experience of personal relationships. When we are thinking of it in St. Paul's secondary sense of the word, as 'the divine influence or influences which operate from within the Christian nature', it is only too easy to slip into thinking of grace as a sub-personal something given by God to work on its own, as a doctor may give a patient a bottle of medicine to be taken three times a day after meals. Unnecessary obscurity has been caused by well-meaning but misguided attempts to picture the irresistible efficacy of God's grace by illustrations drawn from the sequence of cause and effect in the physical world, speaking, for example, of grace as flowing from some reservoir through divinely appointed channels into the human soul, channels from which its entry may be blocked by sin until the free passage is restored by penitence and absolution. One can appreciate and respect the pious intention of nourishing

[1] Vol. I, pp. 189, 205 ff.

[2] Above, p. 61.

faith and devotion by such similes, but the danger of their use outweighs its value. It opens the door to abuses in sacramental doctrine and practice such as in the later Middle Ages developed to the point of provoking the reformation revolt. What is more important for us now is the hindrance it opposes to any intelligent understanding of the doctrine of grace itself. So long as we are thinking in these terms we can find no light on the problem of how at one and the same time an act can both be caused by God's grace and also be the expression of a man's own free will.

It is not so in the realm of personal relationships. We may not be able fully to understand it, but we find no difficulty in accepting as a reality in our experience the fact that one man can help another to be and do what he himself wills to be and do. We know what it means for a man to say 'I could never have been what I am, were it not for so-and-so coming into my life'—speaking with heartfelt gratitude of the coming of so-and-so.

We have to distinguish between two kinds of influence which one man has in the life of another. There is, of course, the 'undue influence' which in a court of law may be held to invalidate a will. This is called undue because it disregards a man's freedom in the sense of his right to run his own life; it is a psychological conditioning which works upon him in a manner similar to the causal efficacy of drink or drugs. In contrast with this there is the influence which approaches him in a fully personal manner, winning him to actions for which he is fully responsible. Here we must make a further distinction, not concerned with the mode by which the influence is exerted but with the end to which it is directed. A man who allows himself to come under the influence of an evil-minded person and be led into evil paths will not have the same ground for gratitude as one who is being strengthened in his devotion to goodness. For, as I was arguing last year, the one course leads to the loss of freedom (*a*) in slavery, the other to growth in self-control and freedom (*b*).[1] It is this last kind of influence which we must take as our starting-point

[1] Vol. I, pp. 184–8.

when trying to think about God's grace in St. Paul's secondary sense of the word. It is the only one which is consistent with His central aim to create a community of persons perfected in their freedom. It has two characteristics of importance for our inquiry.

(i) We know quite well what it means for a man to say 'I could never have been what I am——' or 'I could never have done this deed'—but for so-and-so. We know this from the inside, with an understanding deeper than what understanding we have of the sequence of events in the physical world observed by the natural sciences.[1] And our experience goes to convince us that what the man says may be literally true, that left to himself, by his own strength alone, he could not have been or done what he refers to. I say 'may be', because men can be mistaken: in some cases it may be true, in others not. It is enough for my point if there are any in which it is true, and I am convinced that there are.

(ii) In such a case, a man will neither feel nor think that the help he has received has set him aside and taken out of his hands the running of his own life, that what he has become or done is not the expression of his own will and his true self. The ground of his gratitude is his conviction that he has received help which has given him an increase of the kind of freedom that is really worth having.

From one another we can receive help which enables us to be and do what otherwise we could not, and this in a way which does not infringe but increases our freedom. This may be mysterious. Indeed, it is mysterious in the sense that we do not understand, so to speak, how it works. But it is no more mysterious than the way in which cause produces effect in the physical world. We observe the one process from the outside; we experience the other from the inside. Our difficulty about the doctrine of grace largely arises from our being under the influence of a science *mystique* which can be as destructive of clear thinking as the Bible *mystique* we were reviewing in my first lecture. We

[1] Vol. I, p. 138.

behave as though to say that God's grace is necessary for a man to be and do what he should is to predicate the kind of causal necessity operating in the physical world, a necessity inconsistent with freedom. We behave as though we have to translate our experience of personal relations into terms of sub-personal happenings in order to render it intelligible. When we emancipate ourselves from this illusion we can surely see that in our experience of personal influence at its best we have precisely the analogy we need to lead us towards the understanding of God's grace in St. Paul's secondary sense of the word. When a man ends a letter with such a phrase as 'with my love', or 'X sends you his love', no one supposes that he is enclosing something like a bottle of medicine or a box of pills. It is in this way that we think of God giving His grace to be a divine influence which operates from within the Christian nature. Can we, by following this line of approach, come to think of sacraments as 'means of grace' in a way which will conserve what they stand for in catholic devotion and be immune to suspicion of pelagianism or magic?

III

In his book *The Protestant Era*[1] Professor Paul Tillich discusses, as though he were giving an exhaustive list, three possible types of sacramental theory. He first dismisses what he calls the 'symbolic-metaphoric' view on the ground that it does not involve any 'necessary, intrinsic relationship' between the material element and the spiritual reality. 'The act of baptism is thus a visible representation of the idea of baptism. Obviously, other pictorial actions could serve as representation of the same idea, such as passing through fire, going down into a cave and the like.' He then rejects the 'ritualistic' interpretation of the element on the similar ground that it makes the relation between, e.g., water and baptism 'merely accidental. The connecting of the two is dependent on a divine command. Because of this command,

[1] London, 1951, pp. 106 ff.

water acquires its sacramental significance as soon as it is employed in the properly celebrated rite of baptism'. He comes down in favour of 'a realistic interpretation', which

> explicitly raises the question as to whether there is not a necessary relationship between water and baptism. It questions Luther's view that water is 'simply water', although accepting his repudiation of the magical conception of the sacraments. A special character or quality, a power of its own, is attributed to water. By virtue of this natural power, water is suited to become the bearer of a sacred power and thus also to become a sacramental element. A necessary relationship between baptism and water is asserted. This realistic conception seems to me to be adequate to the true nature of the sacrament. It rejects the idea that there is a merely arbitrary connection between the idea and the material element.

From much that I have said already it will be clear that this discussion seems to me to be misconceived, to be mistaken in its use of the words 'realistic' and 'ritualistic', in its positive grounds for affirming the one view and in its negative grounds for rejecting the other.

For Tillich the 'realistic' view rests upon an attempt to establish a connection between the material and the spiritual realities in the sacrament on the basis of a definition of the material in terms of an analysis of its constituent elements. To repeat what I said last year of this method of definition, 'while it may increase our ability to harness the forces of nature to our own ends, (it) takes us further and further away from understanding the things and events of the world we have to live in'.[1] And while the dismissal of the so-called 'ritualistic' view as implying a 'merely accidental' connection dependent on a divine command may be justified on that description of it, if this be so, Tillich's list is not exhaustive. He has omitted any mention of what emerges from God's revelation of Himself in nature and history to be the true basis of sacramental theory and practice.

The word 'ritualistic' suggests that the connection depends on the correct performance by an earthly minister of a rite in obedience to a command given by Jesus Christ in Palestine some

[1] Vol. I, pp. 159, 164.

nineteen hundred years ago. This ignores the fact that for the Christian believer Jesus Christ is not merely the historic figure who once upon a time gave commands which now we obey in pious memory; He is the crucified, risen, ascended, living Lord, the 'same yesterday, to-day and for ever', whose present activity gives its meaning and reality to all our religious practice, and in particular to the sacraments. We believe the water of baptism to be sanctified to the mystical washing away of sin because we believe Him to be present and to take it and make it so. We believe the bread and wine of the Eucharist to be His body and His blood because we believe Him to be present, alive and active, and to take these material elements to be the vehicle of His continuing redemptive activity in and through His earthly body, the Church; taken to be for Him here and now in His present ministry what the body taken of the substance of His earthly mother was for Him in the opening years of that ministry from Bethlehem to Calvary.

Here note two things. First, that the definition of what is meant in this context by such words as 'body' and 'blood' is not in terms of analysis of their structure but of their function, defined in the same way as we define a pen to be a thing to write with and a chair a thing to sit on. And note, secondly, that in our belief He who takes these elements to be His body and His blood is the Creator of heaven and earth and of all things visible and invisible. Nothing can more truly be said to *be* itself than that which the Creator of all things takes it and makes it to be.

It would wander too far from the course of these lectures to discuss detailed questions of sacramental theology: whether, for example, there is any sense in which the Eucharist can rightly be called a sacrifice, or the sacrament reserved for the communion of the sick or as a focus of devotion. I will say this much. If, as I am maintaining, the ground of our sacramental doctrine is the belief that the living Lord takes the elements to be what He wills them to be in His own use of them, these questions must be considered as concerning what use we may believe Him to will to make of them.[1]

Last year, when we set out on our attempt to make sense of the universe of our experience, we found ourselves driven to postulate a Creator, and to hold that ultimate explanations must be in terms of His will and purpose. To-day the attempt to make sense of the sacramental practice of the Christian Church has driven us along the same road. What gives to the sacraments their meaning and their mode of reality is the use that the living Lord makes of them. In this way we come to a right understanding of them as 'means of grace'. Grace is the word we use for God's activity in Christ towards sinful men, and the sacraments are means of which He makes use in the course of His gracious action.

Now a further point. We have seen that between God and His creatures there can be two kinds of relationship: onesidedly personal, as pictured in the analogy of the potter and his clay, and mutually personal.[2] We have also seen that we men and women are in process of being created into persons: we come into existence as the self-consciousness of our bodies, and have to take over the running of our bodily life as a matter of personal responsibility.[3] Hence at any moment of our earthly life, God stands to us in a mixed relationship. In so far as our behaviour is sub-personal, it is one-sidedly personal: personal on His side, impersonal on ours. We are the clay in the hands of the potter. In so far as we are capable of personal response, of obedience or disobedience, of love or hatred, it can be, and often is, mutually personal. Since our growth into existence as persons is one of those ongoing processes of scientifically knowable change of which we cannot expect to be able to get a clear picture or logical definition of cross-sections,[4] the same is true of the changing gradations in God's modes of relationship to us. All we can say is that God is personally at work in us promoting our growth in freedom into the persons that He wills us to be.

[1] I have discussed these questions further in my *Essays in Christian Philosophy* (London, 1930), Essay IX.
[2] Vol. I, pp. 165 ff., 205.
[3] Vol. I, pp. 161 ff., 180 ff., 234 ff. And above, pp. 80 ff.
[4] Vol. I, p. 174.

God's grace is God at work within us, influencing the direction of our lives. Since His central aim is the development of our growth in true freedom, we can rely on Him not to exercise that kind of 'undue influence' which in despite of our personality seeks to control our behaviour by sub-personal conditioning. This being so, we need have no hesitation in including in our definition of God's grace His activity in us at the sub-personal level, working on and in us after the manner of the potter and his clay. His action is always fully personal, directed towards building us up into creatures capable of taking over the running of our own lives as responsible persons.

If this be true of God's relationship to us in His creative activity, it is surely equally true of His redemptive activity in Christ. The emphasis on the *ex opere operato* activity of Christ in catholic sacramental theology is an attempt to express the truth that He is active at the sub-personal as well as the personal level. If in baptism the true agent is Christ Himself, in whose name His Church is baptizing His children, what limits can we set to His activity in their lives, nourishing their unconscious, sub-personal life with all that they need to become capable of conscious, personal faith when they come to years of discretion? When I come in penitence and faith to receive the sacrament of Holy Communion, I cannot limit the divine activity in me to that of which I am consciously aware. He bids me do this in remembrance of Him. So far all is mutually personal. But when I come, my personal response at its best is poor and meagre. Only too often it is not at its best, but is the response of one who is sleepy, or wandering in thought. My faith has to be shown in trusting God through Christ to give me all the sub-personal growth I need to constitute me a person and enable me to make the personal response of faith. He uses the sacrament to send me forth into the world bound more closely to Himself as a member of the body in which He is carrying on His redemptive work.

Since throughout His action is wholly personal, there is nothing of magic or superstition in the belief that through the sacraments God is nourishing the sub-personal life of His creatures. To deny it would involve the pelagianism of asserting that by its own efforts creation can struggle upwards to personality and only then has need of the grace of God. Moreover, this belief makes provision for the religious nurture of all sorts and conditions of men. Whatever the stage of their development in physical age or spiritual sensitiveness, there is a place for them in the sacramental life of the Church which there would not be if the only offer made to them were the demand for the response of fully personal faith, all or nothing.

There is nothing of magic or superstition in this. But the moment we allow ourselves to forget God's paramount concern for our growth in true freedom the door is opened to both. Forgetting that His purpose in the sacraments is to engender and nourish our fully personal faith, we may content ourselves with a mechanical reliance on the kind of help appropriate only to the sub-personal elements in us, whether or no we go so far as to substitute ritual correctness for moral responsibility.

A degeneration of this kind in the sacramental theology of the later Middle Ages provoked the Reformation revolt against the catholic doctrine of grace. The resulting controversies have been confused by failure to recognize the mixed character of God's relationship to us men at our stage in His creative process. Often, for example, when the doctrines of justification by faith and baptismal regeneration are opposed as alternatives between which we must choose, it is assumed that they are rival descriptions of God's activity and His requirement of response in relation to the same stage of human development. If they are not, if they belong to different stages in the divine creative and redemptive activity, and the temporal order of a man's becoming is not to be ignored as irrelevant to our thought and treatment of him, this is not so. The one reminds us of the heights of personal response to which God calls us, the other of how His love encompasses all sorts and conditions of men.

LECTURE VIII

Prayer and Providence

I

AT this point it will be well to pause, look back over the whole course of lectures, and see where we stand.

In the first series last year we set out to try to make sense of the actual universe of our experience. We found ourselves driven to acknowledge the existence in it of irrational elements which cannot be made to fit into either a materialist or an idealistic metaphysic. Analysis of our experience of freedom led us to see that we live in a world in which dependable orderliness and genuine contingency both have a place. Together they provide the matrix for our coming into existence as self-conscious purposive agents, and the material for our growth in true freedom as persons. The irreducible combination of these two factors produced the postulate of a Creator, in terms of whose personal will we have to seek our ultimate explanations. Within a purposive order we could find a place for both cause and contingency, *as being what they are*, without having to explain either away. We also saw that our attempt to make sense of the universe could only be successful if we could be satisfied that the purpose which is being worked out in it is one which approves itself to us as good.

Among the many loose ends left over from last year were some concerned with the question of evil. We had seen that evil, in its various forms, is the most stubborn of those irrationalities of which, as they stand, no intelligible explanation can be given. What meaning it has in any particular instance is a meaning for action. If irrationalities in general were to be accounted for as incidental to the Creator's will to create persons endowed with freedom, the extent to which evil had been allowed to infect His creation was the measure of His determination that this freedom should be genuinely free.

This year we have been asking what contribution to our further understanding is made by specifically Christian faith, that is, by the interpretation of a certain series of events in the history of this world as embodying its Creator's redemptive activity. What we have discovered may be summed up by saying that it has enabled us to fill in certain details in our knowledge of the Creator whose existence we had been led to believe in from our study of the universe in general. In the events which form the substance of the Christian revelation He has shown that He who is the source and author of the space-time process, to which He has given its own mode of reality, not only works within it, disposing and enabling it to receive the fuller richness of being that He wills to give it, but also, at the human stage, has entered as man into the history of our race, taking upon Himself the doing of the action required to make sense of an unintelligibly evil world. Crucified, risen and ascended, through His continuing earthly body, the Church, He carries on His work of making sense of His creation. To those of us whom He enlists for this service He gives His grace in both senses of the word; He gives us the cleansing from sin which sets us free to engage in it, and the strength that we need for its performance.

I have given this summary of the argument up to date in order to ensure that what I have to say from now onward shall be understood in the context of the position arrived at. Three points must be made quite clear.

1. If we are to try to speak in terms of degrees of reality, to try to distinguish between what is more real and what less real, what is apparently real and what really real, it is in personal relationships that we experience the highest degree of reality known to us. The sub-personal, the material, exists as material for the fashioning of the personal; as it is taken up into the current of personal life it contributes to the creation of something more real than itself. Thus in the popular and pejorative sense

of the word mythology, it is mythological to represent the activity of God by illustrations, metaphors and analogies drawn from the working of impersonal forces; we get nearer to the literal truth when we draw on our experience of personal action.

2. Definitions in terms of purpose and function bring us nearer to understanding the real nature of things than definitions by analysis of constituent elements. The real thing is what it is made for in personal life: a chair to sit on, a pen to write with. When the victim of a joke at a Christmas party lights a trick cigarette which sparkles like a firework, what he is lighting is not a real cigarette. Definition by analysis into constituent elements is definition with a view to making use of the material in constructing something of a higher order of reality.[1] We see things upside down and go hunting a will-o'-the-wisp when we seek to find reality by way of analysis instead of looking for it in the context of personal relationships.

Let me illustrate this point by an addition to what I said in the last lecture about sacramental theology, quoting from what I wrote many years ago in a book now long out of print.

What makes a thing the body of any person is not the material of which it is made, but the fact that it is the means appropriate to the environment in which he expresses himself. When the Person is Christ and the environment the society of believers, the means chosen by the One and accepted by the others are His Body and Blood in the only sense in which the words can mean anything at all. And the full sense in which they are His Body and Blood is that in which He wills to use them as such, not that in which we are aware of their significance.... They must be what He wills them to be before we can discover what they are; and at any moment our discovery may be partial and incomplete....

To view the sacraments as incidents in the social life of communion between God and man saves us from bothering our heads over certain questions which at times have caused distress to Christian minds. If there is no sense in asking what a sacrament is except as an incident in that intercourse, why ask? Suppose, for example, in a celebration of the Holy Communion, a portion of the consecrated Host fall to the ground and be eaten by a mouse. Does that mouse eat 'the Body of the Lord', or does it not? If the answer to the question depended on an analytical definition of the crumb in terms of what it is 'made

[1] Vol. I, p. 159.

of', there might be some point in raising the question. But the crumb is now a different crumb, being no longer a factor in the communion of God and man. It is between God and man that spiritual relationships can obtain, not between God and mice; and it is only within the context of spiritual relationships that bread can be charged with spiritual significance so as to become the Body of Christ. . . . In the Eucharist the living Christ takes the elements offered in obedience to His command and uses them for His Body for the purpose of uniting His followers to Himself; so far as we can tell He has no such intention with regard to mice. . . . Though reverence demands that we take all possible care to avoid accidents, it is morbid to think of our living Lord as being so imprisoned in that which He is using for His own purpose as to be desecrated against His will by a mouse. That way madness lies.[1]

When we define a thing in terms of the will and purpose of its makers and users, and of the part it plays in their life together, we are on the way to describing what it really is. If we want to go further, we must try to discover what part it plays in the will and purpose not of men but of God.

3. If the ultimate truth about things is to be defined in terms of the part they play in the will and purpose of God their Creator, the dependableness of the natural order as the object of scientific study is as integral an element in the reality of the created universe as is the contingency which opens the door to our exercise of freedom. As we have seen, this dependableness is as necessary as the contingency to that growth in freedom (*b*) which is at the centre of God's creative purpose.[2] To the Christian mind the stability of the natural order is rooted in God's concern for this freedom, freedom which is to grow as the web of history is woven by the interaction of human endeavour with the forces of nature. Let me quote again from Fr. Talbot's *Retreat Addresses* to show how here the Christian revelation dovetails into the conclusions of natural theology.

Notice how our Blessed Lord fulfils His obedience within what we may call the recalcitrance and inevitability of circumstances. There is something deeply impressive in those genealogies which occur in the Gospels. The Incarnation of our Lord and Saviour was in utter faithfulness to the great course of history.

[1] From *Essays in Christian Philosophy* (London, 1930), pp. 111, 113.
[2] Vol. I, p. 169.

God does not, as it were, break altogether the course of history and all that it entails. He enters within the course of our human generations and bears the burden which history through these generations brings upon Him. And that is only symbolic of all that happens in His life. You remember how He refuses as one of His temptations any short cut; how He deliberately accepted the opposition, the malignity of the world and His enemies and wrought out His obedience in the face of it. 'How am I straitened', He says, 'until it is accomplished!'[1]

This summary of God's revelation of Himself in His creative and redemptive activity gives us the context in which we must now consider the practice of prayer.

II

There can be few of us who have not at some time or other found ourselves asking whether the prayers we pray are such as can reasonably be addressed to God. Is it any good asking God to interfere with the order of nature or the course of history? If not, is there anything left that is worth praying about? In any case, why should there be any need to instruct God about what we want done? If it is not in accordance with His will, we shall surely not persuade Him to do it; if it is, surely He will do it without waiting for us to ask Him. We have perhaps gone on to think that no one who tries honestly to pray with the understanding can continue to pray for things like rain or fine weather, or, indeed, believe that we can hope by prayer really to effect any change in the divine ordering of earthly events. We have been led to identify understanding prayer with prayer that does not aim at any such thing, but at the harmonizing of our own wills with the will of God. Prayer thus becomes an exercise in self-discipline, a religious experiment in auto-suggestion. The thought of auto-suggestion raises the possibility of explaining intercession for others as working through telepathic hetero-suggestion; but we have doubts whether this is sufficiently proved to justify our putting much faith in it, and we have

[1] L. Menzies: *Retreat Addresses of Edward Keble Talbot*, p. 88.

qualms about the honesty of a kind of underhand interference with our neighbours' right to run their own lives. On the whole it seems safest to regard prayer simply as the practice of bringing ourselves 'in tune with the Infinite'.

The disciplining of our thoughts and our desires to bring them into conformity with the will of God is indeed a very important element in the practice of prayer. But to make it the whole raises fresh difficulties. Sooner or later, if we go on with the honest attempt to use our understanding, we are forced to face the fact that those who wrestle with God in prayer after the manner that we have renounced are growing in a richness and fullness of spiritual life beside which our efforts after self-culture appear intolerably thin and unsatisfying. If we wish to continue to call ourselves Christians, we have to do so as exponents of a Christianity which is unable to enter into any well-established form of Christian public worship without so many mental reservations as to make us doubt our right to the name. Our disquiet grows when we remember that the prayer-life of the Master whose name we bear had more in common with that from which we have cut ourselves off than with our own. For Him the thought that our heavenly Father knoweth what things we have need of before we ask Him is not a reason why we should cease to pray that His kingdom may come and His will be done on earth, that our sins may be forgiven, and that we may be given our daily bread.

We must think again. For the line of thought which issues in this impoverishment of prayer presupposes an idea of God and of His relation to the world different from that which I have summarized at the beginning of this lecture. We must review the situation by setting our thoughts about prayer in the context of our faith that God's aim in creation is our growth in personal freedom. We have seen how orderly development in the physical world provides both the organisms which grow into conscious intelligent purposive individuals and also the environment through intercourse with which they can develop their freedom. We think of the divine control over creation as exercised in two different modes.

In the physical world, from which man springs and which provides him with the medium for his self-expression, we find those uniformities, that dependableness, which are commonly referred to as the 'laws of nature'. The precise nature of these 'laws', and the extent to which they obtain in microcosmic as well as in macrocosmic structures, may be matters of dispute among scientists and philosophers. Whatever the result of the investigations through which alone such disputes can be settled, we may in any case regard the orderliness in nature as due to the Creator giving it such orderliness as is necessary to provide man with a world in which rational study can increase human control.

Apart from that power of conscious, intelligent, purposive action which is characteristic of man, the creatures of the natural world are passive agents of pervading energy, not initiating centres of activity. Like clay in the hands of the potter, they conform willy-nilly to those orderly laws through which the creative process is developed. But in respect to man, in so far as any man has grown up to be a truly personal agent, God's control is exercised otherwise. It operates not through natural law but through grace, by the putting forth of love to win the freely-willed response of answering love.

We think, then, of the divine control over creation as exercised in the two modes of natural law and grace. As in our ordinary experience the world is a place where men and women are developing their freedom through their manipulation of a dependable natural order, so we think of God as exercising over them and their world that mode of control which in each case is appropriate. Stage merges into stage: we cannot draw lines to mark where one ends and the next begins. We have to trust God to know in each case what is required for the furtherance of His creative purpose. Once again we may be helped by the analogy involved in thinking of God as Father. In our experience the art of parenthood is that of transition from external control to free companionship. At first the infant child is of necessity entirely subject to external control. It has to be lifted up, put down, fed, washed, undressed and clothed again. But from the start the wise parent sees as his goal the companionship of free and equal personalities. As the months and years go by he is seeking opportunities for relaxing external compulsion and trying instead to win co-operation, anxious neither to cramp the growing soul by relaxation too long deferred nor to crush it under the burden of responsibilities assumed too soon. So may we think of God as watching over the growth of us men and women, passing with unerring wisdom from the control of law to that of grace as we grow in capacity of response.

In the framework of this view of the relation of God to the world we set the Christian practice of prayer. How does it now appear? We see at once that the difficulty about such prayers as those for rain or fine weather does not lie in any impotence of God to control natural law, for it is in precisely that sphere that His control is most directly absolute. The question we have to ask is not whether God *can*, but whether He *will* vary the ordinary processes of nature. It is here that the real difficulty lies. The orderliness of nature is God's provision for the development of human freedom. We cannot ask Him so to act as to hinder that development. We were thinking last year of how progress in meteorology increases our freedom of navigation by sea and air.[1] This science is developed by the co-ordination of multitudinous messages received by wireless from various directions. If the receiver of them never knew whether a message recorded an item in the orderly network of weather conditions, or a special miracle performed in response to a prayer for fine weather for a Sunday-School treat, the whole possibility of the science would be destroyed.

God wills to develop our freedom by giving us a world patient of study by scientific method, by progress of such study increasingly subject to our control. This truth must be taken into

[1] Vol. I, p. 169.

account in our prayers. We cannot rightly ask God to act in such a manner as to dislocate the order which is the basis and condition of our freedom. Does this mean that we must eliminate from our devotions all prayer of the kind we have been considering? Before we attempt to answer this question, let us consider whether similar difficulties do not arise in connection with the other method of divine control, the grace whereby God works in the world of human freedom.

This grace, as we have seen, is a mode of control which does not set aside our freedom. It reinforces it in its growth to fuller maturity. A few minutes ago I was objecting to the theory that intercessory prayer for others acts by a kind of telepathic hetero-suggestion on the ground that such prayer would be an unjustifiable interference with the freedom of our fellow men, a disreputable exercise of underhand and undue influence. By putting the matter into the hands of God, in prayer, we affirm our repudiation of any such endeavour; we entrust it to One who can be trusted not to undermine the freedom He is in process of creating. Indeed, if there be any possibility of such telepathic influencing of man by man (a question on which I am not competent to offer any opinion) we may believe that by turning our wishes for our neighbours into prayers to God on their behalf, we safeguard them from straying along dishonest ways and insulate our neighbours from the danger of our undue interference in their lives.

But how, then, can such prayer do any good? Surely the more we emphasize the value of intercessory prayer as safeguarding us from unduly influencing our neighbour, the more we empty it of meaning. If we are putting our wishes into the hands of God because we can trust Him not to interfere with our neighbour's freedom, must we not refrain from asking Him to do anything at all? Have we not reached an *impasse* in regard to prayer concerning the divine control both in the mode of grace and in the mode of law? In either case, how can our prayers be anything but requests to God to act in such a way as to hinder the development of that human freedom which we believe to be His central purpose in creation?

Here, at last, we discover what is the real problem of prayer. And, as so often, when we have penetrated thus deeply into the mystery of our existence, the answer to our questioning has to be an expression of our faith rather than the conclusion of an argument proceeding by demonstrative proof. I have tried to make clear the grounds on which I regard it as reasonable to hold certain beliefs about God and His relation to the world. I must now be allowed to speak as one who holds these beliefs, who draws for himself the answer to his own questions from his faith in the omniscience and omnipotence of the God who is both the Author and Source of the order in nature and the Creator of human freedom.

If we believe that both the orderliness of the natural world, and our responsibility for what we do with it, spring from the will and creative activity of God, we must believe that He is able to control the development of His creation without either disorganizing its orderliness or destroying our freedom and responsibility. We cannot rightly ask Him to give us weather which will make the science of meteorology impossible, or the satisfaction of our hopes and desires in ways which would not be for the furtherance of His purpose in history. If, in our ignorance, we ask for things which would hinder His central aim in creation, we would not wish to press these requests or have them fulfilled.

We have to use to the best of our ability the minds that God has given us, trying to discover what we honestly think will be best for the welfare of His creation and of ourselves. But just because we do not know what is and what is not necessary to the achievement of His aim, we are right to bring before Him in our prayers all the people, causes and events which we care about, hope for, or fear. He is God. All the conditions for the fulfilment of His will—the natural world with its orderliness, our freedom and responsibility, the interaction of these with one another—all these come from Him, are known to Him, and are under His control. It may be that there are ways unknown to us in which without disorganizing the natural world or infringing our freedom and responsibility, He can achieve His purpose in one way rather than another, and that He wills to let the choice between them wait on our prayers.

If we cannot be content to think of prayer as wholly concerned with the self-disciplining of our own minds, or as an attempt to cajole God into doing something other than what He intends, or as a futile request to Him to do what He is going to do anyway, there remains only one possible alternative. Our thought about prayer must rest on the foundation of belief that God voluntarily waits upon our asking.

This is the conclusion to which we are driven. It is in keeping with all that God has revealed to us of Himself in His creative and redemptive activity. Why should we find more difficulty about it in the sphere of prayer than in that of action? He has given us an orderly and dependable natural world, and it is His will that we should decide what use is made of it. At every turn the course of history is altered by our decisions. The carelessness of doctor or nurse may cost a patient's life. A bridge which should have been blown up is left intact, and the enemy's troops sweep across to conquer a country. If in other directions God puts the doing of His will on earth into our hands, and lets it wait upon our doing our duty, why should we be surprised if He works in the same manner in the matter of prayer?

The truth about this has sometimes been obscured by a mistaken way of drawing the analogy from the relation of a father to his children. The earthly father, it has been urged, loves to hear his children ask him for their needs, needs he would not think of leaving unsatisfied in any case. Just so, our heavenly Father loves to hear His earthly children prattling to Him of their wants. This is no true analogy; it is a false and misleading caricature of the truth. It is not because God treats us as children that He waits upon our prayers, but because He wills us to grow into our full manhood and to take our place as fellow workers with Him in creation and redemption. If we believe that true freedom, the uncoerced and freely-willed devotion of man to the fulfilment of God's will, is the consummation of His work at which the Creator aims, then it is for this reason and for no other that we think of Him as imposing upon His activity the limitation of waiting upon our response to the call of His love. He is not content that His creation should be completed by the passive conformity of protoplasm, but out of that protoplasm is constituting us true human selves by entrusting to us a share in His creative and redemptive activity. To believe that often He does not act until we ask Him is not the mark of a foolish, a childish, faith. It is the consciousness of growing manhood on the part of the creature, the recognition that God has laid on him the responsibility of deciding whether in this detail the divine creative purpose shall go forward or be delayed. It is one and the same principle which on the one hand prevents us from asking God to modify the course of nature in such a way as to render it impatient of scientific control, and on the other justifies our belief that He may modify creation's history in answer to our prayer.

Prayer is not simply the play of God's children. It is work for grown men and women, work which calls for strenuous endeavour. When we begin to take it seriously we begin to discover how bad we are at it, how much is required of us in the way of self-discipline and effort. Often we cannot even take part in the Bidding Prayer or the Litany without being distracted by thoughts of our own personal concerns from throwing ourselves wholeheartedly into that sharing of God's interests in the world around to which we are being called. How many of us really care deeply about the advancement of learning, about social justice, about international brotherhood, about the unity of Christendom, compared with our own private affairs? The extent to which we can keep our attention fixed on the prayers said in church is a good test of the extent to which we really care about such things as these. How can we expect the God who has given this earth to the children of men to give us these things until we train ourselves to care enough about them to put them in the forefront of our intercessions, caring so much that we cannot keep silence, but must needs voice our aspirations in our prayers?

Intelligent prayer, prayer with the understanding, springs from the faith that all things lie in God's hand, that He can do what He will with them, and that every earthly situation, no matter how hopeless it may appear, can be used to His glory and for the furtherance of His purpose in creation. Such prayer is nerved by the conviction that it does make a difference whether we pray or not, because we believe that in letting His activity wait upon our conscious co-operation God is consistent with His purpose to create in us true human selves whose freedom is to be respected. We shall not seek to persuade God to improve things by actions which would interfere with His revealed method of working, that method whereby He gives us a dependable world over which we can extend our control as we grow in freedom. Nor shall we ask for undue interference with human freedom, whether our own or anyone else's. But neither, on the other hand, shall we despise the use of the intelligence that He has given us and refrain from asking that specific things shall be done.

When to the best of our ability we have thought about the matter that is to be the subject of our prayer, and have formed our honest opinion concerning what needs to be done in order that the present situation may be transformed to the glory of God and the furtherance of His creative purpose, we shall earnestly pray for this with all our powers of body and mind. In this way we shall answer our Lord's call to us to live as His friends rather than as His servants, recognizing our limitations as we close with His own words: 'Nevertheless, not what I will but what Thou willest be done'.

III

In considering prayer we have been led to certain conclusions about God's manner of ordering events in the history of this world. Ignoring for the moment the possible influence of angels or devils,[1] we see history as the interaction of human endeavour and natural forces. We think of the whole process as directed towards the creation of a community of finite persons perfected in the exercise of freedom, and of the divine control as exercised through law and grace. What light can this throw on our understanding of the word 'providence'? Is there any sense in which we can rightly say of a situation in which we find ourselves that it is 'providentially meant'?[2]

We cannot think of God as a kind of celestial chess-player moving men and things about like pieces on a board. That would be to contradict the revelation He has given of Himself both in the dependableness of the natural order as studied by the sciences and in His concern and respect for human freedom. Nor can we think of Him as having favourites whom by some 'special providence' He preserves from catastrophes that befall others. If we eliminate such notions, is there anything left which is worth calling providence at all? Shall we find that we have impoverished our spiritual life as severely as by reducing prayer to auto-suggestion and self-culture?

If I am a Christian believer, I think of my life as coming to me from God in two ways. My own being, whatever powers I may have of body or mind, my share in the life of mankind which has come to me through being born of my parents and has been nourished by food and drink and human fellowship—all this comes to me ultimately from God my Creator: 'whenever I draw a breath or lift a finger I am making use of the power of the Holy Spirit put at my disposal'.[3] Secondly, the various situations in which I find myself, the circumstances which provide me with the material for the life I am to live, come to me from God: they have come about through the interaction of natural forces and human endeavour all subject to the divine control by law and grace. At each moment of my life I am to

[1] Vol. I, pp. 213, 224.
[2] Vol. I, pp. 226–8.
[3] Above, p. 146.

look through beyond the proximate sources of the situation, hold it up before God in prayer, and ask: 'Lord, what wouldst Thou have made of this?'

For practical purposes belief in God's omnipotence means belief that no circumstances can be so evil that they cannot be used for God's glory and the furtherance of His will. Belief in God's omniscience means belief that in them all He can see how they can thus be used. It was thus that on the Cross our Lord used the triumph of the powers of darkness for the glory of God and the rescue of His creation. It is thus that we are to 'endeavour ourselves to follow the blessed steps of His most holy life'.

If this be so, then to the faithful Christian not only this or that special circumstance, but every situation in his life will come to him as 'providentially meant', but the meaning it bears will be what I have called a 'meaning for action'. It is not a meaning which can be explained in words that show how what has happened is as it stands a revelation of God's mind or will or character. It is a meaning which can only be discovered by seeing in the situation what God wants done, and doing it.

Imagine the situation when a man has been killed in an accident, a man in the prime of life and health and vigour, a good husband to his wife, a good father to his children, a good workman and the breadwinner for his family. Imagine yourself called in to try to bring consolation to his widow. What are you to say or do? You may try to explain how what has happened is really a manifestation of the love of God, but I fear me that the explanation will sound rather forced and artificial and unconvincing. You may take the line that God's ways are often inscrutable and inexplicable, but we must accept them and believe that He loves us in spite of appearances. I fear me that this may exasperate more than it consoles. What are you to say or do? I suggest that this may not be the moment for any attempt at words of explanation; that in such a case we should be wise and right to confess ourselves as being as much puzzled, as much in the dark, as is the poor woman herself; that instead of trying to explain what has happened in the past we should do all we can to help her to face the future, to see how best she can rebuild her shattered life and make provision for the fatherless children. The time may come when, looking back, she will say: 'That was the most terrible thing that has ever happened to me in my life. I could never have asked for it nor, taken by itself, is it a thing I could ever thank God for. But through it there have come to me things which have enriched my life, things for which I am deeply thankful: the revelation of unimagined helpfulness and warmth of feeling among friends and neighbours, and above all the discovery that the power of God in human life is not merely a thing one says one believes in, but a reality proven in experience, that when it seemed impossible to go on living I found I could.'

We think then of God's providence as the expression of His omniscience and omnipotence in His control by law and grace of the interaction of natural forces with human endeavours. But if every situation in which a man finds himself is providentially meant, how can anything be called a 'special providence'?

The difficulty here is not peculiar to the idea of providence. It arises whenever we think of God doing things at particular times or places, and of some of His actions being of special importance or significance. Here I may perhaps remark on the curious fact that the catholic Christian seems to think more naturally in terms of place, the protestant in terms of time: it is the catholic who tends to think of God as localized in the eucharistic sacrament, the protestant as converting a man at some particular day and hour. Both are equally difficult: they are instances of the difficulty involved whenever we think of God as doing anything in particular as well as everything in general. About this I can say little more beyond what I have already said in the second lecture of this series.[1] It is one of the difficulties inherent in any attempt to make sense of our experience.

For each of us his own life is made up of a series of events of

[1] Above, pp. 36 ff.

varying degrees of importance. Many days may pass in which everything that happens is of a routine or humdrum nature. We may be growing in stature or wisdom, but the growth, if any, is imperceptible. Against this background other days stand out as those on which we have had to meet emergencies or take decisions in ways that have left a lasting mark on our character and our career. As Christians we regard all our life, all the situations in which we find ourselves, as given to us by God to be used in His service. If among these situations we distinguish some as of greater and some as of less importance, when we speak of the more important as coming by God's 'special providence', we affirm our conviction that their gradation of importance is as much a part of the divine ordering as are the situations themselves.

If we ask in what connections the language of special providence is actually used by Christian people, we must acknowledge that it often gives expression to beliefs of the celestial chess player or favouritism type which will not bear thinking out. But there is another use deserving of more consideration. There are men whose deep conviction of divine guidance is rooted in the fact that as they look back over their lives they can trace a developing pattern in the events of the years gone by. I think it will be found on examination that where this is the case the life has been made up of occasions of which the right use has been made, that the pattern has been woven of responses to situations in which their meaning for action has been perceived and acted upon. The meaning has been brought out by the action and so in retrospect it can be seen. It is at least arguable that if Joseph had not been able to look back on such a life, if, for example, he had not resisted the blandishments of Potiphar's wife, he might never have been able to say to his brethren 'It was not you that sent me hither, but God'.[1]

I have been trying to describe what the word providence can and should mean to a Christian whose thought of God is drawn

[1] Gen. xlv. 5–8.

from God's revelation of Himself in creation and redemption. There remains in the mind a lingering doubt which must be faced before this lecture ends. I may appear to have said nothing about the problems which the use of the word providence commonly suggests, problems arising from the thought that the word implies on the part of God a foreknowledge of events which is inconsistent with the existence of genuine contingency and human freedom. Am I open to the criticism which I have myself directed against those who hold that the biblical religious thought-forms of the Jews should not be disturbed by the awkward questions asked by the more philosophical Greeks?[1] Am I guilty of having taken evasive action, of what on an earlier occasion I stigmatized as the intellectual conjuring trick of professing to talk about one thing and by sleight of mind substituting another?[2]

My answer is that the point at issue has been argued out in earlier lectures. The idea of providence which gives rise to these problems depends in turn on a conception of God and of His relation to the universe other than that which we have come to hold as a result of our examination of the world of our experience and the events of human history. We have tried to make sense of what actually exists and happens. The problems come from the assumption that the only way to make sense is to fit everything into the strait-jacket of either a materialist or an idealist metaphysic. We have found it impossible to account in this way for our experience of contingency and freedom, and have been driven to seek our ultimate explanation in terms of God's will to create a community of finite persons. Our thinking in religious terms is not due to a refusal to ask the philosophical questions. It is the way of thinking to which the asking of them has sent us back. Thinking in these terms, we are far from claiming to have dispelled all mystery. We walk by faith and not by sight, peering into the surrounding darkness by the aid of such light as we have been given. It is indeed mysterious that the limitation of the

[1] Vol. I, p. 78. [2] Vol. I, p. 172.

divine impassibility involved in carrying out His creative purpose should go to the extent of restricting the operation of His omniscience and omnipotence to such exercise of control through law and grace as best contributes to our growth in freedom. But that this is so is what the evidence requires us to believe. It is in our conviction of His care for our growth in freedom that we must ground our faith in His providential ordering of our lives.

LECTURE IX

Eschatology

I

IF, as has been said, words have uses rather than meanings, our first task is to consider how we are to use the word eschatology. It is derived from the Greek: *eschaton*, last; *to eschaton*, the last thing; *ta eschata*, the last things. Now, as Oliver Quick used to point out,[1] the English word 'last' is ambiguous. Strictly speaking, the Greek *eschaton* is a temporal word, denoting what comes at the end of a chronological series. There is another word, *telos*, which means the end in the sense of the achievement of what has been aimed at. So far as etymology is concerned, eschatological should be contrasted with teleological: the one referring to whatever may come at the end of the time-series, whether or no any fulfilment of purpose is involved, the other implying that the ultimate explanation of the evolutionary process is to be found in terms of purpose.

In theological discussion the matter has become complicated owing to the use of the word eschatology in connection with a different set of contrasted views. The result is a certain amount of confusion which we must try to clear up before we can go any further.

More than once I have called attention to the difference between Hebrew and Greek ways of thinking.[2] The Hebrews made their points by the accumulation of images presenting different aspects of the truth rather than through the development of argument by logical steps. Moreover, they thought and spoke in personal, dramatic, religious terms, in which eternity was pictured as the extension of the time series fore and aft. It did not occur to them to raise the awkward philosophical questions

[1] E.g., in *Doctrines of the Creed* (London, 1940), pp. 245 ff.

[2] E.g., Vol. I, pp. 21, 75.

which this way of thinking and speaking involves, questions which have led some in the Greek tradition to think of this world of space and time as the mode in which the unchanging eternal reality appears to us, in which the only conceivable conclusion of the present time-process will be the completion of one revolution in an endless series of circular motions.[1] In such a scheme the *eschaton* of one revolution is the *proton* of the next: there may be processes which express finite purposes and have their own *eschata*, but the idea of the whole time series can neither be eschatological nor teleological.

For the Hebrews it could be, and was, both. The time-space universe was the expression of God's creative will, and its *eschaton* would be the fulfilment of His purpose for it. In these lectures we have tried to face some of the questions raised by the Greeks, and on the main issue, in spite of its difficulties, have found ourselves led to the Hebrew position. Like the Hebrews, we seek our ultimate explanations in terms of God's will. Like them we look for the revelation of His will in the structure and history of His creation. We learn from their prophets that to try to live by our judgments of fact and value is the fundamental act of faith in God, and the path along which He will lead us to fuller understanding.[2] We have accepted their interpretation of their own history as that of the people chosen by God to be the bearers of His redemptive activity. We have seen the preparatory stage of that activity reach its climax in the coming of Christ, whose messiahship requires a reinterpretation of what it means to be the chosen people. For us the coming of Christ is at once the *eschaton* of all that went before and the *proton* of all subsequent history. We are Hebraic in that for us this is not an incident in an endless series of repetitive circles but the decisive moment in the working

[1] Cp. the infiltration of this mode of thinking into the language of Christian devotion:

'For lo! the days are hastening on,
By prophet-bards foretold,
When, with the ever-circling years,
Comes round the age of gold.'

[2] Vol. I, pp. 106, 109.

out of a single purpose which still looks forward to an *eschaton* that shall be its *telos*.

We hold this position with our eyes open. We have seen that the questions asked by the Greeks are real questions which must not be ignored, that eternity cannot be thought of simply as the extension of the time series fore and aft. We speak of Creator and creation because to think in these personal terms illuminates, instead of ignoring or explaining away, both the existence of irrational elements in the time series, and the mystery of its relation to the eternal. We acknowledge the antinomy in our thought of God, that He is the unchanging, eternal, perfect One who nevertheless does particular things at particular times and places in His creation.[1]

We acknowledge the antinomy. I emphasize this because it seems to me that in some quarters to-day there is danger of confusion arising when it is ignored. Living in time and space as finite human beings who look before as well as after, we, like our Hebrew and Jewish ancestors, look for an *eschaton-telos* in which what is now opaque to our understanding shall become intelligible. But because we believe that the eternal God, who is working out His creative and redemptive purpose, is also giving us in the things and events of space and time the material for growing in understanding of His will, we cannot use the word eschatological as a 'smother-word' to excuse us from being troubled by questions that we ought to be asking. We cannot accept the suggestion that our difficulties arise from the fact that we fail to be biblical by not confining ourselves to the eschatological forms of thought used by the biblical writers.

Not long ago I was discussing with a class of students Bishop Nygren's rejection of all attempts at theodicy in connection with the existence of evil. I reproduced from the third lecture of this course my criticism of Nygren's contention.[2] One of those present took up the cudgels on his behalf, saying that Nygren was

[1] See especially Vol. I, pp. 78, 218–24, and above, pp. 34 ff.
[2] Above, p. 51.

the true interpreter of St. Paul in that his outlook was eschatological: if we adopt the biblical, eschatological point of view we realize that we are living 'between the times', that our interim judgments are vitiated by the sinfulness which beclouds our minds, that we must wait for the *parousia* when God's manifestation of the truth will be His own self-justification. On this I would say two things.

In the third lecture I have given my reasons for holding that on this particular point Nygren misinterprets St. Paul. I would now go further and deny that in general their eschatological outlook landed the biblical writers in such absurdity. They were saved from it by their habit of thinking in images, by not asking the philosophical questions involved in their imagery or seeking to draw conclusions by logical argument. From the philosophical point of view they were in the same dilemma as the absolute idealists. To the obfuscation of mind due to sin corresponds the limitation of understanding due to finitude. For both the logical conclusion would seem to be that since nothing can be known for what it is until God tells the eschatologist how He sees it, or the idealist grasps its function in the context of the whole, those of us who believe in a future life must be prepared to wake up in the world to come and find that we had been wrong to rate unselfishness above selfishness or honesty above deceit. Absolute idealists are for ever wrestling with this difficulty, striving to avoid being impaled on this horn of the dilemma. Although they are in it, the biblical writers ignore the existence of the dilemma. Side by side with passages which, taken by themselves, would imply this conclusion are those which bear witness to God encouraging men to use to the full whatever powers of mind they can exert, revealing Himself through judgments that we can make here and now in all our sinfulness and finitude, stripping off from age to age successive layers of obfuscation which distort our vision.[1]

We too are in this dilemma. All human thinkers are. We

[1] Above, p. 63.

differ from the biblical writers in that we cannot ignore it. The philosophical questions having been asked and come within our ken, we have to take notice of them. The besetting temptation of theologians is to try to solve their problems by reverting to the outlook of an earlier age in which they had not arisen. To suggest that we can evade problems of theodicy by adopting the eschatological outlook of the Bible is as misleading as to say that we can avoid those of the consciousness of Christ incarnate by thinking in terms of the ontological categories of the Fathers and Scholastics.[1]

The words eschatological and ontological are both being used as smother words when they are used to conceal the existence of problems that need to be brought out into the daylight and faced. A further instance is the description of the coming of Christ as an eschatological event, as though this made good a claim that Christian faith is both rooted in history and immune to historical criticism. As was discovered at Nicaea in A.D. 325, we delude ourselves if we think to play for safety by confining ourselves to the thought-forms and terminology of some earlier age, or of the Bible itself.

Thinking in personal, dramatic terms, the Jews looked forward to an *eschaton*—the conclusion of the historical time-series—which should also be a *telos*—the fulfilment of God's will to establish His Kingdom, i.e., to have all creation acknowledging His sovereignty and loyally obedient to His rule. Thinking in terms of temporal successiveness, of eternity as time indefinitely prolonged, they spoke of two ages, or 'aeons': the 'present age' in which God's rule was disputed by the powers of evil was to be succeeded by the 'age to come' in which it would be established. Christianity began as a sect of the Jews. The New Testament Christians shared this outlook, these forms of thought, this use of language. Their conviction that in Jesus Christ God had fulfilled His people's messianic expectations, had intervened in history to take the promised decisive action for the establish-

[1] Above, p. 86.

ment of His kingdom, led them to think and speak of that event as the end of the old age and the beginning of the new. This strain in the apostolic preaching is what theologians refer to as 'realized eschatology'. But this was not the whole truth. Although the new age had come, the world—and the Church, for the matter of that—was still far from manifesting to the full the kingly rule of God. They looked forward to the *parousia*, the return of Christ for the final judgment when God should be all in all.[1] There was still an 'age to come'.

So long as we are thinking in purely chronological terms, it would seem simplest to speak not of two but of three ages: the past, the present, and the future. Here, however, another characteristic of Hebrew thought has to be taken into account. Although their imagery presupposed chronological sequence, they distinguished different 'times' by their content as much as by their relative successiveness, if not more so.[2] In their pre-Christian days the Apostles would have contrasted 'the present age', the age of the world's subjection to the powers of darkness, with 'the age to come', the age of the messianic establishment of the kingdom of God. They found themselves living in an intermediate age which combined the characteristics of both. Apparently their imagery had not provided them with a category into which to fit this interregnum. Instead of substituting a three-age for a two-age scheme, they thought of themselves as living 'between the times', in conditions in which the two ages of their imagery overlapped.

It is right that for scholarly exegesis we should try to determine to what extent different New Testament writers thought and spoke of the 'new age' having arrived or being still to come, or of the two ages as overlapping. This provides the material for our further question: what must the truth have been and be if they put it like that? The exegesis reveals the confusion that was inevitable as a result of trying to fit the evidence with which they

[1] 1 Cor. xv. 20–28.
[2] On this, see J. Marsh: *The Fullness of Time* (London, 1952).

had to deal into categories inadequate to grasp it. They are not to be blamed for the confusion. Nor is their witness any the less valuable on its account. But to try now to put ourselves back into their frame of mind is not the way to clear thinking.

In his commentary on *Romans*[1] Bishop Nygren brings out the double strain in St. Paul's teaching about the two aeons. On pp. 144, 159 and 265 the second aeon begins at a definite point of time in the history of this world. On pp. 155, 202, 247, 293–6 the two aeons are two contrasted powers or kingdoms, contemporaneous in time since the beginning of the second. On p. 179 Abraham exemplifies the faith-relationship of man to God which was to be one of the fruits of the coming of the second aeon some centuries later. And on p. 340, in commenting on viii. 18–30, Nygren writes: 'These are mighty affirmations which are closely knit together and stretch *from eternity—through time—to eternity*. The concept of the two aeons is here transcended. *Before* the old aeon stands God's eternal purpose.'

By the use of the words 'transcended' and 'God's eternal purpose' Bishop Nygren betrays the fact that we cannot now put ourselves back into the frame of mind which thinks of eternity as time indefinitely prolonged. The God whose eternal purpose transcends the time-process in which it finds expression is by such language confessed to be the timeless eternal Being of Greek thought. Once again, as so often throughout both series of these lectures, we are brought up against the fundamental mystery of our existence, the relation of time to eternity. We have had to wrestle with various aspects of the problems it presents. We cannot escape them by what is called 'adopting an eschatological point of view'.

Why should we want to? I have a suspicion that we Christian theologians are influenced more strongly than we always realize by the depersonalizing tendencies of much contemporary thought, tendencies which I was criticizing in my concluding

[1] E. Tr., London, 1952.

lecture last year.[1] Elsewhere I have shown how his Gifford Lectures reveal their positive influence on the thought of Archbishop William Temple.[2] We are now concerned with a negative influence which is at times more subtly difficult to detect. If it be thought that metaphysical inquiry must inevitably issue in the subordination of the personal to the impersonal, in regarding religious language about God as the mythological personification of an impersonal ultimate reality, it is not surprising that those for whom religion means an apparently self-authenticating experience of personal communion with God should dismiss philosophy and philosophers as deluded followers of false and misleading trails. Where this is open and avowed we can easily recognize it for what it is, a frame of mind mistaken but understandable.[3] The influence is not so readily detected when it works beneath the surface, when the rejection of philosophy is taken for granted as the unavowed foundation for theological construction, a rejection based itself on a fear of depersonalization which is the hidden underlying motive of the whole.

Here Brunner's criticism of Bultmann is most illuminating. Bultmann had urged that the New Testament must be demythologized in order to make the preaching of the gospel relevant to sinners who think in twentieth-century forms of thought. Brunner assumes that demythologization includes depersonalization and in so far as that is so he will have none of it.[4] Whether or no in this he rightly interprets Bultmann may be open to question. My point is his assumption that an attempt to present the Christian gospel in a form relevant to the scientific and philosophical thought of to-day will involve a re-statement of it in impersonal terms that deprive it of its religious value.

In these lectures I have wasted much ink, paper, time and breath if by this time I have not made clear my conviction that this assumption is unfounded, that, taking full account of progress

[1] Vol. I, pp. 218–24. [2] In *The Doctrine of the Trinity*, pp. 131–4.
[3] See my *Towards a Christian Philosophy*, pp. 11–24.
[4] E. Brunner: *Eternal Hope* (London, 1954), pp. 114 ff., 186 ff.

in scientific research, metaphysical inquiry no less than religious faith leads us to find in terms of personal relations our ultimate categories of explanation.

Nor is it true to say that New Testament theology was exclusively eschatological in the sense of being confined to thinking in terms of successive or overlapping ages. The Fourth Gospel is an integral part of the witness to the way in which the New Testament Christians understood their faith. In it there is recognition of the help that can be gained by exploring the philosophical issues implicit in their eschatological beliefs. To quote from Dr. Lightfoot's Introduction to his Commentary:

> The life of the Church was to fill something more than a brief pause between the penultimate and the final scene, and its endowment, the Holy Spirit, was something more than a first-fruits or pledge of the expected 'Presence' of the Lord. . . . The growth and experience of the Church had shown that the Lord's life was not only an event in Jewish history, but also in world history. Nor was it to be understood only, or chiefly, as a preparation for a future event; it was itself the manifestation in history of the spiritual Power through which the worlds were made, the power which had always been at work, but unseen hitherto, in the course of events. For the expression of these truths a different tradition from the Jewish was at hand. . . .
>
> It is probably true that in no book of the New Testament has the fusion of the two chief and very different elements in Christianity, the Jewish and the Greek, been achieved with a surer touch or with greater thoroughness than in St. John's gospel.

We have earlier noticed the fact that to some thinkers the symbolism of space seems to come more naturally, to others the symbolism of time.[1] Dr. Lightfoot finds in this the clue to understanding the difference between the Hebrew and the Greek forms of thought.

> In the best contemporary teaching, teaching which was mainly that of the later school of Plato, the antithesis, necessary in some form to religion, between that which ought to be and that which is, was not found, as among the Jews, in the contrast of the future with the present, but in the contrast of substance with shadow, of reality with appearance, of mind and spirit with matter, and . . . if the religious Greek sought to envisage his heaven more concretely, he

[1] Above, p. 173.

preferred the image of space to that of time, and spoke of the perfect world as existing 'yonder', not 'here below'.[1]

We need, then, have no fear that to take full account of the philosophical questions implied in Jewish and Christian beliefs and to think and speak of them in terms proper to such an inquiry, will necessarily deprive them of their religious value. 'To adopt an eschatological point of view' is simply to think and speak in the way that is natural to Jews, Christians and other theists who are men and women living in this universe of space and time. To suggest that it refers to something unusual and esoteric, requiring a feat of mental gymnastics by which we assimilate our outlook to that of the biblical writers, is not only untrue but produces in many minds an unnecessary and undesirable sense of mystification. It may sound theologically learned to speak of living 'between the times' in 'overlapping ages', but if we allow ourselves to conclude from this that we are excused from trying to make sense of things while we wait for the *parousia* when God will solve our puzzles for us, we abdicate our claim to be serious theologians. That we are living in the period between the time when Christ 'for us men and for our salvation . . . was made man' and the time when He 'shall come with glory to judge both the quick and the dead' is not a discovery of modern eschatologists. It is what sensible Christians have always believed. The world between these times is the world of which we are trying to make sense, a world which, as we have seen, presents us with puzzles enough and to spare, with irrationalities which cannot be explained away but tempt us to throw up our hands and say that we are 'waiting for Godot'.[2] If I am right in holding that situations inexplicable as they stand may be pregnant with meaning for action, to adopt this waiting attitude will be to cast away our only chance of bringing sense out of nonsense.

In my previous lectures I have done what I can to show how

[1] R. H. Lightfoot: *St. John's Gospel, A Commentary* (Ed. C. F. Evans, Oxford, 1956), pp. 49, 51.

[2] S. Beckett: *Waiting for Godot* (London, 1956).

light can be thrown on our puzzles by seeking to discover from God's revelation of Himself in creation and redemption, the end at which He is aiming. When now I call the subject of this lecture eschatology I use the word in its proper etymological sense. I simply mean that I propose to consider how we may think of the ultimate destiny, the *eschaton* of the creative process as a whole and of men and women as individual persons.

II

I have argued that to make sense of the world of our experience leads us to faith in a Creator, and to the thought of creation as a process in which in increasing measure the Creator is communicating fullness and richness of being to His created universe. Further examination of the details of what is going on has led to the faith that His central aim is the production of a community of creatures whose perfection shall be the perfection of genuinely free finite persons. The content of specifically Christian faith is the gospel that at a certain moment in human history the Creator Himself has entered personally into the process to work from within for the achievement of His aim.

In this we have an interpretation of nature and history in terms of their *telos*, of the end for which they are being created. Can we from the evidence at our disposal learn anything about what is likely to be their *eschaton*, about the actual course of events through which this end will be arrived at?

We know by now that this is not a question to which we can quickly find an answer by asking what the Bible has to say about it. I have shown elsewhere that as a matter of fact biblical support can be claimed for both of two opposed views, for the view that it is God's will to bring His universe to a state of perfection in space and time, and for the view that He is working towards a final cataclysm, the doom and destruction of much that has remained evil to the end, the rescue out of the perishing world of what is to be preserved for eternity.[1]

[1] *The Doctrine of the Atonement*, pp. 125 ff.

The evidence we have at our disposal is that which we have been seeking to understand all along: God's revelation of Himself through the kind of universe He is creating and through His redemptive activity within it.

We look out on the universe from our position within it as Western European Christians of the twentieth century. In the course of discovering that God's aim is to nourish and perfect our growth in freedom we have found that this growth comes by losing sight of ourselves in devotion to things and causes of value in and for themselves. We have to recognize the paradox that our growth as persons may demand the subordination of our personal interests to the service of such impersonal abstractions as truth or justice or beauty.[1] This space-time universe, which is both the matrix and the environment for our existence as persons and our growth in freedom is the sphere in which we find the things and causes that call out our devotion. It provides wildernesses to be turned into gardens, iniquitous customs and institutions to be reformed into just ones, a wealth of undiscovered knowledge waiting to be the illumination of human minds. God wills us to care for these things for themselves. We are not to pursue them because to do so is the way of our own advancement, but because they have a right to our devotion, because they can claim the surrender of ourselves to their service. It seems to me to be arguable that if this be true of us individually, it is also true of us corporately. God's central aim may be the creation of a community of finite persons perfected in their freedom. But to treat the latent and as yet unrealized possibilities of goodness in His universe as having no value for Him beyond what instrumental contribution they may make to the perfecting of this community cuts away from under the feet of each member of it the ground of his devotion to them. We have been led to our understanding of our Creator's central aim by analysing our actual experience of the nature and conditions of our growth in freedom. If we make the central aim the whole aim we destroy

[1] Vol. I, pp. 48, 186 ff.

part of the evidence for its being the central aim, that drawn from the fact that it is in the things and events of this world that the values we seek to serve must be embodied.

If then, both individually and corporately, we are to grow by devoting ourselves to the embodiment of eternal values in the customs, institutions, things and events of space and time, it is hard to resist the conclusion that the *eschaton* willed by the Creator is a perfected universe to be the environment of the perfected community of persons. This conclusion, based on last year's study of the nature of the universe in general, would seem to be reinforced by this year's study of the specifically Christian revelation. 'In His redemptive work God has struck at the heart of the problem (of evil) by action through which men are cleansed from their own sinfulness and won back to share in His interests and to be His agents in the rescue of the rest of His creation. To be sharing in His interest in earthly embodiments of beauty and truth and goodness is to be expressing devotion to Himself. It was to set men free from all that hindered them from this devotion that Christ died and rose again.'[1] The last part of my sixth lecture, from which I have been quoting, suggests that God's redemptive activity has been and is aimed at removing obstacles which block the way to this kind of an *eschaton*, a state of affairs in which everything that exists and happens will be transparent to thought, the consummated union of causal sequence with intelligible purpose.[2]

But there is also evidence which points the other way, and that of two kinds. The one may be called *a priori*, intellectual or theoretical, the other empirical, factual or practical.

(i) It is more than difficult, it is impossible, to imagine what the state of affairs would be which is required by this prognosis. However much this universe may lend itself to the embodiment of eternal values in things of space and time—truth in beliefs and statements, goodness in acts, and beauty in sounds and shapes—in no one of these spheres can the history of this world be regarded

[1] Above, p. 134. [2] Cp. Vol. I, pp. 136 ff.

as progress in chronological sequence towards perfection. The history of the arts is marked by a succession of peaks, which having been attained, we pass on to look for something new. We do not ask our dramatists and musicians to do what Sophocles and Shakespeare, Byrd and Beethoven did and do it better; we ask them to do for our day what those men did for theirs. Is the *eschaton* of this world to be the simultaneous collocation of all these peaks, as when the entire company in a musical comedy or pantomime is assembled on the stage for the final curtain? If so, what then? But the word 'then' has no meaning in connection with the *eschaton*, unless we are to think of eternity as the infinite prolongation of the present time series in which the company continue to sing the final chorus on a stage on which the curtain never falls.

The fact is that both individually and corporately we are conscious of being made for a perfection which is unattainable in any imaginable conditions of space and time. If both corporately and individually we find our true life in the surrender of our selves to the service of the eternal values, what is true for each is true for all. I cannot better express what is involved than in words quoted from Oliver Quick:

> No final or perfect good is attainable in this world at all. For only by the sacrifice which death seals can the work of love be brought to finality. No doubt St. Paul taught that even on this side of physical death the Christian dies spiritually and rises again to newness of life in Christ. Since the resurrection and exaltation of Christ the life of the world to come has begun to be really present and active already. But St. Paul would also have said that the spirit is not the whole man, and the present spiritual resurrection, still imperfect while the spirit is hampered by the mortal and sin-stained flesh of this world, can only give a dim foreshadowing or foretaste of the future glory.
>
> And thus it is that Christianity, alone among the religions and philosophies of the world, succeeds in eliciting from death, i.e., from the actuality of dying, a unique value, so that it is found to make a positive and necessary contribution to the perfection of created life. Other philosophies of immortality suggest either that death is in some way unreal, or that it constitutes merely a release for the spirit through the dropping off of the material body. Not so Christianity. To it dying is an essential part or moment in that act through which

love accomplishes the self-sacrifice which issues in eternal life. And thus physical death, in all its terrible universality, becomes for the Christian a sacrament of the spiritual truth that, because it is love which saves, life must be lost before it be fully won.[1]

To this I may add from what I have written earlier:

> The relation between mankind and the whole physical world is analogous to that between an individual man and his own body. It is difficult to see why what we regard as certain in the case of the one should not be expected as probable in the case of the other. If, as individuals, personally imperfect men yield up their imperfect and sinful bodies and are given a new life in which is fulfilled God's creative and redemptive purpose for them, why should not His cosmic purpose involve the yielding up for destruction of an imperfect and sinful human society?[2]

(ii) Does the actual state of the world give any clue to the nature of the *eschaton* towards which it is moving? It seems to me that the evidence is indecisive. There is no denying, on the one hand, that from the time of Constantine onwards Christian principles have exerted increasing power over the minds, customs and institutions of men. We have developed a conscience about war of a kind which is a new thing in human history. In the League of Nations and the United Nations we have attempted to embody a vision of a new kind of world order, an order in which peace is maintained by the co-operation of free peoples instead of by the dominance of an overlord. If it be urged that as yet the vision has only gripped the minds of a minority of the human race, and that our western nations seem likely to be submerged by Afro-Asian peoples as was the Roman Empire by invaders from the North and East, it may be answered that to a robust Christian faith this will imply only a postponement of ultimate triumph. But can we reckon on the time at our disposal being indefinitely prolonged? Even if the ultimate triumph need not mean the inclusion of all men living in the Church militant here on earth, it will require their conversion to the service of ends of eternal value, the members of the

[1] O. C. Quick: *Doctrines of the Creed* (London, 1940), p. 213.
[2] *The Doctrine of the Atonement*, p. 132.

Church caring for those ends with a wholeheartedness of which our present prayers give poor evidence.[1] Set against this the evidence of our increasing ability to destroy all life on this planet, if not the planet itself, by the misuse of our growing control of natural forces. It is a race against time. Shall we be converted from this misuse in time to give us the opportunity for the further conversion that this idea of the *eschaton* requires?

The more I try to read the signs of the times, the clearer it becomes that this is a question to which at present no answer can be given. Those who hold that by reason of his faith a Christian preacher or theologian should be in a position to pronounce dogmatically in favour of one view or the other assume the existence of a kind of revelation we may feel we would have given had we been God. But it is not the kind that actually He has thought fit to give, which we must be content to accept.

In our present state we ourselves, and the world we live in, are very far from what God wills us to be, from embodying and making manifest the glory of our Creator. I do not have to know whether I shall live to an old age and die in my bed, or be killed to-morrow in an accident, before I can know my present duty. Nor for the world at large is it necessary to know the nature of its *eschaton* before we can see what needs to be done in it here and now. Once again, the kind of meaning to be found in things as they are is a meaning for action, for action which must be taken if their teleological significance, through which alone they can be fully understood, is ever to be brought to light. We must work for the *telos* if we would discover the nature of the *eschaton*.

There is an interesting textual variant in a familiar verse in the Fourth Gospel. According to the Authorized Version, Jesus says to His disciples: 'Whither I go ye know, and the way ye know.' But the better MSS. authority, followed by the Revised Version, simply reads: 'Whither I go ye know the way', and when St.

[1] See above, pp. 133 ff., 169.

Philip asks how they could know the way without knowing whither He was going Jesus replies that to know Him is to know the way, the truth and the life.[1]

Meanwhile, as we wait for the coming years to disclose the nature of their conclusion, and in each generation seek to find and do God's will in the world as we find it, we come, each one of us, to his or her own particular *eschaton*.

III

A year ago I was arguing that, quite apart from Christian faith, the nature of the universe gives us good ground for believing that death is not the destined end for men and women.[2] What more do we Christians mean to assert when we say in our creed: 'I believe in the resurrection of the body'?

By the use of the word 'resurrection' we dissociate Christian belief from doctrines of the immortality of the soul. We have here a good instance of the way in which the Christian revelation has had to make its way among ideas already at home in men's minds at the time of its coming. In the Hellenistic world there was the Platonic tradition maintaining the natural immortality of the human soul on the ground of its being a simple substance. Into this world came the Christian Church, preaching the hope of life after death in such terms as those of 1 Corinthians xv, 1 Thessalonians iv. 13–18, and St. John vi. 40. Just as the attempt was made to interpret Christ in terms of the Logos-Creator,[3] so was this Christian message of hope accepted as endorsing, or endorsed by, the current arguments for immortality. The identification of the two beliefs sank so deeply into the tradition of the Church's teaching that to-day there are quarters in which the confusion still prevails.[4]

Confusion it was and is. Doctrines of the natural immortality of the soul imply thinking of man as a composite structure, as a

[1] St. John xiv. 4–6.
[2] Vol. I, pp. 234 ff.
[3] See above, p. 38.
[4] On this see John Baillie: *And the Life Everlasting* (Oxford, 1934).

combination of a spiritual soul with a material body from which it is to be set free. In those days this was more in keeping with gnostic dualism than with the Hebrew-Christian doctrine of creation with its thought of man as a unity of embodied soul or ensouled body. It is now impossible for us when we realize how we come into existence as the self-consciousness of particular bodies individualized through their existence in space and time.[1] So far as life in this world is concerned, our *eschaton* is not to be the setting free of our soul from our body, but the dying of the whole man in the hope of rising again.

Why, then, the resurrection 'of the body'? When the words *resurrectio carnis* were written into the creed they undoubtedly expressed the belief that at the last day the material particles of bodies buried, drowned, burnt or otherwise disposed of, would be miraculously reassembled and transformed from their previous material into a spiritual mode of existence. Those who rejected gnostic dualism and thought of man as a unity thought of this unity as a unification of matter and spirit, and of the resurrection as the reuniting of elements disunited at death. We can no longer think in this way.[2] What, then, do we mean when we repeat this clause of the creed? Can we honestly take its words on our lips?

Once again, as in our consideration of eucharistic doctrine,[3] we get nowhere if we try to define what we mean by body by analysis of its constituent elements. For each of us his body is the particular organization of material energy through which he comes into existence as the self-conscious subject of its experiences, is given a content distinct from that of all other men and women, is able to express himself in this world of space and time and to grow into a person of definite character. Through my body I am individualized as a person distinct from all others,[4] I am recognizable by my fellows, and I can give expression to my thoughts and intentions. When I speak of having a body in

[1] See above, p. 84.
[2] See Vol. I, p. 164.
[3] Above, pp. 153 ff.
[4] Vol. I, p. 160.

the life to come, and of its being a spiritual body, I mean that I shall have whatever is needed to perform corresponding functions in the conditions of that life. What those conditions will be is to us here unimaginable. We cannot begin to think of what we mean by a 'spiritual body' in terms of what it will look like, feel like, or be made of. Nevertheless, when we speak of the resurrection of the body, we say something worth saying, as can be seen by considering beliefs with which it is contrasted.

I was once talking over these matters with a Lancashire weaver whose name I will disguise as Hulme Pendleton. I had been describing to him oriental pantheistic beliefs according to which we are to be merged in a divine oneness in which we shall lose our personal self-consciousness and individuality. He thought for a moment, and then said: 'That won't do for me. I must be H.P. through all eternity, or not at all.' Again, the thought of a disembodied spirit suggests a pale, anaemic kind of existence, stripped of the powers of self-expression that in a healthy body make life worth living. It means something to say that life will not be less but more fully vigorous and active than anything we experience here. Thirdly, seeing that in this life the measure of our spiritual character and value is that of the quality of our bodily life,[1] it is worth saying that eternally we are destined to be the persons we have become through the way we have lived in our earthly bodies.

In the days when the creeds were being written, these were the positive beliefs which the Fathers were concerned to proclaim in the face of rival doctrines. There were neoplatonists who looked forward to the absorption of personal identity. The Greek Hades and the Hebrew Sheol were peopled by shades whose anaemic existence was a miserable exchange for the full-blooded activity of earthly life. Gnostic teaching about the immortality of the soul, based on the dualistic notion of man as a composite structure of spirit and matter, produced two types of ethic: an exaggerated asceticism exhorting the soul to win freedom from

[1] Vol. I, pp. 224–6.

the body by trampling upon it, and a licence to its indulgence on the ground that the behaviour of the body was irrelevant to the true life of the soul. Against the former the Christian Church maintained that the body must have the respect due to it as God's creation; against the latter that it matters eternally how we live in the body here and now.

These, I repeat, are the positive beliefs for which the Christian Church stood then, for which it stands now. We differ from the Fathers in that we no longer express them in terms of an expectation of the reassembly of the body's physical elements after the manner of the reconstitution of dried eggs in wartime. In the ways of thinking of their time that was the only way in which they could express them. They had to say to the Gnostic libertine: 'It is no good your thinking that when you get out of your body at death you will be done with it. You'll have it turn up again at the Last Day.' We are saying the same thing when we say: 'You will be yourself, and able to express yourself, and the self you will be and be able to express will be the whole self that you have grown into through your life here in the flesh.'

Can we trace any more direct connection between the body in which we hope to be and express ourselves in the life to come and our present earthly body? Can we meet the criticism of St. Thomas Aquinas that it is a misuse of language to speak of the resurrection of the body when we mean the exchange of one body for another?[1] To answer these questions we must consider how from the point of view of a Christian believer we are to think of the relation between the resurrection of Christ and of ourselves.

According to the traditional account of our Lord's resurrection, His body, unlike that of David, 'saw no corruption'.[2] We know too little of the composition either of matter or of spirit to be able to attach any precise meaning to such phrases as 'the spiritualization of His material body' or *non reditus sed transitus*, if to give them meaning requires an understanding of the process

[1] S.Th. III, Suppl. 79, i. [2] Acts xiii. 36, 37.

involved. We have to admit our ignorance in this sphere, to be content to say that by such phrases we express the belief that in the case of our Lord His earthly body underwent some process other than is the destiny of our own, a process of which the nature is completely mysterious to us but which resulted in there being a more direct connection between His earthly body and His resurrection body than we can expect for ourselves.

For Christians, belief in the resurrection of Christ is the ground of their own hope of the life to come. In days when men could think of our resurrection as the reassembling of the particles of our earthly bodies, it was possible to express this as the hope that after going through the process of bodily dissolution and reconstitution we shall rise like Him. In 1 Corinthians xv. 12–19 St. Paul argues from the resurrection of Christ to that of others as though they were parallel instances of a single type of event, and this example has been followed in countless writings and sermons. This argument is, I believe, mistaken. The ground of our Christian hope is the belief that we shall rise not like Christ, but in Christ.

Christianity began as the faith of men who believed that through the coming of the Spirit their crucified, risen and ascended Lord was reproducing in them the way of life which had been His as man on earth. They bear witness to this conviction by speaking of themselves as being 'in Christ', taken by adoption to share in His sonship, members of His body, branches of Christ the true vine.[1] They live as members of His body who, being risen from the dead, dieth no more; He is in them and is their hope of glory, the inward man who shall endure when the outward perishes.[2] We come into existence as the self-conscious subjects of the experiences of perishable bodies. What right have we to think that when these bodies fall away we shall be able to continue without them? The Christian faith is that God offers to man through Christ a share in His own immortality. If in this

[1] Gal. iii. 28; Rom. viii. 15; xii. 5; 1 Cor. xii. 12–27; St. John xv. 1–8.
[2] Rom. vi. 9; 2 Cor. xiii. 5; Col. i. 27; 2 Cor. iv. 16.

life we are united to Him by the surrender of our bodies in His service, we find in that union our hope of a future life.

The 'spiritual body' which is to be the vehicle of our continued personal life in the world to come is the body of the risen Christ into which we are incorporated as members. As each man dies to his natural self by the surrender to Christ of his earthly bodily life, he is 'born again' to become in Christ a 'new man', and finds his own true selfhood as he finds that his true life is to live as a member of the risen Christ. It is the paradox of Christian faith, verified in Christian experience, that the more completely a man surrenders himself to Christ to live as a member of His body, the more fully he finds in that membership a vehicle for his own full, rich, individual, personal life. Thus he can cease to trouble over the fact that his earthly body will perish in the grave. It will live on in the fact that eternally he will be what he has become in and through it; but itself, when considered in terms of the physical elements of which it is composed, it is the 'outward man' that perisheth, leaving its work to be carried on by the body of the 'inward man' who is a member of the body of the risen Christ, his hope of glory.

Here again the witness of Christian faith dovetails into the conclusions of natural theology. Last year we got so far as to see that in order to make sense of the universe we must postulate the continuance of personal life after death. In Christ God reveals Himself as the God who takes the action which confirms this postulate and makes sense of what would otherwise remain nonsensical. Here again we have a belief of which neither I nor any other Christian believer can give a demonstrative proof. As so often, all we can do is to describe as clearly as we may what it is that we believe, offer it as our understanding of the revelatory significance of the events to which the Bible bears witness, and say to those who listen, 'Cannot you see it for yourselves?' For this it must be set in its context in the whole *corpus* of Christian belief. We think of the incarnation as the entry upon the experience of human life on earth by the eternal Second Person of the

Blessed Trinity in order that He may not only win our redemption but also provide the material cause of our bodily resurrection. It is because of this that we believe we have adequate ground for accepting the evidence which ascribes to Him a unique mode both of entering upon and passing beyond His earthly life.[1] Of all this we may not be able to give demonstrative proof. But it is in keeping with the understanding of our experience to which we have been brought by our attempt to make sense of it. We have to seek our ultimate explanations in terms of God's personal activity and will. When we interpret the Christian revelation as God becoming incarnate in order to gather us creatures of flesh and blood into personal relations with Himself, and see in this the fulfilment of His aim in the whole creative process, we are not 'mythologizing' in the sense of symbolizing some more real interplay of impersonal forces in terms of imaginary personification. If as self-conscious human persons men and women are taken into personal union with God in Christ, through them the material universe makes its contribution to a life which is not lived in a lesser degree of reality but in a higher mode.[2]

In view of much that I have said in earlier lectures it should not now be necessary to point out that to think in this way of Christ's resurrection as the ground of our hope of life after death does not imply the limitation of the hope of resurrection to those who are conscious believers in Christ or members of the Christian Church.[3] I may put it like this.[4] That God would take man to share in His eternal life might be, and had been, the pious hope of many. That God has actually initiated such a way of life here on earth, upon which it is now open to men to enter, is the witness of the followers of Christ. With the eyes of their mind illuminated by this 'inside knowledge' they look out and see His working in a wider sphere. In so far as any life, in any age, has

[1] Cp. above, p. 91. [2] See Vol. I, p. 174.
[3] E.g., Vol. I, pp. 234 ff. Above, pp. 106 ff., 133 ff.
[4] In what follows I am largely reproducing what I wrote in the Introduction to *God and the World through Christian Eyes*, published by the S.C.M. Press in 1933.

been given to doing the works of God, it has been moved by the Holy Spirit to be a sharing in the life of Christ. Those who conscientiously oppose the Christian faith, in the honest belief that they are spreading the truth, in their devotion to truth are unconscious champions of Him who is the Lord of all truth. The significance of the Christian way of life is that it reveals the principle of all life. The Christian has the privilege and the responsibility of believing that the life given to God is of eternal quality, and of deepening this faith in the exercise of personal relationship with his Lord. In the light of this assurance he views the lives of others, and often sees God at work in and through them all unknown to themselves. When this is so, their eternal destiny must surely depend on what they actually are, what God knows them to be, rather than on what to themselves they seem to be. For such as these conversion, whether it come in this life or the next, will be the opening of their eyes to acknowledge the Lord whom they have been serving unawares.

IV

We come into existence as the self-conscious subjects of experiences mediated through bodies distinct in space and time.[1] It is questionable whether to begin with, the term 'self-conscious' is accurate. Each of us may be conscious of being not one but many selves, pulled hither and thither by diverse interests and passions distracting the consciousness of the one physical organism.[2] This life is our opportunity of growing into a unified self, a spiritual *hypostasis*. The psychologist speaks of integrating personality round some dominant purpose. The Christian speaks of bringing into captivity every thought to the obedience of Christ, of a man growing into a unified self as he receives his selfhood from Christ. The latter is the Christian interpretation of the former, with the difference that in it the dominant purpose round which the personality is to be integrated must be in

[1] Above, p. 80.
[2] Vol. I, p. 235. Cp. *The Doctrine of the Trinity*, pp. 183 ff.

accordance with the mind of Christ. There are thus three open possibilities in human life: (*a*) to fail in unification, to die without having grown into a self which can hold together as a person when the earthly body falls apart; (*b*) to achieve unity through devotion to some evil end; (*c*) to be unified, either knowingly or unknowingly, as a member of the body of Christ.

(*c*) I need say no more about these last. Their hope of the resurrection of the body and the life everlasting is the hope of the beatific vision, of the joy of sharing in the communion of the saints in heaven. How are we to think of the destiny of the others?

(*b*) The conventional idea of hell as a place or state of eternal torment is inconsistent with God's revelation of Himself in either His creative or His redemptive activity. Through the mechanism of space and time we are individualized into potential citizens of the city of God. Our growth into the kind of selfhood that has more than a space-time mode of reality comes by the exercise of our freedom in devotion to ends of eternal quality. We have seen reason to believe that the history of human thought is the history of God making Himself known to us by stripping off successive layers of misapprehension which miscolour our vision, and that in particular all growth in sensitiveness to moral values is part of God's education of man in knowledge of Himself. If when he comes to the end of his life on earth any one of us has so misused his opportunities that there is left in him nothing of which can be made a citizen of the eternal city, we cannot think of God as keeping him alive, as an individual person, for no other purpose than that of suffering unending torment.

(*a*) We do not know what kind of further training God may have in store for us when we pass from this life. Here once again we have to resist the temptation to claim as a matter of revelation more than God has seen fit to make known to us. We are rightly sceptical about developments of the doctrine of purgatory which suggest that the Church on earth can plan and make arrangements for the journey of its departed members after the manner of a travel agency making reservations for its clients' continental tours. Of that unknown country we have neither time-tables nor maps. Yet we must not in reaction deny the necessity of further training. It is surely beyond question that even the best of us will need both deeper cleansing from our sinfulness, and fuller conformity to the mind and will of Christ. What this will be like we must be content to wait and see.

Universalism, the belief that ultimately all men will be found in the blessed company of the saints in heaven, whatever may have been the manner of their earthly life, is also inconsistent with what has been revealed. We set out to try to make sense of the universe and of our life within it. To hold that in the last resort it does not matter to us eternally what kind of lives we live here and now evacuates both of whatever meaning in them we have been able to discover.

We have here an instance of the kind of problem where we can give an answer to the question of principle but not to questions of empirical fact. We have to put it in a hypothetical form. If there be anyone in whom at his death there is nothing worth preserving as the germ of a life worth living in the world to come, there is no reason for believing in the continuance of his individual personal life. Whether there be any such man or woman is a question of empirical fact to which God alone knows the answer.

I was once talking to an old priest in the lower west side of New York, one of those true shepherds of Christ's flock in whose love and care for his people was reflected his Master's love and care for mankind. 'Our cure of souls', he said, 'is very like the work of doctors of the body. The aim of a surgeon in an operation is to find what there is of healthy tissue and give it a chance to grow. It is to this end that he cuts away what is infected and poisonous. So when we are seeking to bring counsel, advice and absolution to sinners, as we are wrestling, perhaps, with most degraded specimens of humanity, we have to be asking: "How much of this rotten apple can be saved?" ' About the same time there was a report in the press of an inquest on a negro who had been battered to death in a street brawl somewhere in the west thirties. It appeared from the evidence that he was about as low-down a specimen of humanity as could be imagined: witness after witness testified to the effect that he had been more of a brute than a man, a creature of whom the world was well rid. There was one exception, the voice of a woman he had been living with, who said that he had been good to her and she missed him. Only God knows whether that witnessed to some shred of healthy tissue which could be encouraged to grow in some more hygienic sphere than had been provided by this world.

LECTURE X

Freedom and Faith

THE time has come to look back over the whole course of these lectures and try to see what it all comes to. One reviewer of the first published volume remarks that in it I have mixed autobiography with the argument.[1] In a sense that is true, a sense in which, both last year and this, it has been inevitable. I have been trying to put before you what I have come to believe as a result of a life spent in the interpermeating study of theology and philosophy. The argument of these twenty lectures is a kind of map of the course my mind has travelled through forty-seven years. It has often been concerned with questions which are not patient of demonstrative proof, where in each case all that can be done is to state as clearly as possible how one has come to see it asking 'Cannot you see it too?' Where I have included autobiographical detail it has been in the hope that I can most clearly expose to your gaze my present thought by showing what has led my mind to move this way or that.

Moved it certainly has. If any apology is needed for having ruthlessly criticized devotion to cherished forms of words such as justification by faith or the invisible church,[2] it is that I know myself what it means to be called by God to cut loose the ship of faith from its traditional moorings and launch out into the deep. I will not now attempt in one lecture to summarize the contents of the previous nineteen. Instead, I will pick out for emphasis three directions in which I feel myself to have been driven far into the open sea. I will speak in turn of what I now believe about how we should think of God, how we should think of the Church, and how little we know about anything.

[1] *Manchester Guardian*, March 6th, 1957.
[2] Vol. I, pp. 108 ff.; above, pp. 122 ff.

I

For thought about God there are three cardinal passages in what I have said. The first came in the middle of last year's fifth lecture, the other two in the second and sixth of the present series.[1]

In the first of these we had been thinking about the nature of human thought in general, of how our quest is for objectivity, to know the truth about things, to apprehend reality. We had to face the fact that not only is the way in which we ourselves see things coloured by our outlook, but that this is also the case with all those whose works we study as evidence of what they have seen. We came to see the history of human thought as proceeding by the interaction of categories with evidence, the objective logic in the nature of things working itself out in the interplay of human minds, evidence forcing revision of categories. This led to the conclusion that the ultimate object of our study is not what this or that man may have thought or said or meant, but what was the objective truth, the reality, which was seeking to make itself known. We had already thought of natural theology as concerned with God revealing Himself in the manner of His creation. It needed but a small step to see that the true object of our study is God's revelation of Himself, that the history of human thought is the history of God making Himself known in the minds of men, stripping off successive layers of presuppositions which miscolour what is seen.

God in Himself, the eternal author and source of all created being, is unchanging in His perfection. But our knowledge of Him changes as it grows in accordance with His method of revealing Himself to us. Whether or no it ever occurred to the mind of the author of the Book of *Revelation*, there is food for thought in his speaking of God as the Omega as well as the Alpha, the End as well as the Beginning. Is it because of the nature of our theological education in universities and colleges

[1] Vol. I, pp. 114–5, and above, pp. 30 ff., 129 ff.

that we tend in our religious thought to behave like men walking backwards, our eyes fixed upon the past? Corporately we think of God as the Creator who has brought the world into existence and through Moses called the Israelites to be His chosen people; as the Redeemer who died and rose and started the Christian Church on its way; as the Sanctifier who came to inspire that Church at Pentecost. Individually we think of God who has made us and called us, has redeemed us and baptized us into membership of His earthly body, has come in our confirmation to sanctify and inspire us. When we think of Him as present now we think of Him as the God who has done these things, and we ask what we can learn about Him from the biblical writers, the early fathers, the scholastics, the reformers, the carolines, the evangelicals, or the tractarians. How often do we think of Him as standing on before us, calling us on to fuller knowledge, bidding us consider what revision of the categories inherited from all these our forefathers is required by the evidence He is now providing?

Surely this should be an integral element in our thought of God's eternity. Last year we thought of the relation between teacher and pupil as illustrating God's creative activity.[1] The illustration is indeed apposite when we are thinking of His revealing activity. Of a schoolmaster it might be said: 'Boys may come and boys may go, but he goes on for ever'—goes on as one to whom they look up to draw out their capacity for learning, and to share with them the riper knowledge he already has. So our lives are lived in the presence of God who because of His eternal perfection can draw out all our capacities for good and fulfil all our aspirations. The story of creation rolls on through the evolutionary process. At the human stage we make our conscious efforts to struggle onwards. Artists, scientists, inventors seek to discover creation's possibilities for use and beauty. Philosophers seek for a deeper understanding of the universe. Theologians seek for a fuller grasp of God's revelation of Himself

[1] Vol. I, p. 152.

in Christ. All are in the presence of God who has started us on our way, who, as present with us now, with us looks back over the past history of our race,[1] setting us free from our sins and binding us to Himself in personal communion. He is always calling us on to fuller knowledge, and to that use of it through which we may grow in the freedom that He looks for in citizens of the City of God.[2] All the discoveries of our minds, all our fresh powers of control over nature and of self-expression, are given us by God for the shaping of the world and of ourselves in accordance with His will. We press onwards, enriching our minds, increasing our control. Always He is on in front, calling us to fuller knowledge and greater power.

Religious life is stunted and crippled when it loses this sense of God being on before us, calling us to press on into the unknown. The enthusiasm of conversion settles down into the dull routine of conscientious observance. We become timidly afraid of any novelty or change, whether it be in ways of thought, or fashions of dress, or social order. We remember 'Hold fast that which is good', but forget 'Prove all things'. When we say 'Glory be to the Father and to the Son and to the Holy Ghost', we think only of what He has done up to date and the response 'As it was in the beginning, is now and ever shall be' becomes a dull assertion of the monotony of life instead of a challenge to remember the ever-living presence in all ages of the God who is 'making all things new'.

I jump now to my third cardinal passage, the reference in this year's sixth lecture to Donald Baillie's book, *God was in Christ.*[3] In that book Baillie pointed out that when we ask whether Christ was God we put the question in a form which assumes that we know what we mean by God and ask whether Christ was that. But this is logically unjustifiable. For if Jesus Christ really and truly was God incarnate, the answer to our question may require a revision of our existing idea of God. The question

[1] Above, pp. 23 ff. [2] Vol. I, pp. 186–8.
[3] Above, p. 128.

to be asked is no longer whether the kind of God we had previously been thinking of could become incarnate and live a human life of the kind lived by Jesus of Nazareth; it is whether the kind of God revealed to us in Jesus Christ Himself could have done so. This new light on an old question makes the book what I call a seminal book, a book that sows in the mind seeds of thought that continue to grow. For our present purpose its fruit is the principle that in thinking about God we are to bring into captivity every thought to the obedience of Christ.

This gives no promise of early finality in our quest for knowledge of God. As we have seen, both in what He did and what He said, 'Christ gave His life, it is for Christians to discern the doctrine'. This discernment is a process that is still going on, and is likely still to be unfinished at the end of this world's history.[1] By the guidance of the Holy Spirit, who takes of the things of Christ and shows them unto us, successive generations of Christians are enabled to disentangle the revelation of God in Christ from miscolouring presuppositions and gain a fuller grasp of its true import. Whatever growth we may be given in our knowledge of Christ must be allowed to illuminate, and, if necessary, to transform, our way of thinking of God.

Look back now to this year's second lecture. We were thinking of the early history of human religion, how it began in attempts to enter into personal relations with whatever powers control this universe and our life within it, how they were thought of as both hostile and friendly, malevolent and beneficent, needing to be propitiated as well as adored.[2] We have thought of the history of theology as God stripping off layers of misconception which obscure His true nature. Among our own spiritual ancestors the Hebrew prophets were inspired to discard the notion of God as malevolent and hostile to human aspirations. Where He appears to be so, it must be for the upholding of His righteousness in face of His creatures' iniquity. In Christ He revealed Himself as so essentially and perfectly beneficent as to take on

[1] Above, pp. 81 ff., 133 ff.

[2] Above, pp. 30 ff.

Himself the purging of His creation from the evil with which, in order to create persons endowed with genuine freedom, He had allowed it to become infected.

The transformation of our idea of God by the light of His revelation of Himself in Christ is, I believe, one of the growing points for theology to-day. I have hinted at this in what I have said about His sovereignty, His claiming responsibility for the existence of evil, and belief in hell.[1] To go further we must ponder more deeply on the question of the nature of His fatherly love and the grounds of our difficulty in accepting His revelation.

Psychologists are aware of the stubborn power of deep-rooted long-standing mental habits. Our more recently gained beliefs, superior though they may be as apprehensions of truth acquired through the exercise of our reason, lie, so to speak, on the surface. We need to be continually practising ourselves in living by them if they are to penetrate deeply, get a real grip on our minds, and control our thoughts and actions. When they are in conflict with what they find in possession, we are apt to be more swayed by the old occupants than by the new arrivals, especially when under the stress of some emotional disturbance.

It has been my thesis throughout these lectures that the specifically biblical Christian revelation comes to us at the level of the conscious rational mind. God has been educating us in knowledge of Himself by doing things and inspiring men to grasp their significance. The minds of the men before whose eyes He does them are possessed by ingrained habits of thought which colour their vision. The work of the Holy Spirit in the minds of men is never ending so long as the newly-acquired truth is entangled with persisting error and is itself in need of clarification.

How far are our minds still under the spell of the ancestral belief that God is sometimes hostile and malevolent, projecting on Him that fear of the terrible unknown which is one of the most primitive elements in our consciousness? The history of our religion, beginning in Old Testament days and reaching its

[1] Above, pp. 57, 58, 201.

climax in the coming of Christ, is the history of God revealing Himself more and more fully to man as the all-good and all-loving Father who wills the good of His creatures. Yet every now and then one comes upon a Christian who simply cannot bring Himself to accept God's full and free forgiveness, who feels that there is something presumptuous in being carefree and happy, whose life is such that if by inadvertance he allows himself to slip into such a state, afterwards his fears are redoubled by the thought of how he may have imperilled his salvation through his momentary forgetfulness to be anxiety-ridden. To such a one we may surely think of our living Lord as saying: 'What is the good of my having become man, having been crucified and risen again, having baptized you into membership of my earthly body with the gift of the Holy Spirit, if you are still living your life enthralled by the thought of a god who is always wanting to catch you in some misstep, as though to cry: "Now I've got you!"—a blasphemous myth of a god who does not exist at all?'[1]

We must go further. We are not only under the thrall of primitive fears. We are 'bound by the chain of our sins'. Selfishness is so deeply ingrained in us that we find it wellnigh impossible to conceive of love which is wholly free from self-interest. It is extremely difficult really to accept God's gospel of free forgiveness as something we can do nothing whatever to earn but must simply receive. When we have got this far we find it still more difficult to disabuse our minds of the notion that in relation to God we now have in His eyes a status superior to that of other men. What if the revelation of God in Christ shows His essential nature to be love so perfect in its unselfishness as to be unimaginable by us except in so far as fitfully and here and there we catch a glimpse of what it is to lose ourselves in devotion to some person or cause?[2] Problems multiply. We have to remember the danger of a sentimentality which forgets God's revelation of Himself through our judgments of value as the God of

[1] In this paragraph I have largely reproduced a passage from *The Lord's Prayer* (London, 1934), p. 59.

[2] Above, p. 60.

righteousness, which ignores the necessity of believing in His wrath against sin and sinners, in which the doctrine of God degenerates to the level of 'He's a good fellow and 'twill all be well'. But we have to ask ourselves very carefully whether our way of thinking about God's wrath and punishment is to any extent compounded of ancestral fears of hostile deities with desire to escape the doom that will fall on others. How far do we need to disentangle from such relics of the past our apprehension of God's revelation of Himself in Christ? Is failure to do this the chief obstacle to our believing that His care for the genuineness of our freedom moves Him to claim responsibility for permitting the existence of evil as well as taking it on Himself to rescue His creation from its toils?

I have no time to pursue this inquiry further. Nor would it be right for me to try to reach a conclusion on this subject here. Lord Gifford's will directs his lecturers to address themselves to realms so high that a man would be a fool to attempt to do more than point out to fellow searchers after truth directions in which he thinks the way lies open for further advance. Each of us must see what he can, describe it as best he may, and leave it to his successors to discount the error due to his point of view. Let me at this point sum up what I have been trying to say in three sentences. The revelation of God in Christ has to make its way in the minds of men already well stocked with ideas and beliefs that colour their understanding of it. The history of human thought, including Christian thought, is the history of God stripping off layers of misconception which hinder our grasp of His truth. We have always to be asking how far our understanding of the Christian faith needs to be disentangled from hangovers from the past which miscolour our vision, including some so deeply rooted in our mental inheritance that they are only coming to light after nearly two thousand years of Christian faith.

I know no more powerful solvent of theological doctrines

that one may be accustomed to take for granted than to ask: 'What kind of an idea of God does this imply? Is it consistent with His being the kind of God who became incarnate in Jesus Christ?'[1]

II

The character of Jesus Christ is to be determinative for our thought of God. The nature of His messiahship must equally be so for our understanding of the Church, the messianic community, His continuing earthly body. At the end of my sixth lecture this year I was asking questions about what revision of our customary ways of thinking this will require. As on earth our Lord had to put from Him ideas of messiahship taken for granted by His Jewish contemporaries, so to-day He bids us put away the thought of the Church as the body into which men are to come in order to escape the doom destined for those outside and secure their own salvation. This disentangles the question of Church membership from that of the hope of resurrection to life eternal. The use made of this disentanglement in the last lecture shows the necessity of this revision to deal with one of the puzzles with which we set out on our inquiry last year.[2] This led further to our questioning whether in the will and purpose of God the Church militant here in earth is intended ever to include in its membership all the inhabitants of this world.

So far these conclusions are negative in character, the stripping off of presuppositions inconsistent with God's revelation of Himself in Christ. On the positive side are the implications of the fact that Christ 'went about doing good', the thought of evangelization as the enlistment of recruits in a body that exists to set forward the welfare of mankind and to enable creation to manifest the glory of its Creator. It is for this purpose that its

[1] E.g., with regard to revelation, Vol. I, p. 77; to sacraments, my contribution to Baillie and Marsh: *Intercommunion* (London, 1952), pp. 264 ff.; to eschatology, J. E. Fison: *The Christian Hope* (London, 1954).

[2] Vol. I, pp. 54–6; and above, p. 199.

members are His fellowship of forgiven sinners, cleansed from their own sins and seeing their service of the world as their response to His love.

So in every locality the congregation of Christian people is to be foremost in zeal for progress in the arts, the sciences and whatever makes for the good life of man on earth. That in general. In particular the Church has a special work of its own of which in these lectures I have said little or nothing because I have dealt with it at length elsewhere.[1] Christ in His messiahship went directly to the heart of the world's problems by dealing with evil in its manifestation as sin. The specific task of the Church is to act as the continuing earthly body of the Christ who, in biblical language, is the Lamb of God that taketh away the sins of the world. To quote from my earlier work:

> Where there is evil in the world, no matter from what cause, no matter who is to blame, there is the potential source of further corruption of God's creation. Human history shows only too clearly that ignorance, sickness and poverty provide breeding-grounds for envy, hatred and malice, for strife between classes, between races, between nations. What is needed is a body of men and women bound together in a fellowship whose *raison d'être* and vocation is to step in and say: 'Never mind whose fault it is, let it be our privilege, at whatever it may cost us in money, time, energy, health or life, to take these potential sources of corruption and transform them into material for increasing the world's output of good'.[2]

In this its specific task, as in its wider service, Christ calls the Church to a self-forgetful outward-looking attitude, to see the world as our heavenly Father's world in which His work is waiting to be found and done.

Of all the issues that arise from this let me call attention to one of theoretical and three of practical importance.

1. In my second lecture last year I was showing how philosophy is the attempt to make sense of this world as it actually exists. In the following lecture we saw something of the complexity of the puzzles it presents. I do not see how a man who

[1] *The Doctrine of the Atonement* (London, 1951).
[2] *Op. cit.*, p. 96.

has been bitten by the *bacillus philosophicus* can ever be satisfied with a theology for which God is only interested in the salvation out of the world of a certain number of human souls. This limitation of God's interest in His creation, which is characteristic of much continental theology both Lutheran and Reformed, provokes a disastrous divorce between theologians and philosophers. It is idle for theologians to complain that philosophers are indifferent to the preaching of the gospel and the study of theology when they and their God have no interest in the problems of the actual universe which exercise these men's minds, when the gospel they preach has no relevance to them. I hope I have made clear my conviction that the heart of the Christian gospel *is* the message of God's free grace in Christ, of cleansing and forgiveness ready and waiting for all who repent. Let there be no mistake about that. If to a man burdened with the consciousness of his sins there could not be found anywhere in this world someone to say with authority in the name of Christ: 'Go in peace, thy sins are forgiven thee', that would be the final and ultimate failure of the Church, failure in its own specific task. From this root must all its thought and action spring. But we need to reopen the question: What are we forgiven *for*? If we are tempted to stop short at forgiveness and the man's own reconciliation to God and salvation, to treat these as the end and go no further, our gospel is inadequate to God's revelation of Himself in both the Bible of the theologians and the universe of the philosophers.

2. I have used the word 'evangelization' and I have just spoken of the Christian gospel as directly addressed to men burdened with the consciousness of their sins. If the Christian faith be true, all men are sinners; the difference is that some know it and some do not. How can its preaching be relevant to men with no such consciousness of burden, indeed, with no consciousness of sin? It has always been recognized by those engaged in the work of evangelization, in conducting parochial missions or otherwise, that their first task is to 'stir up a sense of sin'. In the

days of the evangelical revival this could be done by what has been described as 'shaking people over hell'. We cannot do that now. What then?

We fail doubly if, dropping hell, we simply speak to men of their own need of salvation. We are untrue to the gospel in urging them to concentrate their attention on themselves, and we do nothing to help them themselves to feel the need of which we are speaking. But a great door and effectual is opened if we turn their minds outward to ask, as we ourselves were asking earlier on,[1] what difference it would make if in the relations between nations, races and classes we could eliminate such factors as national, racial and class pride, ambition, envy and greed. Then let them ask whether they can deny that in their own lives, and in their relations with their fellow-men, there are working those same forces which wreak havoc on the larger scale. From the vision of what this world might be and is not, of how in our homes, our offices, our clubs and elsewhere it fails to reflect the glory of God its Creator because of our selfishness, our grumpiness, our laziness and what not, we learn our need of cleansing and forgiveness. We learn it in a healthy way when we see that the real tragedy of our sins is not that they keep us out of heaven but that they make us useless to God in the carrying forward of His creative and redemptive work.

Once many years ago I was talking to a young nurse who said frankly that she had no religion, that to her the word 'God' simply meant nothing at all. I asked her what she lived by, to which she replied that she tried to do her best for her patients. She was an honest girl, and when I asked: 'Do you?' she said, 'No; sometimes when I'm out of temper or tired I'm short with them or scamp things'. 'What then?' 'I say to myself, "Come on, you must pull yourself together".' There was only one thing to be said, to tell her that if she wished for herself to find true religion she must begin by praying 'O God, if there be a God, help me to do what I know I ought to do'.

[1] Above, p. 73.

3. If we think of Church membership in terms of salvation for eternal blessedness we land ourselves in a dilemma with regard to our creed. We are torn between the claims of charity and faith. The Church exists to be the body of the Lamb of God that taketh away the sins of the world and to proclaim the gospel of God's grace, of forgiveness and the power of the Spirit available to man as a result of what God has done in history incarnate in Christ. It has a definite work to do and a definite message to deliver. For this there must be agreement about what it has to do and say: it must be a body of men and women agreed in believing the central affirmations of the Christian creed. But if we think that to remain outside is to be cut off from hope of heaven, out of very charity we shall be moved so to blur the outlines of the content of the gospel as to leave it with no cutting edge.

By disentangling the idea of Church membership from that of preferential status with a view to the world to come, we make it possible for the Church to be its true self, and to be an effective body, without loss of charity. Imagine yourself to have been attempting to persuade an unbeliever of the truth of the Christian faith, to have got as far as you can by argument and discussion and leave him unconvinced. What are you to say? Something like this. 'I do not pretend always to understand God's ways. Often they are mysterious. If it is His will that for the next stretch of your life you are to serve Him outside the Church, it is not for us to question it. Of one thing I am certain, that His fundamental demand on you is for honesty. From the days of the Hebrew prophets He has made this clear. He would rather have you remain outside until you can honestly come in, than compromise with your convictions for some ulterior motive.' You may have to lose him from the Church Militant here on earth in order to find him in the Church Triumphant in heaven.

4. For the best part of twenty years I was secretary to the World Conference on Faith and Order which became the Faith and Order Commission of the World Council of Churches. In

that capacity, both in these islands and overseas, I have shared in a very large number of discussions between representatives of different churches, discussions aimed at reconciling the differences of conviction which keep the churches apart. This experience has led me to think that we have got as far as we are likely to get on these lines until each and all, in our respective churches, we have radically revised our understanding of what the Church is for. We have explained to one another what we stand for in the tradition of the patristics, the scholastics, and the tridentines, of Martin Luther, John Calvin, Thomas Cranmer, Richard Hooker, William Penn, and John Wesley, of the congregationalist and baptist founding fathers. But all has been on the basis of a common assumption that the Church exists for the benefit of its members, for their rescue out of the perishing world, as the ark in which they are to be ferried over the troublous waters of this life to the celestial shore. So far as this is so we cannot help regarding one another as rivals rather than fellow workers. We shall get no further so long as we continue to discuss the respective merits of what our ancestors thought in terms of bygone ages. We need the new start that can come from revising our thought of the Church in the light of its historical origin as the messianic community of Jesus Christ the Messiah.

III

So to the last lap. How little we know about anything.

More than once I have pictured human thinkers as peering into the darkness of the mystery that surrounds us. As human beings we all look out on the universe from our human standpoint. In each generation we look out with an outlook conditioned by our age and culture. Within each generation each individual is conditioned by his own particular circumstances. Each and all we have to peer into the darkness along the rays of such light as we are given to see by. Knowledge grows by sharing what we see, by comparing our different visions in the faith that they are apprehensions or misapprehensions of a coherent objective reality, that by perseverance in looking and comparing errors can be corrected and the truth discovered. There are two factors to be considered: the extent and the nature of the surrounding mystery and the value of the light at the centre from which we look out.

I have described philosophers as men with so passionate a concern for knowledge that they question the conventions and assumptions commonly taken for granted in the thought and action of their age and culture, seeking for reliable clues to the puzzles that confront us.[1] This year we have set ourselves to examine the nature of God's revelation of Himself in Christ with a view to discovering how far it gives us our central clue to the understanding of all things, what is the value of the light which it gives us to see by. In the course of the inquiry we have learned two things: how much less we know than we want to know, and have often thought that we do know, and something of the nature and value of the light that lightens our way.

Let me remind you of the striking parallel we observed last year between the history of scientific and of theological study in the present century.

> Neither to theologians nor to physicists has God thought fit to give the kind of revelation they feel that they would provide if they were God. Theologians . . . have had to adjust themselves to the fact that God's truth is not given in forms of sound words uncoloured by the outlook of those who bear witness to His revelation. Just so do physicists have to adjust themselves to the fact that all observations of the natural world are relative to the standpoint of the observer. It is equally true of God's revelation of Himself that is given through the sciences as of that which is more strictly the basis of Christian theology that to grasp it we must patiently set side by side our several apprehensions of it, asking what the truth must be if it so appears to men who see it from these various points of view.
>
> When we try to study the universe by scientific method, for a while it seems to respond encouragingly to our inquiries, but when we push these inquiries further in an attempt to grasp its fundamental nature, it seems to slip through our fingers and elude us. It is, I believe, true to say that so far as we are seeking to know enough about it to be able to control it, it is responsive to us. It is when we seek to answer the question of what it is in itself that we are baffled.[2]

[1] Vol. I, pp. 27 ff.

[2] Vol. I, pp. 155, 159.

In so far as scientific research enables us to increase control over sub-human nature and theological study to make more fitting response to God's calls upon us, the distinction between them bears out our observation of their respective descent from primitive magic and superstition.[1] My present point is to call attention to the difficulty we feel in both fields in adjusting ourselves to the realization that we do not know what our fathers, and we ourselves in our youth, used to think we knew. The reaction against acceptance of conventional certainties has produced on the one hand the existentialist emphasis on *angst*, and on the other the dictatorial attempt to impose order on chaos by mass-produced *gleichschaltung*. Those who attribute the present state of affairs solely to decay of religious faith betray an inadequate analysis of the situation. The upheaval of Victorian certainty that science gives us the true description of the real world of nature has as much to do with it as inability to accept Victorian understanding of the divine revelation.

Hence the forms in which a threat to human freedom is actually felt as a matter of practical urgency. 'What kind of freedom is ever conceivable in a technological society? Or in a mass-society governed by all the controls which are now available?' asks Dr. Dillistone in reviewing my first volume.[2] Without specifying what questions he has in mind he goes on to ask whether my discussion had been relevant to 'the questions which are really being asked in this modern age . . . the deepest concerns of our age'. I take this reference to be to the existentialist *angst*. Man can have no deeper concern than the question of his own existence as that is analysed, for example, by Professor Paul Tillich in his book, *The Courage to Be*.[3]

It seems to me that the philosopher, reflecting on the assumptions which men take for granted in their thinking, must come to the conclusion that neither through the natural sciences nor through theology has God thought fit to give us revelation that

[1] Above, p. 31. [2] *The Hibbert Journal*, January 1957, p. 210.
[3] London, 1952.

issues in the kind of knowledge we used to think we had. The light we have is given to enable us to discern in our present circumstances what needs to be done with them: it is in the doing of it that we shall open the door to progress beyond what knowledge we already have. For scientist and theologian alike the field of knowledge can only be cultivated on the basis of faith, faith that the universe 'makes sense', faith that no matter what revision of categories may be required by evidence to come there will be a consistency between the discoveries of the past, the present and the future. Whatever our standpoint, Christian or non-Christian, we find it difficult to adjust ourselves to the necessity of acknowledging this element of faith. A Christian reviewer of my first volume in the *Times Literary Supplement*[1] apparently claims for the theism I have been expounding that it is a matter not of faith but of knowledge; in private correspondence a non-Christian reader of the book has made the same claim for his faith in an impersonal immanent urge working in the universe for its perfection.

As I was saying a few minutes ago, in times of stress and strain we are always in danger of slipping back into our mental habits of longer standing. How happily we could cease from mental strife if we could revert to the belief that God is only interested in the rescue of a certain number of souls out of the perishing universe and has given us the Bible as a manual of instruction for those that are to be saved! For myself the discovery that to see in Christ the revelation of God makes this impossible has been the root of the trouble. It leads on to the question: What then is God aiming at in this universe of His creation? When that question has been asked there is no stopping short of discovering how many and great are the mysteries and how little we know.

I have a strong suspicion that many who are asking Dr. Dillistone's questions are hankering after the kind of knowledge which here and now it is futile to expect. They suffer from a sense of frustration due to the assumption that without such

[1] March 15th, 1957; p. 165.

knowledge they are adrift on a trackless sea with neither compass nor guiding star. They are impatient with theologians who cannot give them what they feel they want. If they are too intelligent to become the prey of either fundamentalist or existentialist prophets, they carry on as agnostics. They exemplify the difficulty we find in adjusting ourselves to the lesson of our age, that God has not thought fit to give us that kind of revelation, that we do not need to be able to picture the *eschaton* of this world's history in order to know what now we ought to be thinking and doing, that without sharing Christ's vision of the end of His journey we can find in Him the way, the truth and the life.[1]

So much for the surrounding mystery. Now for the value of the light we have been given by which to walk and to explore. I have tried to show two things: (i) that, quite apart from Christian faith, we can best make sense of the universe and of our life within it by the hypothesis that it is aiming at the creation of a community of genuinely free persons; and (ii) that if we accept the Christian faith it confirms that verdict and enlists us in the service of our Creator's aim. In considering the first of these we saw how from our experience of imperfect freedom we can get some understanding of what its perfection would be, how from this we can learn what is likely to help and what to hinder its true growth. Then we took note of the fact that for Christian faith the Church is a body called into existence by God not only to learn this lesson but to take the lead in acting upon it. We have seen, too, how the increase of scientific control over natural forces increases our capacity for growth in freedom. But while we are passing through the stage of freedom (*a*) on our way to freedom (*b*), misuse of the freedom we have got leads to its destruction and not its perfection. Thus at this stage increase of power may be for evil as well as for good.

In the light of these considerations we have to face the practical problem of how to promote the growth of true freedom in an

[1] Above, p. 192.

age of mass-society, technology, mind conditioning and brain washing. It helps, I think, to realize that this is one form of the general problem presented by increasing power of control over nature in the hands of men possessed of freedom (*a*). In these lectures I have done what I can to clarify our understanding of the true nature of freedom, and thereby to indicate what kind of actions are likely to help or hinder its growth in human society. To elaborate the practical application of this teaching, to examine, for example, the obligations it implies for those in authority, those who are in a position to exploit the newly-discovered powers of control, belongs, as Aristotle used to say, to another inquiry.

It will be in place, however, to end with some remarks about the contribution to be made by Christian theology to these pressing problems of the day. It should be clear by now that their faith does not enable Christians to provide the kind of knowledge that some people think they have a right to demand from them. What then can we offer?

We will start from the existentialist emphasis on *angst*, the view that an essential characteristic of human nature is a paralysing sense of futility.

> Existentially everybody is aware of the complete loss of self which biological extinction implies. . . .
>
> Non-being is omnipresent and produces anxiety even where an immediate threat of death is absent. It stands behind the experience that we are driven, together with everything else, from the past towards the future without a moment of time which does not vanish immediately. It stands behind the insecurity and homelessness of our social and individual existence. It stands behind the attacks on our power of being in body and soul by weakness, disease and accidents. In all these forms fate actualizes itself, and through them the anxiety of non-being takes hold of us. We try to transform the anxiety into fear and to meet courageously the objects in which the threat is embodied. We succeed partly, but somehow we are aware of the fact that it is not these objects with which we struggle that produces the anxiety but the human situation as such.[1]

For Christian existentialists this sense of insecurity, of being

[1] P. Tillich: *The Courage to Be* (London, 1952), pp. 40, 42.

poised precariously over the abyss of non-being, is transfused and darkly coloured by a sense of sin, of guilt.

Let us assume that there is truth in this, that the Christian is right when he says that all men are sinners, that the actual difference is between those who know they are and those who do not. Let us assume that the Christian existentialist is right when he says that in the depths of their being men have more sense of their sinful creaturehood than they are aware of. What then?

The Christian faith is that down the ages God has been seeking, and is still seeking, to make Himself known to us as our Creator who wills our perfection in freedom. He watches over us with fatherly care, and in Christ offers us entry upon a new way of life of eternal quality. In this life we cease to be concerned about ourselves as we lose ourselves in our share of God's interest in the welfare of His creation. We may be sinners, but God bids us remember that as we answer His call to share in His creative and redemptive work we are to do so as members of Christ's earthly body which is the fellowship of *forgiven* sinners.

Here I would like to quote once again from the Retreat Addresses of the late Father Talbot, a book from which I have learned more than I can say of the true meaning of Christian faith as seen and known from the inside. I quote this passage for its contrast with Tillich's description of the effect of man's realization of the abyss of non-being.

> We are utterly dependent, there is something precarious in our lives; unless we were sustained and embraced by that which is greater than ourselves, we should cease to be. It would be very strange if we thought we made truth by recognizing it; if beauty and truth were exhausted by our little efforts. We do not *make* beauty. It is a visitation to us which we welcome. We are dissatisfied by anything less than the Altogether Perfect. Wake up, then, and recognize this deepest truth: that not only are we made for God, but here and now you are being made, and without Him you are nothing.[1]

Here Father Talbot stands in the true tradition of Christian faith. It was a very early Christian writer who wrote: 'God hath

[1] L. Menzies: *Retreat Addresses of Edward Keble Talbot* (London, 1953), p. 23.

not given us the spirit of fear, but of power, and of love, and of a sound mind'.[1]

We peer out into mystery. For many that mystery is the darkness of the terrible unknown, the terrible unknown which threatens each man's annihilation and paralyses him with the sense of his nothingness. We look back over the history of human thought and see how bit by bit man has sought to understand and make sense of his world and of himself and to gain mastery over the forces of nature. All these efforts depend on his faith that the universe does make sense and will be responsive to his efforts to understand and to control. He discovers the reality and the imperfection of his freedom and comes to see that only by his growth in knowledge and in the mastery of himself and his world can it reach its perfection. His science begins in his attempts to control the forces of nature, his religion in his attempts to enlist on his side the powers of the terrible unknown. For Christian faith God reveals Himself as willing man's growth in freedom, as having acted in the history of the world to rescue it from obstacles to that growth, as calling man to a partnership in which alone true knowledge and full freedom can be found. All knowledge comes from faith of some kind, faith in virtue of which we ask our questions and seek for the answers. I have tried to show that Christian faith, while it forbids us to claim knowledge we have not got, gives us light enough to walk in the way that leads to knowing more. By this faith I have tried to live, and in this faith I hope to die.

[1] 2 Tim. i. 7.

INDEX